The IRA on Film and Television

A History

MARK CONNELLY

McFarland & Company, Inc., Publishers
Jefferson, North Carolina, and London

LIBRARY OF CONGRESS CATALOGUING-IN-PUBLICATION DATA

Connelly, Mark, 1951–
The IRA on film and television : a history / Mark Connelly.
p.   cm.
Includes bibliographical references and index.

ISBN 978-0-7864-4736-7
softcover : acid free paper ∞

1. Irish Republican Army — In motion pictures.
2. Irish Republican Army — On television.   3. Irish Question
in motion pictures.   4. Irish Question on television.
I. Title.   II. Title: Irish Republican
Army on film and television.
PN1995.9.I684C66 2012   791.43'658415082 — dc23   2012008479

BRITISH LIBRARY CATALOGUING DATA ARE AVAILABLE

Front cover: *The Wind That Shakes the Barley*, 2006
(16 Films/Photofest); barley graphic © 2012 Shutterstock

Manufactured in the United States of America

McFarland & Company, Inc., Publishers
Box 611, Jefferson, North Carolina 28640
www.mcfarlandpub.com

Table of Contents

Preface   1

Introduction   5

 1 The Troubles I: The War of Independence and the
    Irish Civil War   15

 2 The Big Fellow: Michael Collins   38

 3 The Shamrock and the Swastika   62

 4 The Troubles II   100

 5 The Classics: *The Informer* and *Odd Man Out*   147

 6 American Angles   161

 7 International Intrigue   198

 8 The Gangster Film: Criminalizing the IRA   204

 9 Themes and Characters   215

10 Post Troubles?   236

Conclusion   242

Chronology   245

Filmography   247

Chapter Notes   251

Bibliography   260

Index   265

Preface

The Irish Republican Army has appeared in more than eighty motion pictures, granting it an unprecedented and ironic cinematic presence. A secret "outlawed" organization for most of its history, the IRA has rarely consisted of more than a few hundred active members. Like Basque separatists in Spain, it is involved in a protracted internecine struggle with few global ramifications. The IRA is dedicated to ending British rule in a corner of a neutral island with a population equivalent to that of West Virginia, a heavily subsidized province Britain has repeatedly stated that it has no selfish, strategic, or economic interest in retaining. An IRA victory would not create a haven for international terrorists, destabilize NATO, disrupt world markets, or endanger British security. The parochial dispute between militant Irish Republicans who want a single unified Irish state and the Unionists who wish Northern Ireland to remain part of the United Kingdom claimed three thousand lives in thirty years, a devastating number for a small community, but far less significant than the loss of life in Kosovo in a single year. Other revolutionary organizations have inflicted more harm, espouse more ominous ideologies, and pose greater threats to international stability. Yet none of these militant forces has captivated moviemakers like the Irish Republican Army.

The IRA commands a greater screen presence than the PLO, ETA, or the FLN because it is Irish. It is not the nature, size, or significance of the organization, or the value of the land in dispute, but the people it involves that attracts attention. As James MacKillop notes, as a small nation, Ireland is uniquely connected to the outside world because of the English language and its extensive diaspora.[1] Unlike a regional conflict in Spain or Serbia, the Irish Troubles reverberate around the world. A film about the IRA can easily star Irish, American, and British actors speaking their native language and draw audiences in London, New York, Toronto, and Melbourne. A nation of only 4.4 million, the Irish Republic has developed a prolific film industry whose producers can rely on overseas markets filmmakers in Hungary or Greece cannot.[2]

The IRA has been a subject explored by major directors from three countries, including John Ford, John Frankenheimer, Carol Reed, David Lean, Neil Jordan, and Jim Sheridan. IRA characters have been portrayed by international stars such as Victor McLaglen, James Cagney, Anthony Hopkins, James Mason, and Brad Pitt. Films about the Irish Republican Army range from realistic docudramas like Paul Greengrass' *Bloody Sunday* (Hell's Kitchen Films, 2002), shot with handheld cameras and natural lighting to create the sensation of watching 1972 newsreel footage, to Joseph Merhi's action farce *Riot* (PM Entertainment Group, 1999) in which a British superhero battles IRA bikers in the streets of Los Angeles during a race riot.

Whether portrayed as a heroic patriot, ruthless terrorist, corrupt gangster, or troubled outcast, the Irish rebel has emerged as a universally recognized cinematic archetype.

This book takes a "history vs. Hollywood" approach to the IRA film, tracing, as objectively as possible, the record of the IRA from its emergence during the Easter Rising of 1916 through the peace process of the 1990s, then examining its depictions on film.

The introduction presents an overview of Irish history, focusing on the eight-hundred-year pattern of invasions and rebellions often referenced in IRA films. Chapter 1 examines the role the IRA played during the Irish War of Independence and the Civil War that followed. Chapter 2 reviews film portrayals of Michael Collins, the charismatic revolutionary who founded the IRA and later fought against former comrades who rejected the treaty with Britain he championed.

Chapters 3 details the IRA's fleeting connections with German intelligence during the Second World War. Though IRA interactions with the Nazis involved small sums of money and the negligible use of arms, filmmakers have found it a compelling sidebar to World War II, creating an onscreen Irish Fifth Column which never existed in reality.

Chapter 4 chronicles the Troubles that ignited in 1969 and led to the reemergence of the IRA both in the streets of Belfast and on film. It was during this time that Ireland began releasing movies about the IRA, offering more genuine and contentious views of the conflict than British and American productions. A Jimmy Cagney movie about the War of Independence made in the 1950s, a period of low-level conflict, generated little controversy. In contrast, Irish films like *In the Name of the Father* (Hell's Kitchen Productions, 1992) or *Some Mother's Son* (Castle Rock Entertainment, 1996) were derided as inflammatory propaganda by Unionists and their Tory supporters.

Chapter 5 discusses two classic IRA-related films, John Ford's *The Informer* (RKO 1935) and Carol Reed's *Odd Man Out* (Two Cities Films, 1947), both of which deleted political references to satisfy British censors. As in many other IRA films, the partisan conflict was muted to serve as a backdrop for a more personal drama to attain wider appeal.

Chapter 6 describes the major role Americans played in both creating the Irish Republican Army and shaping its cinematic image. Fifty years before the Easter Rising in Dublin, Confederate and Union veterans, many calling themselves members of the Irish Republican Army, invaded Canada with plans to seize Montreal to pressure England into withdrawing from Ireland. For generations, America was the source of arms, money, volunteers, and refuge for Irish Republicans. Irish-American director John Ford, whose cousin was an IRA leader, directed several films featuring IRA characters, even inserting them into his romantic comedy *The Quiet Man* (Argosy/Republic, 1952). Later Hollywood filmmakers relied on the IRA to provide terrorist villains in the decade between the end of the Cold War and 9/11. Movies like *Patriot Games* (Paramount, 1992) and *Blown Away* (MGM, 1994), however, made it clear that the heartless terrorist was an IRA renegade, making the actual organization appear more reasonable in contrast and avoiding offending the IRA's American supporters.

Later chapters review representative plots and characters, such as the ubiquitous informer. Chapter 10 evaluates films depicting the status of the IRA since the 1998 Good Friday or Belfast Agreement. Oliver Hirschbiegel's *Five Minutes of Heaven* (Big Fish Films, 2009) presents the Troubles as a past event, while Damian Chapa's *I.R.A. King of Nothing* (BBI Entertainment, 2006) suggests the secret army is merely in hiatus, waiting for a time to strike.

A Note on Terminology

Anyone seeking to write objectively about the IRA faces the obstacle of partisan vocabulary. The contested region can be called Ulster, Northern Ireland, the Province, the Six

Counties, or simply the North, depending on the writer's point of view. In most instances I have used "the North" or "Northern Ireland," terms that are both geographical and more familiar to American readers. For the same reason, I use the Republic of Ireland or the Republic instead of the less common Republican name, the Twenty-Six Counties. For the purposes of this book, the IRA is a generic label for all militant Irish Republicans depicted in films, whose scripts often only refer to unnamed "organizations." To avoid designating members of the IRA as either "soldiers" or "terrorists," I have chosen the more neutral word "volunteer." In addition, IRA appears as both a singular and plural noun, depending on context.

Introduction

Seen from different points of view, the same man may be thought a hero, a freedom-fighter, a terrorist, a gangster, or a murderer.—*Denis Donoghue*

In our age, history is no longer written by the victors. History is written by the film-makers.—*Joan Dean*

The Irish Republican Army (IRA) and its related organizations* have been a feature of Irish life for a century. Initially participants in the War of Independence, their goal since the 1921 Treaty, which partitioned the island, is to unify Ireland into a single sovereign nation, ending British rule in Northern Ireland. On film, the IRA has appeared in mainstream motion pictures such as *The Quiet Man* and *Ryan's Daughter*, action films like *Blown Away*, political dramas, dark comedies, and even a spaghetti Western, *A Fistful of Dynamite*.

Essentially a dispute about the fate of an area the size of Connecticut with a population of 1.8 million, the Troubles of Northern Ireland have attracted filmmakers in a way that the conflicts of Basque separatists and Hamas have not. Although in recent decades IRA organizations have never included more than a few hundred active members, they have inspired moviemakers on two continents. Irish directors like Neil Jordan and Jim Sheridan have made films about the IRA, as have Sergio Leone, John Sturges, John Ford, John Frankenheimer, Carol Reed, and David Lean. Major American stars such as James Cagney, Robert Mitchum, Richard Gere, and Brad Pitt have portrayed IRA characters, as have some of Britain's most distinguished actors — James Mason, John Mills, Dirk Bogarde, Michael Redgrave, Eric Porter, and Anthony Hopkins. Motion pictures about the IRA have stirred passions in Britain and Ireland, sparking editorials and calls for censorship even before the films were released.

The IRA presents both opportunities and challenges to filmmakers who generally try to appeal to the widest possible audience. The IRA continually appears in headlines, generating public interest and debate. As a secret "outlawed" organization, it provides screenwriters and directors with stories of intrigue, espionage, betrayal, suspense, and violence. Directors of action films and thrillers can capitalize on car bombs, spies, secret missions, assassinations, kidnappings, and rescues. The organization's well-known bombing campaigns allow writers to explore ethical debates about the use of terror to achieve political ends and the suspension of civil liberties in the name of national security. The IRA presents filmmakers with a variety of dramatic events that lend themselves to visual expression — ticking time bombs, courtroom debates, demonstrations, car chases, interrogations, and jail breaks.

**For purposes of simplicity, the term IRA is used as an umbrella word to describe all armed Republican organizations. Like gangster films that refrain from using the word "mafia," many motion pictures set in Ireland do not name the IRA directly, instead referring to "rebels" or "the organization."*

Filmmakers, however, also face challenges in bringing IRA stories to the screen. To obtain the largest audience, they have to avoid offending both Irish and British sensibilities, something directors making films about the French Resistance fighting the Nazis or the CIA attacking Al Qaeda do not have to consider. Irish directors risk reopening debates about the Treaty that both founded their nation and plunged it into civil war. Hollywood filmmakers have to overcome several obstacles. To most Americans, Ireland is the Emerald Isle of shamrocks, castles, and leprechauns populated by charming, childlike people given to poetry, drink, and dance. It is hard for many to reconcile these stereotypes with the portrayal of the Irish as ruthless terrorists. Similarly, England is commonly thought of as a peaceful, tidy, hyper-civilized society where rush hour commuters politely "queue up" for double-decker buses and police officers maintain order without guns. England is associated with the Queen, great houses, foxhunting, Sherlock Holmes, Churchill's bulldog resistance during the Battle of Britain, manicured gardens, the Beatles, and Princess Di. American audiences have a difficult time seeing the English, often ridiculed as effete aristocrats, as being capable of the brutality they easily accept in a Southern sheriff from their own country. Complicating storylines is the fact that media accounts about Northern Ireland identify the conflict as one between Protestants and Catholics, something people outside Ireland have difficulty comprehending. Accustomed to seeing racial conflicts in terms of color, Americans cannot easily detect the subtle differences in ethnicity an Irish audience would immediately recognize. Equally problematic for audiences are unfamiliar political labels. Terms like "Unionist," "nationalist," "loyalist," and "Republican" are confusing, as are historical references to the Treaty, the Emergency, Partition, the Six Counties, or the ultimate Irish term of understatement — the Troubles.

The IRA also presents screenwriters with a challenge because of its complicated history. Though an "illegal" or "outlawed" terrorist organization, it once formed the core of Ireland's struggle for independence. Many of its original members were heroes of the Easter Rising and had distinguished professional and political careers in the Irish Free State and subsequent Irish Republic. Michael Collins, the IRA's Director of Intelligence, became Commander in Chief of the newly created Irish Army. Robert Briscoe, who ran guns for Collins, became Lord Mayor of Dublin in 1956 and was a leading figure in the nation's Jewish community. Sean Lemass, reportedly one of Collins' assassins, served as Ireland's Taoiseach, or Prime Minister, from 1959 to 1966. Emmet Dalton, Director of Training of the IRA, became an Irish general and successful film producer. Sean McBride, the IRA's Chief of Staff in 1936, was a founding member of Amnesty International and served as Assistant Secretary General of the United Nations. In 1974 he was awarded the Nobel Peace Prize.

These members of the original or "Old IRA" lend credibility to an organization that in later years would be outlawed in both Britain and Ireland and whose members would be condemned as terrorists.

Ourselves Alone

A conquered nation is like a man with cancer: he can think of nothing else. — *George Bernard Shaw*

The Irish Republican Army (IRA) emerged from Ireland's eight-hundred-year struggle for political and cultural independence from Britain. Ireland's history provides the Irish

Republican Army with precedents for many of its actions and legitimacy for its aims. Much of the enduring support for the IRA, especially among Irish-Americans, rests less on an allegiance to or even an understanding of its neo–Marxist ideology and more on an antipathy for an historic foe and an emotional connection to an oppressed homeland and a sacred cause.

INVASIONS AND DISPOSSESSIONS

For centuries Ireland experienced a series of invasions that shaped its culture and the character of its inhabitants. The Vikings arrived in 895, raiding seaside settlements and burning monasteries. Lacking a navy or a national army, the Irish were unable to prevent these attacks or retaliate against the invaders.

Ireland in the ninth century was not a unified country but an island comprised of a hundred and fifty small kingdoms loosely organized into five greater provincial kingdoms: Connacht, Leinster, Meath, Munster, and Ulster.[1] There were regional differences among the Irish tribes, though most shared common cultural characteristics — a strong oral tradition, a reverence for high art, and a system of laws. Centuries of tribal conflict, however, made it difficult for the Irish to rally behind a single national leader or create a united front against an alien invader.

Viking raids continued into the tenth century. Initially facing little organized resistance, Vikings seized farmland, created earthwork fortresses, and founded towns that later became major Irish cities (including Dublin). The Vikings, however, never fully occupied Ireland or supplanted the existing Celtic tribes. The existence of so many independent tribes meant that invaders might subdue or destroy a single kingdom but leave others intact and able to maintain their religion, art, language, and culture in relative isolation.

The arrival of the Normans in 1169 initiated a series of invasions that would eventually lead to British control over the entire island. The Irish outnumbered their invaders but lacked modern weapons, body armor, and an understanding of military strategy. Often attacking with slings and stones in disorganized hordes, they were routed by knights protected by helmets and chain-mail.[2] In 1171 Henry II landed at Waterford, becoming the first English monarch to set foot on the island. Within a few decades the Normans moved inland from coastal cities, building castles and cultivating land. As conquerors, the Normans considered themselves superior to the indigenous Irish they were dispossessing. In 1216 King John ordered that Englishmen should be given preference as incumbents in cathedral churches.[3] In 1366 the Duke of Clarence, the King's representative in Ireland, called a parliament in Kilkenny, which passed thirty-five laws to buttress English rule. The Statutes of Kilkenny forbade the English from marrying anyone Irish or to employ Irish poets and minstrels. Englishmen were to maintain their English surnames, ride horses in the English fashion, and, above all, speak the English language. Englishmen were forbidden to sell horses or weapons to the Irish. In times of war the sale of food was outlawed. The disdain for anything Irish was proclaimed, and the Irish people were referred to as "enemies." The statutes, designed to keep the English from assimilating with the larger native population, were never uniformly enforced, but they codified prejudicial attitudes about the Irish that would foster division and conflict for centuries.[4]

In 1536 Henry VIII sought to reconquer Ireland. Unable to subdue the Irish and weakened by plague, the English had by the late 1400s retreated to Dublin and its surroundings, known as the Pale. Fearing the island could be used as a base for attacks on

Britain, Henry was determined to firmly reestablish English rule. For now there was a new division separating English and Irish. The conflict between the conqueror and the conquered, once defined by race, customs, class, and language, was intensified by faith. With the Reformation, the English became Protestants, but the Irish remained irrevocably Catholic, making them "pagan as well as savage."[5] In addition, Catholicism aligned the Irish with Britain's longtime adversaries, Spain and France, enhancing suspicions about their motivations and loyalties. The linking of politics and religion would divide the nation and mark its social conflicts into the twenty-first century.

The reconquest of Ireland took many forms and continued through subsequent reigns. The Act of Supremacy made Henry VIII the head of the Church of Ireland as well as England. Now King of Ireland, he launched a series of policies to suppress the Irish. Looking back to the actions of Henry II, he revived the practice of Surrender and Regrant. Under this policy, Irish chieftains yielded tribal holdings to Henry VIII and immediately received them back with an English title and assurances of protection from adversaries. Many Irish chiefs, accustomed to making temporary and questionable alliances with rivals, accepted the offer, not fully appreciating the impact of their decision. Once declaring loyalty to the King, they could not break their agreement without being accused of treason and risking the forfeiture of their lands.[6]

In 1649 Oliver Cromwell, the civil and military governor of Ireland, landed in Dublin with a force of 20,000 men. Telling his soldiers they were like the Israelites venturing into Canaan, Cromwell sought to tame the idolatrous Irish Catholics he described to Parliament as "barbarous wretches."[7] Cromwell's subjugation of Ireland, much like Sherman's March to the Sea, became legendary for its wanton destruction and carnage. He did, however, generally follow seventeenth-century rules of engagement. When a besieged town or garrison surrendered, the inhabitants were treated humanely; when they refused, he gave no quarter.[8] Cromwell's "surrender or die" policy and the resultant massacres would scar the Irish consciousness for centuries.

In addition to pacifying Ireland by alliance or force, the English sought to repopulate the island with loyal Protestants. In 1556 Queen Mary became the first monarch to "plant" English settlers in Ireland. Thirty years later Queen Elizabeth sent English settlers to occupy land confiscated from Irish rebels. Following their defeat at the end of the Nine Years War, many Irish nobles left the island in 1607. Known as the Flight of the Earls, this exodus marked the end of the old Gaelic order. Their vacated lands, mostly in Ulster, were seized.

Settlers from Scotland and England willing to take the Protestant Oath of Supremacy could obtain property in Ulster, lands the Irish were forbidden to purchase. In 1652 Parliament passed An Act for the Settling of Ireland designed to resolve the "horrid rebellion" in Ireland through "a total reducement and settlement of that nation." The Act placed the Irish in ten classifications. The worst of the worst, some hundred thousand, were to be hanged. The rest would be spared but lose their property. Some would be granted land in outlying regions. A second part of the legislation provided that English soldiers and officers owed back pay would be compensated with holdings taken from the Irish.[9]

Parliament passed other laws suppressing Irish commerce and culture. Livestock exports, a major source of income, were restricted. British navigation acts required that all Irish goods shipped to America had to be transported by English ships.[10] In 1695 Parliament made it illegal for Catholics to keep schools, become teachers, or send their children overseas to obtain an education. Catholics were forbidden to wear swords, possess sporting guns, or own horses valued at more than five pounds. Catholic merchants paid higher taxes and were restricted on where they could operate and how many they could employ, hindering their potential for growth. Catholics could not serve in the military, vote, or run for Parliament. Priests were ordered to leave Ireland and threatened with execution if they returned. Masses had to be held as conspiratorial gatherings in forests or bogs.[11] Catholic plaintiffs could only be represented by Protestant attorneys before a Protestant judge and jury. In a noted statement, the Lord Chancellor and Chief Justice declared, "The law does not suppose any such person to exist as an Irish Roman Catholic."[12]

These restrictions, known as the penal laws, had a great impact on land ownership. Catholics could only purchase two acres of land. They could not obtain mortgages to buy land and were restricted on the profits they could derive from rents. When a Catholic landowner died, his estate could not pass to the eldest son but had to be divided equally among his sons. A single son could inherit the property only if he became Protestant.[13] The denial of primogeniture ensured that through successive generations Irish estates were steadily split into ever and ever smaller homesteads, reducing their prosperity and making the Irish vulnerable to the Famine to come.

Finding conditions in their native land intolerable, a large number of the Catholic gentry left Ireland, many settling in France. Like the Flight of the Earls in the beginning of the century, this exodus in the 1690s, known as the Flight of the Wild Geese, saw more lands acquired by Protestants.[14] In 1640 Catholics possessed two-thirds of Ireland.[15] By 1703 the amount of land owned by Catholics fell to seven percent.[16]

As the eighteenth century progressed, many of the anti–Catholic policies were repealed or modified, but the Protestant Ascendancy was clearly established, creating two societies — one compromised of largely landless Catholic peasants, the other dominated by landowning Protestants loyal to the Crown:

> The separate communities were divided not only by religion but by race and, not least, by culture: they learned different poetry, sang different songs, celebrated different victories, mourned different calamities, and, above all, swore different oaths.... Catholic oaths were secret and furtive. Protestant oaths were public and assertive, indeed vainglorious and provocative, being turned into toasts.[17]

In 1800 the Act of Union made Ireland part of Great Britain, ending its status as a separate nation. The Dublin parliament was dissolved. Henceforth, Irish representatives would take their seats in Westminster.*

The most significant event of the nineteenth century (and perhaps all Irish history) was the Famine or Great Hunger (*An Gorta Mór* in Irish) of the mid–1840s, which profoundly changed the culture, economy, politics, social fabric, and destiny of the Irish people. It became a defining chapter in Irish history that fostered the drive for national independence. Although a natural disaster, the Irish came to see it as a crisis caused and exacerbated by British policies, leading some current Irish scholars to declare the Famine a "genocide."

Though not native to Ireland, the potato had become a staple of the Irish diet. For nearly half the population, it served as the sole source of nutrition. Much of the best farmland in Ireland had been reserved for pasturage to supply the growing English demand for beef. Living on small farms, many of which were not much larger than garden plots, the Irish found that the potato, which only required a spade to plant and harvest, could be easily grown in marginal soil. A single acre could produce enough potatoes to feed a family for months.[18]

---

*Though Ireland accounted for nearly half the population of Great Britain, it held only 105 of more than 600 seats.

The potato blight arrived in Ireland in 1845. The fungus spread rapidly, so that potatoes, both those harvested and those still underground, turned into a putrid, blackened, jelly-like mush. Twenty percent of the crop was lost. The following year the entire harvest was lost.[19] In 1847, known as Black '47, the Great Hunger claimed 400,000 lives. Unable to pay rent, farmers were forcibly evicted, landlords often using battering rams to topple their cottages. Thousands died on the open road. Thousands more crowded into coastal cities, where more died of disease in cramped slums and workhouses. In all, a million Irish died,* and over a million emigrated, mostly to America on overcrowded "coffin ships." Within five years the nation's population fell by one-fourth. It continued to fall through successive emigrations so that by 1911 the population dropped to 4.4 million.[20]

Britain's relief efforts — soup kitchens to prevent starvation and public works projects to create employment — were inadequate and often mismanaged. Irishmen, weakened by hunger and disease, were "engaged in useless projects — building roads that led nowhere and walls that surrounded nothing."[21] The Irish resented that some church-based relief efforts encouraged conversion to the Protestant faith. They were especially embittered by landlords who used the crisis as a pretext to clear lands of tenants, often to provide room for cattle. The fact that throughout the Famine Ireland continued to export grain to Britain was seen by the Irish as a crime. Irish nationalists would cite a statement by Charles Trevelyan, who, as Assistant Secretary to the Treasury, administered British relief efforts, as evidence of English cynicism and malicious racism:

> The judgement of God sent the calamity to teach the Irish a lesson, that calamity must not be too much mitigated.... The real evil with which we have to contend is not the physical evil of the Famine, but the moral evil of the selfish, perverse and turbulent character of the people.

The Famine created an embittered Irish diaspora whose poetry and music romanticized the Emerald Isle and heralded the rebels who fought the perfidious English.

Up the Rebels

"Never a generation didn't have its rebel." — *The Nightfighters*

Throughout the conquest, reconquest, and plantation of Ireland there were numerous wars, rebellions, uprisings, and insurgencies. The IRA is often celebrated as the modern tip of a spear that was forged through centuries of armed resistance.

In 1260 Brian O'Neill, the self-proclaimed High King of Ireland, attacked the Normans. His forces were defeated in the Battle of the Down. Brian was executed and his head sent to King Henry III in London.[22] Other kings and chiefs raised armies to oppose the invaders but were generally forced into submission or fled to unoccupied territory. The Earl of Desmond, allied with other Irish clans, led two rebellions from 1569 to 1583 in Munster to prevent the expansion of English rule and Protestant influence. Like O'Neill, he was ultimately defeated and his head presented to an English monarch. During the Nine Years War, rebellious Irish chieftains were defeated in Ulster, leading to the Flight of the Earls and the Protestant settlement of northeast Ireland. In 1641 Catholic gentry attempted a revolt that was ultimately crushed by Cromwell's army.

Most deaths resulted from diseases like cholera and dysentery rather than actual starvation.

In addition to organized military campaigns, there were numerous insurgencies and guerrilla operations. Beginning in the early 1700s, bands of armed men with blackened faces rode through the countryside at night, terrorizing landlords, torching farm buildings, and firing shots through windows. In the 1760s a group calling themselves the Whiteboys tore down fences, punished rent collectors, and warned farmers against taking land from evicted tenants. The Whiteboys were followed by groups like the Rightboys, the Thrashers, the Ribbonmen, and the Lady Clares. These were secret, oath-bound organizations led by Zorro-like figures with romantic sobriquets like Captain Moonlight, Captain Starlight, or Captain Rock who emerged from the night and disappeared with the dawn. They were guided by no consistent political ideology but meted out quick justice on behalf of the poor and dispossessed.[23] They also established among the Irish an esteem for the oath-bound rebel, who, like the American outlaw, would become a romanticized figure celebrated for his daring defiance against the forces of injustice.

THE FIGHT FOR INDEPENDENCE

Physical force Irish Republicanism, the drive to achieve an independent Irish nation through armed resistance and secret societies, began with the 1798 rebellion. Inspired by both the American and French revolutions, the United Irishmen, comprised of both Protestants and Catholics, sought to sever ties with Britain and create a non-sectarian Irish Republic. The leading figure of the rebellion, Wolfe Tone, a Protestant, traveled to the United States and France to secure support. A landing of French troops in Bantry Bay in December 1796 was thwarted by storms.[24] In a subsequent action, Tone was captured wearing the uniform of a French general. Taken to Dublin, he was condemned to death but died of a self-inflicted wound before he could be executed.[25]

In 1803 Robert Emmet, son of a Protestant physician, joined the United Irishmen and, like Tone, went to France to seek support for an Irish revolution. The 1803 Rebellion was limited to a battle in Dublin, and Emmet was executed.

In 1848, radical members of the Young Ireland movement, frustrated by the evictions and sufferings of the Famine, and emboldened by the anti-monarchist revolutions then raging throughout Europe, staged a brief uprising. The leaders, who enjoyed popular support, were sentenced to transportation rather than execution.

In 1867 the Irish Republican Brotherhood, also called Fenians after ancient Irish warriors, planned an uprising among nationalist-minded Irish soldiers in the British army. Its intentions revealed by informers, the Brotherhood could not muster sufficient troops to launch a full revolt. Limited to skirmishes, the rebellion failed but left an important legacy. Seeking to free captured members held in Britain, the Fenians launched a "dynamite campaign." In December 1867 Fenians blew a hole in the wall of Clerkenwell prison in London. The blast failed to liberate the Irish prisoners but leveled nearby houses, killing a dozen Londoners. Special police were recruited to combat terrorism, and public opinion hardened against the Irish, widely caricaturized in cartoons as apelike monsters.[26] The Fenian Rebellion and its aftermath foreshadowed the Troubles of the 1970s.

REFORM MOVEMENTS

Throughout the nineteenth century a non-violent faction of Irish nationalism sought social reforms, repeals of remaining penal laws, and a peaceful end to the Union with Britain. Daniel O'Connell, called the Liberator, was a lawyer and gifted orator who campaigned for Catholic emancipation and a repeal of the Union with Britain. In 1823 he created the Catholic Association which supported Protestants who would fight for Catholic emancipation in Parliament. A small, middle-class movement at first, it grew when O'Connell increased its base by lowering dues and automatically enrolling priests, who encouraged their parishioners to join. Soon dues from a quarter million families funded the first mass movement to rally the Catholic poor.[27]

The politicizing of poor Catholics alarmed the government, which, fearing more Whiteboy-styled violence, banned the movement. O'Connell, however, could not be stopped. He ran for Parliament. On election day, green-clad supporters marched to the polls in organized squads, led by "pacificators" to keep order. Instead of night riders, the British now faced a peaceful mass movement flexing legitimate political power. After O'Connell won in a landslide, Parliament passed the Catholic Emancipation Act, which allowed Catholics to serve as judges, admirals, and members of Parliament.[28]

Once seated in Westminster, O'Connell campaigned to repeal the Union with Britain. Unable to make headway in Parliament, he began holding public demonstrations in Ireland. These open-air rallies, dubbed "monster meetings," drew hundreds of thousands. Many arrived in military-style units, forming an unarmed peaceful army. Though non-violent, the growing movement was viewed by London as a threat. When a monster meeting, expected to draw half a million, was planned on the site of an ancient Irish victory, with posters calling for "volunteers," the government banned the demonstration. O'Connell obeyed the order and cancelled the meeting. O'Connell was arrested, marched through the streets like a common criminal, and tried for sedition.[29] A lengthy trial exhausted O'Connell, whose health and influence ebbed. Once known for his powerful oratory, a dying O'Connell was barely audible when he last appeared in Parliament in 1847 to appeal for famine relief.[30]

The Famine brought attention to the plight of landless tenant farmers. The Land League, formed in 1879, sought to reduce rents, protect families from eviction, and allow tenants to purchase land through a rent-to-own plan. The movement is best remembered for introducing the word "boycott." Land League president Charles Stewart Parnell urged peasants to shun farmers who took land from the evicted. Days later peasants directed this strategy against Captain Boycott. When no locals would agree to harvest his crop, Boycott had to bring in Protestant laborers from Ulster, protected by British troops. Visiting Dublin, Boycott found no hotel would rent him a room.[31]* Though marred by violence by militant members, the Land League achieved its basic mission to help the Irish regain ownership of the land. By 1921, 400,000 of Ireland's 470,000 holdings were occupant-owned.[32]

HOME RULE

Following the failure of O'Connell's attempts to repeal the Union, a more moderate movement emerged and gained widespread support. Led by Isaac Butt, the Home Rule League sought not to break the tie with Britain but to achieve for Ireland limited autonomy within the United Kingdom. Charles Stewart Parnell championed the cause in Parliament, where he deftly used obstructionist tactics to bring attention to Irish issues. Widely popular with the Irish, Parnell won support in both America and Britain as a leader of a peaceful movement that sought to resolve the Irish issue without violence. Parnell's reputation soared

*Captain Boycott *(Individual Pictures, 1947), starring Stewart Granger, Alistair Sim, Cecil Parker (Charles Boycott), and Robert Donat (Charles Stewart Parnell), was shot in County Mayo and at Pinewood Studios.*

after he was jailed. During his incarceration, violence broke out, leading to fears that without Parnell's temperate leadership, secret armed societies would sweep across Ireland. Released from jail, Parnell's image as a responsible advocate was enhanced by his response to the Phoenix Park murders. On May 6, 1882, Lord Cavendish, the new chief secretary, arrived in Dublin. That evening he and his under secretary were stabbed to death by members of the Irish Republican Brotherhood, dubbed the Invincibles. Parnell and others drafted a statement to the Irish people strongly denouncing the assassins. The next day he condemned the murders in the House of Commons.[33]

A Home Rule bill was introduced in Parliament in 1886 but failed to pass. Parnell's popularity remained strong in defeat and was bolstered when a vicious campaign against him collapsed. In 1887 *The Times* accused him of inciting violence and condoning the Phoenix Park murders. A two-year-long government inquiry dragged on until an Irish reporter broke down on the stand and confessed to forging evidence. Entering Parliament following his exoneration, Parnell received a standing ovation from his political opponents.

In less than a year Parnell's life and career unraveled in scandal. In 1889 Captain William O'Shea, a former Irish Home Rule MP, filed for divorce, revealing that Parnell had maintained a decade-long affair with his wife and fathered three of her children. Gladstone, fearful of losing support for Home Rule, told the Home Rule Party to dump Parnell or risk losing the support of the Liberal Party. The Irish MPs voted against Parnell, but he refused to accept their decision, and his party splintered. Parnell married Katherine O'Shea in June 1891, then returned to Ireland in an attempt to rehabilitate his status. He crisscrossed the country making speeches, to little avail. At one event the crowd pelted him with mud. After giving an outdoor address in a driving rain, he returned home ill and exhausted, and died at the age of forty-five.[34]*

A second Home Rule bill failed to pass in 1893.

In 1900 John Redmond assumed leadership of the Home Rule movement. Though he never achieved the prominence or power of Parnell, he was able to solidify disparate groups and political rivals to gain support for Home Rule, which was opposed by Ulster Protestants who wanted to maintain the Union and Republicans who insisted on complete independence. The forces of Home Rule gathered strength, and a third Home Rule bill was introduced in Parliament.

The likely passage of the Third Home Rule bill created a crisis for the Protestants in Northern Ireland and their Conservative supporters in England. The actions of the Land League and the use of boycotts threatened Protestant landowners. Belfast industrialists feared higher taxes. Because a Dublin parliament would be overwhelmingly Catholic, Protestants protested with the slogan "Home Rule is Rome Rule."[35] Central to Unionist thought was the view that Ireland was not one country but two nations separated by "race and religion." For them, Home Rule meant nothing less than "their cultural and political destruction."[36]

On Ulster Day, September 28, 1912, more than 200,000 Ulstermen signed a Covenant in which they pledged to use "all means which may be found necessary to defeat the present conspiracy to set up a Home Rule Parliament in Ireland." Ulsterwomen signed a parallel document. The total signatories amounted to nearly 75 percent of the population over the age of fifteen.[37]

In January 1913 the Ulster Volunteer Force was formed, consisting of 90,000 men commanded by Sir George Richardson, a retired general. The Volunteers illegally imported

*Parnell *(MGM, 1937), starring Clark Gable and Myrna Loy, was a critical and financial failure.*

30,000 rifles. The Unionists were taking up arms, prepared to fight the forces of Great Britain to remain part of Great Britain.[38]

In response to this organized opposition, a group of Fenians created the Irish Volunteers in 1913 to show armed support for Home Rule. Though less equipped than the Ulster Volunteers, the Irish Volunteers quickly outnumbered their Northern opponents. In 1914, as the Home Rule bill headed toward passage, it seemed Ireland was on the edge of civil war.

The Home Rule Bill passed in September 1914, but its implementation was postponed for a year or until an end of the war. The threatened possibility of civil war in Ireland had been diminished by the outbreak of the World War in August. The Great War gave both Unionists and Irish Nationalists what David Fitzpatrick called "a line of dignified retreat under cover of patriotic necessity."[39] Both communities urged their men to enlist, eager to prove their loyalty in order to secure political leverage after the war. The Unionists were pledged to King and Empire. The Nationalists were loyal to a Parliament that had granted but postponed Home Rule.*

The two Irelands appeared to be in uneasy stasis, at least for the duration.

*Irish Catholic enlistment was driven, in part, by sympathy for France and Belgium, Catholic nations attacked by Protestant Germany. Allied propaganda made great use of German atrocities, real or imagined, against nuns and Catholic churches.

1

The Troubles I

The War of Independence and the Irish Civil War

The Irish Republican Army emerged during the Troubles of 1916–1923, which encompassed the War of Independence, also known as the Anglo-Irish War, and the Irish Civil War that followed.

Although Redmond's drive for Home Rule dominated the Anglo-Irish conflict until the outbreak of war, by 1915, more militant movements were coalescing to supplant it. The early Irish enthusiasm for the Great War ebbed with mounting casualties and the prospect of conscription. Irish enlistees found themselves regarded as an inferior race by the British high command, and many soldiers resented that their units were designated as British rather than Irish. Redmond's organization, though still sizeable, had lost much of its strength, as its ablest men had left for service in France, and support for Home Rule declined.[1]

The Irish Republican Brotherhood, though small, resisted Redmond's calls for enlistment in the British Army and provided an alternative to Home Rule. Labor leaders like John Larkin and Socialists like James Connolly were not satisfied with the prospect of national independence alone, envisioning instead a worker's revolution along Marxist lines. In 1913 they formed the Irish Citizen Army to protect strikers. The poet Padraig Pearse, inspired by the Gaelic Revival, believed Ireland required a "blood sacrifice" fueled by religious and nationalist fervor. Arthur Griffith, an Irish nationalist active in the Gaelic League and the Irish Republican Brotherhood, founded a political party and a newspaper with the same name—*Sinn Fein* ("Ourselves").* Much of Griffith's nationalist program was economic. He advocated reforestation and the development of an Irish merchant marine to achieve national self-sufficiency.[2] The Irish Volunteers, formed in 1913, attracted members of the Irish Republican Brotherhood, Sinn Fein, and the Gaelic League.

Though propelled by disparate ideologies, militant nationalists were united in the belief that it was time to strike.

The Easter Rising

England's difficulty is Ireland's opportunity.—*Daniel O'Connell*

The cry that "England's difficulty is Ireland's opportunity" is raised in the old senseless, spiteful way as a recommendation to stab England in the back when she is fighting someone else.—*George Bernard Shaw*, 1916

Frequently mistranslated as "Ourselves Alone."

15

Redmond saw the World War as an opportunity to gain leverage by supporting Britain in her time of need; militant nationalists saw the war as an opportunity to strike Britain in her hour of difficulty. Irish-Americans had met with the German ambassador in 1914 to enlist support for a rising in Ireland. They funded Roger Casement's trip to Germany to gain weapons and recruit volunteers from the ranks of Irish POWs.[3] Casement, born in Dublin, had a distinguished career in the British Foreign Service, achieving an international reputation for his work exposing human rights abuses in the Belgian Congo and South America. Knighted in 1911, Casement retired in 1913 and took up the cause of Irish nationalism, joining the Volunteers and traveling to America to raise funds.[4] His mission to Germany was a disappointment. Only fifty prisoners were willing to enlist, and most of them were simple malcontents seeking a trip home. The German offer of 20,000 rifles seemed inadequate to arm a national revolution. Casement decided to return to Ireland to urge nationalists to abort an uprising he believed destined to fail.[5] A U-boat took Casement to the Irish coast and set him and two others ashore in a collapsible boat. The small craft foundered in the surf, and Casement nearly drowned. He recovered but was quickly arrested and transported to Britain to stand trial for treason.[6] Casement was convicted and sentenced to death. Despite pleas for clemency from Yeats, Shaw, and Sir Arthur Conan Doyle, he was hanged in August.* Casement was in British custody when news of the Rising broke.

On Easter Monday Padraig Pearse led 1500 volunteers, accompanied by 200 soldiers of Connolly's Irish Citizen Army, and seized the General Post Office, known as the GPO, in Dublin. The insurgents raised a Republican flag, and Pearse went outside to declare an Irish Republic "in the name of God and of the dead generations" to an audience of largely bemused passersby. The poorly armed and disorganized rebels (some carried only pikes) occupied a few buildings in Dublin but lacked the resources to expand their attack or defend what they had seized. Newspaper headlines labeled the rising a "crazy rebellion."

The British army brought in artillery and fired on the post office, forcing the volunteers to withdraw. The shelling destroyed and heavily damaged neighboring buildings. In the confusion of battle Dubliners looted stores, but few, if any, joined the rebels. By Saturday the revolt ended. Pearse agreed to surrender and ordered volunteers still fighting in scattered units to lay down their arms.

The Rising was a fiasco. It failed to spark widespread rebellion. If anything, it turned public opinion against the militants. Dubliners resented the extensive damage to their city. Nearly two hundred buildings were destroyed, and a third of the population was forced on relief. The rebels' collusion with Germany was viewed as treasonous while Irishmen were dying in France. As the volunteers were marched into captivity, crowds gathered, urging soldiers to bayonet the traitors.[7] Fearing the British might suspend payments to families of Irish servicemen in retaliation, women pelted the "Shinners"† with rubbish.

Support for the government was short-lived. Determined to teach the Irish a lesson, Major General Sir John Maxwell conducted quick trials in secret and began executing the leaders of the Rising. Pearse and two others were shot on May 3. A week later Connolly was shot. Unable to stand because of a leg wound, he was tied to a chair and placed before

---

*Casement's trial was the subject of Richard Stockton's 1972 play Prisoner of the Crown, which became the first American work to receive a world premiere at Dublin's Abbey Theatre.

†Though Sinn Fein played little direct role in the Rising, the public and newspapers quickly dubbed the rebels "Sinn Feiners" or "Shinners."

the firing squad. In all, fifteen men were executed in Dublin. Roger Casement was hanged in London.[8] Once vilified as crazed rebels, the sixteen took on the status of honored martyrs, courageous men who had not only fought bravely but had published books, written poetry, and even earned a knighthood.

Maxwell's lesson backfired.

The Rising was a defeat that achieved its intended goal. Support for Home Rule collapsed. Consumed by its costly war on the Continent, Britain still sought to pacify the Irish. Then a member of the Cabinet, David Lloyd George was assigned the Irish issue. Realizing he could not hope to get the Unionists and nationalists to compromise, he met with them separately. He urged Redmond to accept a temporary partition of Ireland as a condition of Home Rule, while promising the Unionist leader Sir Edward Carson that any partition would be permanent. Initially satisfied, Redmond rejected the proposal when the Unionist assurance was made public by a member of the House of Lords. Lloyd George offered Home Rule again the following year, and Redmond refused. Eclipsed by events and suffering exhaustion, Redmond died in 1918.

For nationalists, there was only one road left — complete independence.

"A Terrible Beauty": The Troubling Legacy

The Easter Rising was a watershed event in Irish history. But unlike 1776 for Americans, 1916 left a confused and troubling legacy for the Irish. While the Fourth of July is uniformly celebrated by Democrats and Republicans without reflection or apology in the United States, the Easter Rising even now stirs controversy in Ireland. Commemorations are erratic. Depending on the political climate, Irish governments have celebrated, downplayed, or ignored anniversaries of the Rising. The event is credited with leading to the eventual establishment of the Republic, but it is also seen as a sanction for the use of arms. The Rising initiated six years of war and civil war that rent Irish society and culminated in partition and a "Free State" that in general terms differed little from Home Rule status repeatedly offered by the British. Critics of the armed struggle speculate that under Home Rule a united and more prosperous Ireland might have peacefully evolved and eventually achieved independence, not unlike Canada or Australia.

Writing on the fiftieth anniversary of the Rising in 1966, future Taoiseach Garret Fitzgerald noted that England "exploited" Ireland in the seventeenth and eighteenth centuries, "neglected" it in the nineteenth century, but "in the twentieth century ... would have surely subsidized Ireland, as she does the North today."[9] With Home Rule, Ireland could have been more affluent, and been spared violence and terror. But the subsidies Britain might have lavished on Ireland under Home Rule would have come with a price:

> Without the national revival of 1916–1921, would Ireland ever have become a largely self-reliant country, seeking to run its own affairs in its own way, or would it have shrunk like Northern Ireland into dependent provincialism, too concerned about its share of British agricultural subsidies and social welfare re-insurance provisions to want ever to become a sovereign state?[10]

Forty years after Fitzgerald's reflections, the Rising still prompted conflicting responses. For Geoffrey Wheatcroft, writing in *The Guardian* in 2006, the Easter Rising left the "evil legacy" of an armed "reaction against constitutional liberalism into irrationalism."[11] He saw the seizure of the Dublin post office in 1916 as the precursor of Mussolini's March on Rome in 1922 and Hitler's Beer Hall Putsch a year later.* "Looking around today," Wheatcroft concluded, "the Easter rebels have a good deal to answer for."[12] The following April, Kevin Myers insisted in *The Belfast Telegraph* that there was "nothing, absolutely nothing" to commemorate about the Rising which led to the "cold-blooded slaughter of innocent people in the streets of Dublin" and sparked "six lunatic years of civil war ... before a partitioned, independent Ireland marched into a 40-year-long cul-de-sac of isolation and poverty."[13]

But for Sinn Fein's national chairperson, Mary Lou McDonald, the party's first Member of the European Parliament, there was no question about the legacy of the Rising and its proclamation:

> It was a landmark declaration committed to freedom, equality, the eradication of sectarianism, emancipation for all and true democracy. It was a vision of an Ireland where all were equal and where the wealth of the nation would uplift and enrich the lives of all.[14]

Seeing the legacy of the Rising as a blueprint for the future, she urged the Irish in 2006 to "re-dedicate ourselves to finishing the revolution started on the streets of Dublin in Easter Week 1916."[15]

For filmmakers, the Easter Rising was an event to be heralded as a doomed but heroic stand comparable to the American Alamo or dismissed as a foolhardy venture by vainglorious amateurs. John Ford created two distinct visions of the Rising.

THE PLOUGH AND THE STARS (1936)

Sean O'Casey's play *The Plough and the Stars* caused a riot when it debuted in Dublin in 1926 and ended O'Casey's relationship with the Abbey Theatre. Angered by the naturalistic depiction of Irish life and its satirical treatment of Irish nationalism during the Easter Rising, audience members took to the stage and disrupted the performance. Recalling the famous *Playboy of the Western World* riots in 1907, a furious William Butler Yeats told protestors, "You have disgraced yourselves again. Is this to be the ever-recurring celebration of the arrival of Irish genius?"[16]

In bringing this spirited drama to the screen a decade later, John Ford transformed O'Casey's sardonic send-up into a patriotic romantic drama that pitted the tender relationship of newlyweds Jack (Preston Foster) and Nora (Barbara Stanwyck) Clitheroe against the turbulence of the Easter Rising. In O'Casey's play, no historical figures of the Rising are depicted. Instead, working class characters sit in a pub listening to an unnamed speaker in the street delivering a histrionic call for blood sacrifice, "We rejoice in this terrible war. The old heart of the earth needed to be warmed with the red wine of the battlefields ... without shedding of blood there is no redemption."[17]

In his film version, Ford introduced the character of General Connolly, played by mustachioed Moroni Olsen, who bore a striking resemblance to James Connolly. The film opens with a torchlight sympathy procession for the Citizens Army and Volunteers' efforts to establish the Republic. General Connolly delivers an impassioned call to arms, stating dramatically, "Ireland has this night become a nation.... We are a sovereign people ... Ireland will be free."

The signing of the proclamation of the Republic is dramatized with the somber dignity of the signing of the American Declaration of Independence. Connolly then orders rebels

---

Wheatcroft darkly noted the symbolic coincidence that both the Easter Rising and Hitler's putsch produced the identical number of martyrs — sixteen dead men.

to take the GPO, which will provide a "brief advantage" over the British, noting soberly, "I do not know whether we will win or lose, but I do know we are firm in our cause." The volunteers march to the post office, raise the Irish tricolor, and stage a heroic but futile battle against the superior British army. With the GPO under shellfire, a wounded Connolly directs the rebels to abandon the building and fight on. Clitheroe eludes capture by dashing over the rooftops and taking shelter in a garret apartment.

The most dramatic scene shows a hospitalized General Connolly making notes in bed. An attendant in a white coat with a Red Cross emblem salutes Connolly and tells him it is time. Men in military caps and white jackets carefully lift the wounded Republican into a wheelchair, cover his legs with a blanket, and wheel him outside to face a firing squad. Asked by a priest if he forgives the soldiers about to execute him, Connolly nobly states, "I forgive all brave men who do their duty."

With Dublin in ruins, a distraught Nora asks her husband, "What was it all for?" Jack promises that it is only the beginning, telling his wife, "We will live to see Ireland free. And go on fighting until we do." Nora agrees, sobbing, "Aye, and we'll go on weeping."

The seventy-two minute film, badly edited, with reshot scenes, awkward cuts, and post-dubbed lines, lost money and ended RKO's interest in another Ford-O'Casey project.[18]

YOUNG CASSIDY (1965)

Thirty years after *The Plough and the Stars*, John Ford presented a more faithful expression of O'Casey's cynicism in *Young Cassidy* (Metro-Goldwyn-Meyer). The film, based on O'Casey's autobiographies, follows the career of John Cassidy (Rod Taylor) from Dublin day laborer to rebel to playwright forced to leave Ireland following a riot at the Abbey Theatre. Ford began work on the film, holding many conversations with Rod Taylor, who urged the director to abandon his original plan to shoot the movie in black and white. Ford, drinking heavily and in failing health, became ill and was replaced by Jack Cardiff, who directed much of the final film.

The Cassidy family illustrates diverse responses to the Irish condition. Incensed by their poverty, John, a ditch digger, becomes politically active. His brother Archie escapes reality by pursuing art, acting in Shakespearean plays without payment. Dismissive of politics, he advises, "Will Shakespeare could move the hearts of people more by getting them together in a theater than you'll ever do by getting them together in a riotous mass. Don't forget the dreamer in yourself, Johnny." Another brother leaves home to serve in the British army.

Cassidy joins the Volunteers drilling in the hills outside Dublin but becomes quickly disillusioned with the ragtag group of middle-aged men armed with obsolete weapons, leading him to quip, "All the world's a stage ... but some of us are desperately unrehearsed." The whimsical accompanying music underscores the pathetic naiveté of the amateur rebels practicing with wooden rifles.

Arriving late to a meeting, Cassidy joins a discussion about uniforms, rejecting the call for elaborate military dress:

Now look lads, we're supposed to be revolutionaries, not pantomime soldiers. We're not fighting for the right to strut up and down streets in gaudy uniforms. Our only chance is to be irregulars....

The British will regard us as bloody rebels whatever we wear. Uniforms won't help us stand up against machine guns. We got to make up for lack of means by cleverness and cunning. Wear what you got on, but dodge and strike, strike and dodge.

Dispirited by their insistence on waging a conventional war he deems hopeless, Johnny abandons the Volunteers, telling his mother, "I've told them the British will use cannon in the streets of Dublin if need be. I've told them to stop going marching around in big groups. I've told them, and they think I'm daft. I've done all I could, and I've left them."

Watching the smoke of the doomed Easter Rising fill the skies over Dublin, Cassidy proclaims, "The fools, the bloody magnificent fools." Volunteers with bolt action rifles are shown cut down by British machine gun fire and blown apart by grenades. Civilians loot shops and are shot in the crossfire. After massive destruction rakes Dublin, the defeated Volunteers are rounded up. Commenting on the failed Rising, Cassidy's mother tells her son, "What else could anyone expect?"

RYAN'S DAUGHTER (1970)

David Lean's big-budget feature *Ryan's Daughter* (MGM) is a Madame Bovary story of adultery set in a coastal Irish village in 1916 sometime after the Easter Rising. Lean's film captures the narrow jealousies and prejudices of Irish provincial life, its conflict between the villagers and British soldiers providing a fairly accurate depiction of prevailing attitudes. In 1916, before the Black and Tan outrages of the Twenties, the level of animosity was dampened by the fact that hundreds of thousands of Irishmen were serving the Crown by fighting in France. The disdain for the British in Lean's film is initially limited to taunting and refusing to accept a soldier's offer to buy drinks. News of the Rising is supplied when Charles Shaughnessy (Robert Mitchum) stops in a pub and reports on his trip to Dublin, remarking that Sackville Street looks "smashed about" from the rebellion.

The IRA leader Tim O'Leary (Barry Foster) is introduced shooting a policeman in the back. He has arrived in the coastal village to receive a weapons shipment from Germany. At first he is contemptuous of the townspeople, viewing them as unreliable "talkers." When a storm forces the ship to jettison its cargo, the entire village rushes to the rain-swept beach to collect the rifles and dynamite. When O'Leary asks the town's priest (Trevor Howard) what he has done, Father Collins responds, "I didn't, they did it!" Watching children and old women scooping up cartridges and grenades and loading his truck, O'Leary is inspired, noting, "We make speeches about these people, but by God!" Betrayed by an informer, he attempts to escape and is shot. As he's carried off on a stretcher under arrest, the townspeople hail O'Leary as a hero.

Though the Easter Rising is only referred to within the film, *Ryan's Daughter* vividly portrays the changing politics of the early days of the Troubles and the emergence of the IRA as a national force.

The War of Independence

The Easter Rising elevated Sinn Fein to prominence. Although it had little to do with the Rising, most people gave the organization credit for the rebellion, few having heard of the Irish Republican Brotherhood. When Arthur Griffith was released from prison, he found his party filling the vacuum left by the collapse of the Home Rule movement. In 1917 Sinn Fein candidates began winning elections to Parliament and uniformly refused to take their seats in Westminster. By 1918 there were seventy-three Sinn Fein MPs, all of whom refused to go to London. Instead, they formed the Dail Eireann, or Assembly of Ireland, a shadow parliament. The body elected a president and ministers. A declaration of independence was read out, and plans were made to create "a democratic, classless society."[19]

While members of the Dail developed policies for an independent state and sent delegates to seek international recognition, the Volunteers, now known as the Irish Republican Army, staged a guerrilla war. With few men and fewer arms, the IRA relied on John Cassidy's "strike and dodge" attacks. Flying columns raided police barracks to seize weapons, shot up convoys, and assassinated government officials. The IRA systematically destroyed over a hundred tax offices in 1920 to deny the British revenues from Ireland. Republican courts were established to adjudicate civil issues and legal disputes to replace the British administration.[20]

ENTER THE BLACK AND TANS

As the IRA raids continued, the Royal Irish Constabulary (RIC) was unable to cope with the growing military threat. Enlistments fell and resignations soared as its mostly Catholic officers refused to serve British interests, were intimidated by the IRA, or persuaded by family members to quit. Fearful of guerrilla attacks, RIC officers stayed close to their barracks, unwilling to venture out on patrols.

The British were reluctant to send in the army because that would be an admission they were at war, something they wished to avoid. Britain had fought the Great War, in part, on behalf of small nations seeking the right of self-determination. It could not be seen as suppressing a nationalist revolution at home. It could, however, bolster a demoralized police force. Unable to find reliable candidates in Ireland, the British recruited auxiliary policemen in England and Scotland. Some ten thousand men, mostly unemployed veterans, enlisted. There were not enough RIC uniforms available, so the hastily organized force was outfitted with a mix of surplus army khaki and dark green or blue police trousers, jackets, belts, and caps. Their mismatched clothing reminded the Irish of a local hunt, and soon the new arrivals were nicknamed the Black and Tans. Another group of volunteers, typically former British army officers, formed the Auxiliary Division, known as Auxies. Their orders were to support the flagging RIC and mount counter-insurgency operations against the IRA.

Irish propaganda portrayed the Black and Tans as psychotics and convicts released from Britain's prisons to run riot in Ireland. In reality, they were largely ex-servicemen, many of them hardened combat veterans. They were not criminals, but unlike the RIC, they were not Irish. They had little sympathy for or understanding of the country or its people. Accustomed to fighting conventional battles with uniformed enemies, they were ill-prepared to cope with attacks by guerrillas or gunmen in civilian clothing who could toss a grenade or fire a revolver then fade into a crowd. The shooting of a Tan drinking in a pub or buying a pack of cigarettes struck them as murder. Unable to identify their adversaries, and eager to avenge a fallen comrade, they often took their wrath out on civilians, burning houses and farms, torturing prisoners, and shooting suspects on sight. As in many insurrections, traditional soldiers attacked by an invisible enemy came to see no distinction between combatants and civilians. After the IRA shot up a convoy of Auxiliaries in County Cork, Black and Tans attacked Cork City in revenge, burning down much of the business district. In Dublin, fellow Auxiliaries celebrated the event by placing burnt corks in their hats.[21]

The Black and Tan atrocities, many of which were actually committed by Auxiliaries, fueled Republican propaganda for ninety years.*

DE VALERA

The pivotal figure to emerge during the War of Independence was Eamon de Valera. Born in New York City in 1882 to a Spanish father and an Irish mother, he would dominate Ireland in and out of office until his death in 1975. A mathematics teacher by training, de Valera was the senior commander to have survived the Easter Rising, his death sentence commuted.† In 1917 he became president of Sinn Fein and was elected president of the newly formed Dail. De Valera spent much of the Anglo-Irish War in the United States, raising funds and seeking diplomatic recognition for the fledgling republic. Sensitive to the IRA being denounced as a "murder gang," de Valera justified its guerrilla techniques against the English with mathematical reasoning:

> If they may use their tanks and steel-armoured cars, why should we hesitate to use the cover of stone walls and ditches? Why should the element of surprise be denied to us? ... If German forces had landed in England during the recent war, would it have been wrong for Englishmen to ... harass their invader by every means in their power? If not wrong for Englishmen, why wrong for us?[22]

He returned to Ireland in December 1920. In July 1921 a truce was declared. De Valera went to London to discuss a settlement but returned to Dublin days later in dismay, having discovered that Lloyd George had assured the Unionists that Ireland would be partitioned, guaranteeing that the Protestant North would remain part of Great Britain. In addition, the remainder of the country was being offered not independence but something less than full Dominion status.[23] Messages passed between Dublin and London in preparation for official treaty negotiations. When Lloyd George presented a proposal for formal discussion, de Valera, a skilled negotiator, announced that he would not lead the Irish delegation. Arguing that as head of state he should remain in Dublin, de Valera sent Arthur Griffith in his place.

During the weeks of talks and committee meetings it was clear to the Irish delegates that the British were determined to adhere to the basic formula Lloyd George had offered de Valera in July. Ireland would be partitioned, and there would be no republic. The proposal of a "boundary commission" held out the possibility of eventual unification. Despite modifications, the agreement would present the Irish with a compromised resolution. Most of Ireland would be mostly free, but it would not be what Republicans aspired to — a fully independent thirty-two-county republic. Instead, Ireland would be designated a "Free State." On December 6, 1921, the Anglo-Irish Treaty was signed and ratified by the Dail.

In response, de Valera resigned.

---

*In 2006 Ben and Jerry's issued an apology for offending Irish sentiments after marketing a flavor called Black and Tan.

†Many sources claim that de Valera was spared execution in deference to his American birth (Britain, hopeful for American intervention in the war, was reluctant to offend a potential ally). Other sources state that the decision was accidental. The executions were causing a political backlash, so they were called off, sparing de Valera, who was next on the list for the firing squad.

The Treaty and Civil War

To dedicated Republicans the Treaty contravened their core principles. Of particular offense, in addition to partition, was the requirement that members of the new Irish parliament pledge allegiance to King George V. The IRA split over the treaty, and the division was bitter. Former comrades turned on each other. Sinn Fein split into pro– and anti–Treaty parties. In a June election, the Irish people, weary of conflict, voted for the pro–Treaty faction. In a replay of the Easter Rising, anti–Treaty IRA units seized buildings in Dublin. The newly created Free State Army, supplied with British artillery, pounded IRA positions. The Free State forces secured the capital, arresting anti–Treaty volunteers and forcing others to flee the city.

Bitter fighting ravaged the countryside. In October the Catholic Bishops issued a statement formally accepting the Free State as the legitimate government of Ireland and denouncing the anti–Treaty Republicans as illegal rebels. The Free State, which acquired surplus British weapons, sought to establish its legitimacy and interned over 10,000 dissidents.

IRA rebels were outnumbered and lacked resources. Their actions alienated the public because the soldiers they were now killing were Irish, not British. In May 1923 the order came to cease operations, though scattered fighting continued for months.

The anti–Treaty IRA members found themselves isolated from the newly formed government now solidifying around those who accepted the Free State. De Valera, who backed the IRA dissidents in opposition to the Treaty, left Sinn Fein in 1926. He founded a new political party, Fianna Fail (Soldiers of Destiny), and returned to the Dail. Over the next forty years he would dominate Ireland, serving fifteen years as the Taoiseach and fourteen as President.

In 1949 John Costello, who served as Taoiseach between two de Valera terms, changed the Irish Free State, or Erie, to the Republic of Ireland, officially terminating any association with Britain. Hearing the news, a troubled King George VI asked the Irish Minister, "Why leave the family?"[24]

The Civil War left Ireland with a troubling legacy for both historians and filmmakers.

SHAKE HANDS WITH THE DEVIL (1959)

Based on the Reardon Conner novel, *Shake Hands with the Devil* (Troy Films) is a standard Hollywood romance adventure film set in Ireland in 1921. Its cast is tri-national, with American actors James Cagney and Don Murray in the lead roles, supported by British stars Dana Wynter (playing an English hostage), Glynis Johns (portraying an Irish barmaid hussy), and Michael Redgrave (improbably cast as the Irish Republican leader known only as "the General"). Irish performers Cyril Cusack and Richard Harris appear in minor parts to flesh out the ranks of an IRA squad. The director, Michael Anderson, whose previous films included *The Dam Busters* and *Around the World in Eighty Days*, was British.

The film opens with an action sequence of Black and Tans firing machine guns amid burning debris in Dublin. A voiced prologue establishes the setting for a post-war American audience with little collective memory of the Anglo-Irish War:

> Dublin 1921. A city at war. Often it its turbulent history, the men of Ireland had risen to fight for their freedom, only to be crushed. This was the year of total war. It was also the year of the Black and Tans, the army assembled to replace the English regulars who had lost their taste for the suppression of men in search of freedom.

The prologue creates a simplistic and largely depoliticized conflict between freedom-seeking Irishmen and thuggish Black and Tans, who by the late 1950s were non-existent and generally discredited. In the film, the dispute is not one between Unionists and Nationalists, or the Irish and the British Army, but between patriots and gangsters.

Viewers learn about the IRA through the eyes of the protagonist, Kerry O'Shea (Don Murray), an Irish-American medical student studying at the College of Surgeons in Dublin. A veteran of the World War who states "violence never solved anything," he has no interest in joining the fight against the English, minimizing his Irish connections when his classmate Paddy Nolan attempts to recruit him for "the organization." Responding to O'Shea's refusal to join the IRA, Nolan muses, "Ah, it must be a grand thing to be an American, with your war for independence already won."

O'Shea and his classmate are drawn into the conflict when they are fired on by Black and Tans. Badly wounded, Paddy asks Kerry to notify Sean Lenihan (James Cagney). O'Shea is stunned to learn that his medical professor is also a commandant in the secret rebel army. Having dropped a textbook with his name in it, O'Shea fears arrest and seeks shelter with Lenihan after Nolan dies.

The "organization" is portrayed in largely positive terms. In a speech, Lenihan links their group with Irish patriots O'Connell and Parnell, and offers O'Shea two choices: join the organization or accept safe passage to America.

Dressed in a business suit and speaking with an English accent, the General (Michael Redgrave) appears more like a Mayfair banker than a Celtic rebel. Though soft-spoken, he is resolute, calmly threatening to execute a wavering volunteer. Guilt-stricken over shooting a female informer, the young gunman asks to quit the organization. Reminding him that he swore an oath and knew the policy of "once in, never out," the General quietly asks the young man where he wants his body sent, then offers him a chance to withdraw his resignation. "These things are not pleasant," the General explains to O'Shea, but necessary because the rebels are "hopelessly outnumbered."

Taken to a remote farm cottage to await a boat to America, O'Shea meets other members of the organization, which include a swaggering

James Cagney (left) and Don Murray in *Shake Hands with the Devil* (1959).

brawler (Richard Harris) and Chris Noonan (Cyril Cusak), a thoughtful poet. When O'Shea comments, "You don't exactly expect to find a poet with a rifle," Noonan replies, "Patriotism taps at all sorts of doors." Noonan repeats the phrase when O'Shea learns that the stately noblewoman Lady Fitzhugh is transporting an escaped rebel in the boot of her Rolls Royce.

The Black and Tans are wholly depicted as vicious and sadistic, a force apart from the more staid and judiciously humane British army. While British officers debate strategy, a cigar-smoking Colonel Smithson, commanding the Black and Tans, vows he will "burn every house in Ireland down" because it is "the only language these people understand." In one scene Smithson enters a cell to interrogate the captured O'Shea. Filmed in half light, his black tunic resembling a Nazi uniform, he slams his fist directly into the camera. Planning to rescue O'Shea before he can be broken, Lenihan reminds Chris Noonan, "We are not dealing with British regulars. We're dealing with Tans."

In an episode that replays throughout IRA films, the Irish rebels stage a rescue by disguising themselves as British troops, complete with uniforms, rifles, and stolen truck. They free the battered O'Shea, who decides to forgo passage to America to take the oath and join the organization, accepting its "once in, never out" policy. Warned by Lenihan that he will see blood flow, O'Shea states, "I can taste my own right now."

In this film the war, which was marked by outrages on both sides, is presented as one between idealistic freedom fighters and oppressive Tans, who torture prisoners, smash a pub, and take hostages. The politics of the film are summed up by a dramatic statement uttered by the aristocratic Lady Fitzhugh, who, convicted for assisting an escaped rebel, asks, "What is an English judge doing in an Irish court?" Sentenced to two years, the elderly woman starts a hunger strike.

Determined to free her, Lenihan borrows a tactic from Smithson and takes a high-profile English hostage to demand a prisoner exchange. His squad kidnaps Mrs. Curtis (Dana Wynter), a young war widow and daughter of the advisor to the military governor.

The Treaty is presented in a short pivotal scene in which the General informs Lenihan that he has received peace overtures from Downing Street:

The General: They're talking treaty.
Lenihan: What kind of treaty?
The General: Peace with honor.
Lenihan: A Republic?
The General (softly, hesitantly): Free state. Dominion status.
Lenihan: Is that what we've been fighting for?
The General: Sean, both sides must bend a little. We'll be ruling ourselves at last, after seven hundred years.
Lenihan: But still tied to England's aprons strings! That's not peace, that's surrender.
The General: It's a start. The Republic will come later.
Lenihan: I warn you, five out of ten men in the Republican army will split on peace on those terms. If you sign that treaty it will Irishman against Irishman. Civil war bloodier than this one.
The General: And where would you stand, Sean?
Lenihan: Damn well you know.

The General wants to "end the war with dignity and honor" and accept the treaty which will mean an Irish parliament and amnesty for prisoners, asking, "What good is a Republic if there is no one left to enjoy it?" Lenihan, however, insists they must fight "to the last man."

When the truce is announced and rebels celebrate the end of the conflict, Lenihan remains unchanged, denouncing the agreement as "treason." When news reaches him that Lady Fitzhugh has died while on a hunger strike, he intends to execute Mrs. Curtis out of revenge, arguing, "We have no choice."

Kerry O'Shea insists Lenihan is no longer fighting for Ireland or any ideals but "just killing now for the sake of killing." Lenihan announces he will head west to build a new army. One by one, he asks members of the squad to follow him. When they all decline, he calls them "traitors," snarling, "I'll take care of you when the time comes."

O'Shea shoots Lenihan before he can kill Mrs. Curtis, then throws the gun into the sea. The credits then roll over a close-up of the tide washing over the revolver on the beach.

The message of the film is that the Old IRA was a legitimate force of common men, much like American patriots, who fought the British for independence and freedom. By being willing to accept a compromise, they appear reasonable, peace-loving, and hesitant to use violence. The Chris Noonan character, played eloquently by Cyril Cusak, adds a dreamy romantic element to the rebels. The New IRA, represented by Lenihan, is discredited as being stubborn, sadistic, and bent on committing violence for the sake of violence.

The film, produced during the relative calm of the late 1950s, depicts the IRA era as past, the Irish problem resolved. The Irish win their freedom, and the thoughtful and responsible rebels accept peace and reject the isolated fanatic who wants to fight on for the sake of fighting. There is no mention of partition and no hint of the wider civil war that Lenihan predicts. His fifty-fifty conflict becomes the lone struggle of a murderous psychotic.

THE WIND THAT SHAKES THE BARLEY (2006)

Ken Loach's *The Wind That Shakes the Barley* (Sixteen Films) deals with another reluctant medical student drawn into the IRA's war against the Black and Tans. As in the Anderson film, the IRA is shown in a far more favorable light than its Black and Tan adversaries, who engage in outright torture and sadism.

The film opens with a group of hurly-playing Irish youths being harassed by a detachment of cursing Black and Tans who arrive to enforce a ban on Irish gatherings, which includes sports. They demand the boys identify themselves. When one player responds in Irish, he is taken into a stone barn and beaten to death. By opening with a Black and Tan outrage, Loach presents the IRA violence that follows as justifiable retaliation.

In Loach's film the Black and Tans abuse old women, lacerate a woman's scalp as they forcibly cut her hair, conduct mock executions, and torture suspects. In contrast, IRA volunteers stage military attacks, ambushing armed soldiers. They conduct executions of informers with discipline and a measure of sad compassion, allowing their victims to write farewell letters to loved ones. Unlike the Black and Tans, who seem intentionally brutal, the IRA men give warnings before resorting to violence, target only military and police personnel, show remorse for their victims, and retain a level of self-awareness. As in Anderson's film, the IRA appear as freedom fighters seeking independence from a colonial power, using measured violence with great reluctance and soul-searching regret.

Unlike Anderson's film, Loach's plot covers both the War of Independence and the Civil War. The heart of the plot involves two brothers, dramatizing the fraternal conflict featured in Irish stories like Liam O'Flaherty's "The Sniper." Damien O' Donovan (Cillian Murphy) is a young doctor preparing to leave Ireland in 1920 to study medicine in London. Unlike his brother Teddy (Padraic Delaney), who commands a local IRA unit, Damien is not political. Even after witnessing the Black and Tans beat a seventeen-year-old friend to death, he is determined to go to England. The volunteers, he tells Teddy, are hopelessly outnumbered, so armed rebellion is futile. However, after watching British soldiers brutalize a railway worker who refuses to drive a train carrying English troops, Damien returns to take the oath to support the Irish Republic.

Loach depicts the evolution of the IRA as young volunteers practice guerrilla tactics using hurly sticks instead of rifles, raid police barracks to seize arms, and burst into the back room of a pub to kill British officers. This IRA shooting of men in uniform incites a vicious Black and Tan reprisal against civilians. An Anglo-Irish landlord forces a farm worker to inform on Teddy's flying column. Captured by the British, the IRA squad is held in a barracks where Damien recognizes the train driver from the station. Teddy is harshly interrogated but refuses to divulge information, despite having his fingernails pulled out with pliers. Hearing his screams, the rebels begin singing "A Soldier's Song" and stomping their boots in defiance. Questioned by an English officer, Damien maintains that he is an IRA soldier and a democrat. The British, he argues, are engaging in an illegal foreign occupation. In response, the officer counters with the lame assertion that he is simply "following orders." Underscoring the lack of British conviction in the conflict, a soldier with an Irish father allows the O'Donovan brothers and their comrades to escape.

As the war continues, Teddy's flying column becomes better armed and launches larger attacks on British convoys, killing soldiers and seizing weapons. Though dedicated to their cause, IRA volunteers become distraught and disoriented by the sight of their victims, demonstrating a reluctance to use violence not shown by the remorseless Black and Tans.

The O'Sullivan brothers, Cillian Murphy (left) and Padraic Delaney, in *The Wind That Shakes the Barley* (2006).

Unlike *Shake Hands with the Devil*, where only a lone psychotic wants to continue fighting after the Treaty, *The Wind That Shakes the Barley* presents a balanced view of the Civil War. When the truce is announced, it is Teddy, the IRA leader tortured by the British, who accepts the Treaty and joins the newly created Free State Army. Damien, the doctor, continues to fight. Teddy, citing the British threat of "immediate and terrible war" if the Treaty were not ratified, justifies the agreement as a reasonable compromise that ends the conflict and brings Ireland freedom. Damien, radicalized through conversations with the Marxist train driver, insists they must not settle for anything but full independence and a republic.

Loach includes extensive debates in which both sides clash over the Treaty. Teddy reminds the volunteers that Ireland is a small part of the British Empire. Britain, he contends, cannot be seen granting full independence to Ireland without stirring the nationalists in India and the African colonies. While Teddy argues from political realities, Damien clings to the values he took an oath to — the Republic. He insists that under the Treaty, Ireland will only have a "puppet parliament" that will not transform Irish society but continue an economic system that exploits the poor. Part of the split between pro–and anti–Treaty forces concerns arguments not only over partition and dominion status, but promises of social reform. Conservative nationalists wanted independence from Britain; radical Republicans wanted independence and a revolution that would redistribute land and nationalize major industries.

Loach dramatizes the conflict in a scene set in a church. Speaking from the pulpit, a priest exhorts parishioners to embrace "peace and prosperity" by accepting the Treaty endorsed by the Catholic Church. He warns that those who continue the struggle risk excommunication, reminding the congregation that the Irish people ratified the Treaty in a democratic election. His argument is countered by Damien, who rises and states that with the threat "of immediate and terrible war" the vote did not reflect "the will of the people" but instead "the fear of the people." Damien and other Republicans leave the church, demonstrating the widening gulf between the two brothers. When Teddy pleads with Damien to accept the treaty, Damien points to Teddy's Free State uniform and denounces him as a servant of the British Empire who has wrapped himself in the Union Jack, which he calls "the butcher's apron," a phrase used by James Connolly.

Free State soldiers, dismissed as the "green and tans," fill the vacuum left by the British, searching houses and detaining suspects, though with less brutality. The implication is that the anti–Treaty IRA volunteers are the true believers, while the Free Staters, if not traitors to the cause, have diminished it. Damien drills young boys in the hills, while Teddy enforces state policy. Replicating their attacks on the British, the IRA ambushes Irish soldiers and attacks barracks to seize weapons.

After Damien is captured in a raid, Teddy visits him in his cell, wearing a shirt rather than a Free State tunic. He pleads with Damien to stop fighting, accept the Treaty, build a life with his girlfriend, start a family, and practice medicine. He begs his brother to reveal information and accept amnesty. Damien reminds Teddy that he shot their friend Chris Reilly for informing and states, "I'm not going to sell out." Teddy informs Damien that he will be shot at dawn unless he cooperates.

Unwilling to betray his values, Damien is led by Irish soldiers to a courtyard and shot by a firing squad under the command of a tearful Teddy. Just as Damien informed Chris Reilly's mother that he had killed her son, Teddy visits Damien's girlfriend Sinead. And, like Chris' mother, she tells him she never wants to see him again. The film ends with a distraught Sinead weeping over Damien.

The Wind That Shakes the Barley enjoyed great success in Ireland and received the Golden Palm at the Cannes Film Festival. Loach was nominated for best director by the British Independent Film Awards and the London Critics Circle Awards. American reviews were generally positive, with *The New York Times* stating the film "is alive and as troubling as anything on the evening news, though far more thoughtful and beautiful,"[25] and *Newsweek* calling it "dense, brutal, with moments of shattering emotional power."[26] *Variety*, however, found that the "characters get lost in the plot-heavy second half," and the final scene lacked emotional power.[27]

The reception from the British press was less favorable and often hostile. Writing in *The Times*, Tim Luckhurst denounced *The Wind That Shakes the Barley* as a "poisonously anti–British corruption of the history of the war of Irish independence."[28] Loach, in Luckhurst's view, is nothing less than a "leech":

> He still treats the IRA killers like cuddly hippies, still detests the British State that educated him and pays for his films. Loach leeches from the nation that nurtured his talent and spits back in its eye. Unforgivable? No, he is exercising the very freedom his creed would deny all of us.[29]

Luckhurst concluded his review by noting that Hitler's favorite director, Leni Riefenstahl, "did not fully understand the evil cause to which her work contributed." Loach, however, "knows precisely what he is doing."[30]

Four days later Simon Heffer echoed the poisonous leech theme in a brief piece for *The Telegraph* titled "More Poison from Loach the Leech," which asked if anything was more "nauseating ... than ... the bigoted Marxist film director Ken Loach ... winning the Palme d'Or at Cannes, for a poisonous film."[31] Loach, he declared, "hates this country, yet leeches off it, using public funds to make his repulsive films."[32] Heffer ended his comments admitting he had not seen the film and did not need to view it before passing judgment "any more than I need to read Mein Kampf to know what a louse Hitler was."[33] *The Telegraph*'s official film review by Catherine Shoard echoed the same accusation that Loach was a self-loathing Brit. Acknowledging that "the atrocities" Loach depicts "undoubtedly occurred," Shoard argued that "because something's true doesn't mean it convinces as fiction."[34] She was especially sensitive to the film's anti–British tone, noting, "In these troubling times, arthouse audiences appear as eager as the multiplex masses for an easily identifiable bad guy. That's where the British come in useful — we're the oldest villains in the book, both in Hollywood and Europe. And we don't even seem to mind."[35]

Ninety years after the end of the conflict, the Anglo-Irish War could still spark fierce debates. Any film portraying the Old IRA in a favorable light was condemned as propaganda justifying the current armed struggle in the North.

Big House Dramas

Several films set during the War of Independence concern the last days of the Anglo-Irish Ascendancy. Dubbed "big house" dramas by Martin McLoone, these movies generally eschew politics to tell coming-of-age stories set in an era of imperial decline.[36] As mood pieces, they paint romantic murals detailing the dying lifestyle of genteel privilege akin to Vittorio De Sica's *The Garden of the Finzi-Continis*. They also explore the nature of the Irish identity. Most noticeable is that these films are set in the South and feature Protestants who declare themselves to be Irish, in stark contrast to the bellicose Orangemen of the North.

The plight of Protestants in the South remains one of the wounds of the War of Independence, creating distinctly different memories. Tom Barry, leader of the IRA flying column in West Cork, described the social and economic landscape in terms of the great houses:

> In 1919, the "Big House" near all the towns was a feature of first importance in the lives of the people. In it lived the leading British loyalist, secure and affluent in his many acres, enclosed by high demesne walls. Around him lived his many labourers, grooms, gardeners, and household servants, whose mission in life was to serve their lord and master. In the towns, many of the rich shopkeepers bowed before the "great" family, and to them those in the big house were veritable gods. The sycophants and lickspittles, happy in their master's benevolence, never thought to question how he had acquired his thousand acres, his castle and his wealth, or thought of themselves as the descendents of the rightful owners of those robbed lands.[37]

One of the greatest country estates was Puxley Manor. Its destruction, along with that of other big houses, was a hallmark of the war, which still embitters both British conservatives and Ulster Protestants. In 2005 *The Daily Mail Online* published an article describing the ruin:

> It was probably the greatest house in all Ireland, mixing the styles of French chateaux and the practical sturdiness of an old English manor. That was until lame-brained IRA gangsters went there in June 1921 and threw blazing torches inside. Its beauty was destroyed and a thousand people turned out to watch it burn. The IRA went on a spree of destruction, torching the great English houses which were the jewels of the Irish countryside. The Irish country house of today is mostly a hideous lump of cinder blocks and brick in the middle of an open field. These houses have all the architectural flair and charm of those on the upmarket side of a headhunter's village in central Borneo.[38]

The burning of homes of those taking up arms or providing support was characteristic of the conflict. The British burned the homes of Republicans; Republicans burned the homes of Loyalists. For all his resentment against the owners of the "big houses" in the opening pages of his autobiography, Tom Barry later assures readers that the IRA showed tolerance to the Protestants in Cork, executing spies and enemies with ecumenical efficiency while ignoring the homes of the innocent:

> The majority of West Cork Protestants lived at peace throughout the whole struggle and were not interfered with by the I.R.A. We did not press for their support, although we would have welcomed it. We had no doubt that nearly all of them disagreed with our campaign, but we accepted their right to their own opinions as to the wisdom of our cause or the tactics we employed. What we did demand was they in common with Catholics should not commit any hostile act against us and that they should not actively aid the British troops or administration. The majority of the Protestants accepted this position, and let it be said that we found them men of honour whose word was their bond. Aloof from the National struggle, they did not stand with our enemy and they lived their days at peace with their neighbours in spite of all British propaganda.[39]

The "big house" films produced in the 1980s and 1990s depict the men of honor struggling to remain aloof from the war around them.

FOOLS OF FORTUNE (1990)

The past is always there in the present.

Fools of Fortune (Polygram), based on the William Trevor novel and directed by Pat O'Connor, chronicles the downfall of a Protestant family destroyed by the violence of the Anglo-Irish War. It is also, as Hal Hinson's review notes, "a passionate, mystifying awkward bit of filmmaking" that blends flawed romance, improbable politics, and psychic phenomenon, with the IRA making an unusual appearance.[40]

In 1920 Quinton (Michael Kitchen) and his wife (Julie Christie) are the proud owners of Kilneaugh, a country estate with a big house. Unlike the Loyalist baron described by Tom Barry, Quinton is an open-minded Protestant who has taken in a defrocked priest, Father Kilgarrif (Tom Hickey), to tutor his son Willie (Sean McClory). The younger Quinton enjoys a charmed boyhood, playing with his sisters and listening to music performed by the family's Irish servants. Quinton passes onto Willie his father's tolerant view of Irish Catholics, calling them friends. "We're Irish, Willie, and so are they," he explains, "but you see, it hasn't always been easy to be an Irishman in Ireland." For the enlightened Quinton seeking to be aloof from the struggle, the Black and Tans, not the IRA, are the ones to fear. Riding home from church, the Quintons pass Black and Tans conducting a search, and Quinton tells his son they have a bad reputation, prompting Willie to ask if they are the "ones released from jail?" Mrs. Quinton despairs about the men sent to protect her interests, wondering, "Why can't they leave us in peace?"

Hearing of the Black and Tans, Father Kilgarrif tells Willie he wishes there was another Daniel O'Connell because "he showed there could be freedom without violence." Pointing to a portrait on the wall, he tells Willie that his great grandmother, Anna Quinton, was a "marvelous woman" who during the Famine begged people to help the starving Irish and urged her husband "to give away most of his land to those who had suffered." Disowned for her efforts, she died young, her ghost appearing on a nearby lake. The priest tells Willie that "it can be love and mercy that changes things, not men with swords and guns."

The IRA makes a brief, courteous appearance at Kilneaugh. A touring car arrives bearing men dressed in suits and ties rather than the characteristic trench coats and flat caps. With the solicitous air of an insurance salesman, one of the men enters the home and suggests they "get down to business." Although identifying herself as being English, Mrs. Quinton tells him, "We want to do anything we can to be of help to you." After the visitor thanks them and leaves, Willie overhears his parents arguing. Quinton tells his wife that he will provide money, but he will not allow "IRA fellows" drilling or storing guns at Kilneaugh. His wife insists they must do more. Doyle, a Quinton employee, observes the IRA men drive away. In a reverse of a typical action of the war, the three IRA men are killed when the Black and Tans ambush their car.

In retaliation, the IRA hang Doyle and cut out his tongue. Quinton muses that Doyle may have been killed because he was a friend of a Black and Tan sergeant named Rudkin, who served with him in France. Passing Rudkin in town, Quinton tells Willie he does not like the man.

One night the Protestant manor is set afire — not by Irish rebels but by English Black and Tans. Rudkin and a fellow Tan, seeking revenge for Doyle, torch the house. As flames consume the home, the portrait of Anna Quinton is shown burning. When Quinton emerges from the house, Rudkin shoots him, along with two servants. Only Willie, his mother, and a maid survive.

A decade passes and Willie (Iain Glen) has become a shy, troubled young man struggling to cope with his mother's ongoing grief and alcoholism. He falls in love with his second cousin Marianne (Mary Elizabeth Mastrantonio) who visits from England. While showing her the ruins of his old home, he is overcome with remorse. Discovering his mother's body after she commits suicide, he is driven to seek revenge. Tracking Rudkin to Liverpool, he confronts the former Black and Tan, reminds him of his crimes, stabs him, then goes into an alcoholic exile in a remote seaside cottage. Marianne, pregnant with Willie's child, moves in with Quinton aunts and raises their daughter Imelda. As a schoolgirl Imelda experiences flashbacks of events she never witnessed. Walking through the woods, she visualizes Doyle hanging from a tree. At school she cowers on a stairway, shrieking in horror as she envisions the burning of Kilneaugh and her grandmother's suicide. At home she wakes screaming from a nightmare of her father stabbing Rudkin.

Returning home, Willie discovers that his daughter has ceased speaking and "lives in her own world." While Irish neighbors believe Imelda is "gifted," Marianne bitterly declares her daughter to be "insane." Visiting Kilneaugh, a tearful Willie and Marianne despondently contemplate their destroyed lives in front of the ruins. Imelda wanders inside the burnt walls and imagines the big house restored to its prewar beauty, including the portrait of Anna Quinton. Smiling, she gazes out the window, envisioning her happy parents playing like children on the lawn.

While portraying the pain of the war, *Fools of Fortune* creates a nationalist fantasy, suggesting that if only the British left them alone, the Catholics and Protestants (at least enlightened ones like the Quintons) could work together and live in peace. The IRA dress like businessmen and kill a single informer. In contrast, the thuggish Black and Tans murder children and burn a jewel of a country home, destroying an idyllic world.

THE DAWNING (1988)

Robert Knight's *The Dawning* (Lawson Productions) presents a romantic depiction of an IRA gunman amid a coming-of-age story set in the West of Ireland in 1920. The film opens with the birthday celebration of Nancy Gulliver (Rebecca Pidgeon), an orphan living with her aunt Mary (Jean Simmons) and her elderly retired general grandfather (Trevor Howard) in the shabby gentility of cash-poor Anglo Irish aristocracy. Colorful landscapes, rock shores, great houses, and sunsets form the backdrop of Nancy's life. Finished with school and anticipating university, she questions her beauty and shows a growing curiosity about adult life. She flirts with Harry (Hugh Grant), a priggish Great War veteran and stockbroker. Carefully groomed and dressed in each scene, Harry is a vapid upper crust Englishman of detailed manners and little insight. The violence of war is only hinted at, with Aunt Mary warning Nancy about the Black and Tans and curfews.

Nancy encounters Angus Barrie (Anthony Hopkins), who has taken up residence in her private hideaway, a beach cottage. Although he dodges her questions and refuses to provide his name, Barrie becomes Nancy's tutor. Enamored with the older man, she brings him food and whiskey. Speaking softly, Barrie reveals himself to be a tormented man, disillusioned and thoughtful. An artillery major in the British Army, he tells her he fought for four years "for the rights of the small nations," noting, "I thought we were striking a million blows for justice. Of course, I was wrong." He speaks of a failed marriage, his loss of convictions, growing doubts, and being haunted by "voices from the past." Thoughtful and contemplative, the Shakespeare-quoting Barrie acts more like a vacationing college professor going through a midlife crisis than a rebel on the run.

In the cottage he shows Nancy his gun, telling her, "I use it when I have to. I make no apologies. See, my war isn't over yet." Realizing that Barrie is in the IRA, Nancy insists she must inform on him, but says nothing and returns to visit.

Barrie reflects quietly on his past and his current status as a "truly seedy revolutionary." When Nancy remarks her distaste for "this killing business," Barrie states that he feels no guilt for his actions. "After all," he tells her, "your grandfather was a killer ... but they gave him medals to wear and a pension and he was off plundering other people's land.... Indeed, if he'd been younger, he'd be down the street now killing his fellow countrymen."

As Nancy shifts her affections to Barrie, she enjoys defying Harry's stiff manners, calling him an informer, and announcing that she plans to lose her virginity and join the Republicans. With Barrie she engages in philosophical discussions about life, love, marriage, youth, and beauty. He explains to her that he once knew her Aunt Marie, warning that "nostalgia is a disease ... avoid it. Nothing of value gets lost with change." Barrie becomes her surrogate father as she faces changes both within herself and in her way of life. In saying farewell, she asks, "May a daughter kiss her father goodbye?" Barrie enlists Nancy to assist the rebels by passing a message to a man named Joe Mulhare in a restaurant.

The IRA appear in two scenes near the end of the film. In one, a group of middle-aged upper-class women are stopped by a roadblock manned by a flying column composed of teenage boys intent on commandeering their car "for the cause." Recognizing one of the youths, the driver threatens to tell his mother and orders him to remove the cart blocking their way. Humiliated, the boys retreat and let the car pass. At a horse race, Nancy spots Joe Mulhare in the crowd, then watches his older and more disciplined gunmen slip through the crowd and shoot twelve British officers with pitiless efficiency. At dinner, when Aunt Mary discusses the shootings, a servant mentions, "Twelve less to torture our poor boys." Nancy agrees. When her aunt states she is too young to understand such things, Nancy responds, "I'm learning."

British soldiers arrive at the house with a photograph of Barrie, described as "armed and extremely dangerous" and a "ruthless killer" suspected of planning the racetrack shootings. When shown Barrie's photograph, Aunt Marie pretends not to recognize him. The British officer calls Barrie a "ruthless man" and the rebels "just animals."

Nancy flashes back to the shootings, immediately followed by the memory of a smiling Barrie standing by the sea. Even after witnessing the killing she professes to detest, Nancy rushes to the cottage and urges Barrie to flee. In a romantic gesture, Barrie kisses her hand and departs. Spotted by Black and Tans on the beach, Barrie declares Nancy's innocence, raises his hands in surrender, tosses his weapon aside, and is shot down as Nancy is held back, crying.

The audience is left with Nancy's grief over the tormented gunman, not his twelve faceless victims. Anthony Hopkins' moving performance creates the impression that the IRA was justified in its violence and guided by noble convictions its privileged and shallow adversaries were incapable of appreciating.

THE LAST SEPTEMBER (1999)

This is the story of the end of a world.

Based on the Elizabeth Bowen novel, *The Last September* (Matrix Films), directed by Deborah Warner, is the most lavish and complex of the Big House films. Set in County Cork in 1920, its basic plot parallels *The Dawning*. A young virgin orphan, Lois Farquar (Keeley Hawes), comes of age on the lush estate of her uncle, Sir Richard Naylor (Michael Gambon), and her Aunt Myra (Maggie Smith). Though courted by an English officer, she develops a fascination with an IRA rebel. Deborah Warner devotes much of the film to capturing the genteel world of Twenties Anglo-Irish aristocracy, described in a prologue as "a tribe" that is "caught in the bloody conflict between the Irish Republicans and the British Army." Her characters walk through immense over-decorated rooms, stroll across rolling lawns, play hide and seek in glens, ride horses, play tennis, motor in pricey convertibles, and dine in great halls or under massive tents. Lois spends much of her time gazing through a telescope, which narrows her vision to the small world of her uncle's estate. The Irish fade into the background as servants, farm laborers, and shopkeepers, with the exception of a lone rebel, Peter Connelly.

As the War of Independence swirls around the edges of their delicate world, Sir Richard and Lady Myra live in privileged denial, dismissing the Troubles to their English visitors as "tomfoolery" and "nonsense." When their houseguests suggest rounding up the rebels and transporting them to the tropics, Sir Richard complains, "This country is altogether too full of soldiers with nothing to do but dance and poke old women out of bed to look for guns." Responding to the comment that he sounds like he is "on their side," Naylor remarks, "Why wouldn't I be? I am Irish. We all are here."

This Anglo-Irish identity is lost on the English, particularly Lois' suitor, Captain Colthurst (David Tennant), who cannot follow Naylor's train of thought on the Irish situation:

Colthurst: They won't win, you know, sir.
Naylor: My dear chap, they will. It's only a matter of time. But we've got to make it as hard for them as possible. That's important for afterwards, you see?
Colthurst: Sorry?
Naylor: We've got to spoil it for them, that's the point. You're losing a bit of the jolly old Empire — territory, revenue, subjects. When that's gone, England will still be there. But we are losing a country ... a world. The difference is that you don't care. Flanders saw to that. But we do. We care. Do you follow me?
Colthurst (*puzzled*): "We"?
Naylor: Well, the Irish.
Colthurst (*confused*): But they're Irish, too.
Naylor: Exactly!

Colthurst is infatuated with Lois, courting her and writing her letters. Lois finds the army officer amusing, but is intrigued by Peter Connelly (Gary Lydon), a childhood playmate who is now a rebel taking refuge in an abandoned mill on the estate.

"Wild" Connelly is less a modern revolutionary than a throwback to the Whiteboys of a previous century. He appears almost feral, crouching in the cave-like mill, hiding in the woods, and skulking near walls. Wolfish, he exists on the edge of civilization, coming out at night to attack. Like Nancy in *The Dawning*, Lois brings the rebel in hiding a basket of food, leading Connelly to call her "Little Red Riding Hood." Like Nancy, Lois claims to hate violence but is fascinated when she watches Connelly load his revolver and asks what it feels like to kill. "Ah," he states diffidently, "you get used to it." Like Angus Barrie, Connelly has no regrets about taking life. When questioned, he readily admits to killing a Black and Tan sergeant.

Visiting Connelly in the mill, Lois questions his motives, surprised that her childhood friend sees no place for her in her native land:

Lois: Why do you keep on?
Connelly: To get rid of your crowd. Why else? We want our chance.
Lois: Where will we go?
Connelly: Wherever you like. Back to England.
Lois (*perplexed*): Back?

The Big House Drama: (left to right) Maggie Smith, Jane Birkin, Lambert Wilson, and Michael Gambon in *The Last September* (1999).

Colthurst approaches the mill, and Lois breaks away from Connelly, insisting he wound her so she can claim she was taken hostage. Connelly fires his last round into her hand and escapes. "Rescued" by Colthurst, Lois returns home, where Sir Richard warns her to stay away from the mill, suggesting that he knows about her relationship with the Irish rebel.

In a final confrontation at the mill, Connelly kills Colthurst. Distraught over the captain's death, Lois leaves her childhood world for London. Sir Richard contemplates moving to Canada, telling his wife, "We must all learn to live with our losses."

The Big House dramas present an ironic depiction of the Anglo-Irish aristocracy: Their enemies are portrayed more sympathetically than the forces of the Crown assigned to protect them. The acts of violence are disproportionate. In *Fools of Fortune* the IRA hang a single suspect. In retaliation, Black and Tans set a house fire that kills two small girls, and they shoot three innocent men. In *The Dawning* the IRA kill twelve officers, but the audience only sees a few nameless figures from the back falling like bowling pins. In contrast, the death of the man who orchestrated their murders, the poetic Barrie, is dramatized with haunting poignancy.

Troubled Legacies

The legacy of the Troubles is explored in films set in the 1950s as middle-aged IRA veterans grapple with the outcomes of their youthful struggle. With independence won, Ireland established a national identity and solidified the role of the Church. What emerged was a socially conservative nation that banned birth control, censored movies, and saw a steady flow of emigration as its young people went abroad for better opportunities.

BROKEN HARVEST (1994)

"Civil war is the worst kind. It leaves scars that never heal."

Written, produced, and directed by Maurice O'Callaghan, *Broken Harvest* (Destiny Films) explores the lingering effects of the Troubles. Growing up in the 1950s in rural Ireland, Jimmy O'Leary (Darren McHugh) discovers how events of the Twenties he only read about in school still divide Ireland and fuel ongoing feuds between people of his parents' generation.

His father Arthur (Colin Lane) recounts how in the 1920s he fought the Black and Tans who ransacked his house and killed a neighbor. In response, he tells his son, "Me and fellows like me, we took up rifles and fought for freedom." They lived in the hills for weeks and were welcome in any home until "it all went wrong" and they fought among themselves in the Civil War, which "leaves scars that never heal." Though Jimmy's parents emigrated to New York, they returned to Ireland after his father inherited a debt-laden farm. Believing that one of Ireland's problems was that the best people left, Arthur is an idealist, giving up a good job in America to pursue the hard life of a small farmer who uses a horse instead of a modern tractor. An embittered Republican, he derides British comic books as "propaganda" and is upset when Jimmy listens to the BBC.

Jimmy finds that the adults in his town are still divided over the Civil War. While "Uncle" Josie McCarthy (Niall O'Brien) tells him to forget the past, his father, who nostalgically cleans his rifle, insists "sometimes it's wrong to forget." The schoolmaster, who never fired a shot during the war, remains a zealous Republican who despairs when his snickering pupils fail to appreciate their history. "I will tell you what happened whether you want to hear it or not," he hectors them. He joins Jimmy's father at a commemoration ceremony where IRA veterans wearing medals and dressed in trademark trench coats fire a volley over a memorial to Republican dead.

Standing apart from the crowd, Josie suggests, "It's time we moved on from all this," prompting the schoolmaster to denounce him for abandoning Northern Ireland and "selling out" the past. At mass the priest pleads with his parishioners to "face the serious task" of "putting aside all the animosities that have divided us since the Civil War." But even drinking in the pub, the men separate into two mutually suspicious groups.

Arthur O'Leary insists on passing his views onto his son, telling his wife, "He doesn't know, and he doesn't care. But he will someday." When she reminds him that the war is over, he responds, "It's not over yet, by God."

Standing in the grain fields with Jimmy, O'Leary contemplates the harvest that will help him pay his debts, reminding his son about a time "when an Irishman couldn't even own a horse. We changed all that.... All we wanted to is look across our own fields and say 'these are our fields' and ... do things our way, not their way."

His harvest "broken" by a rainstorm and unable to repay the bank, O'Leary faces eviction, reenacting a tragedy from the Famine. Forced to sell his cattle for a fraction of what he owes, the IRA veteran sighs, "We were better off under the British." Provoked by an adversary, Arthur gets into a fight and is arrested. The police sergeant tells him, "We admire and respect you for what you did in the past, but we're the law now. The old days are gone."

But the past is something Arthur can never escape. Experiencing flashbacks to fighting the Black and Tans, he fires on the police escorting the banker to seize his farm. The unarmed Garda call on the army for support. Shot by an Irish soldier, Arthur falls from his horse, which gallops through the town, signaling his death. His widow and son then leave for New York.

In the 1990s Jimmy (Pete O'Reilly), now in his late thirties, returns to Ireland to bury his mother. An aging Josie tells Jimmy he plans to leave him the farm. Only after seventy years are the wounds of the Civil War able to heal as the last participants die off.

AMONGST WOMEN (1998)

"The family is the center of everything."

Amongst Women, a parallel production of BBC Northern Ireland and RTE, is an award-winning four-part television mini-series set in rural Ireland in the Fifties that follows the lives of the Moran family over a decade. Michael Moran (Tony Doyle) is a grim, taciturn patriarch presiding over his three daughters and two sons. A widower, he struggles to keep his family together, although his elder son has already emigrated to London. Emotionally remote, muttering mixed messages, he is a distant father who shows little sensitivity. His speech at a daughter's wedding extols the importance of family life but is as joyless as a politician's resignation address. A man of small vision, he values the civil service because it means "a good dry job stretching to infinity with a pension at its end."

Moran's bitter disillusionment stems in part from his experiences in the IRA during the Troubles thirty years before. Driving through the countryside with his second wife Rose, he recalls fighting the Black and Tans, marching from one safe house to another in wet weather, waiting for an ambush. Contemplating present-day Ireland, he mutters, "I get sick to see what I fought for." When Rose suggests he apply for an IRA pension, he bitterly states, "I'd throw it in their teeth. Look where we are now, a country run by a small-minded crowd of gangsters out for their own good. It was all for nothing."

When a nun discusses his daughter's plans to study medicine, Moran asks, "Didn't we fight a war so doctors and their like could take the fat, while the rest of us got the lean? I didn't notice many doctors in the brigade when we were fighting the British. But they were quick enough to take the soft jobs for themselves when the coast was clear."

As his children leave home for work and marriage, sensing his influence eroding and his health failing, he bitterly recalls the Troubles:

Don't let anybody fool you, the war was a bad business. Oh, we didn't shoot at women and children like the Tans, but we were a bunch of killers alright. Of the twenty-two men in the original column, only seven of us were alive at the Truce. What did we get for it? A country if you'd believed them. Some of our people in the top jobs instead of a few Englishmen. And now half my family live and work in England. What was it all for? The whole thing?

2

The Big Fellow

Michael Collins

Collins' career is a paradigm of the tragedy of modern Ireland: the suffering, the waste of talent, the hope, the bedeviling effect of history and nomenclature whereby one man's terrorist is another man's freedom fighter. Like Prometheus, Collins stole fire. Like Prometheus, he paid for his feat.... But his name burns brightly wherever the Irish meet. — *Tim Pat Coogan,* The Man Who Made Ireland

Michael Collins' story was made for Hollywood. Young, handsome, brave, witty, daring, inventive, and romantic, he emerged as the most dynamic, most colorful, and most tragic figure of the Anglo-Irish War. His feats were so varied and legendary that in popular history and Irish political mythology he appears to have single-handedly won the war against Britain and established the Free State. Like an American Founding Father, his interests and achievements were multi-faceted. In a public career of just six years he played innumerable roles — editor, party whip, public speaker, leader of a squad of assassins, the intelligence chief who caught spies at their own game, the wanted man who hid in plain sight, the man of mystery who dodged adversaries with the skill of Houdini, the mastermind of an underground communications network, the innovator of guerrilla techniques that inspired Begin and Mao,* the Minister of Finance who bankrolled a revolution, the diplomat who negotiated with David Lloyd George and Winston Churchill to gain Irish independence, the founder of an insurance company, the economic visionary who championed energy independence, the organizer of Ireland's national police force, the creator of a political party, the gunman who saw peace and prosperity as the ultimate way to unity, and finally the romantic martyr slain by former comrades in his home county at the age of thirty-one, leaving behind a grieving fiancée and a nation bereft.

His historic achievements were so immeasurable that Peter Hart, whose biography seeks to demystify Michael Collins, concludes that "he became the most ruthless, the most powerful, the most calculating and the most successful politician in modern Irish history."[1] His brief career symbolized a pivotal transition in Ireland. As Director of Intelligence of the IRA, he led a rebel force to win a war of independence against Britain; as Commander in Chief of the Irish Army, he fought those same rebels who refused to accept the peace. As Hart notes, in accepting the Treaty with England, Collins left the Irish with the "triple legacy of independence, partition and the IRA" that has shaped Irish life and politics for nearly a century.[2]

Yitzak Shamir studied Collins' tactics and used "Michael" as a code name during Israel's war of independence against the British.

The Making of a Revolutionary

Born in West Cork in 1890, the youngest of eight children, Michael Collins was raised in an atmosphere of Irish nationalism. But like many of the Irish, including his older sister, Collins sought employment in Britain. At fifteen he took a civil service examination and moved to London to work in the Post Office Savings Bank in West Kensington. In the bank's Writing Room, Collins wrote out deposit and withdrawal receipts, and addressed envelopes at the rate of seventy an hour.[3] The work, though clerical, demanded concentration, speed, and accuracy. In London, Collins immersed himself in Irish culture. He joined the Gaelic Athletic Association* and in 1909 became a member of the Irish Republican Brotherhood, precursor of the IRA.[4] The following year he went to work for the brokerage firm of Horne and Company supervising messengers. In 1914 he joined the Board of Trade as a clerk.[5] With the outbreak of the Great War, Collins left Horne's and took a position with the London office of the Guaranty Trust Company of New York.[6] This exposure to financial institutions, especially American business methods, like his work for the Post Office, would aid Collins during the coming war for independence. During his London years he read extensively and attended the theater, Shaw being one of his favorite dramatists.[7] Steeping himself in the history of Irish nationalist movements, Collins also developed opinions on a range of interests, including military strategy, socialism, and Einstein's latest theories.[8] Living in London for a decade introduced Collins to a cosmopolitan world, expanding his education and helping him develop a sophisticated sense of himself and Ireland's future. These years in the heart of the British Empire also gave him insights into his adversaries without developing a narrow inflexible hatred of the English.

The Easter Rising

Sensing that events were stirring at home, Michael Collins returned to Ireland early in 1916. He took a part-time job handling business accounts for the wealthy Plunkett family, becoming closely associated with Joseph Plunkett, an organizer of the coming uprising. Though only twenty-eight, Plunkett was tubercular and underwent surgery that spring. Often bedridden, he depended on his athletic aide-de-camp to deliver messages, attend meetings in his absence, and run errands. On Easter Monday Collins donned an Irish uniform, then helped dress the ailing Plunkett. Arriving at the General Post Office, Collins promptly took a British officer prisoner, then assisted Plunkett upstairs to find a safe refuge.[9] Collins played a marginal role in the following days, standing guard and doing little fighting. With the building burning on Friday, the volunteers were forced to abandon the GPO. Collins led men across the street to a grocery store. Surrounded by British troops, they ultimately surrendered, joining the ranks of other disarmed volunteers marched down O'Connell Street into captivity. Though Collins was not a major figure of the Easter Rising, he was among the few hundred men who had taken up arms against the English for a few days, and this alone provided him with revolutionary credentials.

Collins' stature was heightened in defeat. Among the thousands of Irish rebels held in the Frongoch camp in North Wales, Collins demonstrated leadership abilities and honed

*To foster Irish identity, the GAA proscribed members from playing games associated with the English: soccer, hockey, rugby, and cricket.

his views. Although he personally admired the leaders of the Rising, he criticized their lack of organization and their overall strategy.[10] He recognized that ill-equipped rebels could never achieve independence waging a conventional war against the superior British Army. Given their small numbers and limited weaponry, they would have to use the hit and run guerrilla methods employed by the Boers in South Africa. Collins advocated the use of "flying columns," bands of fifteen or twenty minute men who could quickly assemble and make fast, punishing assaults on outposts and convoys, then disappear to limit their own casualties.[11] He also realized that true sovereignty required economic as well as political independence. It was in prison that Collins conceived of establishing an Irish insurance company to prevent the export of premium income to Britain. At Frongoch, Collins earned his nickname "the Big Fellow," a term of affection for those who admired his strength and determination, and a term of derision for those who regarded him as a showoff and braggart.[12]

Intelligence Warrior

Released in December 1916 as part of a general amnesty, Collins returned to Dublin and became Secretary of the National Aid Association providing financial assistance to veterans of the Rising. He used the position to reorganize the Irish Republican Brotherhood and the Irish Volunteers and within a year was a member of the Brotherhood's Supreme Council.[13] Collins became Director of Organization of Sinn Fein, whose military wing would evolve into the Irish Republican Army. In 1918 Michael Collins was elected to Parliament, representing Cork South. Like other Irish MPs, he refused to take a seat in the British Parliament and joined the newly formed Dail Eireann established in Dublin in 1919 and was elected Minister of Finance. That year he became Director of Intelligence and Adjutant General of the Irish Volunteers.

With an expanding portfolio of titles and offices, Collins became a major organizer and instigator of a revived struggle against British rule. As Minister of Finance, he launched a public loan to raise funds for the Irish Parliament. With an eye for publicity, Collins used the wooden block on which Robert Emmet had been beheaded in 1803 as a table to launch the loan. Family members of men executed in 1916 were filmed queuing up to make donations. When the loan closed, £379,000 had been raised.[14] Money also came from American sources. To protect funds from seizure by the British, money was deposited in personal bank accounts. Collins assiduously collected gold sovereigns and secreted them in a child's coffin.[15]

As Director of Intelligence, Collins developed an unconventional but highly effective security organization. The size and extent of this network is difficult to assess because he kept much of it in his head, not letting one group know what another was up to. His agents were largely volunteers. Some were assigned routine but important tasks, such as combing through the society pages of newspapers to clip articles and photographs of police and military personnel. Others shadowed British agents at their favorite clubs and restaurants, gleaning information overheard by waiters and barmen.[16]

Collins was able to penetrate the heart of British intelligence. Men like Ned Broy and Dave Neligan worked in Dublin Castle, supplying him information about impending arrests and raids. Assigned to typing up reports about IRA personnel and activities, Broy slipped in an extra carbon sheet and supplied Collins with a copy of what the British knew about him and his forces.[17] The British provided Collins with an intelligence coup when they assigned his second cousin Nancy to decode highly sensitive messages from Whitehall.[18] Collins' spies were not espionage professionals but policemen, hotel clerks, prison guards, telegraph operators, post office sorters, and typists who made copies of reports, intercepted letters and telegrams, passed on comments overheard while serving drinks, and smuggled the information out of Dublin Castle. In April 1919 Broy brought Collins into Dublin Castle to observe the British intelligence unit at work and examine their files firsthand.*[19]

Collins established his intelligence headquarters, called the Brain Center, in a lawyer's office less than 200 yards from Dublin Castle. Here, volunteers compiled dossiers and reports on British personnel and maintained files of stolen documents and cipher material.[20]

Collins appreciated that intercepted intelligence was time sensitive. Warnings about raids or the identification of an informer had to be delivered quickly. Collins relied on his experience supervising bank messengers to create a high-speed communications network. To enforce efficiency, hand delivered messages were accompanied with a tracking slip that required messengers to record the time they received and passed along a document. Many IRA men avoided arrest when a hastily scribbled warning initialed MC was thrust into their hands as they stood in a pub or left church.[21] Collins corresponded with volunteers outside Dublin using the British mail with a double-envelope system. A letter directed to an IRA headquarters or a man under surveillance would be placed in a second envelope addressed to an innocuous residence where a messenger would collect and hand deliver Collins' instructions.[22]

In April 1918 Collins was arrested for giving a speech "likely to cause disaffection."[23] Released on bail, he never appeared in court and lived on the run, a wanted man, for the next three years. Collins led a frenetic life, operating a complex, fluid organization from a chain of safe houses and cubbyholes. Though portrayed in legend as a daring gunman, much of his time was spent handling a stream of letters, reports, and messages. According to one biographer, "files and memos were his medium."[24] Holding meetings in taxis, pubs, and hotels, he spent nights in the homes of sympathizers. Moving about Dublin alone, often on bicycle, dressed in a business suit and bowler, he looked more like a stock broker than a rebel and was able to chat his way past sentries and checkpoints. Dublin Castle had no photographs of Collins and relied on sketchy written descriptions.†[25] Collins could safely assume that many of the policemen who did spot him did not attempt to arrest him out of sympathy or fear of reprisal. Noticing an officer on a streetcar, Collins would sit next to him, then affably ask about his family, mentioning his wife's name or his children's school as a friendly form of intimidation.[26]

Collins' success depended on his ability to locate talented people, win their loyalty, and coordinate their activities without being detected. In 1920 Collins contacted Robert Briscoe through an attorney. Aware of Briscoe's business dealings in Germany and his knowledge of the language, Collins sought him out for a gun-running operation. On the appointed evening, Briscoe was instructed to go to the headquarters of the Gaelic League where a messenger led him to a small hotel. Though he had never seen Michael Collins, Briscoe recognized him at once when the "door flew open" and a "swift moving" figure announced that

---

*Collins' penchant for accurate record keeping backfired when his files listing names of his Dublin Castle contacts were captured by the British.

†In group photographs Collins appears turning his face from the camera. He altered his appearance by sometimes growing a moustache.

Briscoe was being attached to his GHQ and would take orders only from him personally. Collins had prepared a cover for Briscoe's gun-smuggling mission, set aside funds for his activities, assigned seven pounds a week support for his wife during his absence, and ordered him to leave immediately. The entire encounter, Briscoe recalled, lasted forty minutes.[27]

Collins kept on the run, managing to elude the British. Demonized by the English as a brutish murderer, Collins' business attire proved valuable camouflage. In one incident police stormed into Sinn Fein headquarters and Collins escaped, calmly walking past a policeman who assumed he was a minor clerk.[28]

Collins' cat and mouse game with the British had comic flashes. His Squad raided a post office and carried off sacks of mail addressed to Dublin Castle. After searching for classified information, they resealed routine letters and dropped them in mail boxes for delivery. Days later, Lord French, the General Governor of Ireland, opened an envelope to find the contents bearing the stamp "Opened and censored by the Irish Republic."[29] Learning the address the British were using to collect anonymous tips, Collins' agents sent a flood of fake messages naming loyalists as rebels to divert police resources and mask genuine clues.[30]

With information from Dublin Castle, Collins waged war against informers, spies, police officers, and secret agents. He told an American reporter that "to paralyze the British machine it was necessary to strike at individuals. Without her spies England was helpless."[31] In May 1919 Collins directed his Squad to ambush convoys and attack police barracks throughout Ireland. Within this group was an elite corps of assassins called the Twelve Apostles. Often posing as traveling businessmen, they served as Collins' hit men, targeting informers and spies who formed the eyes and ears of the British government.[32] Irish policemen were warned in advance and given the opportunity to resign their posts. Secret Service officers, once identified, were tracked down and shot. Families of policemen were pressured to get officers to cooperate or at least turn a blind eye to IRA activities.[33] In addition to carrying out assassinations, the Squad conducted raids, such as stealing army vans for IRA use.[34]

With the arrival of the Black and Tans and the police auxiliaries from England in 1920, the intelligence war intensified. Frustrated by the IRA's hit and run ambushes and assassinations, the Tans and Auxis burned villages and shot hostages. Members of the Essex regiment forced neighbors to burn the Collins home in County Cork.[35]* In reprisal, the IRA enforced boycotts, threatened sympathizers, and increased actions by the flying columns.

Bloody Sunday

As the year passed, the British intensified their measures to counter Collins, who now had a £10,000 price on his head. Colonel Ormonde Winter established a network of English agents in and around Dublin who lived undercover, often with their wives, in houses and hotels. They called themselves the "hush-hush men" but were known as the Cairo Gang by the Irish.[36] They carried out raids and attacks, having obtained the identities of Collins' men through coercion and rewards. Collins, determined to get the upper hand, helped engineer a major attack on the British network. Sunday, November 21, 1920, was planned as the date of a major assault on British intelligence in Britain and Ireland. London timber

*The officer in charge of the raid, Major Arthur Ernest Percival, made headlines in 1942 when he surrendered his command in Singapore to the Japanese, a British defeat many Irish celebrated.

yards, Manchester power plants, and Liverpool docks were targeted for sabotage, while simultaneously Collins' men would eliminate Winter's "hush-hush" men.[37]

In Britain, only the Liverpool attack took place, the plans for sabotage in London and Manchester having been seized in a raid. In Dublin, Collins' Twelve Apostles carried out their campaign with military precision.

Members of the Twelve Apostles attended mass, then formed eight groups that fanned out over the city, knocked on doors, brushed past maids and wives, and executed their targets, often catching their prey still in their pajamas. Twelve British agents were killed, as were two Auxiliaries who ran into the IRA apostles. None of the assassins were killed.[38] The shooting of a dozen agents in their homes less than two weeks after Lloyd George declared that he "had murder by the throat" stunned Dublin Castle.[39]* Initial reports inflated the death toll to fifty.[40] "Panic reigned," recalled Dave Neligan. Terrified British agents and their wives rushed to Dublin Castle, seeking safety. Learning his comrades had been slain, an agent committed suicide. The "effect was paralyzing."[41] The fallen officers were given a state funeral in London, though Lloyd George expressed little sympathy for intelligence men done in by their rivals, stating, "They got what they deserved. Beaten by counter-jumpers."[42]†

The day earned the name Bloody Sunday not because of the IRA executions but for a controversial shooting by police and military forces that afternoon. According to British accounts, the police suspected IRA members would attend a Gaelic football match at Croke Park. The game had been widely advertised as a fundraiser to assist dependents of dead or imprisoned IRA men.[43] Policemen, Auxiliaries, and British soldiers arrived in separate groups to conduct a search. Shot at by an IRA guard, the police and soldiers returned fire. An armored car blocked an exit and fired its machine gun into the air for effect, triggering a deadly stampede.[44] Afterwards, the British claimed thirty revolvers were found on the grounds.[45] Irish witnesses maintained no shots were fired from the stadium, asserting it was an unprovoked revenge attack in which drunken Black and Tans sprayed Irish civilians with machine gun fire. Twelve people, including a football player, were killed and seventy injured.[46]

To the British, the Croke Park shooting was a reasonable police action gone awry; to the Irish it was a reprisal massacre.

The impact of the Squad's punishing attack elevated Michael Collins' status among the Irish to the point that he was celebrated as "the man who won the war" and subsequently hailed as "the founder of modern guerrilla warfare" and "the first freedom fighter."[47] The English condemned him as the bloody mastermind of a murderous terror network.

With de Valera out of the country for eighteen months, Collins became the dominant leader of the Anglo-Irish War. As Peter Hart notes, in reality, Collins did not play the role ascribed to him by either his admirers or his foes. Collins rarely left Dublin after 1919, so IRA flying columns in the rest of Ireland operated independently. As guerrillas, they could not wait for orders but had to seize opportunities for attack and retaliation. In addition, the IRA did not wage the war alone. Resistance to British rule came from many sources. Collins did paralyze British intelligence, but Irish railway workers who refused to transport munitions and troops helped paralyze the British army.[48] Still, the CIA concluded in a 1996

---

*Though the British were stunned by the attack, IRA planners were disappointed. They had intended to assassinate thirty-five officers; two-thirds of their raids that morning failed to locate their targets or were aborted.

†One of Collins' "counter-jumpers" was reportedly future Taoiseach Sean Lemass.

review of Bloody Sunday that Collins' "intelligence service was one of the architects of the victory."[49]

Collins' significance as a warrior derived from his understanding of war's limitations. He realized that a sustained campaign, even one marked by victories, could jeopardize the goal of Irish independence. Continued conflict risked British escalation and the introduction of regular army units, heavy artillery, and aircraft that could overwhelm poorly armed guerrillas. Ongoing violence also risked the possibility that a war-weary Irish public would acquiesce to offers of Home Rule to achieve peace.[50]

Collins' ambushes and assassinations also brought him into conflict with Republican leaders like Cathal Brugha and de Valera. Fearful that guerrilla techniques would cause nationalists to be dismissed as terrorists, they advocated conventional warfare that would better represent a legitimate government. De Valera wanted "one good battle about once a month with about 500 men on each side."[51]

In May 1921 some of Collins' men took part in the burning of the Dublin Custom House, an operation ordered by de Valera. Over a hundred and twenty volunteers set fire to a major government center, disrupting administrative services and income tax collections. The action proved to be a propaganda coup but a military debacle. Six IRA men were killed and seventy were captured.[52]

Though costly to the IRA, the dramatic attack led, in part, to negotiations. Lloyd George faced increasing domestic and international pressure to end the conflict. In June King George V visited Belfast and appealed for reconciliation and peace. Contacts between Lloyd George and de Valera were made through intermediaries. A truce was announced on July 11, 1921. Learning that Britain would never allow a fully independent Ireland, de Valera announced he would remain in Dublin and delegated Arthur Griffith and Michael Collins to negotiate a settlement with Lloyd George. Collins objected, seeing himself as a soldier rather than a diplomat. Meeting with the British face to face would humanize the man of mystery, reducing the ability for negotiators to use Collins and the IRA as a threat to push the Irish agenda.

The Treaty

Collins arrived in London with members of the Squad serving as body guards. Apprehensive about the visit to Britain, Emmet Dalton created the Irish Air Force when he purchased a surplus Canadian airplane to fly Collins out of England if needed. Formal talks began at No. 10 Downing Street on October 11, 1921, which lasted two months. In addition to formal discussions, Collins met with Winston Churchill in the home of artist John Lavery.*[53]

On December 5, 1921, Lloyd George presented the Irish with an ultimatum promising "immediate and terrible war" unless the treaty was signed by ten o'clock that evening. The Irish arrived and, after some discussion, both parties signed the treaty at two-thirty the next morning. Michael Collins was noticeably troubled. When a British delegate suggested he was signing his political death warrant, Collins responded, "I may have signed my actual death warrant."[54]

---

*Collins' frequent visits to the Laverys led to rumors of an affair between Michael Collins and the painter's young American wife Hazel, whose image later appeared on Irish banknotes.

While the delegates had been in continual contact with Dublin, many in Ireland assumed that the negotiators had acted largely on their own. To staunch Republicans, the agreement to partition and dominion status was a betrayal and surrender. Michael Collins was held up for particular vilification. Robert Briscoe, who considered a summons to see Michael Collins "a tremendous thing" a year before, was outraged.[55] The treaty, he declared, was a "shameful surrender" that would "forever sunder Ireland into two antagonistic states."[56] He maintained that dominion status and partition could have been achieved without conflict, so that "Ireland lost all she had won by five years of war."[57] Briscoe reserved his greatest condemnation for Michael Collins. While Arthur Griffith, Duggan, and Duffy were seen as parliamentarians, Collins was, in his words, "our man of steel and granite, our fearless fighting leader."[58] What, he wondered, had happened to the "trusted and beloved" man of steel? Had he been "ill-prepared," "seduced" by English diplomats, fallen ill, or "betrayed his country for personal ambitions? ... We could not understand the man at all," Briscoe concluded.[59]

As Peter Hart notes, Collins, though leader of the Irish Republican Army, "had never attached himself publicly to the full Republican demand," noting that in all his correspondence the word "republic" rarely appeared.[60] Collins also well understood the limited resources the IRA could muster in the event of full war.

Collins campaigned for ratification of the Treaty throughout the island, while de Valera and Cathal Brugha rejected it. After a series of heated debates, the Dail approved the treaty on January 7, 1922, establishing a provisional government, with Collins as chairman. De Valera resigned as president and was replaced by Arthur Griffith. The Black and Tans and British troops quickly departed, as did the civil administrators from Dublin Castle.[61]

Commander in Chief

On January 16, 1922, General Michael Collins entered Dublin Castle to officiate the transfer of power. According to his nephew, when Collins arrived, the British commanding officer reproved the new Irish general, noting that he was seven and a half minutes late. Collins reportedly responded with the quip, "After seven and a half centuries, you're welcome to the seven and a half minutes."[62]

Michael Collins was now the Commander in Chief of the Irish Army and the most powerful man in the country. During the treaty discussions he had been transformed from a wanted man in hiding who shunned photographers to a celebrity stalked by paparazzi and swarms of fans in both Dublin and London, where girls rushed forward to kiss him and celebrities like George Bernard Shaw and T. E. Lawrence were eager to meet him.[63] But Collins, who had ambitious plans for the economic and cultural development of Ireland, faced a maze of challenges.

Border conflicts occurred on the newly bifurcated island. Minorities were harassed. Cattle were driven off Protestant farms in the South; Catholics were evicted in the North. Many IRA volunteers opposed the treaty. Disillusioned and jobless, they still bore arms. With the quick departure of the British, rebellious volunteers filled the vacuum before Free State forces could be put in place.[64] To secure funds, IRA men robbed banks and held up cars on the roads. In April 1922, a band of anti–Treaty IRA irregulars occupied the Four Courts and other government buildings in Dublin. At first Collins took no actions to dislodge them.[65]

In a general election, those opposed to the treaty won only thirty-six of a hundred and twenty-five seats, giving Collins a clear mandate. Lloyd George pressured Collins to uphold the treaty and suppress dissidents. Free State troops, armed with British artillery, fired four hundred shells into the occupied buildings until the irregulars surrendered. Other troops eliminated IRA snipers who had taken positions on Dublin rooftops.[66]

A War Council was created by the new government, and Michael Collins was named Commander in Chief of the Irish Army. He resigned from the cabinet to dedicate himself to waging a campaign against his former colleagues. The IRA was driven from most of Ireland's cities, though irregulars held out in Collins' home county Cork and neighboring Kerry.[67]

The Mouth of Flowers

On August 19, 1922, Collins set out to Cork to inspect troops and engage in talks with neutral officers with hopes of defusing the growing civil war. Telling General Dalton he would be safe in his home county, Collins remained edgy, grabbing his sidearm when an amateur photographer approached to snap his picture.[68]

On August 22, Collins and General Dalton left Cork in a small convoy consisting of a motorcycle, a tender with a dozen troops, and an armored car. Collins and Dalton rode in the back of an open touring car. Outside the small village of Béalnabláth (The Mouth of Flowers) the convoy came under fire from IRA guerrillas. Emmet Dalton told the driver to "drive like hell," but Collins ordered him to stop, saying, "We'll fight them." Collins took a rifle and returned fire. The machine gun in the armored car pinned down the IRA men in the hills. When the machine gun jammed, a number of volunteers broke cover and ran. Collins, seeking better aim, stepped from behind the armored car and was killed by a single bullet to the head.*

Collins' body lay in state in Dublin, where tens of thousands, including British officers, paid their respects. Half a million lined the streets during his funeral. Two days after Collins' death, George Bernard Shaw wrote to Johanna Collins, telling her:

> I rejoice in his memory, and will not be so disloyal to it as to snivel over his valiant death. So tear up your mourning and hang up your brightest colors in his honor; and let us all praise God that he had not to die in a snuffy bed of a trumpery cough, weakened by age, and saddened by the disappointments that would have attended his work had he lived.[69]

Collins' death at thirty-one, less than a year after the creation of the Free State, raised the question of what would have happened had he lived. He saw the Irish Free State as both an old and a new country. He wanted to revive the Irish language and foster traditional

---

*Like the Kennedy assassination forty years later, Collins' sudden death sparked immediate speculation and gave birth to a conspiracy industry and a stream of books and videos. Suspicion fell on de Valera, who had spent the previous night in a house near Béalnabláth. General Dalton was accused of killing Collins on behalf of the British Secret Service. The machine gunner in the armored car, who later deserted to the IRA, was blamed. Other theorists suggest that Collins' was felled by friendly fire. As with the Kennedy assassination, there were questions about entrance and exit wounds and the direction of the fatal shot. The fact that his body was first taken to a private hospital used by British troops and that the post mortem report prepared by surgeon-poet Oliver St. John Gogarty subsequently disappeared from a safe in the Royal College of Surgeons in Dublin led to charges of a coverup.

Irish culture while encouraging new commercial ventures and technological advances. He envisioned a "co-operative" economy that would avoid the excesses of both "old capitalism" and "State Socialism," which he dismissed as "a monopoly of another kind."[70] To free Ireland from its dependence on British coal, he advocated harnessing the "white coal" of Ireland's rivers. "I can see in the future very plainly prosperous cities, both old and new," Collins imagined, "fed by the greatest river in the United Kingdom — the Shannon."[71] For a man who was willing to use violence to drive the British out of Ireland, he did not see military action as a tactic to end partition. The way to reclaim the lost counties of Ulster was to build a new country Unionists would want to be part of. "A prosperous Ireland will mean a united Ireland," he wrote. "With equitable taxation and flourishing trade our North-East countrymen will need no persuasion to come in and share in the healthy economic life of the country."[72]

Harry and Kitty

Two figures in Michael Collins' life added to his cinematic potential. Hollywood screenwriters would not have to invent a romantic backstory to humanize a political figure. Michael Collins' own life contained a romantic triangle worthy of a Warner Brothers production.

Harry Boland was one of Michael Collins' best friends and closest comrades in the Anglo-Irish War. "They were two of a kind," Tim Pat Coogan noted, "brave, energetic, unscrupulous, jolly buccaneers."[73] Harry and Mick had fought in the Easter Rising and worked as a team on the run during the guerrilla war, sometimes sleeping in the same bed with revolvers in their hands.[74] Both were elected to Parliament in 1918 but were absent at the opening of the Dail in 1919 because they had gone to England to help de Valera escape from Lincoln Jail. De Valera's prison break was full of cinematic stereotypes, including items hidden in cakes, wax impressions of stolen keys, and cross-dressing to slip past the enemy.

In 1917, while Harry and Mick were visiting Longford, Collins met and fell in love with Boland's girlfriend, Kitty Kiernan. Unknown to Boland, Kitty and Michael Collins began a protracted courtship, exchanging hundreds of letters and arranging visits while Boland was out of the country. In October 1921 Boland wrote Kitty, wishing she could accompany him to America to "spend our honeymoon in perfect bliss." Now aware of her interest in Michael Collins, Boland declared to Kitty, "I need not say to you how much I love him," noting "no what manner our Triangle may work out, he and I shall always be friends."[75]

Michael Collins and Kitty Kiernan's engagement in 1922 was featured in society pages. Boland wrote Kitty, wishing her "long life and happiness."[76]

As in a B film, the two friends were separated by the Civil War. Boland sided with de Valera, rejecting the Treaty Collins had signed. On July 28, 1922, Collins wrote a letter to Boland, stating:

> Harry, it has come to this. Of all things it has come to this. It is in my power to arrest and destroy you. This I cannot do. You are marching under false colors. If no words of mine will change your attitude, then you are above all hope, my hope.[77]

On July 31, 1922, Harry Boland was fatally wounded by a Free State soldier as he attempted to escape arrest. Three weeks later Michael Collins was killed in Cork. Kitty

Kiernan symbolized the trauma of Ireland's ongoing Troubles, having lost the two men she loved within a month on opposite sides of Ireland's fratricidal Civil War.*

Michael Collins remains a figure of continued controversy. In 2007 Lord David Puttnam spoke at a gathering marking the 85th anniversary of Collins' death and compared him to Gandhi and Mandela, "men who, having freed their own people from the shackles of oppression, became icons for peace and reconciliation everywhere."[78] In response, the Irish commentator Kevin Myers derided Collins as a "cold-blooded killer" who "injected a toxin into Irish life" that promoted the "cult of murder."[79]

Colors and Shadows

Michael Collins has been the subject of numerous biographies and television documentaries in both Britain and Ireland.

HANG UP YOUR BRIGHTEST COLOURS (1973)

> One of the optimistic facts about human affairs is that it usually takes a lot of people on the wrong side to beat a few people on the right side. —*Kenneth Griffith*

Hang Up Your Brightest Colours: The Life and Death of Michael Collins (ITC) earned the distinction of being "banned for twenty-five years." The film was written and narrated by Kenneth Griffith (1921–2006), a popular Welsh-born character actor whose credits include *A Night to Remember* and *Four Weddings and Funeral*. In addition to appearing in over eighty motion pictures, Griffith made eighteen documentary films. A passionate anti–Imperialist, Griffith became a supporter of the IRA in the 1970s and produced a biographical film about Michael Collins.

Taking the title from George Bernard Shaw's letter to Collins' sister, Griffith created an unconventional documentary, a blend of archival footage and dramatic impersonations. The film contains no interviews or customary monotone voice-overs but dramatic impersonations by Griffith, mimicking Irish and British accents with histrionic poses, gestures, and shouts.

Griffith's narration is highly polemic. Collins is championed as a man of "extraordinary talent" who possessed a "great capacity for love" of children and old people, while Churchill and David Lloyd George are belittled as "imperial bully boys" who, confronting Collins during the Treaty negotiations, were "in the presence of their better." Griffith offers a passionate account of the executions of the Irish patriots following the Easter Rising, noting in contrast, "The executions Michael Collins carried out against the English later were never without a terrible reason. We must give him credit for that." Commenting on Collins' imprisonment after the Rising, the Welsh-born Griffith notes that Collins was taken, "*to my country's shame,* to Frongloch Prison Camp in North Wales."

Griffith's film applies the word "terror" to describe English oppression rather than Irish resistance, stating that among Churchill's "jolly ideas" was the introduction of the Auxiliaries, who were "comparable to Nazi SS troops" who "murdered and tortured freely." In contrast, he sarcastically calls the 1922 IRA assassination of General Henry Wilson in London a "nasty little knock."

---

*Kitty Kiernan subsequently married Felix Cronin, naming one of her sons Michael Collins Cronin. She died in 1945 and was buried in the same cemetery as Michael Collins.

Griffith's account of Bloody Sunday compares the methodical "execution" of English "spies" with the "lorry loads" of Auxiliaries who drove to Croke Park Stadium, "pointed their machine guns" at an Irish crowd, "and fired point blank" in revenge. No mention is made of the stampede or the possibility of precipitating gunfire from the stadium.

In discussing the Treaty, Griffith is unreservedly hostile to Lloyd George, whom he decries as taking "the most terrible political action" of dividing the country "against the will of the vast majority of the Irish people" for "strategic and economic" reasons. He portrays Griffith and Collins as fall guys sent on a doomed mission to negotiate with the British knowing that they could not bring back a Republic. Cathal Brugha is depicted as a jealous "fanatic" who resented Collins' popularity.

The British offer of dominion status, in Griffith's words, contained "the residual of shame" in an oath of allegiance to the Crown and the partition of the island. In Griffth's view, the Scottish settlers in Northeast Ireland were "rejecting the offer of warm hospitality from the Irish people" and "threatening an armed insurrection if they failed to get a border." Lloyd George was "grossly dishonest to the Irish people" in that he pledged there would be no permanent partition of the country after promising Sir Edward Carson that Ulster would not unite with the rest of Ireland. The mistake the Irish delegates made, in Griffith's view, was trusting the duplicitous British.

Though often referred to as a "banned film," *Hang Up Your Brightest Colours* was not technically censored. According to Griffith, the film was not offered to the Independent Broadcasting Authority for review to save the IBA from being accused of political censorship. In response, Kenneth Griffith made a documentary, *The Public's Right to Know*, in 1974 about television censorship, which discussed his Michael Collins film. Accused of bias, Griffith responded, "I could no more be detached about Ireland than I could about Auschwitz and Buchenwald."[80] Griffith named his London home Michael Collins House.

THE SHADOW OF BÉALNABLÁTH (1989)

The Shadow of Béalnabláth: The Story of Michael Collins (RTE) is a four-part documentary produced by Irish television and distributed in the United States in a VHS format by Rego Irish Records & Tapes. Written by Colm Connolly, the film won an Irish television award. In contrast to Kenneth Griffith's hagiography, Colm Connolly's biography is factual and objective. Though it presents Collins as "a giant of Irish history," it does not demonize the British as imperialists and avoids inflammatory rhetoric. The opening sequence recreates the death of Michael Collins in a music video tribute. Much of the film follows the traditional documentary format, blending current interviews with members of the Collins family, biographers such as Tim Pat Coogan, and archival statements of leading figures of the Anglo-Irish War, including Emmet Dalton and Dave Neligan.

Cathal Brugha is described as a "tough Dubliner and ardent Republican" rather than a jealous fanatic. The film disputes the IRA claim that the Black and Tans were criminals and psychotics, describing them as "ex soldiers home from the Great War to a jobless Britain" who "fought terror with terror." Frustrated with IRA guerrilla attacks, however, they "committed atrocities" that were denounced by the press in both Ireland and Britain. The Auxiliaries, the film states, were respected by the IRA for their refusal to surrender and willingness to fight to the last man.

In recounting the events of Bloody Sunday, the film follows Vinnie Byrne, then the sole surviving member of the Twelve Apostles, as he retraced his steps and reenacted the shooting of two British officers. The description of the Croke Park incident presents the conflicting accounts concerning shots coming from the stadium.

The film dramatizes the romantic attachment of Michael Collins and Kitty Kiernan through readings from his letters. It also addresses speculations about Collins' affairs with other women, including Lady Lavery. An interview with Sir Shane Leslie, however, purports that the reason for Collins' visits to the Lavery home was to meet secretly with Winston Churchill.

The last episode consists of a ten-minute reenactment of the fatal ambush, with costumed actors riding in vintage vehicles, followed by extensive interviews addressing conflicting theories about Collins' death. The allegation of de Valera's involvement is dismissed as a "malicious rumor." John M. Feehan, author of *The Death of Michael Collins*, asserts a massive coverup occurred after Collins' death, raising suspicions that Collins was either killed by his own men by design or by an act of friendly fire. Detailed accounts of Michael Collins' head wound are presented by Patrick J. Twohig, author of *The Dark Secret of Beal-nalbath*, who believes Collins was killed by a bullet ricocheting off the armored car. The statements by a pathologist and diagrams of entrance and exit wounds are reminiscent of History Channel documentaries about the Kennedy assassination in Dallas. And like many Kennedy assassination investigators, Colm Connolly claims to finally solve the mystery "once and for all," naming Dennis "Sonny" O'Neill as the IRA man who fired the fatal shot.

BELOVED ENEMY (1936)

"What do you know about love? ... You're married to a cause."

The first feature film based on Michael Collins' life, *Beloved Enemy* (MGM), was released fourteen years after his death. The film, directed by H. C. Potter, opens with a written prologue and a disclaimer:

DUBLIN, 1921
    A time of Ireland's bitter struggle for freedom from English rule....
    A time of night raids and ambushes, of guerilla warfare against British military occupation....
    A time of horror and heroism, with men on both sides dying bravely for what they believed was right.
    This story is not taken from the pages of history. Rather, it is legend inspired by fact, and all characters are fictional.

The protagonist, Dennis Riordan (Brian Aherne), is drawn from the legend of Michael Collins. The Chief of Staff of an Irish rebel army with a £10,000 price on his head, Riordan bicycles around Dublin in a business suit and felt hat, hiding in plain sight because "nobody knew what he looked like." Like Collins, he lives on the run, dodging capture by ducking through windows and escaping over rooftops. Like Collins, Riordan bedevils the British because he has "spies in the post offices, telephone exchanges, army, police, even in the Castle." In a reference to Bloody Sunday, he is denounced as leader of "a murder gang, pulling our men out of bed in the middle of the night and slaughtering them." The film portrays Riordan as being clever rather than ruthless. Cornered in a marketplace, he tosses a handful of coins among the poor to create a distraction rather than use a gun to evade British agents. When members of his movement suggest blowing up a visiting diplomat, Riordan rejects the idea, reminding them, "We're not a handful of conspirators but the government of a free people." Like Collins, he travels to London during a truce to negotiate a Treaty, which offers a compromise that is bitterly rejected by hardliners. To avoid imminent war and an invasion of Ireland, Riordan agrees to the Treaty, stating he is "signing his own death warrant." He returns to Ireland and, now dressed in the military uniform of the new nation, speaks at a pro–Treaty rally. After urging the Irish to abandon "gunpowder and hatred" for a "bright future" that is "built in peace," he is assassinated by a former comrade. This original ending proved to be unpopular with audiences, so a new version was added in which a wounded Riordan promises his lover and viewers that he will survive, delivering the film's last line, "I'm not going to die. An Irishman never does what is expected of him."

Brian Aherne portrays the rebel leader as a dreamy idealist rather than an athletic man of action. His nationalism is more romantic than political. His torment over the treaty appears more spiritual than strategic. Dennis Riordan wears the costume of Michael Collins and goes through the motions but is more effete than ruthless, more whimsical than determined.

Overall, the film provides only a superficial pastiche of images. There are shots of Black and Tans trolling Dublin in armored cars and brief scenes of heated treaty debates. The words "IRA," "republic," "partition," or "dominion" do not appear in the script. The treaty debate is limited to generic statements. Told "you are reaching for the moon, gentlemen, and we can't give it to you" by the British, Riordan replies, "You knew what was in our minds when we came." In private, the Irish delegates talk about "compromise" and "getting all we want." The impasse comes down to "a few words in the treaty," but there is

Brian Aherne as Denis Riordan, with Merle Oberon in *Beloved Enemy* (1936).

never an explanation what those words imply. In *Beloved Enemy* the political struggle between Ireland and Britain is of secondary importance, providing a turbulent backdrop for what Michael Gray called a "cupid-inspired delirium."[81]

The heart of the film is the on-again off-again relationship between Irish rebel Dennis Riordan and Lady Helen Drummond (Merle Oberon), daughter of Lord Athleigh (Henry Stephenson), a Lloyd George–like British diplomat assigned to resolve the Anglo-Irish crisis. The storyline plays in part on the rumored relationship between Hazel Lavery and Collins, though in the film the young English beauty is partnered with an elderly father rather than an elderly husband. Athleigh and his daughter arrive in Dublin. Riordan calls off a planned attack on Athleigh and rescues Lady Helen when their armored car runs into a rebel ambush on a munitions convoy. Not knowing his identity, Lady Helen is smitten with her rescuer, who woos her with Irish poetry and dreams of an untroubled family life on a farm in Galway. Learning that he is indeed Dennis Riordan, Lady Helen informs her father but is relieved when Riordan escapes capture.

As their relationship develops, the lovers fall under suspicion. Riordan's comrades begin to question his dedication to the cause. Confronted by one of his men, Riordan promises never to see Lady Helen again. Reunited in London during the treaty talks, Riordan and Lady Helen contemplate peace and a life together in Galway. Learning that her father plans to launch a major military action against Ireland if Riordan won't agree to the treaty, Lady Helen urges her lover to accept the compromise.

The film's message that love can triumph over ethnic and national conflicts no doubt resonated with 1936 audiences troubled more by current events than recent history. It also explains why audiences wanted a more optimistic ending.

THE TREATY (1991)

The Anglo-Irish television docudrama *The Treaty* (Merlin Films) offers a fuller and more authentic portrayal of Michael Collins. With its narrative focused on the events surrounding the 1921 Treaty, the film makes no reference to Kitty Kiernan, and though Lady Lavery is depicted, there is no suggestion of a romantic relationship. The film opens with Collins (Brendan Gleeson) in business suit and felt hat cycling through the Dublin streets in 1919 to deliver an order to shoot an inspector and his bodyguard. A following scene dramatizes a characteristic Collins trick of getting past an army checkpoint by confidently approaching the captain in charge, offering him a cigarette, and feigning Loyalist sympathies.

Audiences learn of Collins' effectiveness when Sir Henry Wilson (Liam O'Callaghan) tells Lloyd George (Ian Bannen) that Collins is "destroying our intelligence network with impunity" and is "no simple gunman" but a mastermind "running an army while on the run with a price on his head."

Brendan Gleeson captures the excitable, boisterous adolescent nature of the Big Fellow in scenes where political discussion turns into boyish horseplay, or a cool, coy Mick chats up a star-struck waitress.

Though the film opens with a dramatic depiction of his use of assassination, Collins is portrayed as a thoughtful pragmatist, sensitive to military and political realities. Unlike Cathal Brugha (Ronan Wilmont), who urges continued war until the ideal of a full Republic can be achieved, Collins persuades de Valera (Barry McGovern) to accept the British invitation to negotiate. His army, he explains, "is down to counting bullets" and can hold out only a few weeks. "If the British knew how perilous our position is," he argues, "they'd be for going on…. We have driven them to the table, so lets talk…. We must achieve the maximum limit of freedom."

Disappointed that he was not selected to negotiate in London during the preliminary discussions, Collins becomes apprehensive and resentful when de Valera suggests he accompany Arthur Griffith (Tony Doyle) to the treaty talks. "If you sup with the devil you get to know him," he tells de Valera. Meeting the British in person, Collins realizes, would compromise his image so that he would be transformed from the "elusive Pimpernel they could never capture or defeat" into a man "with feet of clay." De Valera maintains that he should remain in Dublin as the "symbol of the Republic" who must "never be seen to compromise that position." Brendan Gleeson captures Collins' energy with his finger jabbing and gesturing as the aloof de Valera, stiff and schoolmasterly, delivers his reasons for distancing himself from the peace process.

The film accurately portrays a conflicted Collins moving uneasily from underground guerrilla leader to diplomat. Riding his bicycle to a pub for a meeting with the Irish Republican Brotherhood, he angrily rolls his bike to a lookout, demanding that a car be sent for him, stating, "I'm no longer the man on the bicycle. Sell it, take it home, throw it the River Liffey." Collins explains to the Supreme Council of the IRB that if he goes to London he will be unable to bring back a Republic. Recognizing that they cannot defeat the British militarily, Harry Boland urges Collins to go to London because "a gunman will screw better terms out of them than an ordinary politician." Collins agrees but insists on keeping in daily contact with the IRB so he can be aware of the "twists and turns" going on in Dublin. An IRB member warns Collins, "Watch they don't make a scapegoat out of you, Mick."

Concerned that he might be arrested and shot if the talks break down, Collins orders Emmet Dalton to have a plane ready for him at Croydon Airport. In heading to London, Collins is portrayed as a sober realist, appreciative of the domestic pressures confronting Lloyd George. Asked by Arthur Griffith what he would be willing to settle for, Collins states that "the idea of a twenty-six county Ireland without a single English soldier or civil servant in it — imperfect as it may be — has a great attraction. It could be the stepping stone to a unified and free Ireland."

During the London negotiations Collins is invited to the Lavery home where Sir John paints his portrait. Like Lady Helen in *Beloved Enemy*, Hazel Lavery serves as Collins' confidant and intermediary between Irish and English interests, hosting a dinner party for delegates from both nations.

Meeting alone with Lloyd George, Collins works through the details of the treaty, accepting a free state status within the British Empire. Faced with the prospect of war (Churchill suggests sending 100,000 British soldiers into Ireland if the talks fail), Collins agrees with Griffith to sign the treaty. The film ends with Birkenhead and Collins shaking hands, and Collins stating that he had "signed his actual death warrant."

Overall, Michael Collins is portrayed as a conscientious, rational delegate who makes a painful but reasonable compromise while hardliners like Brugha are willing to risk war, and de Valera, having told delegates to get the best they could, remains an obdurate purist, rejecting compromise.

MICHAEL COLLINS (1996)
"Some people are what the times demand."

The most ambitious and most successful film biography of Michael Collins is the Neil Jordan eponymous production *Michael Collins*. Nominated for two Academy Awards, the film was the second largest grossing motion picture in Irish history, surpassed only by *Titanic*. The film did less well in the United States and in Britain, where newspapers criticized it for historical inaccuracies and its implied support for the current Irish Republican Army. The film signaled a new era in Irish filmmaking and sparked fresh debates about the IRA, particularly its celluloid image.

Jordan's script, though closer to Collins' actual life than the fictional *Beloved Enemy*, lacks the accuracy and detail of *The Treaty*. The film covers the six years of Michael Collins' public career, from the Easter Rising in 1916 to his death in 1922.

The opening words of the film, spoken by Joe O'Reilly (Ian Hart), evoke the last line of *Beloved Enemy*. Comforting a grieving Kitty Kiernan (Julia Roberts), Joe tells her, "He never did what anyone expected. He got the British out of here, and no one expected that."

The film begins with the doomed Easter Rising. Michael Collins (Liam Neeson) is shown firing a handgun, fighting alongside Harry Boland (Aidan Quinn). Surrendering to the British, the Volunteers march off in defeat and are held with Eamon de Valera (Alan Rickman). Extras bearing remarkable resemblances to Padraig Pearse and Thomas Clarke are pulled from the lineup of prisoners as ringleaders for execution. Collins assures Boland that next time, "We won't play by their rules, Harry, we'll invent our own."

Returning to Ireland from prison in 1918, Collins builds his network, sending his guerrillas to raid a police barracks to seize arms and giving nationalist speeches, which are observed by Dublin Castle agent Ned Broy. Collins tells followers, "We'll be an invisible army. Our uniform will be that of the man in the street, the peasant in the field. We'll come out of the crowd, strike the enemy, and vanish back into the crowd again."

After the Easter Rising: (left to right) Alan Rickman, Liam Neeson, and Aidan Quinn as Eamon de Valera, Michael Collins, and Harry Boland in *Michael Collins* (1996).

In Jordan's film, Ned Broy serves as a composite of double agents who pass on information from the British. Collins asks Broy to let him see British files and instructs him to make an extra copy of the reports he types. Collins hones his strategy, realizing that "files are no good without the G-men who compile them." He orders his men to collect information on "every member of the British administration," examining the society pages to find names, addresses, and clubs to produce reports that are updated weekly. He also assembles the Twelve Apostles, asking for the twelve best men in the Dublin division of the IRA. His men shoot British officials in the streets in scenes reminiscent of *The Battle of Algiers*.

"I want peace," Collins tells Harry Boland, but warns, "You haven't seen anything yet." Contemplating further violence, he tells Boland about the English, "I hate them. Not for their race, not for their brutality. I hate them because they've left us no way out.... I hate them for making hate necessary." An Ormonde Winter–like character named Soames (Charles Dance) arrives from London with intelligence agents to neutralize Collins, urging his men to hunt him down. Collins shadows these British agents, boldly approaching Soames on the street to ask him for a light. Having identified the British agents, Collins' Twelve Apostles spring into action.

The events of Bloody Sunday are related in an abbreviated form. Pairs of gunmen kill British agents while shaving, exercising in a park, or having breakfast. The scene of IRA men machine-gunning two men in a restaurant is wholly invented; the actual Squad used handguns. The shootings are interspersed with romantic scenes of Collins and Kitty Kiernan, who refers to Collins' assassins as "so many Valentines delivering bouquets." The Valentines, Collins tells her, say "Leave us be."

With "the flowers delivered," Kitty wonders if the British will get the message. The message, Collins tells Kitty, is "give us the future, we've had enough of your past. Give us our country back."

The British respond by hanging Ned Broy* and shooting up Croke Park. In Jordan's version, a convoy of angry Black and Tans storm the stadium. The armored car rolls onto the playing field, machine gunning players and civilians in the stands.

De Valera announces that the British have made overtures toward negotiations and demands a change in tactics because the British press calls them "murderers." He reasons, "If we are to negotiate as a legitimate government, our armed forces must act like a legitimate army" making large-scale engagements, which Collins denounces as "marching in step to slaughter." De Valera orders a traditional assault on the Customs House, which leads to the killing of six IRA men and the capture of seventy. Collins tells Boland the IRA can hold out for only a week. Boland calculates there are two thousand IRA volunteers opposing a hundred thousand British troops.

Calling himself a "yob from West Cork" with no gift for talk, Collins rejects the idea of negotiating in London. De Valera, nevertheless, assigns Collins to head the team, holding himself in reserve as a "final arbitrator." Collins agrees reluctantly, sharing with Boland his view of de Valera's rationale. Appearing in London will end Collins' anonymity, making him a known quantity and a target.

There are no scenes of Collins negotiating with Churchill or Lloyd George. Instead, the film cuts to his return from England four months later with the compromised treaty in hand. Jordan implies the terms of the agreement come as a shock to Republicans in Ireland.

*In fact, Ned Broy (1887–1972) survived the Anglo-Irish War and served as a police commissioner in the Irish Free State.

Liam Neeson firing a weapon in *Michael Collins* (1996).

Harry Boland reads about the terms in a newspaper, despairing over the loss of Northern Ireland and the required oath of allegiance to the British Crown.

In stormy Dail debates, Collins pleads for peace:

> Make me a scapegoat if you will. Call me a traitor, if you will. Please let's save the country. The alternative to this treaty is a war which nobody in this gathering can even contemplate. If the price of freedom, if the price of peace is the blackening of my name, I will gladly pay it.

De Valera and his supporters leave the Dail in protest against the treaty. As the deputies leave, Harry Boland follows, leading Collins to say, "Not you, Harry."

Collins next appears in the uniform of the new government, taking command of Dublin Castle from the British. Remonstrated for being seven minutes late to the ceremony, Collins responds, "You've kept us waiting seven hundred years, you can have your seven minutes."

The anti-treaty forces are presented as inflexible fanatics, like Cathal Brugha, and naïve "kids" who seize the Four Courts. Collins meets with Harry Boland, now de Valera's "right hand man," who asks if it is true that he is engaged to Kitty. Collins repeats his suggestion that de Valera wanted to break up the Collins-Boland team because "we were too dangerous together." Still divided by the treaty, the friends part, symbolizing the start of the Civil War.

Collins supervises the shelling of the Four Courts where Harry is fighting. Attempting to escape, Boland dashes through the Dublin sewers. Emerging from the tunnels, Boland is spotted in the river and shot. Arriving just as Harry's body is lifted from the water, Collins tells the soldier who killed him, "He was one of us."

Leaving for a tour of Cork, Collins says, "They won't kill me in my own county."

The final scenes of the film emphasize two elements. The doomed engagement of Collins and Kitty Kiernan is dramatized with the scenes of Collins' death interspersed with images of Kitty trying on wedding apparel. The involvement of de Valera in Collins' death is also implied when a young IRA gunman (Jonathan Rhys Meyers) notices the Collins party in a Cork pub and reports to de Valera, who is huddled in a candlelit stone cottage. Informed that it appears Collins is willing to negotiate, de Valera wonders, "Can I trust him?" His youthful gunman responds, "Can you trust anyone these days, Chief?" The young man returns to the pub and asks Collins what he would have to say to de Valera. Angered, Collins defends his actions:

> Tell him that Harry Boland's death was enough. Tell him that Mick Collins says he wants to stop this bloody mayhem. Tell him I am sorry I didn't bring back the Republic, but nobody could have. He was my Chief always. I would have followed him to hell if he asked me ... and maybe I did.

Embracing the boy, Collins sighs, "But it is not worth fighting for anymore. We have got to learn to build with what we have."

The young IRA man returns to an anguished, weeping de Valera. Asked for a reply, de Valera says nothing. The courier returns to the pub and tells Collins to attend a meeting in a farmhouse outside Béalnabláth the next day.

The final sequence cuts between the ill-fated convoy in the Cork countryside and Kitty Kiernan shopping for her wedding dress. Riding in an open car, Collins jokes about his upcoming wedding, suggesting that Lloyd George and Churchill serve as bridesmaids. Aerial shots show IRA gunmen taking positions on a hillside and firing down upon the Collins convoy. De Valera's messenger is depicted firing the fatal shot.

The film concludes with newsreel footage of Michael Collins' funeral, with titles heralding his importance to Irish history as a man whose death united the country in grief as he tried to "remove the gun from Irish politics." Appearing over scenes of the funeral cortege is de Valera's famous 1966 quotation, "It is my considered opinion that in the fullness of time history will record the greatness of Michael Collins, and it will be recorded at my expense."*

The Making of *Michael Collins*

> *Michael Collins* will forever change the American perception of Irish films and perhaps even of Irish history. And only for the better.—*Joan Dean*

Michael Collins intrigued filmmakers for decades. At various times John Ford, John Huston, and Robert Redford expressed interest in bringing his story to the screen.[82] In the 1980s two major Collins projects were launched. Kevin Costner visited Ireland and hired Eoghan Harris to write a screenplay, but the film was never made. After being appointed to head Columbia Pictures, British producer David Puttnam planned a Collins film and commissioned Neil Jordan to write a screenplay in 1982. The director assigned to the movie, Michael Cimino, contemplated casting Liam Neeson as Eamon de Valera and had begun designing sets and preparing screen tests when the project was terminated.[83] Columbia's parent company, Coca-Cola, had advised Puttnam that the British Army might switch its soft drink contract to rival Pepsi if Columbia released a Collins film.[84] Jordan maintained his interest in the project, envisioning Liam Neeson playing the lead. A decade later, both

---

*The Irish historian Joe Lee has questioned the authenticity of the de Valera quotation.

In an image producers selected for the movie poster, Liam Neeson is shown sans weapon in *Michael Collins* (1996).

Jordan and Neeson had come to prominence in Hollywood. Jordan's films *The Crying Game* and *An Interview with a Vampire* had been highly successful, and Neeson had received critical acclaim for his performance in *Schindler's List*. Now supported by David Geffen, Jordan was able to sell his idea to Warner Brothers and secured a $28 million budget. Adding star power to the film was Julia Roberts, who agreed to play Kitty Kiernan for $125,000, less than one percent of her typical fee.[85]

The production of *Michael Collins* became a national event in Ireland. It was an ambitious big-budget production, shot on eighty-four locations.[86] In addition, filming took place during the 1994–1996 ceasefire, when Ireland was being transformed from a poor, rustic country to the high-tech Celtic Tiger known for its booming real estate market, computer software, rock bands, and movie stars. Relatives, biographers, and historians debated how Collins should be depicted on film.[87] Warner Brothers' promotional material quoted Jordan as saying, "I have never lost more sleep over the making of a film than I have over *Michael Collins*, but I'll never make a more important one."[88] Newspapers reported on the progress of the film, much of it shot on location. The making of a big-budget bio-epic by an Irish director with an Irish leading man signaled Ireland's emergence in world cinema. Thousands of people agreed to work as unpaid extras. The largest film set ever constructed in Ireland was assembled to recreate the GPO for the Easter Rising sequence. After filming was completed, the set was opened for public tours, leading some to suggest that the Irish government should purchase the structure as a national monument.[89] Irish authorities cooperated with the production, allowing Jordan to shoot street scenes in Dublin, which required blocking traffic in the center of the city. Producer Stephen Woolley found local officials so accommodating it seemed "like we're performing some service.... Because it's Michael Collins, whatever we do seems OK."[90] The Irish film censor Sheamus Smith played an important part in the film's success by granting *Michael Collins* a PG certificate to "make the film available to the widest possible Irish cinema audience."[91]* The film was endorsed by former Taoiseach Garret Fitzgerald and the Minister for Justice, Nora Owen, a grand-niece of Michael Collins.[92]

The British response to the anticipated film was guarded and often hostile. The actor who had played Oscar Schindler, the heroic savior of Jews during the Holocaust, was now cast as a figure many considered a terrorist. English critics condemned the film as "anti–British" and an "I.R.A. film" sight-unseen.[93] Concerned about its reception in the British market, Warner Brothers previewed the film for English pundits and government officials and was surprised by their generally positive responses. Still nervous about the film's image, Warner Brothers softened its advertising. An early movie poster depicting Liam Neeson holding a rifle was replaced with the image of Michael Collins giving an energetic but unarmed speech.[94] Warners' concerns mounted when the Provisional IRA exploded a bomb in London that killed two people and injured a hundred others. Fearing that a movie of Michael Collins could incite violence, conservative commentators denounced the film as incendiary and "dangerous."[95] In press interviews, Neil Jordan repeatedly insisted that his film was not pro–IRA, stating that the present IRA would condemn Collins as a traitor for accepting the treaty that partitioned the country.

In August 1996 *Michael Collins* received the Golden Lion award for best picture at the Venice Film Festival. Liam Neeson won for best actor. In Ireland the widely anticipated film earned IR£ 4 million, an amount surpassed only by *Titanic*.† It opened in 800 theaters in the United States and 200 in Great Britain, including Northern Ireland.[96] Warner Brothers invited Irish groups, including NORAID, to film premiers in major American cities.[97] Although Liam Neeson was nominated for a Golden Globe, the only two Academy Award nominations *Michael Collins* garnered were for cinematography and best musical score.‡ Though many in the British press were troubled by the film, the Evening Standard British Film Award for Best Actor was given to Liam Neeson. Alan Rickman was nominated for a BAFTA Award as Best Supporting Actor. The movie won no American Academy Awards, and despite the inclusion of Julia Roberts, *Michael Collins* earned less than $11 million dollars in twelve weeks.[98]

For American reviewers, many less knowledgeable about the historical events behind the film, *Michael Collins* drew a range of criticisms and observations. *U.S. News & World Report*'s Thom Geier saw *Michael Collins* as a "Celtic version of Spike Lee's Malcolm X, a sympathetic portrait of an advocate of violence who was killed just as he embraced peaceful methods."[99] Terry Golway's review in *America* saw the film as a lesson: "If the story of Michael Collins tells us anything, it is that today's gunman may be tomorrow's peacemaker, and that democratically elected leaders must do all they can to encourage such conversions."[100] Writing in the same publication, Richard A. Blake saw Michael Collins as a character operating "in a moral vacuum" in a film in which violence is "not only justified but glorified."[101] Barbara Shulgasser of the *San Francisco Examiner* regarded Collins in his "shiny military uniform" with cynicism, noting, "It's tough not to envision Collins as a German

---

In the United States the MPAA gave Michael Collins *an R-rating.*

†*Given Ireland's population, the U.S. equivalent would be $300 million in ticket sales.*

‡*Chris Menges received the most award nominations for his cinematography, winning the Los Angeles Film Critics Association Award for Best Cinematography.*

officer who thinks Hitler's all right because, after all, his life has improved since the Nazis came in."[102] Michael Null summed up the film as "being just another over-indulgent sermon by a misguided preacher. Think of your $6.50 as an offering."[103] Jonathan Coe's review in *New Statesman* extolled the film as "a breathtaking piece of cinema, a wonderfully crafted narrative, and therefore Neil Jordan's first real screen masterpiece."[104] Coe dismissed accusations that the film glorified violence, claiming *Michael Collins* to be "the most deeply questioning films about political violence that I have ever seen.... The fact that this honest and powerful work should have been so vilified by commentators with an unbending agenda is also, one could argue, a tragedy of a minor sort."[105]

Deconstructing *Michael Collins*

In Ireland and Britain, any film about Michael Collins was destined to arouse immediate and pointed responses, both ideological and artistic. For the politically minded, the film was subject to contrasting ideological interpretations. Was Michael Collins the ruthless innovator of urban guerrilla warfare or the peacemaker "who wanted to take the gun out of Irish politics"?

A single fifty-second scene sparked divergent responses from audiences and reviewers. After a number of G-men are assassinated, a bowlered Ulster police detective (Ian McElhinney) marches through Dublin Castle telling a cowed Ned Broy in a pronounced Northern accent, "Since you Dublin boyos can't sort out this Collins, I suppose it is up to us." He tells Broy to "fergit" his files and lift anyone connected to "this geezer" that night. "There is a new regime in here, and it's startin' now!" he announces. Muttering, "A bit of Belfast efficiency is what they need," the black-hatted officer climbs into the back of a car, slams the door, and is promptly blown up in a ball of fire.

This scene sparked cheers in Boston; in Northern Ireland the Disabled Police Officers Association urged boycotting the film, largely because of the car bomb scene.*[106] The scene was condemned as an anachronistic political statement. Car bombs were not a feature of the Anglo-Irish War of 1920 but an IRA weapon used in Northern Ireland from the 1970s–1990s. The antique car bombing appeared to legitimize the modern-day IRA by visually linking its tactics with the War of Independence. In addition, the Belfast policeman was the single Northern Protestant depicted in the film. For Unionists, *Michael Collins* "reaffirms the anti-imperialist myth: that republicans need deal only with Britain and not with the Ulster Protestant and the Unionist voter.... For the Unionist audience of Northern Ireland ... *Michael Collins* ... visualizes them out of history."[107] For British conservatives and Northern Loyalists, the film ignored the undeniable fact that a million people in Ireland want no part of either Michael Collins' Free State or Eamon de Valera's Republic.

Eoghan Harris, whose Kevin Costner screenplay about Collins was never produced, took exception to Jordan's film. He maintained the car bomb scene "is like a forensic clue to Neil Jordan's political agenda — to make an artistic comment, however oblique, on the armed struggle." Jordan, he argued, was giving audiences "a Northern Collins."[108] He repeatedly attacked the film for its historical inaccuracies and alleged pro–IRA stance.

In October 1996 Neil Jordan responded to Harris' criticisms in an *Irish Times* article entitled "Tally Ho! Mr. Harris." "Film," Jordan reasoned, "is not history, cannot be history, but every now and then makes use of history for its own purposes."[109] The only meaningful

*The association's chairman was unable to review the film, having lost his eyesight and hearing in an IRA bombing.

assessment, he believed, was one that "compares different, filmic versions of the same subject."[110] Jordan then dissected Harris' screenplay, detailing historical inaccuracies and fictional events, abandoning his analysis after thirty-one pages, noting, "It seems fruitless to continue with historical comparison, since they are few and far between."[111] Jordan's article concludes that the Harris screenplay's "relation to history, under any definition of the term, is non-existent."[112]

Three days later *The Irish Times* published a response by Eoghan Harris which excoriated Jordan's "sneering and self-serving synopsis of *Mick,* my screenplay for Kevin Costner."[113] Harris then informed readers that Costner had paid him a million dollars for his screenplay, taking a pass on Jordan's. Jordan's script, Harris asserted, was a "metaphor for some aspects of the armed struggle in the North."[114] The car bomb scene, the "casting of so many familiar Northern faces," Stephen Rea's Northern accent, even the décor, in his view, evoke modern-day Belfast rather than Dublin of the Twenties. Jordan "gives us ... a Northern Collins, a most modern Collins, a savage Collins, a basically Belfast Collins."[115] Gone from Jordan's script, he asserts, "is the organizational genius, the man who ran a government out of bits of paper in his pockets."[116] Gone, too, was the "whole powerful romantic sweep, sweet and bittersweet, of the Irish revolution." Instead, Jordan, gave audiences "a gangster movie."[117]

The parrying of critical reviews and historical reexaminations led commentators to see the film as an historical event of its own. Lance Pettit noted, "*Michael Collins* demonstrated that film had become the preeminent medium through which Ireland both examines itself and projects its image to the wider world."[118]

Ghost Story

In assessing *Michael Collins* in her book about Neil Jordan, Maria Pramaggiore sees ghosts as an important element in the film. Meeting Harry Boland on his return from America, Collins jokes, "You look like a gangster." Boland responds, "You look like a ghost." Collins, in Pramaggiore's view, commands "a ghostly and deadly army" that remains "invisible."[119] Collins himself remains a specter to the British, leading Soames to ask the Dublin G-men, "Doesn't he have a face, this Collins? Doesn't he have corporeal form?" Pramaggiore suggests that the ghostly artistic imagery of the film, with its silhouettes and washed out colors, reinforces the politics:

> *Michael Collins* suggests that we ignore ghosts at our peril. This is the lesson the British forces learn, with the respect to the IRA's shadowy assassins and its imagined republic. Irish Republicans, de Valera wrote to Collins, must "act as if the Republic is a fact." They unseat the British empire by denying its political legitimacy and by substituting their own belief in and performance of a mythical Irish Republic. By performing — by acting as if the Republic is a fact — these ghosts of the Irish nation "ghostify" the British empire itself, causing it to vanish into thin air.[120]

In bringing these ghosts to life, Neil Jordan reminded the Celtic Tiger generation of their nation's violent birth pangs and Collins' troubling legacy of the partition and the IRA.

Collins' ghost shadowed the Irish movie industry itself. Emmet Dalton, who cradled the dying Collins in his arms on a roadway in Cork, resigned from the Irish Army in December 1922, objecting to the execution of Republican prisoners. Dalton became a film producer, working in both the United States and Britain, before founding Ardmore Studios in County Wicklow. The studio was officially opened in May 1958 by the Minister of Industry and Commerce and future Taoiseach Sean Lemass, who, according to Tim Pat Coogan, was among Collins' gunmen on Bloody Sunday.[121]

3

The Shamrock and the Swastika

Today England is locked in a life and death struggle with Germany and Italy.... The lesson of history is plain. England's enemy is Ireland's ally.—*The IRA's* War News, *1940*

The diseased ethos that embraced Hitler as a friend 65 years ago remains intact within Sinn Fein–IRA today.... All those who died for Ireland were good; all deeds done for the republican cause, no matter how terrible, and all alliances, regardless of the nature of the allies, can be justified, provided England suffers.—*Kevin Myers,* The Daily Telegraph, *2005*

The IRA's wartime association, however tentative and ineffectual, with Nazi Germany embarrassed Irish nationalists, antagonized the British, perplexed Irish-Americans, and generated numerous opportunities for filmmakers. Because they are instantly and universally recognized as evil, the Nazis provide a cinematic shorthand that spares screenwriters tedious and sometimes clumsy exposition. The ability to link the IRA with the Nazis gave Unionists and the British a propaganda coup to discredit Irish Republicans by juxtaposing their timid bombing campaign of the early Forties with the excesses of the Third Reich.

After the end of the Civil War the Irish Republican Army foundered, its movement fractured by dissensions over leadership, objectives, and tactics. The use of violence was a source of continual debate. Force was essential in both demonstrating the organization's relevance and attracting new members. As Tim Pat Coogan notes, "The guns, the excitement and the secrecy attract new members thirsting for adventure.... Take away the guns and the excitement and how do you ... attract new members?"[1] Sean O'Callaghan opened his book *The Easter Lily* by recounting the excitement he felt when he joined the organization:

I joined the I.R.A. in November 1934. To me it was the fulfillment of all my aspirations, for to be sworn in as a soldier of the Irish Republican Army had glamour, and there was a thrilling sensation in belonging to it which only a secret, oathbound society can give.[2]

In addition to the question of methods, the IRA was divided on its objectives. Should Republicans target the Six Counties of Northern Ireland, the Free State government in Dublin it refused to recognize, or England itself?

IRA actions tended to be sporadic and disorganized. The Army Council complained to the Clan na Gael that it lacked arms, ammunition, and money.[3] Large-scale military operations were unfeasible. Instead of mass revolution or dramatic acts of sabotage, there were marches, declarations, occasional raids on police barracks, robberies to secure funds, and isolated shootings of informers and Free State officials. In some Irish towns shopkeepers were intimidated into boycotting British goods. In Dublin a shipment of Bass ale from Britain was destroyed. A movie theater in Dublin was blown up after showing a film the IRA deemed "British propaganda." In Galway, another film was seized and destroyed, and cinema operators were threatened.[4] In January 1931 Patrick Carroll, a suspected informer, was shot dead in Dublin. Two months later John Ryan, who had provided evidence against the IRA, was found dead in Tipperary with a note around his neck reading "Spies and informers beware. IRA."[5] These actions often backfired, turning public opinion against Republicans. Attacks against law enforcement now targeted men wearing Irish, not British, uniforms. De Valera's *Fianna Fail* retained the veneer of Republicanism, and the Free State exuded a patina of Irish identity, giving Gaelic names for government boards, agencies, and institutions in a largely English-speaking country.* Some IRA efforts were symbolic, designed to humiliate or discredit the Free State government. De Valera's 1936 St. Patrick's Day radio broadcast was interrupted by a voice saying, "Hello, everybody, this is the IRA."[6]

With the onset of the Depression, the IRA became involved in land and labor disputes, which created a further schism. The February 1931 IRA convention called for the creation of a workers' and farmers' organization. At an IRA parade in Dublin that June, Peadar O'Donnell argued that Republicans should suspend their struggle to end Partition and concentrate on creating a Republican Workers Party, with the aim of establishing an Irish "Peasants' Republic." In September one hundred and fifty delegates attended a congress in Dublin, proposing the nationalization of banks and foreign trade.[7] Many in the Republican movement were troubled by the shift in priorities, maintaining the IRA's sole objective was to end the British occupation of the Six Counties. Devout Catholics were wary of the organization's emergent Marxist ideology. Vigilantes, inspired by angry sermons denouncing the "plague of Bolshevism," attacked IRA members and burned Republican meeting halls.[8]

The leftward tilt of the IRA also brought it into conflict with the militant rightist organization, the National Guard, established in 1933 by General Eoin O'Duffy. The decision to select blue shirts as a uniform immediately led the public to nickname the conservative organization the Blue Shirts, linking them with Mussolini's Black Shirts and Hitler's Brown Shirts. The National Guard held military-style parades, espoused the corporate state, sided with anti–Communists, used Fascist symbols, and adopted the Nazi raised arm salute. O'Duffy later organized an Irish Brigade to fight for Franco. Fourteen hundred volunteers went to Spain but saw little action and returned to Ireland within a few months.[9]

The conflict between the IRA and Blue Shirts, mostly veterans of the Free State army, threatened to reopen the wounds of the Civil War. When O'Duffy announced plans to parade in Dublin, de Valera feared a replay of Mussolini's 1922 March on Rome and banned both the parade and the organization. The Blue Shirts faded from the scene. To circumvent the ban, O'Duffy renamed his group the Young Ireland Association, which joined other conservative but less militant organizations to create a new political party, Fine Gale.

The collapse of the Blue Shirt movement failed to strengthen the IRA, still torn with dissension over its ends and means. The IRA was officially outlawed by de Valera in 1936. Leaders were arrested. Garda records made public in 2009 revealed that throughout the 1930s Free State police had IRA informants, many of them receiving regular payments, in nearly every county in Ireland. IRA mail was routinely intercepted, examined, and sometimes photographed.[10] Many leftists in the movement, like Frank Ryan, volunteered to fight Franco's Fascists in Spain, which deprived the IRA of some of its most committed activists. Ryan joined the International Brigade and was taken prisoner by Italian troops in 1938.

As tensions mounted between Britain and Nazi Germany in the late Thirties, another IRA leader, soon to be its Chief of Staff, saw a new opportunity.

The Irish Free State was officially Saorstát Éireann; *the armed forces were called* Óglaigh na hÉireann; *the Irish national police force, founded by Michael Collins, was named* An Garda Síochána.

The S-Plan

In the summer of 1936, Sean Russell announced a grand plan to members of America's Clan na Gael, which had financed the Easter Rising. In a newspaper interview that August, Russell first denounced de Valera as a traitor, then outlined ambitious designs for a repeat of the 1916 uprising twenty years before:

> ... De Valera has betrayed the trust of the Irish nation by becoming the tool of Great Britain.
>
> Instead of fighting, as he promised, for the Republic of Ireland, he has been content to allow her to become a nation subject to a foreign King.
>
> Republican forces are awaiting an opportune moment to fight with all their might for the nation's freedom.
>
> When the moment will come I do not know. It may come when the British become embroiled in a European conflict. But our plan of campaign is ready.
>
> As de Valera knows only too well, we have splendid military forces in Ireland, with cleverly hidden arsenals.
>
> Then, over in England, where we shall also take the offensive, we have another secret army of Irishmen, who meet quietly, for drill and target practice.
>
> We have also quantities of ammunition and other war material in England.
>
> Our Air Force may be small, but it is reasonably efficient.
>
> When hostilities start we shall certainly send planes to bomb England.
>
> It is a very definite plan in our scheme for an offensive.[11]

Russell's claims were fanciful. The "secret army" in London was equipped with a half-dozen handguns and a single submachine gun.[12] The "small" but "reasonably efficient" air force was wholly fictional.

The secretive Clan, however, was a receptive audience. It, too, harbored fantastic plans for international terrorism. One scheme discussed in New York in the late Thirties consisted of loading a large airplane with fuel and explosives, flying over the Atlantic to bomb the House of Commons, then making a forced landing in northern France.[13]

On January 16, 1939, Sean Russell declared war on Britain, signing an Army Council statement that called on the English to withdraw from Northern Ireland "in the name of the unconquered dead and the faithful living."[14] Supplied with funds from the United States and Germany, IRA men traveled to Britain to wage war.

Over the next several months over a hundred and twenty bombs exploded across Britain.* Fifty-seven explosions occurred in London alone. Throughout the English Midlands IRA bombs damaged train stations, post offices, power plants, and gas mains. Bombs were left in public lavatories, letter boxes, and cloak rooms. Tear gas bombs cleared cinemas in Liverpool.[15] In Manchester, incendiary bombs set fire to a major department store.[16]

The IRA bombing campaign, designated the S-Plan for Sabotage, though alarming, was amateurish and amounted to more of a "nuisance campaign" rather than a "reign of terror." Many of the bombs failed to detonate because budget-minded IRA agents used cheap alarm clocks as timing devices.[17] The most commonly available explosive material was gelignite, which was bulky and degraded quickly. With little access to sophisticated weapons or industrial chemicals, the IRA relied on unreliable, unstable homemade devices.[18] As J. Bowyer Bell pointed out, even a few well-placed explosions could have crippled Britain's vital aircraft production. Small, recurring attacks on the London Underground would have disrupted commercial life in the hub of the British Empire. But there was no central strategic

*Some sources place the total number of explosions in Britain in 1939 at nearly 300.

planning. Targets were chosen by local commanders.[19] The casual and haphazard nature of the bombing campaign is illustrated by Brendan Behan's depiction of an IRA bomber:

Jerry Gildea was a clerk in Guinness's brewery, and had volunteered to "go active in England" for the period of his annual summer holidays. A fast whip over *via* the L.M.S., a time bomb planted in a railway or an incendiary package in a dock warehouse, and back to the office. "Have a nice hols., Mr. G?" Smiles, little do you know.[20]

The bombing campaign scored minor victories, such as Northern Ireland postponing a visit of the Duke and Duchess of Kent to Belfast.[21] The main impact was to harden British opinion against not only the IRA but the entire nationalist movement. *Time* magazine satirized the logic of Russell's S-Plan:

The political reasoning behind I.R.A.'s English bombings is about as involved as a Rube Goldberg invention: 1) one of I.R.A.'s 15,000 members gets a job in England as a mechanic, poster painter, motorman; 2) he plants a bomb in a place where it will raise merry hell but probably will kill no one; 3) the terrified English people put pressure on the Government; 4) the Government cedes Northern Ireland to Eire; 5) a unified Irish Republic is formed, which will be so anti–British that it will take sides against Britain in the next big war. So far, of course, I.R.A's eccentric machine has worked only so far as Step 2.[22]

These attacks, although targeting property rather than the public, raised concerns in Ireland as well as Britain. For de Valera, Sean Russell's campaign in the name of Ireland challenged his legitimacy as the nation's leader. Furthermore, the violence undermined de Valera's peaceful campaign to end Partition and directly contravened his promise that Ireland would not be used as a base for attacks against Britain.

In April 1939 Russell returned to the United States, a continual source of IRA funds. In his speeches (now attended by German-American Nazis) he openly took credit for the bombing campaign, claiming it would continue until the British withdrew from Northern Ireland and released Irish political prisoners.[23] In June he was taken into custody in Detroit, possibly as a precaution because King George and Queen Elizabeth were touring North America. Russell's detention became a *cause célèbre* among Irish-American Congressmen. Pennsylvania Representative MacGranery denounced Russell's arrest as "a very stupid blunder" that "demonstrated British influence in the U.S."[24] Seventy-six Irish-American Congressmen pledged to boycott the royal couple's American visit in protest. Russell was freed on bail but ordered to leave the United States.[25]

As the bombings continued throughout the summer of 1939, de Valera took action to curtail the IRA. In June 1939 the Offenses Against the State Act went into effect, allowing detention without trial. On July 26 a bomb exploded in a London train station, blowing the legs off a Scottish physician. That day de Valera denounced the bombing campaign in the Irish Senate, declaring that "no one can think that this Government has any sympathy with it."[26]

De Valera's condemnation of the IRA campaign did not mean, however, he was willing to cooperate with the British. The bombs, after all, were going off in England, not Ireland. When Scotland Yard sent agents to Dublin to arrest terrorist suspects who had fled Britain, they found the Irish government unwilling to honor their warrants.[27]

The worst attack took place on August 25 when a bomb in Coventry killed five people and wounded dozens of others. Two IRA men, Peter Barnes and Frank Richards (aka McCormick), were sentenced to death for their involvement. De Valera condemned the attack but sought to stay their executions. An *Irish Times* editorial admitted the men's guilt but argued there were "higher considerations than stern justice" in their case. When Barnes and Richards were hanged in February 1940, demonstrators marched in Dublin, cinemas closed, and athletic events were cancelled in protest. In New York City, Irish-Americans placed a wreath outside the Irish pavilion at the World's Fair to "honor the martyrs."[28]

The Abwehr Takes an Interest

The start of the Second World War signaled what could have been a repeat of the 1916 Easter Rebellion when Republican forces seized buildings in Dublin while Britain was pre-occupied with the war in France. Germany had long been seen as an Irish ally, a source of weapons and support. If World War I helped spark events that freed the Twenty-Six Counties, perhaps, some hoped, the new war would provide an occasion to free the Six Counties of the North and drive the British out of Ireland altogether. The IRA of 1939, however, was not the IRA of 1916. It was much smaller and much less organized. It enjoyed less public support in Ireland. Its American sponsor, the Clan na Gael, was much smaller as well. As a result of the S-Plan, many IRA men were either jailed in Britain or interned in Ireland. The IRA was in no position to become what the British feared and the Nazis hoped, a militant Fifth Column providing an organized resistance army challenging the British on their own soil.

Although the declaration of war intensified IRA activities, their characteristics remained more criminal than military. In Northern Ireland the IRA staged robberies to secure funds, ambushed police cars, and occasionally planted small bombs. In 1942 two policemen were killed in a shootout near the border. In a robbery similar to the one portrayed in *Odd Man Out*, the IRA raided a flax mill for its payroll and killed a policeman.[29]

When war broke out, the IRA's Chief of Staff was not even in Ireland. Although ordered to leave the United States, Russell had remained in New York. With the beginning of hostilities, passenger service to Europe was disrupted. After making overtures through intermediaries, Russell secured permission to travel to Germany. Passing first through Genoa, Russell arrived in Berlin in May 1940. Within weeks he was being trained by the Nazis in sabotage and commando techniques. Russell asked the Germans to secure Frank Ryan's release from a Spanish prison. The head of German intelligence was a personal friend of Franco and arranged for the Leftist Republican to be escorted to Germany. Though Ryan was in poor health and nearly deaf, he was selected to accompany Russell on his mission to Ireland, which the Germans dubbed Operation Dove. In preparation for the proposed invasion of England, Russell was to organize the IRA to attack Northern Ireland, which it was hoped would lead Ireland into occupying the Six Counties.

Russell and Ryan never reached Ireland. The day after their U-Boot put to sea, Russell fell ill and died on August 14 of a perforated ulcer. His body, covered in a Nazi flag, was buried at sea.* Having not been fully briefed by Russell, Frank Ryan was in no condition

*For many years a much mutilated statue of Sean Russell stood in Dublin. Right-wing vandals chopped off the right arm, claiming its upward pose was a Communist salute. The statue was repaired, with the arm pointed downward. In 2004 left-wing vandals decapitated the statue and removed the restored arm, denouncing Russell as a Nazi sympathizer. In 2009 a new bronze version was unveiled. Wearing a trademark trench coat, the new Russell statue is equipped with alarms and a tracking device in its head to deter vandals.

to pursue the assignment on his own. The submarine returned to Germany. Ryan suffered a disabling stroke a few months later and died in a Dresden sanitarium in 1944.

The failure of Operation Dove was emblematic of the Nazi-IRA alliance. In the early years of the war a few Nazi agents were inserted into Ireland by parachute or submarine. Many had poor English skills and lacked familiarity with Irish life and customs. They were a strange assortment of diverse characters. Ernest Weber-Drohl was a chiropractor and former circus strongman. Henry Obed, perhaps the oddest Nazi agent to be inserted into Ireland, was an Indian national whose dark complexion drew immediate attention after he and two South African Germans rowed ashore in a dinghy. Spotted by Irish police walking with suitcases, the three agents claimed to be visiting students. Irish police immediately called Dublin about the suspicious foreigners who had "appeared from nowhere."[30] Like most of the other Abwehr agents, the three were quickly detained and interned.[31] The attempt to create an "Irish Brigade" by recruiting British POWs of Irish extraction was abandoned. After the invasion of the Soviet Union in 1941, German interest in Ireland diminished.

After the war Hermann Görtz, a major in the Abwehr, provided a glum assessment of the IRA's value to the Nazis. Parachuted into Ireland in 1940, Görtz eluded capture for over a year, staying with sympathizers and deliberately avoiding contact with IRA members, whom he grew to distrust. In Görtz's opinion, Stephen Hayes, who replaced Sean Russell as Chief of Staff of the IRA, was little more than a cowardly alcoholic.[32] In November 1941 Görtz was arrested in Dublin and interned for the remainder of the war. Released from prison with the end of hostilities, Görtz took a job with a German charity in Dublin. Learning that he was going to be deported to Germany, Görtz committed suicide, evidently because he feared the Allies would turn him over to the Russians. Before his death he bitterly reflected on his failed mission to Ireland and the uselessness of the IRA in a series of articles printed posthumously in the *Irish Times*. In his estimation, the IRA was "worthless":

> Inside the I.R.A. nobody knew what game was really played, not even their leader. Their internal means of communication were as primitive as boys playing police and brigands. They got no further than the open message in the sock of a girl. And what messages! There was no code — they did not want to learn the most simple code.... They had not a single wireless operator; they made no attempt to learn message discipline; their military training was nil. I once said to one of them I admired for his personal qualities: "You know how to die for Ireland, but how to fight for it you have not the slightest idea."[33]

The IRA's opening wartime action signaled its pitiful disorganization. With the declaration of war, the IRA ordered Daniel O'Connell's famous maxim to be painted on walls in Northern Ireland as a warning to the British. Evidently the instructions were misconstrued, and walls in Belfast soon bore the less menacing and somewhat capricious message "England's difficulty is Ireland's opera tune."[34]

The Emergency

The IRA-Nazi alliance was exaggerated as a focal point of Ireland's wartime neutrality, which is still a sore point in Britain. Long after the end of the Second World War, British resentment against the Irish was stirred by rumors that Ireland refueled Nazi U-boats and supplied weather reports to the Luftwaffe. De Valera was accused throughout the war of allowing German and Japanese spies to operate openly from their Dublin embassies.

On September 1, 1939, Nazi Germany invaded Poland. In response, Great Britain declared war. Ireland declared neutrality.

A country of four million with few strategic resources, Ireland was bound to play a marginal role in any European conflict. For a country on the brink of world war, Ireland was sparsely armed. In 1940 the Irish defense force had fewer than eight thousand regular soldiers.[35] The Irish Air Corps consisted of sixteen attack planes, all of them obsolete and many unserviceable.[36] Although an island nation, Ireland maintained a naval force of four ships. Ireland could offer little more to either side than its geography.

But declarations of neutrality are not always neutral. Britain still considered Ireland part of the Commonwealth and expected Eire to join its war effort like its sister dominions.* The British took de Valera's stance as an affront and a serious obstacle to their national security. Germany never expected Ireland to join the Axis, but benefited from Ireland's neutrality that denied Britain use of its ports and airfields. Neutrality meant that Axis embassies would remain open in Dublin, and that Germans would be able to operate in a country bordering Great Britain. Neutrality denied the British the usufruct of territory they anticipated and gave the Germans access they hoped for but never took for granted.

The British reacted to Ireland's neutrality with shock, anger, and disappointment. In the face of Hitlerism, de Valera's stance seemed highly parochial and petulant. For the Irish, who had just eighteen years before managed to achieve independence from Britain, the presence of British troops on Irish soil or even ships in Irish ports both endangered the nation by making it a target and represented a retreat from sovereignty. Realizing that temporary wartime concessions could easily become the post-war status quo, de Valera refused to grant the British the use of key seaports. "It took 600 years to get the British out of this country," he reasoned. "We don't want them or any others to come here again."[37] In addition, he understood that any cooperation with the English would erode domestic support and add credibility to the IRA's claim of being the "true Republicans."

In September 1939 the Emergency Powers Bill gave de Valera powers over nearly every aspect of national life, including press censorship, transport, agriculture, and the military. Officially, the Second World War would be known in Ireland as the Emergency. In keeping with its stance of neutrality, Eire interned German and Allied air crews that crashed on Irish territory.†

The IRA continued its war on Britain and began mounting attacks at home. On December 23, 1939, the IRA raided a Dublin fort and stole a million rounds of ammunition, much of which was recovered. A week later a Garda officer in Cork was killed. De Valera began interning and executing members of the IRA.[38] During the Emergency, Ireland interned some six hundred Republicans. Many threatened with internment were released if they signed declarations to abandon activities against the Irish government.[39]

These actions made little impression on the English, who were angered by de Valera's declaration of neutrality and the continuation of IRA bombings, which now coincided with the start of Luftwaffe air raids. Memories of the 1916 rebellion and previous arms shipments

---

*Australia, New Zealand, and India declared war on Germany the same day as Great Britain; Canada followed a week later.

†Axis and Allied personnel were treated as "internees" and not prisoners-of-war. Granted passes, they frequented a nearby race track, swam in local baths, and went to movies. Officers could be seen dining in Dublin's upscale restaurants. Terence Ryan's film The Brylcreem Boys (Opix Films, 1998) pits two internees, one German and the other Allied, as romantic rivals for a local Irish girl. Roger Tucker's Waiting for Dublin (Corsan, 2007) involves a downed American and German pilot stranded in a rustic Irish village.

from Germany raised concerns about the potential of both sabotage and espionage. The large Irish population in Britain meant that IRA operatives or sympathizers could move freely throughout the country without detection. Fluent in English and knowledgeable of British customs, they could easily obtain and pass on information with a facility few highly trained foreign agents could achieve. In the First World War Michael Collins had built a comprehensive intelligence network that relied on ordinary clerks, typists, railway men, drivers, and merchants that helped him neutralize Dublin Castle. A similar network could provide the Nazis with a British underground that could carry out sabotage, monitor troop movements, and obtain military and industrial secrets.

In fact, Ireland's breaches of neutrality tended to favor the Allies. Whatever political and diplomatic poses Dublin might take in the name of national sovereignty, England and Ireland were inextricably linked by economic realities: 50 percent of Ireland's imports came from Britain, and 90 percent of its exports went to Britain.[40] Economic realities also continued the long-established pattern of Irish men and women migrating to Britain to seek employment. Fifty thousand Irish citizens served in Britain's armed forces during the Second World War, and tens of thousands worked in its factories. Throughout the war Ireland provided Britain with a valuable source of manpower. To maintain its neutral stance, Ireland downplayed the role of its citizens' military service. Irishmen who served in the British forces were discouraged from wearing their uniforms when home on leave. When a Dublin journalist serving in the British navy survived the sinking of *The Prince of Wales*, Irish newspapers reported that he had "recovered from his recent boating accident."[41]

Ireland was hardly as independent as de Valera proclaimed. All ships bound for Ireland first docked in Britain. All mail from Ireland passed through British censors. In 1940 the British took control of the undersea cable connecting Ireland to the Continent so that communications were monitored.[42] Because de Valera claimed that all the Irish in Northern Ireland, whether Protestant or Catholic, were rightly "our people," he felt obliged to help when their lives were threatened. After a major German air raid on Belfast in 1940, de Valera sent men and equipment from the Dublin fire department north to help quell the fires. In other instances, badly needed RAF pilots forced down in Ireland were escorted to the border and allowed to return to British territory. In contrast, German pilots remained interned until the end of the war. In 1943 a B-17 carrying American General Devers crashed in Ireland. Instead of being detained, he was feted at a special dinner by local residents, then driven to Northern Ireland to continue his mission for the Allies.[43] These breaches were monitored by the Germans who, eager to keep Ireland from fully joining the Allies, only filed protests.

Although Britain and America pressured de Valera on the issue of neutrality, Ireland's refusal to join the Allies actually benefited their cause. Had Ireland declared war, many of the 50,000 Irishmen who joined the British armed forces would likely have stayed home to defend their island. In addition, the RAF, stretched thin during the Battle of Britain, would have had to extend its air cover to protect Ireland.

These facts could not fully overcome British resentment about de Valera's refusal to declare war, his cordial relations with German diplomats, and his objections to the arrival of American troops in Northern Ireland, or the suspicion that he gave free reign to Nazi and Japanese agents. With the outbreak of war, Churchill contacted the First Sea Lord, calling for a special report regarding "the so-called neutrality of the so-called Eire." Specifically, Churchill wondered if "Irish malcontents" might supply Nazi submarines in the West of Ireland. "If they throw bombs in London," he asked, "why should they not supply the U-boats? Extreme vigilance should be practiced."[44] The British sent a representative to Ireland to investigate Churchill's concerns. When he began asking too many questions of the locals, the officer was taken into custody by Irish intelligence and sent back to England.[45] The Irish had no access to the kind of fuel used by submarines, but Churchill's question led many in Britain to suspect Ireland's motives and generated conspiracy theories still surfacing in blogs and letters to editors seventy-five years later.

The ability of the Irish to regard Nazi Germany through a lens of neutrality was viewed by many in Britain as a vicious, self-serving version of "the enemy of my enemy is my friend" philosophy. Few could appreciate the actions of Robert Briscoe. Although an orthodox Jew and dedicated Zionist, he traveled to Germany to negotiate a trade deal with the Nazis, noting in his autobiography, "I would do business with Hitler if it was for Ireland's good."[46]

If de Valera's announcement of neutrality at the start of the war disappointed the British, his behavior at war's end, in the wake of the liberation of Nazi death camps, incensed London. On May 3, 1945, de Valera called on Eduard Hempel, the German minister, to express his "condolences." He evidently called on the minister's personal residence and did not, as widely reported, visit the German legation to sign a book of remembrance for Adolf Hitler.[47]

Understanding the firestorm that this act might unleash, de Valera defended his visit, refusing to feign a "diplomatic illness" to evade his duty as head of state. Writing to the Irish minister in Washington, he maintained the necessity to follow protocol:

> To have failed to call upon the German representative would have been an act of unpardonable discourtesy to the German nation and to Dr. Hempel himself. During the whole of the war, Dr. Hempel's conduct was irreproachable. He was always friendly and invariably correct — in marked contrast with Gray. I certainly was not going to add to his humiliation in the hour of defeat.[48]

David Gray, the American ambassador, was a persistent critic of Irish neutrality, who saw the Irish as jeopardizing an Allied victory and threatening a post-war Anglo-American hegemony. He particularly angered de Valera in 1944 with his demand that Ireland not become a refuge for Nazi war criminals after the war. Determined to maintain national sovereignty, de Valera was irritated at foreign attempts to influence Irish policies.* The Dail, the Taoiseach reminded critics, had adjourned on learning of Roosevelt's death the month before. As a neutral nation, Eire was bound to follow diplomatic etiquette and recognize the loss of heads of states.[49]

Neutralizing Irish Cinema

Ireland had a long history of rigorous film censorship, banning and censoring motion pictures for partial nudity, suggestive language, or depictions of extra-marital relations. During the Emergency, film censors sought to "neutralize" Irish cinema fare, banning and editing films for political content. The number of films proscribed in Ireland rose from 10 in 1939 to 77 in 1943; the number of films cut increased from 36 to 275. Joseph Connolly, the specially appointed Controller of Censorship, delineated films for special examination,

---

*Otto Skorzeny, the SS commando best known for rescuing Mussolini in 1943, purchased a farm in Ireland in 1959. In January 2007 the RTE documentary Ireland's Nazis, hosted by Cathal O'Shannon, revealed that Ireland granted asylum to Nazi war criminals, including the Croatian mass murderer Andreij Artukovic. In May 2007 the Jewish National Fund celebrated the fortieth anniversary of the planting of the Eamon de Valera Forest in Israel.

including those "dealing with war preparations, parades, ... pictures of shelters" and "all references for or against any of the countries involved as belligerents."[50] Much of Connolly's censorship was designed to stem any pro–British influence, particularly films that, in his words, "tend to glorify the empire or British rule — White man's burden — spreading the benefits of white (British) civilisation — Kiplingesque — Gunga Din — Bengal Lancer — Four Feathers type of stuff."[51]

As a result, movies such as *A Yank in the RAF* were heavily censored to eliminate shots of Union Jacks, derogatory comments about the Germans, dialogue identifying Nazi aircraft as "the enemy," and a scene of a Dunkirk evacuee celebrating the sight of Spitfires appearing over the Channel. Other major American "war movies," such as *Sergeant York* and *Casablanca*, were banned outright.*

In addition to banning and censoring fictional films, Connolly's office insisted that "All news films ... must be free from war news or anything of a propagandist or partisan nature."[52] The Germans, Connolly insisted, were not to be called "the enemy" or portrayed in a negative light. Any affinity with England by referring to British soldiers as "our troops" or using the collective pronoun "we" to suggest a linkage between the Eire and Britain was to be avoided.[53]

As a result, Movietone newsreels, widely shown in Ireland, were cut. The September 9, 1939, reel that covered the outbreak of World War II was censored to remove shots of Hitler and images of cheering Londoners. The sinking of the British passenger ship *Athenia* was cut as well. Irish censors sought to eradicate the most innocuous references to World War II, in one instance cutting a scene of English schoolchildren visiting a zoo because they were carrying gas masks.[54] When Dublin was bombed in 1941, Irish censors edited a Pathé Gazette newsreel to cut inflammatory lines such as "Murderous attack from the sky" and "Shocking attack."[55] Rather than an act of war, the bombing was presented as a natural disaster in order to dampen public reaction.

Irish censors banned or cut songs from musical short features to eliminate war references. The popular song "When the Lights Go on Again" (suggestive of a wartime blackout) was cut from a Columbia film, along with "Bless Them All" and lyrics from "Rosie the Riveter" that mentioned "victory" and "the red, white, and blue" (which were also the colors of the British Union Jack).[56]

The exclusion of World War II images from Irish screens had an impact on the public consciousness. The German author Heinrich Böll recounted an incident that occurred on a trip to Ireland in the 1950s. In Dublin he was stunned to see a bright red van bearing a swastika. The van, he discovered, was operated by the Swastika Laundry. Founded in 1912, the firm had adopted the name and logo before the advent of Nazism and evidently saw no need to change. So for decades after World War II, the red vans, which would ignite controversy in any other European capital city, rolled through the streets of Dublin, unnoticed except by tourists.

Hitler's Irish Movies

> "Ich bin kein Verräter"—*Patrick O'Connor,* My Leben für Irland

The first motion pictures to capitalize on the idea of a German-Irish wartime alliance were produced in the Third Reich in the early years of the Second World War. Before the

---

*In 1945 Casablanca *was released in Ireland, with romantic scenes between Rick and the married Ilsa deleted.*

Soviet Union and the United States entered the conflict, Britain was Germany's principal adversary. Recognizing the Anglo-Saxons as fellow Aryans equally opposed to and threatened by Slavic Communism, Hitler embraced lingering hopes for reconciliation between the two racially superior nations. Although dismissed as a lunatic stunt, the Hess flight to Britain in 1940 and German overtures to the exiled Duke of Windsor underscored the desire some Nazis harbored for a merger of British and German interests. Dr. Josef Goebbels, the Reich's Minister for Propaganda and Public Enlightenment, was less enthusiastic about a rapprochement with Britain. Seeking to discredit British imperialism and dispel Germans' lingering affection for the English, Goebbels, who supervised German film production, saw an opportunity in exploiting the Irish Cause.

Nazi Germany produced two Irish films designed to be anti–British propaganda. Both were directed by Max Kimmich, who later insisted his films were meant to be pro–Irish rather an anti–English. Born in Ulm in 1897, Kimmich initially intended to pursue a medical career, writing movie scripts to support his university studies. He soon abandoned his plans to become a physician and took a writing job with Ufa, Germany's largest motion picture company. By the early 1920s he was operating a small studio of his own, producing low-budget films in rapid succession.[57]

Carl Laemmle, the diminutive founder of Universal Pictures, saw some of Kimmich's work and returned to his native Germany (he had been born in a village twenty miles from Ulm in 1867) to meet the young filmmaker. Laemmle put Kimmich under contract for his newly formed Deutsche-Universal production company, assigning him to recruit German actors for work in Hollywood. In the silent era language barriers did not exist, and Laemmle, who constantly complained about Hollywood stars' rising salaries, repeatedly raided German studios in search of cheaper talent. Kimmich traveled to California in the late Twenties, where he wrote and directed a series of comedy shorts. Dubbed the "drugstore cowboy" series, the one-reelers starred Arthur Lake, who would become better known as Dagwood Bumstead a decade later. But directing fifteen-minute films entitled "The Love Wallop" and "The Speed Sheik" left Kimmich frustrated and unchallenged. Unable to secure the opportunity to direct feature films at Universal, Kimmich returned to Germany in 1929. Here he wrote and directed a German film set in America called *Kennst Du das Kleine Haus am Michigansee?* (*Do You Know That Little House on Lake Michigan?*) in 1930.[58]

With the rise of the Nazis, Kimmich found himself ostracized by the film community and blacklisted, tainted by his relationship with Hollywood and Carl Laemmle, who was Jewish.[59] Laemmle, who never forgot his roots in his small German town, was distressed when he learned that a street that had been dedicated in his honor was renamed for Hitler. Though he retained much of his personal fortune (he aided the emigration of hundreds of Jews from Germany), he had lost control of financially-strapped Universal in 1936 and could no longer serve as a mentor to Kimmich.[60] Blacklisted and unable to find directing assignments, Kimmich supported himself by writing. Though shunned by Germany's Filmwelt for his Hollywood Jewish associations, his talents were still highly regarded. When the actor Paul Wegener encountered problems directing the adventure film *Moskau-Shanghai* in 1936, Kimmich was called in to assist but was denied screen credit.[61]

Kimmich's fortunes improved markedly in 1938 after he married Josef Goebbels' younger sister Maria. Now brother-in-law to the Nazi Propaganda Minister, he was cleared to direct films under his own name. His feature *Der Vierte Kommt Nich* (*The Fourth Will Not Come*) was well received when it was released in the spring of 1939. The Academy Award–winning actor Emil Jannings hired Kimmich to direct a pacifist drama, *Der Letze Appell*

(*The Last Roll-Call*). A major film with an eminent cast and a large budget, it told the tale of a World War I German ship captured by the British and destroyed by a mine, along with the principal characters. Lavish naval battle scenes were photographed on the Baltic Sea. While the film was being edited, relations between Germany and Britain worsened, and the government ordered all work on the project shut down. Kimmich arrived at the studio to find that all prints of the film had been seized and apparently destroyed, leaving historians with nothing but still photographs of Emil Janning's grand production.[62]

Though many critics assume Goebbels initiated the Irish films, Kimmich maintained in post-war interviews that the film ideas were his.* As wartime propaganda, both are cinematic curiosities. Besides the irony of the Nazis producing movies that champion freedom fighters battling foreign occupation is their strangely muted attack on British imperialism. In Kimmich's films the English debate their treatment of the Irish, with some urging policies of moderation. In one scene British officers show a deference toward an Irish baron the Nazis would never extend a nobleman in any nation they occupied.

THE FOX OF GLENARVON (1940)

The Fox of Glenarvon (Tobis) was written by Hans Bertram and Wolf Neumeister, based on the German novel by Nicola Rhon. The image of Ireland in Kimmich's film contrasts sharply with the charming Hollywood vision of the Emerald Isle. Kimmich's Ireland, characterized by dark mists, treacherous bogs, and grim, torch-bearing peasants, resembles the Transylvania of a Thirties Dracula movie. In addition, there are perplexing anachronisms in plot, costuming, and set design. Although the novel was set in 1884, the film's action appears to take place in the mid–twentieth century. Interiors feature 1940s furnishings, electric table lamps, and telephones, yet, inexplicably, no motor vehicles appear in exterior scenes. British troops patrol on horseback and transport condemned men in a horse-drawn prison van. The Irish rebels are referred to as Ribbonmen, an organization that was most active from the 1830s to the 1850s. More puzzling to modern viewers familiar with *Riverdance* is Kimmich's stilted, mechanical version of Irish folk dance.

The film opens with a topographical model of the British Isles. The camera zooms in on Ireland, then cuts to a series of shots showing the sea crashing on rocks as sonorous music accompanies a sequence of titles:

> Ireland — the green island — is one of the oldest victims of English despotism!
> For eight centuries fraud and deceit, plunder, murder and arson have been the methods of British politics.
> Millions have been starved, banished and executed in the life of suffering of these people.
> But the pride and love of freedom of the Irish could not be broken.

In the first scene, O'Riordan (Friedrich Kayssler), the stern leader of the Fenian-like group called the Ribbonmen, engages his followers in a dour, cadenced chant:

> O'Riordan: How long is your staff?
> Ribbonmen: Long enough to gain our freedom.
> O'Riordan: The road is bad.
> Ribbonmen: We will make it better.
> O'Riordan: With what?

Kimmich had attempted, without success, to bring The Fox of Glenarvon *to the screen in Hollywood in the 1920s.*

Ribbonmen: With the bones of our enemies.
O'Riordan: Who is our enemy?
Ribbonmen: ENGLAND!*

The film pits O'Riordan's rebels, who use ribbons as an insignia, against Philip Grandison (Ferdinand Marian), the corrupt English Justice of the Peace of Glenarvon. Although Grandison is not openly identified in the script as being Jewish, Eoin Bourke suggests German audiences may have assumed as much because of Marian's title role in the anti–Semitic film *Jud Suss* released the same year.[63]

Baron Ennis (Karl Ludwig Diehl), an Irish nobleman, returns to Glenarvon after seven years in exile and encounters a wrecked prison carriage that had been ambushed by the Ribbonmen. Inspecting the body of an English officer, he picks up a swatch of ribbons as the police ride up. Grandison confronts Ennis, who identifies himself and explains his presence. Cordially accepting Ennis' story, Grandison allows the baron to continue on his way.

At his home, Ennis gazes sadly at the portrait of his dead wife Fleur, telling a servant that she was cut down by British machine guns during an insurrection. The camera closes in on the portrait of Fleur, who bears a striking similarity to Grandison's wife Gloria (Olga Tschechowa), a secret member of the Ribbonmen. After Ennis' valet informs him of the worsening situation in Ireland, including the burning of a village in reprisal for harboring rebels, two Ribbonmen appear, requesting horses to draw the hearses of two fallen comrades. Ennis lends them the horses and attends the nighttime funeral. At the wake, Gloria sings over the bodies of the dead, and Ennis is struck by both her resemblance to Fleur and her nationalist passion.

At a reception Ennis learns that Britain is sending Sir Tetbury (Werner Hinz) to Ireland. Having served with Tetbury in India, Ennis denounces him as a tyrant, telling Grandison that England will regret the day he arrives in Ireland. Hearing Gloria singing in another room, Ennis enters and immediately recognizes her as the woman from the funeral. He asks her to dance and is shocked to learn that she is married to Grandison.

Grandison is next shown discussing his financial plight with an underling. Living beyond his means, he has fallen deeply into debt. To secure funds, he conspires to sink a ship to collect the insurance money. He arranges to extinguish a lighthouse and create a false beacon that leads the *New Zealand* to crash on the rocks. Grandison then blames the shipwreck and death of thirty crewmen on the Ribbonmen, arguing they destroyed the vessel because they believed Sir Tetbury was aboard. Ennis rejects this accusation, claiming the Ribbonmen are not murderers but "decent Irish patriots" who would not sacrifice thirty innocent lives. Realizing that Grandison wants to frame the Ribbonmen, Ennis meets Gloria at a hunting lodge to warn her. Gloria declares her love for Ennis but states she cannot bring herself to leave her English husband.

When the guard who detected the false beacon is found dead, Grandison blames his murder on Ennis. Refusing to provide an alibi that would implicate Gloria, the baron is placed under arrest. Gloria begs her husband to release Ennis, admitting that she was with him at the hunting lodge at the time of the murder. Grandison agrees to free her lover, provided she promises never to see him again.

Tetbury arrives in Glenarvon intent on suppressing the rebels. His soldiers smash into

---

*The chant echoes an actual Ribbonmen password exchange, which began:
  Q: How long is your stick?
  A: Long enough to reach my enemies.

a church while the Ribbonmen hold a secret meeting in a back room. The rebels flee through a tunnel, leaving behind their symbolic swatch of ribbons. Running through the woods, the Ribbonmen spot a country pub and rush inside to hide among local folk dancers. Joining the festivities, the rebels stamp their boots loudly on the floor in a slow tattoo. Then, hands clapped on the shoulders of the man in front of him, each dancer marches in a glum lockstep. Tramping solemnly, they tread across the floor like convicts on a chain gang. When Tetbury demands to know how long he has been dancing, an Irishman dryly responds "about twenty years."

Accused of collaborating with the English because of his quick release from jail, Ennis is tried by the Ribbonmen for revealing details of their secret meeting. Ennis defends himself and denounces Grandison for the wreck of the *New Zealand*. Gloria appears and warns the Ribbonmen that Tetbury's soldiers are on their way. Questioned by O'Riordan, Gloria reluctantly admits that her husband was responsible for the attack on the church. The Ribbonmen put a rope around Grandison's neck and haul him out to be lynched.

Tetbury's soldiers arrive and discover Grandison's body hanging inside a burning cottage. Chasing after the Ribbonmen, Tetbury's horsemen fall into a bog and drown. O'Riordan apologizes to Ennis for doubting his loyalty, while Ribbonmen celebrate the destruction of English troops. O'Riordan reminds the rebels that "It is still a long way to freedom!" and Ennis proclaims, "This night will be a signal for all of Ireland." The film ends with Riordan, Ennis, and Gloria joining a parade of torch-bearing Ribbonmen singing about freedom.

MEIN LEBEN FÜR IRLAND (1941)

Kimmich followed *The Fox of Glenarvon* with a more pointed attack on the British. He both wrote and directed *Mein Leben für Irland* (*My Life for Ireland*), released by Tobis the following year. The story, woven together by a locket inscribed with the film's title, tells of two generations of the O'Brien family's struggle against British occupation. Although banned briefly after the war as a Nazi "propaganda" film, Kimmich's movie mirrors Hollywood features like *Thirty Seconds Over Tokyo* or *Mrs. Miniver*, blending action, romance, and suspense with a few brief words about justice and freedom. The depiction of the British as oppressors differs little from Hollywood's portrayal of the redcoats during the Revolutionary War. There are no heavy-handed scenes of overt sadism or villainous lechery which Hollywood ascribed to the Germans and Japanese. Ironically, the only torture scene in the film is conducted by Irish nationalists. While the British calmly question and present evidence to IRA suspects, Irish students water torture a classmate they consider a traitor.

The film's opening scene, which serves as a prologue, is set in Dublin in 1903. An English official, flanked by rifle-bearing policemen, enters a thatched cottage on a foggy marsh to evict an Irish family dwelling in nineteenth-century squalor. The stone house, plain furniture, and threadbare peasants evoke scenes of the Famine fifty years before. The household includes well-established film victims — a terrified, hand-wringing grandmother; tattered children; an exhausted, downcast mother clutching an infant; and a proudly defiant father. When the father challenges the official and complains about the lack of money and food, the British police begin to remove the family by force. Irish rebels, led by Michael O'Brien (Werner Hinz), appear on the scene and begin firing at the British.

In the ensuing shootout, reminiscent of an American Western, Michael O'Brien is wounded and captured, along with several other rebels. Next shown standing in handcuffs before a military court, Michael O'Brien, wearing a heroic bandage around his forehead, and his companions are sentenced to death. O'Brien bitterly rails against the injustice of British oppression and the death by hunger of "thousands and thousands." Rejecting the charge of treason, he declares he is fighting for his homeland. The judge reads out the names of the condemned, along with their professions — including a student, author, and university professor — signaling to audiences that the prisoners represent more than a simple peasant rebellion.

As the rebels await execution, O'Brien's fiancée, Maeve Flemming (Anna Dammann), arrives at the prison, and there is a poignant scene of the lovers embracing through the cell bars. Informed that she is carrying his child, O'Brien agrees to marry her to give their child a name. The death-row wedding is conducted by a priest and witnessed by handcuffed prisoners. O'Brien hands Maeve his father's locket, which springs open to reveal an inscription. After a final embrace (with a soaring soundtrack), the groom and his comrades are led (to the sound of a rolling drumbeat) through a medieval corridor to a courtyard where the shadows of gallows are silhouetted against a stone wall.

The film flashes forward to 1921. Michael O'Brien Jr. (Will Quadflieg), now eighteen, is a student at St. Edwards College, an English school designed to Anglicize its Irish students. The *Mr. Chips* schoolmasters in Oxford gowns and mortarboards, mandatory lessons in British "civilization," rugby games, and school uniforms present a benign form of Dickensian imperialism and suppression of indigenous culture (a pale version of Germany's brutal oppression of the nations it then occupied). Michael's classmates include an Irish-American, Patrick O'Connor (Heinz Ohlsen), who develops a crush on Michael's widowed mother. Maeve actively supports the IRA, harboring Robert Devoy (Rene Deltgen), a wounded leader.

The name Devoy is an interesting choice. In World War I John Devoy (1842–1928), a leader of the Irish Republican Brotherhood, met with the German ambassador in Washington to propose that the Irish would prove a valuable German ally in the fight against Britain. Though often wearing a trench coat, Kimmich's bearded Devoy looks more like a Bolshevik as he paces about in underground hideouts and later commands a barricade.

Visiting the O'Briens, Patrick notices Devoy looking from a bedroom window and realizes the house is used by the IRA. He later slips out of the school dorm late at night to spy on the O'Brien home, peering through a window at Maeve and Devoy, who now wears the O'Brien family locket. Returning to the college, he is spotted by a fellow student, a bespectacled toady and squealer, who inquires where he has been, then relates their conversation to the school master, who informs the police.

After the British raid the O'Brien home and arrest Michael's mother, Patrick is taken to police headquarters. At first he refuses to identify a photograph of Devoy or admit seeing him in the O'Brien home. Confronted with his statement to the toady that he had seen a man in Maeve's bedroom, Patrick admits the report is true. The British attempt to turn him into an informer, but he leaves the college (wearing a trademark IRA trench coat) and dodges British machine gun-fire to track down Devoy in a hideout and explain his role in Maeve's arrest and pledge his loyalty. Devoy realizes that Patrick's interaction with the police gives him access to Dublin Castle and provides the IRA with a valuable double agent and swears him to secrecy. Patrick complains to Devoy about playing informer, but the IRA leader stresses the importance of his part in the struggle and presents him with Michael O'Brien's locket as a token of his patriotism.

Unaware of Patrick's role as double agent, Michael suspects him of being a traitor when he spots him passing a letter to a policeman. He leads a group of students to snatch Patrick from his bed and subject him to water torture to make him confess. In an eerie scene shot with exaggerated shadows and flickering lights highlighting the students' faces, Patrick is bound and lowered into a swimming pool, repeatedly questioned and dunked until he loses consciousness.

At a ceremony marking the end of the school year, the students, dressed in top hats and proper British schoolboy uniforms, assemble before their professors. A bonfire is lit, and the national anthem is played, with the Irish students refusing to join their English classmates in singing "God Save the King." Hearing shots from the Dublin insurrection, they throw their school papers on the bonfire (which mirrors a Nazi book burning), followed by their top hats. Students tear a Union Jack from a faculty platform and hurl it into the flames. Then, joined by one of their professors, who tosses aside his mortarboard, the young Irishmen storm the college armory, grab rifles, pistols, and ammunition, and join the street fighting. Patrick discovers a wounded Devoy, who dies before he can reveal his true role to anyone. Patrick accompanies the rebels breaking into Dublin Castle. Still trusted by the British, he is able to convince an English officer to open a door, allowing the Irish to storm through. Patrick and Michael encounter each other fighting side by side and rush to free Maeve. Shot by a secret policeman, Patrick slumps to the floor. Examining his wound, Maeve discovers her husband's locket and asks him where he got it. Patrick tells her that he received it from Devoy, whispering, "I am no traitor." Michael now realizes that Patrick is truly his friend and takes possession of his father's locket. Patrick dies in Maeve's arms, and the film ends with a close-up of the locket's inscription, *Mein Leben für Irland*.

Kimmich's script incorporates generic IRA themes and characters — notably, informers and Irish-Americans. The inclusion of Patrick O'Connor suggests to viewers that the Americans, or at least members of a large ethnic group in the United States, are opposed to British interests. Germans may have found this reassuring in 1941, hoping that the United States might remain neutral. The overall message of the film is that the Irish are irrevocably opposed to the English, indicating that Britain in World War II might be threatened by the kind of insurrection it faced in 1916. The climactic ending, which shows the British fighting street battles within the United Kingdom and eventually being defeated by a mob, was no doubt designed to hearten wartime German audiences.

Except for the appearance of a World War II-era tank, the film's depiction of street battles is fairly accurate. The shop fronts resemble those of 1921 Dublin. Black and Tan troops ride in armored tenders firing bulky, circular drummed Lewis guns at Irish rebels who barricade streets with sandbags and household furniture. The scene's realism, however, came at a high price.

The special effects technician hired to plan the battle sequence was recalled to the front and left before completing a diagram showing where he had placed charges. When the director called action, scores of extras ran onto the set and began activating the explosives. Unaware of the disaster unfolding before him, the director kept the cameras rolling. Several extras were killed and others seriously wounded in the blasts. News of the deadly mishap was suppressed, and some of the accident footage appears in the final cut of the film. Max Kimmich was not on the set that day and claimed in interviews in the 1960s that he never learned of the incident until after the war.[64]

The film, targeted at the youth market and featuring some of Germany's future stars, was popular with wartime audiences. The propaganda value of Kimmich's films was lost on audiences in the occupied countries who saw the movies not so much as attacks on British imperialism but celebrations of resistance to the Nazis themselves. A 1940 SS memo deemed *Der Fuchs von Glenarvon* as "totally unfit, even dangerous for the Polish population. It has been pointed out that the story in these films can be misinterpreted by the Poles and Czechs as an encouragement for their own freedom fight against Germany."[65]

These films were not shown in Ireland during the war. They were screened at an Irish film festival, and in 2007 the RTE television show *Hidden History* broadcast an episode called "Hitler's Irish Movies."

The View from Albion

I SEE A DARK STRANGER (1946)

The first British film to link the IRA and the Nazis was *I See a Dark Stranger* (Individual), produced by Frank Launder and Sidney Gilliant, best known for their 1938 film *The Lady Vanishes*. Released a year later in the United States under the title *The Adventuress*, the film brought critical acclaim to its twenty-six-year-old star Deborah Kerr. In stark contrast to Kimmich's scenes of machine gun–fire shattering shop windows, tanks crushing barricades, and mobs storming Dublin Castle, Launder describes the Anglo-Irish conflict only through the boozy memories of an Irishman holding court in a pub.

I See a Dark Stranger portrays Irish Republicans as childish and naïve, almost clownish figures. Though on one level a story of wartime intrigue, the film is laden with a patronizingly dismissive attitude toward Irish nationalists. The Republican movement is depicted as quaint parochialism based on barroom heroism, dreamy romanticism, and petulant grievances. Above all, the film's message is one of reassurance for a wartime British audience — that the Irish will put aside their provincialism and petty differences with the English and see themselves unified against the common threat of Nazism. In case viewers might have trouble getting the message, the film includes a voiceover. Though using whimsy and humor, as a propaganda vehicle it is far more ideological and blatant than either of Kimmich's productions.

I See a Dark Stranger opens with an ominous, oversized shadow cast against a wall featuring a French street sign. A mysterious figure darts through what appears to be a French village, complete with kiosks and billboards advertising Byrrh. A gunshot causes the figure to flee. Walking along a country road, a man with a scarred cheek casts a flashlight on a signpost that reveals he is on the Isle of Man. The narrator, stating the obvious, comments on the irony of a French village being on the British Isle of Man, then announces that "we have started this tale at the wrong moment." The film backtracks to the West of Ireland in 1937 to tell the story of "a very strange little character named Bridie Quilty," who "grew up hating everything British."

Fourteen-year-old Bridie (Deborah Kerr) is introduced standing in the doorway of a pub, overhearing her father Dan Quilty relive his heroic fight against the English in the 1916 Rising. As a score of drinkers surround him, Danny Quilty tells his spellbound listeners that he and Mick O' Callaghan fought "countless thousands" of Englishmen till their last bullet. Throughout the battle, Quilty recalls, he was thinking of Cromwell and "all the death and destruction, the poverty and persecution, the suffering and starvation that he brought on the sacred soil of Holy Ireland." Forced to surrender, the rebels, "worn, torn, and bedraggled," in Quilty's words, were marched "down O'Connell Street, the city we

Deborah Kerr as Bridie Quilty, spying for the Nazis in *I See a Dark Stranger* (1946).

loved burning around us, the crowd silent and sad." Then a "miracle" happened when an Irish girl broke through the line of English soldiers to take Mick's hand and sing a revolutionary song, giving the defeated IRA men hope. Bridie listens to her father, mouthing the words of his well-worn story. The narrator tells viewers that "night after night Bridie listened to that same old tale ... nursing a bitter hatred of everything British."

The next scene is set seven years later at Bridie's twenty-first birthday party in 1944. Inspired by her late father's hatred of the English, Bridie sets off to Dublin to join the IRA. When her motives for going to the "sinful city" are questioned, she states she can take care of herself, hinting that she has fended off the advances of several men at her party. Her announcement that she hopes to become as great a figure as her father is met with quiet derision. An old woman blames Danny Quilty for putting "all that nonsense into her head." Another jokes that if all the men in Ireland who claimed to have participated in the 1916 uprising had actually fought, the General Post Office could have never held them all. If Danny Quilty's heroics are imaginary, the audience is led to believe that his claims of British injustice are equally false.

On the train to Dublin, Bridie shares a compartment with a distinguished, middle-aged gentleman, whom she finds initially appealing until she notices the name "Miller" on his bag. Once she identifies him as English, her mood changes, and she tells herself the man resembles Cromwell. Miller (Raymond Huntley) speaks with a crisp British accent and defends the English in a conversation with Bridie that leads to a joke about Irish neutrality:

> Bridie: My father fought for Ireland against the English in 1916, and if I ever get the chance, I'll do the same.
> Miller: For the subject of a neutral country, aren't you being a little belligerent?
> Bridie: There is nothing belligerent about it. It's entirely a question about which side I'm neutral on.

Once in Dublin, Bridie visits her father's old comrade, Michael Callaghan, who is now the deputy director of an art museum. While waiting, she joins schoolgirls on a tour. The guide points out paintings of Irish Republican heroes, including Sir Roger Casement, "a lovely man, knighted by the British for his fight against the Belgian tyranny over there in Africa, hung by the British for his fight against British tyranny here in Ireland." Among the portraits of Padraig Pearse and James Connolly is a picture of a young, black-haired Michael Callaghan in a Republican army uniform.

The camera cuts from Callaghan's Michael Collins–like portrait to the museum director of 1944, a dignified, gray-haired man in a business suit. The interaction between Callaghan and Bridie contrasts her eager, naïve Republicanism, fueled by her father's colorful imagination, with the mature wisdom of an elder statesman, a rebel turned Founding Father. Callaghan's calm propriety (and his acceptability to a British audience) is enhanced by his manner of speech. While Bridie talks in country girl Irishisms ("Ah, me heart's beatin' like a drum"), Callaghan (Brefni O'Rourke) speaks with the measured, resonant accent of a BBC announcer.

When Bridie excitedly announces her desire to join the IRA, Callaghan smiles patiently and quietly attempts to dissuade her:

> Bridie: I want you to get me into the Irish Republican Army.... I want to fight against the English the way yourself and father did.
> Callaghan: But my dear child, we're not at war with Britain.
> Bridie: Ah, I know they've a separate war on with somebody else, and we're neutral, but that's no reason why we shouldn't carry on our own private war that's been going on for the last seven hundred years.
> Callaghan: But in 1921 Ireland signed a treaty with England.
> Bridie: But what has a treaty to do with it?
> Callaghan: Well, we got a good deal of what we wanted by it — not everything, mind.
> Bridie: Ireland is still partitioned!
> Callaghan: I'm aware of that. But I believe when England and Ireland come together and discuss it on a friendly basis, partition won't last very long.
> Bridie (nonplussed): A friendly basis? It can't be you sayin' these things, Mr. Callaghan! ... After all the English have done to Ireland since Cromwell!
> Callaghan: Child of grace, Cromwell has been dead for three hundred years.
> Bridie: Well, not in Ballingarry!

Callaghan kindly suggests that her hometown is "very romantic and very remote" and apart from the modern world and political realities. He tells her that "times have changed" and that the Anglo-Irish conflict should be resolved through "constitutional means." He tells her to "forget this wild notion" and return home.

The mention of Cromwell continues a theme established in the opening scene. Recent British abuses, such as the Black and Tans just twenty years before, are not mentioned in the film. Bridie's hatred of a seventeenth-century figure suggests that her Republicanism is based on archaic grievances and quaint folklore, not present-day injustices.

Disappointed by Callaghan's response, a downcast Bridie leaves his office, then pauses before the portrait of Sir Roger Casement and reads the nameplate on the frame noting his execution by the British in 1916, the year of her father's imaginary battle with the English. Casement's link with the Germans in the First World War provides Bridie with an inspiration.

The next scene, in a Dublin bookshop, reveals that Miller is a Nazi agent. His contact tells him that a spy with important information named Oscar Price is being held in a prison in the English village of Wynbridge Vale. Miller remarks that he must recruit a new team of unknown spies to free Price. Preparing to leave the bookshop, he overhears Bridie asking a clerk about German language books and follows her.

The film shifts to Wynbridge Vale, where a pair of female hands are seen dumping a bucket of white paint over a statue of Oliver Cromwell. The staunchly anti–English Bridie is now employed at an inn catering to British servicemen. Playing the role of a virginal Mata Hari, Bridie solicits information about the prison to pass on to Miller, who poses as a cattle buyer from Argentina. Miller suspects that the inn's newest guest, Lt. David Baynes (Trevor Howard), is an intelligence officer and directs Bridie to keep him distracted. On a date in the countryside, Bridie misleads Baynes about the time and tries to keep him interested in her. Her flirting becomes strained when her date announces his intention to write a thesis about Cromwell.

That night English-speaking Nazi agents (presumably IRA men) wearing British army uniforms stage a cunning deception by providing the English with a decoy prisoner in order to take charge of Oscar Price, the scar-faced German spy. When a soldier realizes the trick, the British give chase. In a shootout Price is killed and Miller is wounded. Before dying, Price tells Miller that vital information is contained in a notebook hidden on the Isle of Man.

Having completed her assignment of keeping Baynes out of the way, Bridie breaks off their date and heads back to the inn. In her room she discovers a dying Miller, who orders her to complete his mission and pass on news about the notebook to a contact she is to meet on a train. Not knowing what the agent looks like, she is to identify herself by asking to lower a window. Miller then instructs her to dispose of his body after he dies to prevent suspicion.

In a Hitchcock-like scene, Bridie places Miller's corpse in a wheelchair and pushes it through crowded streets to reach a deserted cliff, where she dumps it into the sea. The next morning she heads to the station, with Baynes following her. In the train compartment Bridie finds herself seated with a British officer, an elderly lady, a businessman, and two middle-aged women. Following her instructions, she requests to lower the window, but none of the passengers responds with the appropriate reply. The old lady, evidently the Axis agent, is taken off the train before Bridie can pass on the information. Miller's bookshop contact observes the interrupted mission. Bridie decides to return to Ireland, now pursued by Baynes, who tells her he witnessed her pushing a wheelchair through town the night before. With tightened security, travel to Ireland is suspended. Bridie decides to go to the Isle of Man herself, locate the notebook, stowaway to Ireland, and turn it over to the German minister in Dublin.

Having discovered Miller's body and wheelchair tracks on the cliff's edge, British intelligence officers pursue Bridie to the Isle of Man, where she has discovered Price's notebook describing a French village near the town of Ramsey. Bridie follows the directions and discovers an area sealed off with barbed wire. She reasons that the British must have recreated a French village in order to rehearse the expected invasion. If the Germans could obtain Price's description, they could identify the actual town on the French coast and ambush the invading troops. Visualizing British soldiers being mowed down on the beach and speaking her thoughts in a voiceover, Bridie has an epiphany: "That must be it! What desperate thing are you about girl? You're holding thousands of lives in your hands. British lives! Irish lives! It's the book of fate itself you're carryin'!"

Bridie returns to the hotel to destroy the notebook but is followed by Miller's bookshop contact. Baynes appears, and Bridie confesses she is a "retired spy," having burned the notebook and abandoned her plans to help Germany. Baynes informs her that she is still in danger. Having read the notebook, she could be forced to reveal the description of the village. She cannot be allowed to fall into German hands, which means she must be turned over to the British, who might execute her for espionage.

Bridie and Baynes are captured by the Nazis and taken to Ireland, where the agents plan to rendezvous with a U-boat. After escaping from the Germans, Baynes tells Bridie they must head to Northern Ireland. She objects to being taken "out of a neutral country where I belong so that I can be tried and shot." Entering an inn, Baynes has a change of heart. Believing they are still in Ireland, he tells the barman to call the police, who will intern Bridie rather than try her for espionage. While waiting, Baynes notices a waitress chewing gum and spots American GIs in the pub. Realizing they must have crossed the border and that Bridie will be picked up by British police, Baynes suggests they flee south. A radio newscast announces the invasion of Normandy, so Bridie's information is no longer of any value. Baynes rushes her upstairs into a bathroom and lowers her out a window to make a dash across the border. Turning around, he finds himself face to face with the Nazi agents. In a comic fight scene, Baynes subdues the spies with help of the police.

The movie ends with scenes of people celebrating VE Day. Newlyweds Mr. and Mrs. Baynes register at an English hotel. Discovering the name of the inn, a furious Bridie storms out, refusing to spend her honeymoon at the Cromwell Arms.

The "strange little character" Bridie has married an Englishman but retains her Irish pride in a diluted, symbolic fashion. Her epiphany about Irish and British soldiers dying side by side on the beaches suggests that, given exposure to the wider world, she, like Callaghan, will accept the 1921 treaty and see that England and Ireland can settle their differences through friendly discussion. The need for violent Republicanism has passed, and its echoes, generated by rebel tales and barroom boasts, have no place in the post-war world.

Ironically, the motion picture designed to reassure British audiences can now be used by militant Irish nationalists as a testament to the failure of compromise, noting that since Callaghan's 1944 calm assurance that partition will soon end by "constitutional means" the border has not moved a single inch.

THE GENTLE GUNMAN (1952)

The Gentle Gunman (Ealing Studios), directed by Basil Dearden, is a little seen film starring John Mills and Dirk Bogarde that presents a darker, more malevolent vision of wartime Irish nationalism than *I See a Dark Stranger*. The characters are motivated not by dreamy romanticism or barroom bravado but a mean, poisonous ideology that embraces violence and celebrates martyrdom. The film's most notable scene, depicting the IRA planting a bomb on an Underground platform during the Blitz as part of the S-Plan, was clearly designed to incense post-war British audiences, demonstrating both the organization's cowardice and cruelty. For recent viewers, the scene eerily presages the 7/11 terrorist bombings in London subways that claimed over fifty lives in 2005.

The film, based on a play by Roger MacDougall, presents an ongoing debate between an Irishman and Englishman, interspersed with action scenes focusing on a conflict between two brothers in the IRA. The political context of the film is established with a highly staged opening discussion between an Irish physician and his English guest in Northern Ireland in 1941. The two middle-aged men discuss politics over whiskey and chess, exchanging bromides about freedom and terrorism:

> Dr. Brannigan: Northern Ireland is occupied territory ... and as long as that state of affairs continues, you'll always have trouble. Check.
> Truelhome: That's your excuse is it for a gang of IRA hooligans who try to terrorize us by setting off bombs in half the cities of England?
> Dr. Brannigan: It's not an excuse, it's an explanation!
> Truelhome: And I suppose you wouldn't object if Englishmen started chucking bombs about all over Ireland?
> Dr. Brannigan: Sure, isn't that what you've been doing for the past three hundred years?

The old friends comment on their contested but long-standing relationship, with the doctor pouring fresh drinks and suggesting that the English will never understand the Irish character, which sparks a heated response from his guest:

> Dr. Brannigan: The trouble with you Englishmen is that you haven't got the imagination to know what it's like to be an Irishman.
> Truelhome: Maybe you have to be an Irishman to see the point of setting off a bomb in a crowded tube station.... Good heavens, man, we had enough to put up with in London at the time without your young hooligans coming over with their suitcases full of bombs!

The film then cuts to a closeup of two Irishmen, Tim Connolly (Liam Redmond) and Patsy McGuire (Jack MacGowran), placing a time bomb in a suitcase. When their London landlady knocks to introduce a visitor, she chides Connolly on his "blarney" and takes the opportunity to ask the Irishmen to donate to a Spitfire fund. She notes that although they are neutral, she assumes "you would not be working over here if you didn't want to help us" and assures herself that the Irishmen are "all really British at heart."

The visitor, Matt Sullivan (Dirk Bogarde), has arrived in London to find his brother Terry (John Mills), who has been reported as being unreliable. Terry has failed to appear as scheduled to plant the bomb. Matt volunteers to fulfill his older brother's mission. Connolly instructs him to carry the bomb to a tube station, cautioning him to locate it carefully. The intent of the bombing, he points out, is a "gesture of protest" with "no unnecessary loss of life."

With anti-aircraft fire booming in the background, Matt descends to the Underground platform where London families seeking shelter from the air raid are camping out for the night. He walks to an empty portion of the platform and puts the suitcase on a table. As he leaves, children playing hide and seek cluster around the table. Hearing ticking from the suitcase, a child alerts a policeman, who picks up the bag. Matt flees in fright. Terry, who observed his brother placing the bomb, rushes forward, grabs the suitcase, and tosses it down the tunnel where it explodes harmlessly. He later reassures Matt that no one was hurt except a few rats, "but none of the English variety."

Matt is followed, but Terry helps him elude the police, who nab Connolly and McGuire.

When Matt accuses him of being a traitor, Terry denies informing the police, then suggests that a traitor is "only a man who's changed his mind." Called a coward by his brother, Terry claims that it is not cowardice that led him to abandon violence. "It is not easy to say you have been a fool all your life, condemn things you've grown to believe in..." he tells his younger brother. "There are better ways of serving your country than dying for it." He assures Matt that the ends remain the same, only the means are different. He still believes in Irish freedom but no longer sees "leaving a handful of bombs around in tube stations and lavatories" as a "crusade."

Rejecting Terry's explanations, Matt warns his older brother, "If you value your life, don't ever set foot in Ireland again."

Ireland, though neutral, is portrayed as being less safe than wartime Britain. Molly Fagan (Barbara Mullen), an IRA widow, urges her teenage son Johnny (James Kenney) to go to Northern Ireland where he can find work on the docks. She is eager that he escape the influence of the local IRA leader Shinto (Robert Beatty), who uses the Fagans' isolated roadside garage as a headquarters. Shinto is a dark, brooding figure in a slouch hat and black leather coat, and Molly blames him for husband's death at the hands of the English. For Molly Fagan, Irish nationalism is a contagion, which has already infected her elder child. Maureen Fagan (Elizabeth Sellars) is a dark-lipped siren of violent Republicanism. Formerly in love with Terry, she has been disillusioned by news of his becoming a traitor and burns his love letters. When Shinto tells her Matt is going on a job for the IRA, Maureen transfers her affections to the younger brother. As she watches Matt practice with his gun, Maureen's face lights up with sexual arousal. Kissing Matt passionately, she tells him she will be thinking about him while he fights the English.

Learning that Connolly and McGuire are being transported to Belfast, Matt enlists Johnny Fagan to learn the details of their arrival so they can stage a rescue. Terry returns to Ireland, where Maureen denounces him as a traitor, accusing him of going soft while in England. Realizing that he has lost her affections, Terry asks if she would rather have Matt with a steady job and a paycheck instead of a gun. Shinto remarks, "If it means forgetting your country, I'd rather have the gun." This dialogue sets up a debate. While Terry and Molly reject violence, hoping to save Johnny and Matt from the fate of a gunman, Shinto and Maureen insist that action, not talk, will gain Ireland her freedom. Maureen sits, hard-faced and determined, refusing to see Matt as a simple "gunman":

> Maureen: He's a soldier fighting in an army.
> Terry: Ah, sure that's what I thought when I went over to England. But you know what I felt like after a bit? I felt like an anarchist in the middle of an air raid with a parcel of home-made bombs and a bagful of answers to questions that people have stopped asking.
> Shinto: Maybe the question of Ireland's freedom is out of date in England, but we're still looking for the right answer over here....
> Molly: You killed his father, Shinto. Leave Johnny alone.
> Maureen: It was the English killed our father.
> Molly: No, it was Shinto. Joe was happy enough until he told him he was unhappy. And he was free, too, till you told him he wasn't.... That was the end of his happiness and his freedom, and it was the end of his life.
> Shinto: He died for Ireland.
> Molly: Better he had lived for it, Shinto. The way he did before you came along.

Shinto warns Terry not to let Matt go soft because "talk" did not free the Twenty-Six Counties, and talk will not drive the English from Northern Ireland. Terry insists he will save his brother from being a gunman, destined to die in a useless cause.

Matt calls the garage, telling Terry that Johnny has been wounded in Belfast. Terry rendezvous with his brother and helps him carry Johnny to Dr. Brannigan, who is still debating his English guest when they arrive:

Truelhome: You seriously telling me that you would defend the IRA?

Dr. Brannigan: I'm not defending them, I'm attacking you.... Down there, Henry, only two miles away is Ireland. Free Ireland. The men who are criminals in England are martyrs down there.

Truelhome: There're a bunch of hooligans...

While Brannigan treats Johnny, Terry again appeals to Matt to give up violence and renounce Irish Republicanism. Terry insists he is still a good Irishman but now realizes that nationalism causes trouble. An Irishman, he claims, is the same as an Englishman, a Russian, or an American. Having lived and worked among the English, he tells Matt that they are people like the Irish, with the same hopes and fears, and who "pay too much rent and too many taxes just like we do.... It's not against people like that we should be working, Matt, it's with them.... It's peace we want and security and a decent life."

The wounded Johnny regains consciousness and tells Matt and Terry the name of the ship carrying Connolly and McGuire to Belfast. Shinto tracks Matt and Johnny to Brannigan, the only "safe doctor" in the district. Suspecting that Terry has been trying to undermine his brother's resolve, Shinto regards him as a traitor and a "rotten apple." After an ambulance removes Johnny to a hospital, Shinto forces Matt and Terry to accompany him, taking Dr. Brannigan and Truelhome hostage to prevent them from contacting the police.

At the garage, Shinto locks Terry in a makeshift cell to await court-martial and forces Brannigan and Truelhome into a stone shed. When Truelhome protests against being mistreated by Irish ruffians, Shinto curses him, telling the Englishman that "Ireland's a place apart, something you've got no right to, something sacred." Truelhome, he states, should be ashamed of trespassing on "holy ground."

After Matt and Shinto leave, Molly frees Terry, who, posing as a stranded sailor, boards the ship carrying Connolly and McGuire and helps them escape. At the dockyard Terry tells Matt that Connolly and McGuire have been rescued and are on their way to the garage over the border. Unconvinced, Shinto plans to carry out his assault on the prison van as it leaves the waterfront. Terry insists that the van will be empty, but Shinto and his men, armed with guns and grenades, take positions on a crowded street. In a scene reminiscent of his experience on the subway platform, Matt finds himself surrounded by children at play. He pulls the pin on his grenade, but, seeing the children, replaces it and refrains from joining the attack. Shinto, unconcerned about civilians, tosses his grenade and begins shooting. Unable to stop the van, he flees, leaving two fallen comrades in the street.

Arriving at the garage, they discover that Connolly and McGuire have not appeared. Shinto holds an IRA court-martial and condemns Terry to death as a traitor. Molly returns from the hospital with news that Johnny has died, killed, she insists, not by the English but by Maureen and Shinto. As Terry is led to his execution, Connolly and McGuire, drunk and singing, roll up in an old car, celebrating Terry as their rescuer. When police cars are spotted heading toward the garage, Shinto, Connolly, and McGuire speed off, chased by gunfiring policemen in the style of an American Western.

Terry and Matt remain behind, then walk off down the road together, leaving dark-lipped Maureen behind them.

The film concludes with a scene of comic relief as Brannigan and Truelhome, still locked in the shed, finally end their heated but friendly debate with a binational toast:

Truelhome: To England, where the situation may be serious but is never hopeless.
Dr. Brannigan: To Ireland, where the situation is always hopeless but never serious.

Like *I See a Dark Stranger*, the film suggests that Irish nationalism is an obsolete concept in the post-war world. Island-bound, Shinto clings to an ancient, almost cultish view of Ireland as a sacred realm, a "place apart," whereas the more cosmopolitan Terry sees the common humanity of all peoples. The isolation of the Irish character is symbolized by the remote, windswept Fagan garage, the only location viewers are given of Ireland. Brannigan and Truelhome, despite their outbursts, maintain their caustic friendship, aging men who agree to disagree, suggesting that Irish are not so much a race apart but irksome British cousins capable of redemption.

The ending of the film, like that of *I See a Dark Stranger*, suggests that the IRA has come to an end, its last efforts sputtering out in a humiliating and inexcusable decision to align its fate with the vanquished Third Reich. As Ed Moloney notes in *A Secret History of the IRA*, "by 1945 the IRA had effectively ceased to exist." With its leaders jailed or discredited, "not even a membership list had survived defeat."[66]

A Gentle Gunman was little seen in Britain within a few years of its initial release. The British hope that they were finished with the IRA ended when a revived IRA staged border raids into Northern Ireland in the late Fifties.

The Irishman Who Never Was

In 1943 the British executed one of the most successful deceptions of the Second World War. Hoping to convince the Germans that the Allies intended to invade Greece rather than their actual target, Sicily, a small team of intelligence officers devised a novel scheme to allow German agents to intercept bogus documents they would assume to be genuine.

Flight Lt. Charles Cholmondeley initially suggested placing the false papers on a corpse that would be dropped from an airplane with a defective parachute. This idea was quickly rejected because post-mortem injuries would be readily identifiable, and it would be obvious that the body was dead before it hit the ground. Lt. Commander Ewen Montagu, a Royal Navy intelligence officer, came up with an alternative plan — having the body wash ashore in Spain as an apparent victim of an air crash at sea. Immersion in water for several days would mask decomposition that would occur during transport.[67]

Codenamed Operation Mincemeat, the hoax was planned in great detail. First, Montague and Cholmondeley had to locate a suitable body. Obtaining a corpse, even in wartime, proved difficult because of their particular specifications. It had to be the body of a man of military age whose cause of death would simulate an air crash at sea and who would be unclaimed by friends or family. A search located the body of a derelict who had died of pneumonia after an accidental ingestion of rat poison. The presence of fluid in the tramp's lungs would be consistent with drowning.

Equipped with a suitable body, Montagu focused on developing fake documents the Germans would accept as authentic. To create a plausible explanation why the papers would be carried by hand, Montagu suggested they consist of letters containing personal comments the author would want to keep from going through normal channels. The key document was a letter written by Lt. General Sir Archibald Nye, Vice Chief of the Imperial General Staff, to General Sir Harold Alexander, commander of the 18th Army Group in North

Africa. In the letter Nye referred to the upcoming invasion of Greece, then discussed a delicate problem they were having with their American allies who were improperly issuing Purple Hearts to British servicemen. The letter was typed on Nye's notepaper and signed by the general himself.[68]

Montagu and Cholmondeley then labored to create a personality for their dead courier. They decided to name the corpse Major William Martin of the Royal Marines. The phantom major was issued a naval identity card. To make the major appear capable of human error and therefore more believable, Montagu decided that the card would be a replacement bearing the notation that the original had been lost.[69] To dissuade the Spaniards from conducting an autopsy that might reveal the true cause of death, the body would wear a cross and carry an identity disc labeling him a Roman Catholic.[70] To make Major Martin even more credible, Montagu suggested they invent a full life for the dead officer. In addition to the usual personal items such as money, wallet, cigarettes, and keys, Major Martin would carry a bill for an engagement ring from a well-known London jeweler, love letters from his fiancée, her snapshot, postage stamps, a bill from a London tailor, letters from his father, theater ticket stubs, and an overdraft notice for £79 19s. 2d. from Lloyd's bank. To make the overdraft note seem even more convincing, Montagu had it misaddressed. The envelope bore a handwritten note: "Not known at this address. Try Naval and Military Club, 94 Piccadilly." The Naval and Military Club prepared a bill for William Martin indicating that he had been in London shortly before his ill-fated trip. Not sure he could draft a convincing love letter from a woman, Montagu had an office girl compose the phony letters. To suggest that the dead major had read and reread them, Montagu folded and unfolded the love letters several times and rubbed them on his clothes to give them a bit of wear and tear.[71]

The body was carefully dressed in a Royal Marine uniform and Mae West, and the briefcase containing the documents was attached to his waist with a leash used by bank messengers. The body was then sealed in an airtight steel canister packed with dry ice and placed aboard the submarine *Seraph*, which headed to the coast of Spain where Franco's government was known to cooperate with German intelligence. Being a neutral nation, Spain would turn the body over to the British consul, allowing Montagu to verify that the dead major had been discovered.

On April 30, 1943, the officers aboard *Seraph* set Major Martin adrift off the coast of Huelva, where currents would predictably carry the body ashore. On May 3 the British Vice Consul in Huelva reported to London that Spanish officials had recovered the body of a Major Martin that was presented to British officials, who gave the dead officer a military funeral. There was no mention of his briefcase. With this information, Montagu placed Martin's name on the casualty list and sent urgent inquiries to British officials in Spain about the missing briefcase. After ten days the Spanish presented the British attaché with the rest of Major Martin's effects, including his briefcase, which appeared intact, its letters apparently unopened. When the documents arrived in London, lab technicians determined that the crucial letters had been opened and laid flat, most likely to be photographed. A message was flashed to Churchill, then in Washington: "Mincemeat swallowed whole."[72] Expecting an invasion of Greece, the Germans diverted forces from Sicily, weakening Axis defenses on the eve of the Allied landings.

THE MAN WHO NEVER WAS (1956)

Ewen Montagu published an account of Operation Mincemeat in 1953. His book *The Man Who Never Was* inspired a film version of the same name, released three years later.

Directed by Ronald Neame, *The Man Who Never Was* (Sumar Film Productions) presents a highly accurate dramatization of the first stage of the hoax. Ewen Montagu was portrayed by Clifton Webb. Montagu himself was given a cameo role as an officer disparaging his own plan during an early staff meeting. Because Charles Cholmondeley was still on active service, his name could not be used, so the character of Lt. George Acres (Robert Flemyng) was created. Early in the film Montagu and Acres watch a practice parachute jump, which leads the younger officer to suggest dropping a body from an airplane. Montagu rejects that idea, then proposes casting the body adrift at sea to be recovered onshore.

The first half of the film recreates the hunt for a corpse, the fabrication of the misleading documents, and the creation of Major Martin's backstory. Historical figures, such as Winston Churchill and Louis Mountbatten, are represented in the movie. To add human drama, the film depicts Montagu having to secure permission from a grieving father to use the body of his son who had died of pneumonia. The character of the office girl who wrote the love letters is built up, and she is given an amorous American roommate, Lucy Sherwood (Gloria Grahame). Accustomed to playing with men's affections, Lucy dictates a passionate love letter to the more staid Pam (Josephine Griffin). The preparation of the body, its packing in a container filled with dry ice, and the launching at sea are faithfully reenacted with almost documentary-like accuracy.

The opening title assures viewers that aside from a few disguised names, "in all other essentials this is the true story of 'Major William Martin.'" The second part of the film, however, departs markedly from historical events. In reality, Operation Mincemeat was "swallowed whole" by German intelligence. In the film, however, the head of German intelligence, Admiral Canaris (Wolf Frees), doubts the authenticity of the intercepted documents. Realizing that "there is no way in which we can check the genuineness of these papers," he determines "to check the genuineness of the bearer" and advises that "someone had better ask a few discreet questions in London just to make sure there was such a man."

The film then introduces a wholly fictional Irish element to Operation Mincemeat. Patrick O'Reilly (Stephen Boyd) is shown arriving in Britain from Dublin. He takes a cab driven by an Irishman (Cyril Cusack), who asks him if he had a pleasant journey. O'Reilly responds with a password and repeats that he is from Dublin. The driver gives him an emergency number to call, noting that his "instructions" were simply to pick him up and deliver him to his destination. When the driver asks him why he had been selected for this job, O'Reilly sarcastically smiles, "Because I'm so fond of the English."

The appearance of an agent from Dublin, the Irish cab driver, the use of a password, the mention of "instructions," and the question of why O'Reilly was chosen from a presumably larger pool of potential spies all imply that a well-organized ring of Irish agents was actively spying for the Nazis in wartime London. O'Reilly's connection with Ireland is firmly established, with the word "Dublin" mentioned three times in the script. Arriving at his flat, his landlady greets him as "the gentleman from Dublin."

Stephen Boyd's Irish agent is two-faced. Chatting with his landlady, he is charming and affable. Once she leaves his room, his face hardens and he opens a suitcase given to him by the cab driver which contains a shortwave radio and a German Luger. After setting up his antenna, he begins tapping out messages to the Nazis.

Speaking softly with an obvious Irish accent and always smiling, O'Reilly follows up leads provided in Major Martin's personal effects, making inquires at his tailor, the Naval and Military Club, and his bank. Still unsure of Martin's authenticity, O'Reilly studies photostats of the love letters signed "Lucy" and the accompanying snapshot and goes to the address listed on the letterhead. Encountering Lucy's roommate, he tells Pam he is a friend of the late Major Martin and gives her his actual name and address. Lucy then arrives home, drunk and distraught. She matches the girl in the snapshot, and, having just heard of the death of her current RAF boyfriend, gives a convincing performance of a grieving fiancée.

Back in his flat, O'Reilly taps out the message "Martin probably genuine." He warns the Nazis to stand by for confirmation in one hour, noting that he has deliberately revealed his identity to "the enemy." If no message is sent from London at that time, it will mean that he has been arrested and that Major Martin is false. With Luger in hand, a grim-faced O'Reilly waits for the police to arrive.

Alerted by Pam, Montagu and Special Branch officers race to O'Reilly's flat. While en route, Montagu realizes what the agent may be up to and calls off the chase, allaying Nazi suspicions about Major Martin by allowing their agent to leave the country undetected. When the hour passes without his arrest, O'Reilly makes the sign of the cross, then sends the confirming message: "Martin genuine."

The phrase "Martin genuine" is echoed by a chorus of German-accented voices as black arrows emblazoned with swastikas indicate the transfer of forces on a map of Sicily. The film ends in Spain, with a newly decorated Ewen Montagu placing his medal on the grave of the fictitious Major Martin.

The addition of a Nazi agent on English soil adds suspense to an otherwise static storyline. In reality, Montagu only learned how fully the Germans accepted his ruse after the war when captured German documents were examined by the Allies. Having the enemy checking up on Major Martin in London creates a cat and mouse drama and sets up the suspenseful confrontation between the spy and Lucy.

Nigel Balchin's screenplay, which received a Best British Screenplay BAFTA award in 1957, weaves fact and fiction so artfully that audiences are left with the impression that Irish agents actually played a critical role in Operation Mincemeat. Alan Stripp notes in his introduction to Montagu's memoir, "It is a tribute to the scriptwriter ... that an audience can accept the whole combined operation of suspense and entertainment so uncritically."[73] For British audiences the image of an Irish spy in a London flat tapping out messages to the Nazis is wholly "acceptable," attesting to wartime attitudes about both the IRA and Irish neutrality. Having the Irish spy cross himself before relaying a critical message to the Nazis reinforces the stereotype of the Irish as the other — a people apart.

British films capitalized on the IRA's superficial links to Nazi Germany to discredit both Irish nationalism and Irish neutrality. Given Britain's needed alliance with the United States during and after the Second World War, English films about the IRA ignored the fact that most of the organization's support came from America and not Germany.

Hollywood Takes

The IRA-Nazi connection, the bombing campaign, and Irish neutrality were marginal issues in the United States. Outside of Washington diplomatic circles, few Americans were aware of the difficulties de Valera raised for the Allies. Films associating the Irish with Nazi Germany would counter the prevailing Hollywood vision of Ireland as a nation of leprechauns, shamrocks, castles, and colleens — and upset millions of Irish-Americans.

Hitler's man in London, Stephen Boyd, in *The Man Who Never Was* (1956).

The United States, however, did produce two films highlighting IRA collaboration with the Nazis.

A Terrible Beauty / The Night Fighters (1960)

A Terrible Beauty (Raymond Strauss Productions) is based on Arthur Roth's 1958 novel of the same name. Born in New York, Roth grew up in Northern Ireland and served in both the IRA and the Irish Army before seeing service in the U.S. Air Force. Unlike *The Gentle Gunman*, *A Terrible Beauty* (retitled *The Night Fighters* for its American release) focuses the debate about the IRA on the Irish themselves.

Set in the Catholic village of Duncrana in Northern Ireland in 1941, the film provides a greater insight into the complexities and contradictions of Irish life. Dermot O'Neill (Robert Mitchum) is a hard-drinking thirty-five-year-old bachelor still living at home with his parents and postponing marriage to his impatient girlfriend Neeve (Anne Heywood). While his father listens to German radio broadcasts and delights at the news of British sinkings ("lovely, lovely, lovely"), Neeve urges Dermot to travel to Britain and get work so they can marry. The local priest supports an IRA raid on a British army arsenal as an "old Irish game" but is compelled to read a letter from the bishops declaring "that it is a mortal sin for a Catholic to bear arms illegally or to fight against lawful authority."

To establish the setting for American audiences in the Sixties, the film opens with a series of explanatory titles:

> With England at war, the Irish Republican Army sought once more to free the Six Counties of the North from British Rule and unite all Ireland under the flag of the Free State.
> In a campaign timed to coincide with the German invasion of England, I.R.A. groups were reformed all over the North.
> Even in farming communities where the war, as yet, was little more than newspaper headlines.

In the first scene, a lone figure trains a flashlight on a signpost identifying the location as Northern Ireland, then signals a plane that drops IRA agent Tim Malone (Christopher Rhodes), along with weapons packed in canisters emblazoned with swastikas. A series of explosions and the sound of machine-gun fire follow.

After "extensive training" in Germany, Tim Malone has returned to Ireland to coordinate an attack on the North in conjunction with a German invasion of Britain. He appoints Duncrana's most fierce nationalist, Don McGinnis (Dan O'Herlihy), to be the leader. McGinnis, who is club-footed like Goebbels, tells pub mates, "This time we'll drive the Englishmen right into the sea!" McGinnis helps Malone recruit "patriots" to join the IRA campaign, including a reluctant Dermot, who claims that there was a rebel in every generation in his family.

Unlike Shinto, who is driven by a cultish nationalism, McGinnis has a highly personal agenda for urging action against the English — namely, Dermot's younger sister. Bella (Marianne Benet) is a coy flirt who delights in exciting advances from the village lads but ignores the lame McGinnis. Self-conscious about his disability, McGinnis watches a folk dance from the sidelines, burning with frustration. He hopes his role as commandant will enhance his status, making him desirable. Outside the dance, he urges Dermot and the other lads, including Protestant Sean Reilly (Richard Harris), to join the IRA.

Dermot O'Neill casually offers to enlist. His girlfriend Neeve urges him to make something of himself, to go to England to get a job with good wages. "There is money to be made across the water," she reminds him. Dermot refuses, noting his father would never let him in the house again if he went to England. Instead, he says he will go to America after the war and make enough money for them to marry.

O'Neill's lack of political conviction is demonstrated by his late arrival to an IRA meeting. McGinnis announces that the IRA is secretly allied with Germany. He warns his men that they may face prison and execution if caught. Malone selects Dermot and Sean for a raid on an English arsenal. Driving an army truck in British uniforms, Dermot and Sean help Malone steal cases of Bren guns and ammunition.

After the raid, Dermot discusses the bishop's statement condemning the IRA with the cobbler Jimmy Hannafin (Cyril Cusack), who questions the justification of allying Irish ambitions for freedom with Nazi Germany. Unlike Maureen Fagan in *The Gentle Gunman*, Neeve is angered by Dermot's involvement in the IRA, reminding him of its "kill or be killed" history.

Although the first raid believably reenacts the type of operation the IRA conducted during the war, the second assault is wholly fictional. The Nazis provided funds and some weapons in hopes the IRA would attack Northern Ireland, but there was no operational coordination. Meeting in a basement, a dozen IRA men plot the demolition of a power plant to coincide with a German invasion. The IRA–Nazi alliance is openly declared with the rallying cry, "Germany sits on the Channel. The invasion of England. Tonight she strikes. Soon all Ireland will be ours!"

In the movie the IRA stage a commando-style attack analogous to the French resistance or the Polish underground, fighting a pitched gun battle with British troops with an intensity and a casualty count far greater than any actual IRA raid staged during the entire war. O'Neill helps Reilly, who is wounded in the leg, flee across the border into Ireland. While taking shelter in a barn, Dermot expresses doubts about the IRA, noting, "We talk about fighting to make Ireland whole, and I sometimes wonder if we're not helping to keep it torn apart."

Dermot leaves Sean in an Irish hospital, urging him to stay safe in the Free State until the war is over. With the failure of the Nazis to invade England, their raid accomplished nothing. Sean thanks Dermot for standing by him, leading Dermot to remark that their friendship is "the only good thing to come out of the whole affair."

Returning to Duncrana, Dermot finds his mother distressed that he has taken lives. His brother urges him to quit the IRA and head to England. Learning that Sean was captured trying to cross the border, Dermot is disillusioned with the IRA for refusing to attempt a rescue. When McGinnis tells him, "You can't put the cause in danger for the sake of one man," Dermot wonders, "What kind of a cause is it that allows its comrades to rot behind prison bars?" Dermot believes in personal loyalty and comradeship, while McGinnis sees the Cause as an abstraction above personal considerations. Dermot decides to leave the IRA when McGinnis plans a retaliatory attack on a police barracks. Dermot objects because the

Robert Mitchum (top) and Richard Harris in *The Night Fighters* (1960).

police are Irishmen, not British. McGinnis remains resolute, claiming the officers are "traitors to their country, and they deserve to die." When he announces the name of the police barracks, Dermot informs McGinnis that a policeman's family lives upstairs. "I'll have no hand in the shooting of women and children," Dermot declares and leaves the IRA, stating, "I didn't join to make war on innocents." He tells McGinnis that if he intends to follow through with his plan, he will tell the police without naming names.

McGinnis brands Dermot an informer and beats him, but only when held by others, allowing the lame commandant to demonstrate his manhood by striking someone who cannot defend himself.

Dermot tells the police about the raid and plans to head to England. Grabbed by the IRA, he is taken to a midnight court-martial. Facing possible execution, Dermot maintains his droll sense of humor. Noting that McGinnis' men are wearing the characteristic trench coats, he muses, "Sometimes I think the IRA was invented by a manufacturer of trench coats to keep up sales."

The trench coat becomes a prop for both comedy and tragedy. Rescued by his brother, Neeve, and Jimmy, Dermot immobilizes his teenage guard by suspending him by his trench coat. Lying in wait for the escaped Dermot, McGinnis sees a trench-coated Bella riding her brother's bicycle. Crying "Informer!" he mistakenly shoots her. Discovering that he has killed the girl he loves, a shaken McGinnis drops his gun and runs away.

The film ends with Dermot and Neeve aboard a ship sailing away from their beautiful but troubled island. This reinforces the emigration theme established in *The Informer* and *Odd Man Out,* suggesting that the cause of Irish nationalism is doomed, and that protagonists' only hope is a life in exile.

THE EAGLE HAS LANDED (1976)

The leading American film to deal with the IRA-Nazi alliance is *The Eagle Has Landed* (Associated General Films), directed by John Sturges. An action and suspense feature based on the novel by Jack Higgins, *The Eagle Has Landed* blends historical figures — Admiral Canaris (Anthony Quayle) and Heinrich Himmler (Donald Plesance) — with fictional characters to add credibility to an implausible plot. Unlike *The Man Who Never Was*, which dramatized a factual event, Sturges' film creates a wholly fictional "what if" storyline.

In 1943, with the fortunes of war turning against him, Hitler (in Higgins' story) approves a plan to kidnap Winston Churchill and fly him to Berlin. Considering the operation a mad scheme, Admiral Canaris assigns Colonel Max Radl (Robert Duvall) to develop a feasibility study, assuring him that Hitler will probably forget the idea within a few days. Unlike Canaris, Himmler embraces the project and wants to make the plan operational.

Informed that Churchill will spend a weekend in a village near the sea, Radl realizes that the implausible scheme might work. Agents could be parachuted into the village, seize Churchill, and make their escape on an E-boat waiting offshore. He selects British-educated Colonel Kurt Steiner (Michael Caine) to lead the commando team. To make a Nazi officer more acceptable to American audiences, Steiner is shown trying to save a Jewish woman from the SS in Poland. Court-martialed for his efforts, Steiner and his men are sent to an island penal colony. Though dubious about the plan, Steiner agrees to lead the mission because it will reinstate his men. He insists, however, that his troops will wear German uniforms under their disguises, so that if discovered they will fight as soldiers and not as spies.

Another essential member of Radl's team is Liam Devlin, an Irish Catholic university lecturer in Berlin. Devlin (Donald Sutherland) is a charming, hard-drinking, womanizing, poetry-quoting, red-haired Irishman who initially greets Radl by saying "top of the morning" with a drink in his hand. Asked by Radl if he is still a "supporter of the Irish Republican Army," Devlin corrects him, repeating the oft-repeated catchphrase "Soldier of, Colonel. Once in, never out." Questioned why he is not with his compatriots in England, Devlin answers with a reference to Sean Russell's bombing campaign, "I don't want to spend my days in Bayswater mixing up explosives in my landlady's saucepan to blow the arms and legs off a couple of passersby. My fight is with the bloody British Empire. And I'll fight it on my own two feet." His goal, he asserts, is a "united Ireland." Offered the opportunity to participate in the operation to kidnap Churchill, Devlin eagerly agrees — for twenty thousand pounds.

Although the plot of the film is wholly imaginative, the character of Liam Devlin is a far more credible IRA figure than the imaginary Irish spy in *The Man Who Never Was*. While there were no IRA agents following operational orders from the Abwehr, the backstory of Liam Devlin parallels, in many ways, the wartime experiences of the Irish novelist Francis Stuart (1902–2000). During the Irish Civil War Stuart ran guns for the IRA and was interned until the end of hostilities. In the 1930s he became friendly with Helmut Clissmann, a German intelligence officer stationed in Dublin. Stuart assisted in developing academic exchanges between the Irish Free State and Nazi Germany. In 1940 he traveled to the Reich to deliver messages from the IRA. He remained in Germany until the end of the war, lecturing in Berlin, making anti–British propaganda radio broadcasts, and visiting the ailing Frank Ryan before his death.[74]

Devlin is dropped into Ireland near the Ulster border in advance of the operation. Once in England he assumes the job of marsh warden near the village Churchill plans to visit and contacts South African Nazi agent Joanna Gray (Jean Marsh), who supplies him with a shotgun and a motorbike. Arriving at the village, he immediately takes an interest in eighteen-year-old Molly Prior (Jenny Agutter).

Devlin marks a drop zone on a beach and radios weather conditions to the plane carrying Steiner's raiding party. Dressed in Polish uniforms, Steiner's detail enters the village and takes up positions as if conducting maneuvers. Steiner's English and knowledge of British manners is genuine enough to fool the local priest (John Standing) and an American army captain (Treat Williams).

Steiner's plan goes awry when a small girl falls into a mill race. A German rescues her but is killed by the mill wheel, and his jacket tears open to reveal his Nazi uniform. Now exposed, Steiner's men take hostages and hold them in the church. Confronted by Captain Clark (Treat Williams), Steiner is told that Churchill is safe and his plan is foiled. Clark asks him to surrender. Prepared to fight to the end, Steiner nobly releases the hostages. Devlin appears at the church and informs Steiner he has discovered a tunnel leading from the church to the vicarage, providing an escape route.

Steiner parts with Devlin, intending to continue on the mission alone. Reaching the home where the Prime Minister is staying, Steiner waits outside. When Churchill steps onto a balcony, characteristically puffing a cigar with a glass of brandy in his hand, Steiner shoots him and is immediately killed by British officers.

Captain Clark is mystified when a British officer states no one will know what has happened. The dead man, Clark learns, is not Churchill but George Fowler, an impersonator who had been used as a decoy to provide cover for the Prime Minister's flight to the Tehran Conference. The failed assassination attempt will remain a secret.

The film ends with Devlin walking through the English woods, with the voiceover of his love letter to Molly declaring he has "suffered a sea change and that nothing can ever be the same again."

With Steiner, Radl, and Gray killed, Devlin is the sole survivor of the operation, noncommittal, romantic, and magical. He fades from the scene, leaving the English and Germans to continue their war, going back to Ireland to wage his own battle against the British Empire (with half of his twenty thousand pounds in a Swiss bank).

The production of *The Eagle Has Landed* was not without controversy. Concerns about the current IRA led to a cast change. Richard Harris, who was slated to appear in the film, was replaced after he attended an IRA fundraiser in the United States.[75]

Irish Images

For Irish filmmakers, the IRA's wartime bombing campaign and Nazi associations were largely ignored. The events of the 1940s lacked the drama, historical significance and revolutionary legitimacy of the heroic 1920s and were of less immediate concern than the renewed Troubles of the 1970s and 1980s. In addition, Ireland's neutrality remained a subject of debate. There were, however, a few Irish dramatizations that explored the IRA's actions during de Valera's Emergency.

CAUGHT IN A FREE STATE (1983)

Caught in a Free State (RTE) is a four-part mini-series produced and directed by Peter Ormond depicting the actions of Nazi intelligence operations in wartime Ireland. A strong attempt was made to interest German networks in co-producing the series. Changes were made in scripts to overcome German objections, but no German network was willing to invest in the production, and it was not aired in Germany after its Irish release.[76]

The series stars Peter Jankovsky as the German agent Hermann Görtz, Barry McGovern as Eamon de Valera, and Joan O'Hara as Iseult Stuart, wife of Francis Stuart. Benno Hoffman plays Dr. Ernst Weber-Dohl, the strongman-chiropractor, and Tariq Yunus appears as the Indian agent Henry Obed. Because some figures of the era were still living, names were changed so that Colonel Dan Bryan, head of Irish Army intelligence, became Colonel Brian Dillon (John Kavanaugh).[77]

Caught in a Free State follows the arc of Hermann Görtz's Irish adventure, from his arrival and internment to his suicide after the end of the war. De Valera's high wire act of maintaining neutrality is depicted, indicating that some government officials, in addition to the IRA, expressed Axis sympathies. Serious scenes are juxtaposed with farce, creating what critics viewed as a "jarring" and uneven contrast of intrigue and slapstick.[78]

Nevertheless, the series was aired in Britain on Channel 4 in 1984 and 1986.

BORSTAL BOY (2000)

Among the IRA bombers arrested during Sean Russell's S-Plan campaign of 1939–1940 was sixteen-year-old Brendan Behan. Born into a staunchly Republican family in 1923,* Behan later claimed Michael Collins handed his pregnant mother a five pound note on O'Connell Bridge because her husband was in prison for IRA activities.[79]

---

*Behan's uncle, Peadar O'Cearnaigh, wrote the Irish national anthem, "A Soldier's Song."

Behan joined the Republican youth organization Fianna Eireann when he was eight.* While waiting to become a full-fledged member of the IRA, he went on courier missions, delivering messages in Belfast and London. The S-Plan was underway, and Sean Russell needed volunteers. Russell approved sixteen-year-old Behan's acceptance into the IRA. In May 1939 Behan was sent to the IRA training camp in Killiney Castle, learning how to mix explosives in a saucepan, using a wooden spoon to prevent sparks.[80] That same month his seventy-seven-year-old grandmother sold her Dublin home and moved with her two daughters to Birmingham where she prepared bombs for the IRA campaign. An accidental explosion led to the discovery of sticks of gelignite, fuses, and detonators. Granny Furlong was sentenced to three years; her daughters Emily and Evelyn received three to five years.[81] Eager to play a more active role himself, Behan traveled to England with a stolen travel permit and homemade explosives. His trip may have been unauthorized by the IRA command, which usually provided bombs to volunteers after their arrival in Britain. Detected as he left Dublin, Behan was arrested within ten hours of landing in Liverpool.[82] At his trial, Behan gave an impassioned political speech and then, because of his age, was sentenced to three years in a Borstal reform school.

Behan, who had begun writing poetry and contributing to Republican newspapers, devoted much of his time to reading in prison. Returned to Ireland in 1941, Behan continued writing and participating in Republican activities. At the 1942 Easter Uprising commemoration in Dublin, Behan fired several shots at Special Branch officers. Sentenced to fourteen years in prison, Behan was released in 1946 as part of a general amnesty of IRA prisoners.

Behan effectively left the IRA in 1947 at the age of twenty-three, though he remained closely associated with leading members for the rest of his life. After spending a few years in Paris, Behan returned to Ireland and pursued an active literary career, writing poems, stories, radio plays, and articles for the *Irish Times*. In 1954 his first major play, *The Quare Fellow*, was produced in Dublin and ran for six months. A London production followed in 1956. By the late 1950s Behan had become a major figure on the international literary and dramatic stage. His witty and often drunken appearances on talk shows in Britain and the United States made him a celebrity. *The Hostage* opened on Broadway on September 9, 1960, and ran for 127 performances.[83]

In 1958 Behan's memoir, *Borstal Boy*, was published. Banned in Ireland for profanity, the cynical and sometimes ribald account of his juvenile prison experiences received rave reviews in Britain and the United States. Behan described his autobiographical account as one of "innocence and experience":

> It's the story of an Irish boy of sixteen arrested and sentenced in England for I.R.A. activities, of his fears, hopes, and relationships with the other boys in an English reformatory.... Some people may say that my book shouldn't be read, then I say that adolescence should not be lived.[84]

The book traces Behan's "coming of age" as he moves from a dedicated bomber full of Republican talking points, rebel songs, and grievance history to a more sophisticated young adult who recognizes the common humanity of the English and learns to distinguish the British people from the policies of their Empire. The book recreates the smug sarcastic Holden Caulfield adolescent state of mind. Behan captured the boys' colorful and often complex rhyming slang in such detail that the book was published with a glossary.†

Frank Ryan, who accompanied Sean Russell on the failed mission Operation Dove, led the organization for several months in 1933 when Behan was a member.

†For example, the juveniles use "china" for "friend," a shortened form of "china plate" which rhymes with "mate."

A dramatization of *Borstal Boy* by Frank McMahon opened in Dublin at the Abbey Theater in 1967, with Frank Grimes playing Brendan Behan. Grimes reprised his role three years later in a Broadway production, directed by Thomas MacAnna, which opened March 31, 1970. Running for 143 performances, *Borstal Boy* received the 1970 Tony for Best Play, and nominations for Best Actor and Best Direction.

Peter Sheridan's *Borstal Boy* (Hell's Kitchen) offers a twenty-first-century version on Behan's adolescent prison experience during the Second World War, de-emphasizing his Republicanism to create a politically correct bisexual coming of age story. Written, produced, and directed by Peter Sheridan, brother of Jim Sheridan, the film took a decade to bring to the screen. Described as being "inspired by" Behan's memoir, the movie accurately follows the book in only the opening and closing scenes. Sheridan recreates Behan's arrest and courtroom political speech and his eventual return to Ireland, using much of Behan's dialogue. The events at the reform school itself, which take up the bulk of the film, depart radically from Behan's account, presenting an escape attempt and a student play which never occurred. Though the book briefly recounts some homosexual horseplay among the inmates, the film makes Behan's emerging and often confused sexuality a key theme, depicting his affections wavering between an English sailor and the warden's daughter.

The opening scene establishes the time and place, with Behan (Shawn Hatosy) descending a gangplank and walking past sand-bagged anti-aircraft gun emplacements, wartime propaganda posters, and British soldiers. As in the book, Behan is arrested when officers storm into his room and discover his "Sinn Fein conjuror's outfit" (a suitcase full of explosives and detonators). In the police van he meets Charlie Milwall (Danny Dyer), an English sailor arrested for theft. During his interrogation, Brendan insists that the IRA is "not a murder gang" and that the bombers hanged for murder are "dying for their country." In jail Behan salutes two condemned IRA men by saying, "Up the Republic." The two prisoners return the salute with military precision. In reality, Behan never met the men hanged for the Coventry bombing but wrote about them, contemplating them on the day of their execution and commenting on the expected reaction in Dublin and New York. Waking from a nightmare that he is being hanged, Behan is comforted by Charlie, who reveals himself to be gay by kissing him. Behan rejects his advance but maintains his friendship as they are sent to Borstal, a juvenile school presided over by a schoolmasterish superintendent named Joyce (Michael York).

Whereas Behan's memoir focuses on the Anglo-Irish conflict, with numerous mentions of historical events, Republican poems and songs, and literary allusions, the film softens the IRA angle while emphasizing the sexual nature of Brendan's Borstal days. Brendan's attentions shift back and forth between Charlie and Joyce's daughter Liz (Eva Birthistle), an artist who feels trapped by her father's refusal to let her live in London during the Blitz.

The IRA-Nazi alliance is wholly absent from the film. In the memoir Behan mentions meeting Polish Jewish prisoners only in passing. The film presents Brendan befriending a Polish Jew imprisoned for stowing aboard a British ship. When the refugee states he wants to go to Palestine, Brendan tells him he would be safer in neutral Ireland. This is the first of several scenes in which Brendan displays sensitivity toward a Jew, who is variously called "brown eyes" by a guard and "Jewboy" by a fellow prisoner. He is the first inmate Brendan invites to join his escape attempt. Brendan, who considers himself a POW rather than a juvenile delinquent, plans a breakout by obtaining maps from the school library. His escape crew is multi-national, including Charlie, the gay Englishman; Jock, a Scot; a Canadian; and a Polish Jew.

Brendan's softening of his Republicanism is symbolized by his attitudes toward rugby. At first he stands on the sidelines, refusing to play, stating, "I leave English games to the English." He later changes his mind and joins fellow Borstal boys in a match against British soldiers, rallying the scoreless team to victory.

Brendan's antagonist is Dale (Lee Ingleby), a perfect villain — a weasely, anti–Semitic, homophobic, misogynistic sex offender. Sentenced for raping an underage girl, he immediately assaults a fellow inmate, claiming his bed and job as head boy of the barrack. When one boy mentions that a sixteen-year-old married friend "gets it every night," Dale laughs, "Married? What a mug! See, the best part is takin' it when it's not being offered."

Dale overhears plans for the escape and finds the boys' cache of civilian clothes. He announces that he and a friend will join the breakout, replacing Charlie and the Polish Jew. When Charlie objects, Dale pulls a knife. "This is my escape," he announces, "No Jews and no queers." Brendan shakes hands with Dale, agreeing to his demand, but fools him by leading the escape with his original team ahead of schedule. Realizing that he has been deceived, Dale immediately snitches to the warden, who calls out the army to search for the boys.

The boys reach the sea and run in the surf. This moment of adolescent freedom and celebration is shattered when the Jewish refugee and another inmate are killed by a landmine. The intrusion of the Second War World marks a distinct departure from the book. For a teenager living in wartime Britain, Behan took no interest in the progress of the war, mentioning Hitler only in the lyrics of an impromptu prison song.

The next scene depicts a rabbi and parson officiating at joint funerals. Joyce, ever indulgent, offers Brendan and the surviving escapees the choice of three months' detention or their word to make a new start.

Brendan's budding bisexuality emerges as his friendship with Charlie deepens. He gives the British sailor a Brendan-the-Navigator medallion. He asks Liz to secure permission from her father for the inmates to mount a production of *The Importance of Being Earnest*. Liz assists in the production and seemingly encourages a homosexual relationship between Brendan and Charlie. As she puts lipstick on Charlie, who plays a female part, Liz tells him, "It's so hard to tell someone that you like them ... it's so hard to find the right words."

Brendan and Charlie (in drag) have a lingering onstage kiss, but immediately after the play Brendan shifts his attentions from Charlie to Liz, inviting her to a party in the dorms. When she explains she can't attend, Brendan gets drunk at the graves of the boys killed by the landmine. Charlie joins him, and Brendan states that it was "strange" kissing him during the play but admits it "felt all right."

Charlie returns to the dorm where he is confronted by Dale who has opened his kit and discovered stolen items. Dale grabs Charlie and orders his pals to bend him over a bed. Dale pulls his trousers down and is about to rape the gay sailor when Liz arrives to join the party. Spotting her, Dale assures her there is no trouble, then seizes the opportunity to sexually assault a female.

Brendan arrives and prevents both rapes, beating Dale senseless. Despite protestations by Liz, Brendan is placed in solitary for assault. When he is released, Behan discovers Charlie leaving Borstal to rejoin his ship, headed for Singapore. In Charlie's absence, Brendan becomes romantically involved with Liz, reading her poetry and posing for a portrait. Learning that Charlie's ship has been sunk, Brendan is grief-stricken but resists Liz's attempts to comfort him.

Brendan is offered an early release if he is willing to denounce the IRA. He refuses, stating that betrayal does not suit him. Instead, he offers a compromise, pledging, "I'll promise not to take up arms against England until you finish this bastard Hitler. Beyond that, I reserve me options." When asked to put this assurance in writing, he refuses. Joyce intercedes, stating, "A Borstal Boy's word is good enough for me."

Before leaving Borstal, Brendan says farewell to Liz, who unveils a painting of Charlie and Brendan. Looking at the portrait, Brendan comments on what he has learned in prison. "I was brought up to hate the English," he says. "I had to come here to learn about love." Love, he tells Liz, is much stronger than hate, noting, "I learned that from you and Charlie. I had it both ways, just like Oscar Wilde." Liz asks him to write not to her but "for everyone."

Brendan, the budding writer, returns to Dublin, his Republican ideals intact but tempered by an understanding of the common humanity of the English.

It served both British and IRA propaganda to exaggerate the organization's activities during the Second World War. It also served the needs of scriptwriters and directors seeking a dramatic storyline. As a result, motion pictures, especially those made by British studios, tended to lend credence to the false impression that the IRA maintained a sophisticated spy network in Britain directly coordinating with German intelligence.

Seventy years after the war, the link between the IRA and the Nazis and de Valera's declaration of neutrality during "the Emergency" are still used by Unionists and their Tory supporters to discredit not only the IRA but Irish nationalism and the Republic.

4

The Troubles II

By the end of the Second World War the Irish Republican Army was a moribund organization, reduced to scattered and disorganized units. Arguments and splits divided the leadership and dispirited the ranks. By the late 1940s their numbers had dwindled to some two hundred active members. In 1950 the Dublin unit had a "paper strength" of less than forty men.[1] Attempts to recruit volunteers met with some success, but the tradition of "once in, never out" could no longer be enforced. Bored with aimless drills and doctrinal meetings, new members quickly lost enthusiasm for the cause and dropped out. The IRA, according to J. Bowler Bell, faced a crisis in the early Fifties. It "was either going to decay into a bitter little group of ageing and unsuccessful fanatics, conspiring pointlessly at odd corners, or act even when unready."[2]

Beginning in the early 1950s the IRA raided British army bases and seized arms needed to launch a new campaign in Northern Ireland. Some attacks were carried off successfully. Others ended in comic failure. Raiding an officers' training school in England, the IRA loaded up a van with weapons, only to discover their truck was so heavily weighted it was unable to move. They were forced to discard half their haul, then rumbled off. Still overloaded, the truck wobbled and took a wrong turn, attracting police attention. Caught with nearly a hundred rifles and a machine gun, the three volunteers were sentenced to eight years in prison.[3] In a more serious incident, four IRA men and a civilian onlooker were killed when a mine exploded prematurely.[4]

Lacking resources, the border campaign that started in 1957 failed to disrupt life in Northern Ireland. Though some attacks killed and wounded British personnel, the operation, like the wartime bombing campaign, devolved into intermittent vandalism and petty sabotage before being suspended in 1962. In all, eighteen lives were lost. Hundreds of IRA men were interned without trial or sentenced to prison. Having failed to unite Ireland, the greatest victories the IRA could claim were budgetary: Their actions forced two governments to spend millions on security. Most disillusioning to its advocates was the campaign's failure to ignite widespread support. Although their purpose was to liberate the Six Counties, the IRA bombers had to operate from the Republic, finding no sanctuary in Northern Ireland.[5] Most nationalists agreed with Robert Briscoe's assessment that the "New IRA," though "not hooligans or criminals," had succumbed to a "misguided patriotism" that led them "to die for Ireland when ... they would better live and work for her."[6] By reverting to violence, the IRA only opened old wounds and suspicions that would further delay any end to the partition they claimed to abhor. By 1961, Gerry Adams reported, the IRA in Belfast had fallen to twenty-four men and two handguns.[7]

The IRA failed to excite much interest south of the hated border. When nationalists demonstrated in front of the Dublin post office, site of the 1916 Rising, few passersby took notice. Ireland, plagued by continuing unemployment, low wages, and continued emigration,* showed little public and less official interest in the old cause.

During the fervor of the bombing campaign of 1958 the Republican organ *The United Irishman* claimed a circulation of 144,000. By the mid-sixties circulation dropped to 14,000.[8]

The IRA of the early 1960s was of little interest to filmmakers, save as a comic byline.

THE LEAGUE OF GENTLEMEN (1960)

Released the same year as *Ocean's Eleven*, Basil Dearden's *The League of Gentlemen* (Allied Film Makers) is a strikingly parallel action comedy about a team of army veterans using their wartime training to stage a daring robbery. Deardon, who directed *The Gentle Gunman* in 1953, created an English caper movie laced with satiric asides, running gay gags (Oliver Reed makes an uncredited cameo appearance as an over-the-top effeminate chorus boy), and quips about Billy Graham and California cults. Among the droll comedic elements is a sardonic IRA subplot.

Forcibly retired from the British army, Colonel John Hyde (Jack Hawkins) assembles seven cashiered officers with expertise in demolitions and communications to rob a London bank. Hyde tells his men that stage one of the mission is to secure weapons and equipment, to be "supplied by our late employer." Their target will be an army command training center in Dorset. Given recent events, Hyde has discovered a tactic to deflect suspicion:

> We shall have to provide the authorities with a scapegoat. In this case I'm relying on the British character. We British will always give the Germans, the Russians, the Japanese, or even the Egyptians the benefit of the doubt, but never the Irish. So throughout this exercise if we use our accents judiciously, the IRA will get the credit and the blame.†

Dressed in British uniforms, Hyde and two conspirators impersonate senior officers making a snap inspection of the base to distract army personnel, while their comrades, posing as utility repairmen, break into arms lockers and seize submachine guns, explosives, and gas masks. The following day, one of Hyde's men (Richard Attenborough) reads a newspaper headlined "Daring Raid by Irish Rebels."

In 1960 the IRA appeared harmless enough for a British filmmaker to parody without offense. Within a decade, the IRA would reemerge in some of the most violent clashes since the Troubles of the Twenties.

Never-Never Land

By the early 1960s Northern Ireland had become, in J. Bowyer Bell's words, a "never-never land — never visited, never noticed."[9] Ever sensitive to their minority status on the island, Protestant Unionists created an administration to ensure their dominant status in the six-county Province where they constituted a two-thirds majority. Stormont, the North-

---

*In 1961 the population of the Irish Republic fell to 2.8 million, the lowest since the Famine.

†The "blame-it-on-the-IRA" tactic appears in A Prayer for the Dying *(Samuel Goldwyn, 1987) when London gangster Jack Meehan (Alan Bates) plans to kill a witness with a bomb carefully constructed using trademark IRA components. In* Midnight Man *(VisionView/Carousel/Telescene, 1995) Arab and Russian conspirators plan to leave "the fingerprints of the IRA" on a royal assassination to end the peace in Ireland and shake the British empire. In* Hidden Agenda *(Helmdale Film, 1990) British intelligence kidnap, kneecap, and kill a British army captain threatening to reveal a political scandal in order to blame his murder on the IRA.*

ern Ireland Parliament, was a bastion of Protestant Unionism with little Catholic representation. Gerrymandering and voting restrictions (Protestants were able to cast multiple ballots) limited Catholic political power. Protestants received decidedly preferential consideration for welfare benefits, public housing, and jobs. Fearful that high Catholic birth rates would weaken their demographic hold on Ulster, Unionists hoped discrimination would spur emigration.

The ruling Protestants treasured their British connection, expecting the London government to subsidize their province, which could not sustain itself—without interfering in the way they governed it. In general, London cooperated, turning a blind eye to overt discrimination in Ulster it would never countenance closer to home.[10]

Above all, what unified the Unionists was fear:

> They feared today and tomorrow and so focused on preserving the immediate past — that was the purpose of politics. Nothing else mattered as much as the constitutional issue — the security of the majority in the six counties to maintain their traditions. Nothing else mattered at all, not class nor caste, not everyday differences, not personalities, not the usual bread-and-butter issues. Fear had permitted, had encouraged, the formation of a sectarian state within the United Kingdom, a political relic ignored by London, detested by Dublin, unknown elsewhere, and a marvel to its supporters.[11]

The more militant Unionists, called Loyalists, fiercely embraced their British/Protestant identity, declaring allegiance to the Crown with a Victorian jingoism that led critics to question what they were loyal to. Their Union Jack–draped streets, drum-banging parades, and angry denunciations of Popery seemed archaic and out of step with a growingly diverse Great Britain. Watching a procession of speakers at a Protestant rally denounce the Pope and the Kennedys, John Conroy saw in the Orange pageant a surreal celebration that could only occur in Ulster:

> It occurred to me that the Orangemen assembled were proclaiming their Britishness in terms no one on the British mainland considered a twentieth-century sentiment, in outfits no one else in Britain would consider wearing, all the while proclaiming a history that hadn't happened.[12]

In addition to the fear of the Irish, the Unionists feared the very nation they were proclaiming loyalty to. A half century before they had been willing to take up arms to fight Home Rule, ready to fire upon British troops for the right to stay British. They remained ever apprehensive that liberal elements in Westminster would force them into concessions and compromises, even possibly abandoning their costly province altogether.

Although the IRA was broken, disorganized, and dispirited in 1964, Loyalists felt compelled to remain vigilant. There was a fear that the upcoming fiftieth anniversary of the 1916 Easter Rising would spark a renewed nationalist attack on the Union. In addition, they felt threatened by a growing Catholic civil rights movement. Inspired in part by American blacks demanding voting rights in the South, Catholics had begun marches and demonstrations.* Although its goal ostensibly was to secure equal rights for Catholics as British subjects, Loyalists saw the movement as a menace to their political power and a threat to the Union. The majority of Catholics did not condone the IRA's armed struggle, but they were nationalists seeking an end to partition. Most supported the Social Democratic and Labor Party (SDLP), which shunned violence but advocated the creation of a united Ireland through peaceful means.

---

*Catholic marchers often carried banners reading "We Shall Overcome."

In 1966 Loyalists formed the Ulster Volunteer Force (UVF), a paramilitary organization that announced it was declaring war on the IRA, promising to execute its members and punish those who gave them succor. It was quickly declared illegal by the government of Northern Ireland but continued its armed struggle against the IRA until it declared a ceasefire in 1994.* Like the IRA, the UVF conducted bombings, killing fifteen in a pub explosion in Northern Ireland and thirty-three in a pair of attacks in the Republic.† This organization was followed by the Ulster Defense Association (UDA), which carried out attacks under the name Ulster Freedom Fighters (UFF).

Tensions mounted in Northern Ireland in the late 1960s, culminating in pitched street battles between Protestants and Catholics. In August 1969 Northern Ireland erupted into violence and spats of ethnic cleansing. Catholic homes and shops were burned by Loyalist mobs. The RUC was unable or unwilling to contain the disorder. Nearly 1,500 Catholic families were forced to flee their homes. Images of burned-out houses and refugees riding atop trucks hastily piled with whatever household goods they could salvage enraged the Catholics in the Republic and shocked British public opinion. It marked a devastating blow to the Irish Republican Army, which was unable to protect the community it claimed to represent. IRA, it was mockingly claimed, stood for "I Ran Away."

In Ireland, Taoiseach Jack Lynch went on television to denounce attacks against Catholics, stating, "It is evident that the Stormont Government is no longer in control of the situation," and that "the Irish Government can no longer stand by and watch innocent people injured and perhaps worse."‡[13] Lynch ordered army medical units to the border to treat displaced nationalists. Members of the Irish government considered sending troops into the North to protect Catholic neighborhoods. Given the Irish army's lack of manpower and vehicles, any military incursion into Northern Ireland would have been fragmentary and of little duration. Contingency plans included commandeering civilian buses to transport soldiers and sending special forces into Belfast to launch diversionary guerrilla attacks, blowing up docks and the BBC offices, among other targets.** Lynch called for United Nations peacekeepers, a demand rejected by London. London did send in troops.

At first, the beleaguered Catholics greeted the British soldiers as neutral protectors. Grateful housewives were photographed serving tea to Her Majesty's Forces. The image of Irish Catholics heralding British troops as saviors was a humiliating blow to Irish nationalists, especially the IRA. The arrival of the British Army, however, changed the nature of the conflict and would soon be used to validate IRA ideology.

British forces could not remain neutral for very long. Though directed from London, the military had to cooperate with the RUC and Ulster officials. The soldiers first sent to protect stayed to patrol, often searching Catholic homes for weapons without warrants, manning checkpoints, and providing security for Protestant enterprises. As the barricades, sandbags, and barbed wire went up, and the streets began to rumble with heavy armored vehicles, Catholic Belfast took on the look of occupation.

Sporadic operations continued until it officially disarmed in 2007.

†*The "Dublin and Monaghan bombings" on May 17, 1974, marked the greatest loss of life on a single day during the Troubles.*

‡*Lynch is often misquoted as having said "stand idly by." The word "idly" appeared in the text but did not appear on the teleprompter, though many viewers insist they heard him say it.*

**The prospect of a 1969 Irish invasion of the North was the topic of a 2009 RTE program,* If Lynch Had Invaded.

As London intervened in Northern Ireland, it pressured Stormont to make reforms. Unionists expected the British army to provide security in what they claimed to be part of the United Kingdom but resented political interference in what they considered local matters.

Birth of the Provos

With the outbreak of violence in 1969, young Belfast Republicans wanted arms to protect their neighborhoods from Loyalists. The IRA in Dublin was hesitant. Marxist in orientation, its leadership was loath to condone a sectarian conflict rather than a class struggle. The idea of working-class Catholics battling working-class Protestants violated their view of the Irish problem.

In 1970 both the Irish Republican Army and its political party, Sinn Fein, split, the younger militant volunteers becoming the Provisional IRA or "Provos." The Official Irish Republican Army, which maintained its vision of a thirty-two-county socialist state, conducted a few shootings and bombings before suspending military operations in May 1972. Still hoping to frame the conflict in terms of class, the officials adhered to leftist hopes expressed by Republicans like Cathal Goulding, who argued in July that "we need those million Protestant working people on the workers' side in the Irish revolution.... They are still thinking on bigoted, sectarian lines, but the potential exists for growth of consciousness of the common cause between Protestants and Catholics."[14] But like the Wolfe Tone Society, which included Catholics, Protestants, and a Jew, the Official IRA could not reconcile its ideology with events unfolding in the streets.[15]

Loyalist violence against Catholics gave the newly-armed IRA support, recruits, and something the border campaign failed to engender — legitimacy. The IRA grew in stature, but the nature of the conflict condemned it, no matter how powerful or large it might become, to being an armed force that could not extend support beyond the Catholic community. Less dedicated to notions of class struggle, the Provos wanted to define the conflict as one between the Irish and British occupiers. In Republican mythology Ireland had been and must eventually become one nation. It denied the concept of two Irelands.

If Unionists were united in their dedication to their ties to Britain, the Republicans were wholly focused on severing those links. Kevin Toolis defined the obsessional nature of the IRA:

> As a philosophy, Irish Republicanism is the unqualified belief that a United Ireland is an intrinsic good, and the demand for Irish national self-determination so pressing, so overwhelming, that this goal must be pursued at all costs but principally and immediately by force of arms. Ireland must be reunited and the illegitimate British Crown Government forced to leave that portion of the country, Northern Ireland, over which it rules and claims jurisdiction. All other political questions and struggles in Ireland are secondary and inferior to the resolution of the "national question."[16]

Republicans saw Northern Ireland as the Six Counties occupied by the British, a last colony of the Empire. The Unionists were not seen as an obstacle to unification, being simply "puppets of British imperialism." As always, for Republicans "the real enemy was Britain, and once Britain had been defeated Unionist resistance would simply collapse."[17]

The Troubles became dominated by three conflicting narratives. The Unionists fought to maintain their heritage and the union that assured that Londonderry was as much a part of Britain as London. The Irish people had approved the Treaty creating a two-state solution, accepting Ulster as part of the United Kingdom. The violence, in their view, was caused by a minority of criminals, Marxists, and Republican fanatics whose ideology was undemocratic. The IRA was something to be defeated, not negotiated with or placated.

For Republicans, the enemy was Britain, an imperialist power that, after eight hundred years of domination, was still holding onto a portion of Ireland it had no legal claim to. The Irish, in the Republican view, were fighting for independence and the right of self-determination. The demographic realities of Northern Ireland were dismissed, as "Ulster" was deemed an artificial and illegitimate "statelet."

For the British, who repeatedly stated (much to the chagrin of Unionists) that they had "no selfish, strategic, or economic interest" in Northern Ireland, the conflict was one between Irish nationalists and Irish Unionists. As a democracy, Britain had to acknowledge the principle of majority rule. As long as the Unionists prevailed, Britain could not abandon its troubled province.

After 1970 the conflict moved beyond street fights and fire bombs. In 1971 the first British soldier serving in the North was killed by the IRA.

That August internment began. Thousands of British troops and RUC officers swept through Catholic neighborhoods to round up the IRA. Supplied with outdated lists and vague descriptions, soldiers often raided the wrong home or arrested relatives or volunteers who had been inactive for years. Subjected to interrogation methods later characterized as "inhumane and degrading" by the European Court of Human Rights, those mistakenly detained were released "traumatized, radicalized, and infuriated by the experience."[18] The abuse of wholly innocent men angered Catholics, who bitterly noted that no Loyalist suspects were arrested. Internment without charges or trial became a leading Catholic and nationalist grievance.

In January 1972 thirteen Catholics demonstrating against internment were shot dead by British soldiers in Londonderry. In March Britain suspended Stormont, introducing direct rule of the Province from London. In July, Belfast was rocked by blasts from twenty-two IRA bombs that claimed nine lives.[19]

As the conflict continued, the bombs became larger, the attacks more sophisticated, and the assassination of opponents and suspected informers more vicious.

No Go Land

As the violence escalated, Belfast cleaved into two separate and armed communities:

Protestants flew the Union Jack and painted their curbstones red, white, and blue; Catholics flew the Irish flag and painted their curbs orange, white, and green. Men in one part of the city wore bowler hats and carried silver-knobbed canes; men just a block away wore green and carried shillelaghs. Belfast felt more British than London, and more Irish than Dublin.[20]

But unlike Berlin, cleanly divided by a single wall, Belfast became a warren of improvised barricades. Some were created by the authorities. Other, illegal, barriers were erected by the IRA to block police surveillance, or by residents wishing to wall off a Protestant or Catholic neighbor. With the mounting violence, once integrated neighborhoods became monolithic as minority families moved out, often relocated by public housing authorities to "safer" districts. In 1970 over 320 Protestant families were moved from the predominately

Catholic housing estate of Ballymurphy over a single weekend.[21] Protestants and Catholics attended separate schools, learned separate histories, celebrated separate holidays, drank in separate pubs, and took separate cabs.

Belfast became a city apart from the rest of the English-speaking world. Armored vehicles patrolled the streets. Police stations were surrounded by sandbags and barbed wire. Telephones were tapped. Surveillance cameras were omnipresent. Helicopters churned over the city. Soldiers in flak jackets searched cars and houses. Shoppers and commuters became accustomed to pat-downs and bag searches. Building codes were amended for heightened security. Sidewalks in Catholic housing estates were designed to support the weight of military vehicles.

Belfast became the most patrolled, most observed, most monitored city in Europe. Names, photographs, addresses, arrest records, and car registrations were entered into databases to provide officers with instant profiles of suspects stopped at a checkpoint or spotted leaving a building under surveillance. Many joked that British intelligence knew the wallpaper pattern of every dining room in Belfast.

The violence continued, becoming a feature of daily life. Explosions were routine. Belfast's twelve-story Europa Hotel opened in 1971 and became known as the "most bombed hotel in Europe."* The luxury hotel was a prime IRA target and would be bombed over twenty times in its first four years of operation. Visiting reporters joked they could cover the Troubles without leaving the hotel bar.[22] After being bombed eighteen times, one merchant opened a separate bombing account at his bank to track his rebuilding costs and compensations.[23] By 1992 the British government had paid out £657 million in compensation for some ten thousand explosions in Northern Ireland.†[24]

The belligerents waged war with mutually self-defeating strategies. The more the British provided security, the more Northern Ireland resembled an occupied country. The watch towers, armored personnel carriers, sandbagged police stations, and barbed wire bolstered the Republican narrative that the IRA was an insurgent guerrilla army fighting a war of national liberation against foreign occupation. The more the IRA bombed and killed, the more they made it difficult for the British to withdraw, and the more they inflamed the antipathy of the Unionists whose acquiescence they would need to achieve their ultimate goal of unification.

Paisley and Adams

Two political figures dominated the Troubles for decades. Born in 1926, Ian Paisley became a founding member of the Free Presbyterian Church of Ulster and the Democratic Unionist Party. A strict fundamentalist, Paisley achieved prominence for his militant anti–Catholicism, staunch pro-life views, and his outspoken denunciation of homosexuality.‡

*The Europa Hotel is featured in Hidden Agenda (Helmdale Film Corporation, 1990) as the base of operations for two Americans investigating human rights violations in Northern Ireland.

†This scheme created a new kind of arson-for-profit venture, as merchants torched failing businesses then filed compensation claims as victims of terrorism. Other business people doubled up, filing for both compensation from the British government and their private insurance companies.

‡In 1977 Paisley launched his Save Ulster from Sodomy campaign to protest calls for decriminalizing homosexual acts between adults.

In 1963 he organized protests against the lowering of flags in Belfast following the death of Pope John XXIII. In 1988 he was ejected from the European Parliament after interrupting a speech by Pope John Paul II, accusing him of being the Anti-Christ. His demand that police remove an Irish tricolor from Sinn Fein's Belfast offices sparked rioting in 1964. Paisley helped establish several Loyalist organizations, which formed paramilitary wings. In 1969 he was jailed for organizing an illegal counter-demonstration against a Catholic civil rights march. In 1981 he founded his own paramilitary organization called Third Force to oppose growing cooperation between Northern Ireland and the Irish Republic. A member of Parliament for thirty years, he consistently opposed any British suggestion of power sharing in Northern Ireland. Though claiming fidelity with Britain, he was temporarily suspended from the House of Commons and once ejected from a meeting at No. 10 Downing Street. His confrontational demeanor, strident rhetoric, and distinctive voice made him a caricature of the uncompromising Orangeman.

Gerry Adams, born to a West Belfast nationalist family in 1948, was active in the civil rights movement in the late 1960s and Sinn Fein. Adams has consistently denied membership in the IRA, but both British and Irish state papers, as well as leading journalists, have identified him as a leading figure of the Provos. Adams was interned and released on several occasions. As an IRA commander, Adams was instrumental in promoting two weapons that would become hallmarks of the armed conflict: the American Armalite and the car bomb.[25] Soon recognized for his leadership, Adams earned the nickname "the Big Lad," a sobriquet he reportedly enjoyed because it evoked memories of Michael Collins, the Big Fellow.[26] He was elected to Parliament, serving from 1983 to 1992 and 1997 to 2011, but abstained from taking his seat in Westminster. As president of Sinn Fein, he was a leading spokesman for the Republican cause. Like Paisley, Adams had a distinctive presence. His beard, glasses, and soft, evasive speeches gave him a professorial image which clashed with Loyalist depictions of him as a dangerous terrorist. To deny terrorists "the oxygen of publicity," Margaret Thatcher banned Gerry Adams' voice from British media. The ban only enhanced Adams' prominence among Republicans and led to farcical television. Interviews with a voiceless Adams were aired with subtitles. Later, actors were hired to imitate his voice, creating the bizarre experience of watching a man being dubbed in his own language.*

The appearance of Paisley and Adams together during peace talks in the late 1990s, more than any other image, signaled the end of the Troubles.

The Long War

The IRA adopted a "long war" strategy. The IRA could never defeat the British Army, but, like the VC or the FLN, it believed it could wear the enemy down by making the Six Counties ungovernable. Eventually, the IRA's Army Council assumed the British would tire of securing their costly province and leave Ulster the way the French abandoned Algeria. But unlike the Vietnamese or the Algerians, the Republicans were not seeking political independence but unification with another country. As they struggled to make Northern Ireland ungovernable for Britain, they made it increasingly unpalatable for the Irish Republic to absorb.

At the time of partition in 1922, Northern Ireland contained most of the nation's indus-

---

*John Major lifted the ban in 1994. A similar ban against Adams existed in the Irish Republic.

try and 40 percent of Ireland's tax base, but by the 1980s it was a rust belt of decaying and inefficient industries.[27] Ulster's costs to the United Kingdom far outstripped its revenues. By 1995 the Crown was paying £3.4 billion annually, or $3,500 for each subject, to maintain the Province.[28] For one of the largest economies in the world, it was a bearable drain. For the Republic, a nation of four million, the cost would have been formidable.*

As the long war continued from the 1970s into the 1990s, the Republic was changing. Ireland's Celtic Tiger economy transformed a once sleepy nation known for whiskey and tourism into a high-tech country exporting computer software. With a stream of Irish writers, actors, musicians, and motion pictures reaching international audiences, Ireland commanded a position on the world stage that rivaled nations ten times its size. The humiliation of partition was something of the past. The North, with it violent tribalism, crumbling industry, crime, and unemployment, was less and less appealing to a nation forming a global identity.

Though publicly committed to a united Ireland, Irish politicians were always reluctant to pursue the issue. Early in the conflict, Harold Wilson met with the Irish Taoiseach and proposed a strategy to unify the island. A Wilson aide recalled the surprising reaction of the Irish politicians when, over lunch, Harold Wilson "put forward a plan for turning the dream of unity into reality. I had thought they would jump for joy, but their reaction was more akin to falling through the floor."[29]

Northern Ireland was becoming more and more a Never-Never Land no one wanted. Filmmakers, however, saw opportunities in depicting the Troubles onscreen.

Normal Abnormalities

The contested region took on a multiplicity of names, reflecting the loyalties and identies of its residents. In *Divorcing Jack* (Scala, 1998) Dan Starkey (David Thewlis) drinks whiskey with a visiting American reporter, Charles Parker (Richard Gant), whose naïve comment prompts a geopolitical lesson:

Parker: It tastes better in Ireland.
Starkey: It's Northern Ireland to you. Or Ulster, if you're a Protestant. Six Counties or the North ... of Ireland if you're a Catholic. And if you're the British government you call it the Province.
Parker: And what do you call it, Mr. Starkey?
Starkey: I call it home.

The acceptance of "abnormal normalities" in Northern Ireland is depicted in Mike Leigh's *Four Days in July* (Water Bearer Films, 1985), which follows the parallel but distinctly different lives of two couples, one Protestant, the other Catholic, facing the birth of a child. Amid the gossip and ordinary conversations are offhand references to internment and violence. The Protestant soldier starts his morning commute by looking under his car for bombs. The disabled Catholic casually recounts his wounds from a Loyalist drive-by shooting, a ricochet bullet fired by British soldiers at a checkpoint, and a bomb blast injury.

The Big Brother atmosphere of Northern Ireland is illustrated in the opening sequence of Jim McBride's *The Informant* (Hallmark Entertainment, 1997). Gingy, an IRA veteran, returns to Belfast, his car passing security towers, high walls, and military checkpoints. The

---

In addition, many in Ireland were dubious about the prospect of absorbing a million Protestants who would have little or no loyalty to the Republic.

moment he hands his ID card to an officer, his picture appears on a computer screen in army headquarters, revealing his address and prison record. In the first scene of Kari Skogland's *Fifty Dead Men Walking* (Future Films, 2009) Special Branch intelligence officer Fergus (Ben Kingsley) sits before a bank of security monitors following the movements of a potential informer.

TITANIC TOWN (1998)

Based on the Mary Costello novel, Roger Michell's *Titanic Town* (BBC Films) captures the never-never land atmosphere of Belfast in 1972 as Bernie McPhelimy (Julie Waters), a working class Catholic mother, struggles to raise her children "without hate" in West Belfast. The film opens with her ineffectual husband Aidan (Ciarán Hinds) fumbling with the door of their new townhouse in Andersonstown, a semi-suburban housing estate resembling American garden apartments. While their family and friends sing "Danny Boy" at a conventional housewarming party, the camera moves outside to reveal a British soldier posted in their front yard.

Although Aidan's brother is a low-level official in the IRA, the McPhelimys are largely apolitical. In one scene Aidan suggests letting an IRA gunman take shelter in their home; in another he rushes out to provide first aid to a wounded British soldier. He laughs off having his house searched by soldiers and smiles when the army photographs him as a potential terrorist. Having her home searched without warrant does not offend Bernie as much as embarrass her because the beds are unmade. As they watch the British round up elderly residents, Aidan and his son joke about the British using "an old list."

Julie Waters (left) and Elizabeth Donaghy in *Titanic Town* (1998).

For the McPhelimys the IRA are simply "the boys." Noticing a British soldier in front of their home during a downpour, Bernie's daughter Annie casually remarks, "He's wasting his time. The boys don't come out in the rain."

After a friend is shot by the IRA walking home from a butcher shop, Bernie becomes politically active, arguing with her brother-in-law that the IRA is losing support because of civilian casualties. She insists they must "get the shooting retimetabled" to avoid gunfire during the daytime when women are shopping and children are coming home from school. Asked to speak at a local women's meeting, Bernie is warned not to mention the IRA. Taking the stage alongside Unionist women, she argues the "one issue is to get the shooting stopped." Claiming that the IRA is "defending their homes," angry Republican women disrupt the discussion, denouncing Bernie as a traitor for cooperating with Protestants.

Bernie is interviewed on television. Watching his wife on the news from his hospital bed, Aidan calls her, troubled that her statements sounded "anti–IRA" rather than "pro–peace." Annie writes a statement for her mother to read in public to mollify the nationalist community.

Introduced on a morning talk show as being critical of the IRA, Bernie awkwardly reads Annie's statement, telling the interviewer, "We need the IRA to defend us, and we need them to maintain law and order ... because we can't rely on the RUC." When the talk show host reminds her that the IRA killed her friend, Bernie agrees, stating she condemns them for that single action but maintains the IRA has lowered crime in her neighborhood. "What I want is to try to get them to reschedule the shooting," she explains, causing the puzzled host to ask, "So you don't mind if they shoot people, it's just a question of the time of day?"

Bernie and a friend arrange a meeting with the IRA. The two housewives are politically unsophisticated but savvy enough to expose the IRA's amateurish security measures. Taken to one residence, they are told they are being moved to another location. After a car ride through the countryside, they are led into a house. The women stun the IRA when they immediately recognize that they have simply been taken to a different room in the same building. The curtains, they inform the men, are a dead giveaway.

The IRA offers to reduce the shootings in their neighborhood if the women will deliver a message to the British government. Bernie and her friend meet with officials in Stormont and announce the IRA will agree to a ceasefire provided their conditions are met. They then read a list of conventional Republican demands that constitute a full British surrender. Unaware they have been used to deliver a boilerplate message, the women are equally naïve when the British encourage their suggestion of circulating a petition to influence the IRA to cease using violence.

Angered by the petition campaign, a masked gunman threatens to kill Bernie and hang her in front of her house for children to find. Undaunted, Bernie speaks at a church, urging people to sign the petition:

> We've failed this generation. Every time a soldier is shot, we keep quiet. Every time a civilian is shot, we condemn the security forces. We're so predictable. I'd like to see a real chance. I'd like to see us have the humanity to condemn the shooting of a soldier.

Bernie collects 25,000 signatures in ten days and appears on TV with greater confidence. With her growing fame, she feels she has come into her own and that this "is her time." Although thousands sign her petition, many in the community resent her claim of representing Catholic concerns. In protest, a mob storms Bernie's house, breaking windows and injuring her son.

British officials congratulate her on her petition, but she refuses to comment when a reporter suggests that anyone who wants peace must be against the IRA. Realizing that she has been co-opted, Bernie resigns from the peace movement. She tells Annie that all she wanted was peace for her children, maintaining "because I was naïve doesn't mean I was wrong."

Forced to leave Andersonstown, Bernie's family packs their belongings into a truck. The final scene presents a Brueghlesque mural of the Troubles. As they drive off, a bomb explodes behind a neighboring house, and army vehicles and soldiers appear on the scene. Two youths, presumably the IRA bombers, take cover, then run across the street as a woman pushes a pram down the sidewalk, a man on a ladder cleans his windows, and a neighbor mows his lawn, his back and forth movements uninterrupted by the action around him.

A title appears at the bottom of the screen — "These things happened over twenty-five years ago" — to indicate the duration of the conflict.

NOTHING PERSONAL (1995)

Thaddeus O'Sullivan's *Nothing Personal* (Channel Four Films) is one of the few films that focuses on a Loyalist paramilitary group. Set in Belfast in 1975, the story opens with an IRA bombing that demonstrates the organization's inept cruelty. A volunteer leaves a bomb in a Protestant pub where several uniformed policemen are seated at the bar. The officers finish their drinks and depart before the explosion, so that only civilian patrons are killed and maimed. In retaliation, Loyalists kill a Catholic leaving a Catholic pub.

Nothing Personal depicts the Loyalists as being a mirror image of the Republicans, collecting protection money, kneecapping miscreants, drinking in pubs, listening to patriotic songs, and savoring the power that comes with a gun. Like the IRA, Loyalists speak about their "cause" and "country" while clearly enjoying the thrill of violence. Tommy (Ruaidhri Conroy), a sixteen-year-old Protestant, tells a girl about participating in a street fight with Catholics because it "beats watching television." Like a young Henry Hill in *Goodfellas*, Tommy is excited to be embraced by powerful older males. He is delighted when he is given a gun and assigned to guard a door in a club.

The Loyalist leader Leonard Wilson (Michael Gambon) meets with his IRA counterpart Cecil (Gerard McSorley) to discuss a planned truce and violations of their rules of engagement. Cecil regards the murder and mutilation of the Catholic civilian in response to the pub bombing an "unacceptable attack" on his community. Leonard claims to know nothing of the murder but later questions a young Loyalist named Kenny (James Frain) how a man could live with himself after committing something so "low and dirty." Kenny insists that the Catholic was in the IRA and therefore a "legitimate kill." Wilson, however, accepts Cecil's position that the victim was not political, telling an irritated Kenny, "His word is good enough for me ... bring your men under control."

Most difficult for Kenny to control is Ginger (Ian Hart), an obvious psychotic who relishes humiliating victims and engaging in violence. He needlessly mutilates a corpse, sets a man on fire in a street battle, and shoots at fellow Loyalists for sport. While Kenny asks Tommy to act as a security guard, Ginger puts a gun in the boy's hand and tries to get him to shoot a Catholic held for interrogation. Learning of the truce, Ginger explodes with rage, arguing, "We have to make life for them so ... miserable they get down on their hands and knees and crawl across the fucking border." Unlike Kenny, he feels no remorse when a nine-year-old Catholic girl is accidentally killed, dismissing her as being nothing more than "fucking vermin."

Recognizing Kenny's inability to curtail Ginger's mayhem, Leonard calls a major in the British army. When their car is stopped by soldiers, Kenny shoots Ginger, sparking a fussilade of return fire that rips apart the vehicle, killing all occupants. Leonard arrives on the scene, supervising the army's action to remove a dangerous renegade threatening his control of the Loyalist community.

Both the Loyalists and the IRA are portrayed as ethnic mobs rather than political organizations, their cause being a thin veneer masking parallel cults of violence. Leonard and Cecil, like rival mafia dons, respect each other's territory and share the problem of keeping their young gunmen in check. As Mick LaSalle of the *San Francisco Chronicle* suggests, the film is not so much about politics as it is about "male nature." "The men," he notes, "give themselves over to a culture of violence that runs amok and becomes an insane, degrading machine. The machine is so much bigger than any of the people involved that there really can be nothing personal."[30] Like Richard Wright's story "The Man Who Was Almost a Man," *Nothing Personal* is a powerful illustration of the appeal the gun has to young, disenfranchised males seeking power and respect. The Troubles may produce "an insane, degrading machine," but that machine does serve very personal agendas of power and identity.

BELFAST ASSASSIN / HARRY'S GAME (1982)

Lawrence Gordon Clark's *Belfast Assassin* (Yorkshire Television) narrows the Troubles to a deadly "game" played between two assassins. With its focus on suspense and action, the film's politics provides little more than a premise and background color.

Following a voiceover set of instructions, IRA volunteer Billy Downes (Derek Thompson) travels to London and shoots the Right Honorable Henry Danby (Robert Morris) on his doorstep in front of his wife and two young daughters. Downes methodically collects his spent cartridges, then flies to Dublin via Amsterdam. An IRA telephone call to the BBC offices in Belfast announces that the IRA had issued a "court martial execution order" on Danby for his creation of the Long Kesh "concentration camp."

Returning to Belfast, Billy is treated as "a bloody jewel" of a hero and promised protection because "each day they look for you and don't find you, we hurt them some more." The thin, curly-haired Billy looks more like a graduate student than a hit man and appears more troubled than celebratory. Billy's wife is angered at his actions, telling him what he can expect, "They'll shoot you and then write a bloody song about you just right for Saturday nights when they're pissed, so keep the verses short and the words not so long."

In London the Prime Minister (who is never named) orders that a special agent be sent to Belfast to locate the assassin. A British general argues that such a mission constitutes "a death sentence" because "the place is quite tribal. They know who belongs and who doesn't."

The agent selected is Captain Harry Brown, who grew up in Northern Ireland and has worked undercover in the Middle East. Posing as a merchant seaman who had been overseas for years to explain his softened accent and ignorance of recent events, Harry returns to Belfast.

Agent and assassin meet in passing at a dance and study each other. Their dates ask their partners about the other man, and both Billy and Harry answer with an identical line: "I dunno."

The RUC pick up the girl Billy was seen with. Fearful of being labeled a tout and punished by the IRA, she hangs herself in her cell. In retaliation, the IRA decides to kill Rennie, the officer in charge of her interrogation.

Assigned to the task, Billy enters Rennie's home and is confronted by his wife, who, like Danby and himself, has a young child. Unafraid of the intruder, she denounces the IRA gunman with confidence and certainty. Like his own wife, she sees Billy as a man with no future:

> You go through with this, they'll get you. They always get the man. You'll spend the rest of your life in the Kesh. People are sick and tired of you. Even in your own ratholes they've had enough of you.... They don't want you anymore living off their backs. Without your guns, you're nothing. You're a creeping disease-ridden little rat. Is that what your great movement's about? Killing people in their homes?

Arriving home, Rennie suspects something is wrong and draws his weapon. Spotting Billy, he fires. Billy takes aim at Rennie but hesitates when his young daughter gets in the way. Clearly pained at the situation, Billy struggles to push her aside, then runs off, smashing through a window rather than endanger a child. Rennie fires shots, wounding Billy in the arm.

When British soldiers search Billy's home, smashing furniture and ripping up floorboards, his wife confronts the soldiers, sounding much like Rennie's wife:

> Bloody brave aren't you? ... All these men in one wee house and one wee girl alone with kids? And it takes all of you with your bloody guns and Saracens.

Billy's failure to shoot Rennie because of the child is understood by the IRA leadership, but he is warned that in order not be seen as "going soft" he must be the one to execute Harry. Accompanied by two IRA men, Billy attempts to grab Harry on his way to work. Taking them by surprise, Harry shoots two IRA men. Billy drives off with a wounded volunteer in the back seat. Harry flags down a car and forces the driver to give chase. Billy loses Harry in traffic, then abandons the car in front of a hospital. Wounded and exhausted, Billy runs home, collapsing in front of his wife. Harry finds him and orders Billy to surrender. Billy tries to run, and Harry shoots him. Billy's wife screams that there was no reason to kill her unarmed husband. Harry tells her, "He would have known we had to get him.... A test of wills. No way we could afford to lose."

Observing the shooting from a distance, two British soldiers in a lookout post mistake Harry for a Provo and shoot him. Harry falls to the street and crawls past the Catholic residents who stand impassively as he struggles to escape. Noticing Harry's gun on the pavement, Billy's wife picks it up and confronts her husband's killer: "You came to our street to kill him." Harry looks up at her and tells her, "He had to die." Billy's wife shoots Harry just as British armored vehicles arrive.

Though Billy is denounced as a "disease-ridden rat," he is more humanized than Harry. Like his victims, Billy has a home, a wife, and small children. He is shown feeling distraught for his actions. In contrast, Harry is only given a military resume, with no scenes of a family life. In *Belfast Assassin*, the assassin is human, the secret agent representing justice is emotionally remote, cold, and mechanical. Although the film does not suggest a moral equivalency between the IRA and the British government, it does depict parallel organizations using similar tactics. As in *Nothing Personal*, the conflict is more about masculinity than politics, with women and children as the terrorized pawns in "Harry's Game."

CAL (1984)

Adapted from the novel by Bernard Maclaverty, Pat O Connor's *Cal* (Enigma Productions) traces the doomed love affair between young Cal (John Lynch) and Marcella Morton (Helen Mirren), the Catholic widow of a slain Protestant policeman.

Cal and his father Shamie (Donal McCann) endure continuing harassment in their predominately Protestant neighborhood. Cal is beaten by Loyalist youths. A threatening note is thrust under their door, and eventually their home is firebombed. The loss of the uninsured house devastates Shamie, who falls into a deep depression and is ultimately committed to an asylum.

Despite these injustices, Cal remains politically uninvolved, troubled by his past role in an IRA shooting. After falling in love with Marcella, he realizes she is the widow of the policeman shot by his friend Crilly (Stevan Rimkus), who enlists him to serve as a getaway driver in a holdup.

The leader of the local IRA unit, Skeffington, is portrayed as a hypocritical and cruel gang leader. Crilly takes Cal to meet Skeffington, who at first appears to be a thoughtful patriot. Trying to recruit Cal into playing a more active role and commit himself to the Cause, he states his case reasonably, "Not to act is to act. By doing nothing, you're keeping the Brits here." He then relates a moving narrative about witnessing thirteen of his countrymen slain on Bloody Sunday by British "trespassers." He claims to see potential in Cal's reticence in taking part in violence (Cal is too squeamish to work alongside his father in an abattoir):

> I'm a teacher, Cal. I know the kind of boys who join the army. Idiots, the psychopaths, the one class of people who shouldn't be given a gun.

Crilly, however, acts like a young hoodlum, engaging in robberies and shootings more for the excitement than patriotism. In addition to shooting an off-duty policeman, he shows no regard for the lives of innocent civilians. Running into Cal in a bookshop, he smirkingly shows him a bomb hidden in a book. When Cal asks why the IRA would want to blow up a bookstore, Crilly shrugs off the question, asking, "Why not?"

Skeffington's true colors are revealed when Crilly taps Cal to go on an assignment. Skeffington's elderly father has been badly injured by a car driven by a sixteen-year old. In retaliation, Skeffington "wants to make an example" of the boy, telling Crilly, "I don't want this bastard to walk again." The plan is to shatter the teenager's kneecaps with a power hammer while Skeffington watches.

Their car drives past an army checkpoint and crashes. Cal manages to escape. The apprehended Crilly calls out his name, identifying him to the British, who arrest Cal in the final scene.

The actions of the IRA match the brutality of the Loyalists, underlining the comment made by Cal's Protestant employer that "there are bad bastards on both sides." The idea that the IRA is no different than the Loyalists is also illustrated by Crilly's comments after a holdup. Jumping into the getaway car with the cash, he jokes to Cal that his victims asked him, "Which side is it this time?" Both the Loyalists and the IRA are portrayed as little more than flag-waving thugs, using politics as a justification for criminal sprees and personal vendettas. Cal's dispirited father states at one point that Northern Ireland "is rotten to the core."

Bobby Sands

> "There is no such thing as political murder." —*Margaret Thatcher*

Bobby Sands emerged from the ranks of entry-level volunteers to become a Republican martyr and the iconic figure of the Troubles, his face emblazoned on walls, posters, and t-shirts around the world. Born in 1954, Robert Gerard Sands joined the IRA in 1972. Later that year he was convicted on a weapons charge and sentenced to four years in prison. Released in 1976, he continued participating in IRA operations. In 1977 he was convicted of possessing a firearm and sentenced to fourteen years.

At Long Kesh he became commanding officer of the Republican prisoners protesting the repeal of Special Category Status, which had been granted in 1972 during British negotiations with the Provisional IRA. Under these rules, IRA convicts were viewed as "political prisoners" who were housed in separate units, allowed additional visits and food parcels, and exempted from wearing prison uniforms and doing prison work. Republicans held meetings and drilled in prisons, using them as training facilities.*

Following protests, attacks on prison personnel, and a major fire in Long Kesh, the British government changed tactics, denying Republicans political status and treating them instead as convicted criminals. By labeling IRA prisoners as convicts they hoped to discredit and criminalize the IRA. On March 1, 1981, the fifth anniversary of the abolishment of special status, Bobby Sands began a well-publicized hunger strike. A hunger strike is a long, painful self-imposed torture with deep significance to the Irish. In ancient times aggrieved peasants would fast on the doorsteps of noblemen as a way of shaming their overlords. To its supporters, the IRA was staging a moral crusade. To its critics, the hunger strike was a cynical, calculated strategy to recast terrorists as victims.

As weeks passed, Sands' self-imposed suffering elevated him from the ranks of the unknown to an international media figure. A hunger strike is protracted self-denial that demonstrates discipline if nothing else. He soon became the face of the IRA, recognized by most of the world by a single photograph of a smiling young man who "looked more like a drummer in a rock band than a ruthless terrorist."[31]

As time passed, the hunger strike sharpened the divide between Catholics and Protestants. Even those Catholics who were unsympathetic or even opposed to the IRA came to see Sands as a victim of British intransigence. To the outside world, the controversy appeared puzzling and cast the British government as obdurate and heartless. The prisoners were not proclaiming their innocence or demanding freedom. Granting their requests would endanger no one. Whether terrorists or freedom fighters, the inmates in question would remain securely behind bars.

For Sands and the IRA the strike was not about the demands but "the will of the just against the power of empire."[32] As his fast continued and daily reports chronicled his protracted decline in detail, Sands attracted more attention. Christ-like images of a bearded, emaciated prisoner appeared on murals in West Belfast. The concern for a man starving himself conflated and galvanized the Irish, blending reverence for Catholic martyrs, grievances against the British, and recollections of the Famine. Because it took so little for the British to put an end to this suffering, opponents of the IRA saw it as an issue of universal human rights separate from the armed conflict in Northern Ireland. For Republicans, Sands' hunger strike refuted the British claim that the IRA prisoners were simply gangsters. Criminals, Republicans argued, do not starve themselves for a principle.

Nor do they get elected to Parliament. On March 5, 1981, Frank Maguire, a Northern Ireland MP, died suddenly. Sinn Fein quickly persuaded and pressured nationalists not to run in the upcoming by-election so the imprisoned Bobby Sands could be entered as a

---

Because IRA volunteers spent so much of their time behind bars studying and engaging in political discussions, British prisons became known as "Republican universities."

protest candidate. Although many nationalists distrusted and detested the Provos, they fell into the campaign's general tone. A vote for Sands was not a vote *for* the IRA but a protest vote *against* the British government and the Protestants. For many it was an election about life and death. A vote for Sands was not so much an endorsement of his ideology but an appeal to the British to spare a young man's life. The fact that each day Bobby Sands was inching closer and closer to death energized the campaign. The turnout for a by-election was high. Over 86 percent of voters went to the polls, and Bobby Sands received over 30,000 votes, defeating Unionist candidate Harry West, who was shocked that "decent Catholics ... would vote for a gunman."[33]

The Republicans could hurl a second repudiation at the British. Criminals don't starve themselves for a principle, and terrorists don't get elected to Parliament. Now the British faced a perplexing dilemma. The skeletal man dying in a prison cell for the right to wear his own clothes was not simply an inmate but an elected member of their own Parliament. The Thatcher government remained steadfast in its refusal to compromise.

On May 5 at 1:17 A.M. Bobby Sands died. His hunger strike had lasted sixty-six days. Margaret Thatcher's comment on the death of the new MP was terse. "Mr. Sands," she announced to the House of Commons, "was a convicted criminal. He chose to take his own life. It was a choice his organization did not allow to many of its victims."[34] Technically accurate, it nevertheless seemed harsh, especially to the international press who did not associate the ultimate form of passive resistance with the violence Thatcher was trying to suppress.

The attempt to marginalize and criminalize the IRA produced the opposite result, creating just the kind of spectacle the British did not want to see. Bobby Sands' funeral on May 7 received international media coverage. A hundred thousand people lined the streets, adorned with black flags. Thousands marched in the procession, including members of the clergy, human rights activists, three members of the European Parliament, and Iran's ambassador to Sweden.* To prevent violence, police erected twenty-foot-high canvas barricades to shield the procession from the view of Protestant neighborhoods. Watching the long procession pass, a Protestant minister wondered if there was such a thing as a moderate Catholic.[35]†

At the graveside an IRA honor guard in uniform fired a volley of shots over a flag-draped coffin. To television viewers around the world, the ceremony had the pageantry of a state funeral. The IRA men, though masked, looked more like soldiers officiating at Arlington than ruthless terrorists. Demonstrations erupted in Paris, Milan, and Oslo. In India members of Parliament stood in a moment of silence. The lower house of the New Jersey legislature approved a resolution honoring Bobby Sands' "courage." In New York longshoremen announced a twenty-four-hour boycott of British ships, Irish bars closed for two hours, and a thousand attended a special mass at St. Patrick's Cathedral.

Still, the British held fast. Nine other hunger strikers followed Sands' example, dying one by one over the following months, creating "a series of deaths that offered ever decreasing power to shock, to move, to have a political impact."[36] The hunger strike was called off on October 3. The British quietly acquiesced to the inmates' demands without officially restoring political status.

In Tehran the newly established Islamic Republic changed the name of the street outside the British embassy from Winston Churchill Boulevard to Bobby Sands Street.

†*This minister, the Rev. Robert Bradford, was assassinated by the IRA six months later.*

The British claimed victory. Margaret Thatcher had withstood tremendous international pressure and refused, at least openly, to negotiate with terrorists. In the process, however, she became a Cromwellian hate figure the IRA could exploit in its propaganda. The hardness of her position alienated the Catholic moderates the British were trying to separate from Republicans. The IRA, however, was unable to transform the widespread sympathy for Bobby Sands into widespread support for its armed struggle. The process of recasting Bobby Sands from Republican martyr to symbolic victim of injustice made him internationally famous but also depoliticized him by universalizing him and separating him from the specific struggle. Moderate Catholics might hate Margaret Thatcher but rejected militant nationalism. The election of Bobby Sands, however, introduced a political element into the struggle, strengthening the influence of Sinn Fein.

Bobby Sands was featured in several motion pictures and television dramas, two of which use his story to frame very different dramas about the Troubles and the IRA.

Some Mother's Son (1996)

In *Some Mother's Son* (Castle Rock Entertainment) Bobby Sands is portrayed by John Lynch, though in Terry George's film he is a supporting character in a wider drama that explores the complexity of the Troubles, demonstrating conflicts within the Irish Catholic community and splits between British authorities. At its heart is the relationship that develops between two very different Catholic mothers brought together by their sons' participation in the hunger strike. Kathleen Quigley (Helen Mirren) is a widowed school teacher with little political consciousness. A middle-class mother, she has little in common with Annie Higgins (Fionnula Flanagan), a working-class farmer and staunch Republican.

The film opens with news footage of Margaret Thatcher's election. A government official, Farnsworth (Tom Hollander), tells prison officials that the Prime Minister wants a "new approach" in Northern Ireland, which he describes as a "three-pronged strategy — isolation, criminalization, demoralization." Roads along the border are to be blockaded and Catholic communities isolated. Key to the new strategy is "criminalization" of the IRA. "These people are criminals," Farnsworth declares, "They are not soldiers. They are not guerrillas. There is no war. There is only crime." To demoralize the IRA, prisons, he argues, must become an asset, a place where "we will break the back of the IRA."

The new policy prompts IRA retaliation. Gerard Quigley lies to his mother to borrow her car for an operation. Joining Annie's son Frankie, he fires a rocket, blowing up a British army vehicle. After a gun battle with RUC officers and British soldiers, Gerard and Frankie are arrested.

Gerard is an atypical volunteer, and his actions are held up to question. He is not the product of a Catholic ghetto, raised with few options in small rooms in narrow streets patrolled by soldiers. He has grown up in a substantial, symbolically white seaside home with sweeping vistas and large windows. His mother is a teacher, and his sister works in a bank. On the surface their lives differ little from middle-class family life in Britain or North America. A university dropout with long hair, the jobless Gerard seems more like a Sixties radical, a dilettante in a cause the rest of his family ignores. Visiting her son in custody, Kathleen is shocked that Gerard was involved with the IRA and stunned by his uncaring disregard for a wounded man:

Kathleen: Gerard, a man was shot.
Gerard: But he was a soldier.

Kathleen: He was somebody's son, like you're mine!

Gerard: He was waiting to kill us. He got shot.

Kathleen: You lied to me.

Gerard: I had to ... I had to lie because I wanted to protect you.... I didn't think you could handle it. You spent years like running away from all this stuff, OK?

Kathleen Quigley can be seen as the voice of mature reason struggling to comprehend the motives of a misguided juvenile — or a symbol of complacent denial, narrowing her concern to the success of her middle-class children while ignoring the social injustice around her. Gerard, who sees himself as a soldier fighting a war, can be accepted as a rebel fighting oppression — or a callous delinquent.

When Kathleen tells Gerard her attorney hopes to have the charges reduced from attempted murder to conspiracy, he declines the suggestion with a smile. Because he will refuse to cooperate by recognizing the court, he expects to receive a long sentence.

Kathleen blames Danny Boyle (Ciaran Hinds), head of Sinn Fein, for her son's plight. At their trial Gerard and Frankie reject the legitimacy of a British operating in Ireland and declare themselves to be prisoners of war. Frank Higgins is sentenced to life, and Gerard receives twelve years. In prison, Gerard is placed in a cell with Bobby Sands.

After her brother's conviction, Alice Quigley feels compelled to resign her job because the bank has been robbed four times by the IRA. Feeling no one will trust her, she leaves home.

Although Frank and Gerard remain comrades, their mothers stand in marked contrast. Agreeing they need a drink, Kathleen stops at a Loyalist pub, where Annie refuses to sit beneath a portrait of the Queen. Looking up at the picture, she raises a glass in toast:

Annie: Tiocfaidh ar Lar.

Kathleen (impatiently): And what does that mean?

Annie: Our day will come.

Kathleen: And what day is that, Annie?

Annie (whispering): The day the Brits go home.

Kathleen: The day the bloody Brits go home is all you people can think about. Well, my life won't change either way.

Annie: Your life and my life are two very different things, Mrs. My son was shot dead by the British!

Kathleen is moved by the loss of Annie's son, and the two women develop a strained friendship. The complexity of life in Northern Ireland is illustrated in an ironic scene. While Kathleen tries to teach Annie how to drive along a beach, their car gets stuck in the sand. With the tide coming in, the women panic but are rescued by passing British soldiers.

Conflict within the British government is shown in debates between the unyielding Farnsworth and Harrington (Tim Woodward), a Foreign Office official who is willing to "compromise" with the prisoners' demands. The British decide to respond to the refusal to wear convict uniforms by granting the concession to all prisoners, creating a distinction without a difference, since criminals and Republicans would be clothed in matching civilian shirts and sweaters. Harrington is angered by this tactic:

Harrington: Now you listen to me. I'm a diplomat in Her Majesty's Government. I do not break agreements.

Farnsworth: Well, this is war, not diplomacy.

Harrington: Really? I distinctly remember you saying to me that it wasn't war.

Farnsworth: Look, I want you to start treating these people for what they are. A bunch of terrorists. You do what it takes to draw them out into the open, and you finish them off!

When her son joins the hunger strike, Kathleen becomes politically involved. Though she never becomes a supporter of the IRA, she joins Annie in campaigning for Bobby Sands. Her activities bring her into conflict with her Catholic school, but she refuses to be dissuaded from supporting Sands. With Sands' election to Parliament, Kathleen hopes the British will negotiate to end the hunger strike. Seeking a compromise "for our sons' lives," the mothers meet with officials in London.

Farnsworth insists the government "does not negotiate with terrorists." He deftly shifts the responsibility of the prisoners' fates from the British to their mothers, reminding them that if their sons lapse into coma they have the legal authority to intervene and grant nourishment and treatment. "Surely, no mother," he tells them, "would allow her son to die."

As Sands nears death, a candlelit vigil is conducted outside the prison. When his death is announced, British troops break up the demonstration. The film recreates Sands' massive funeral, with its IRA honor guard firing a volley over a flag-draped coffin. Watching the news coverage, Harrison tells Farnsworth, "This is a disaster," and accuses him of creating another Irish martyr.

Harrison meets with Kathleen and urges her to help him "stop this madness" and take him to see Danny Boyle. Escorting the Foreign Office official to Sinn Fein headquarters, Kathleen plays the role of diplomat. Harrington agrees to meet the prisoners' demands to end the hunger strike provided the IRA does not claim to have won prisoner-of-war status. Boyle is skeptical, stating that Thatcher would never accept such a concession. Harrington assures him that "senior concerned parties within the government" are convinced the Prime Minister will accept the terms.

Back in his office, Harrington speaks on the phone, presumably with London, reporting that he has struck a deal, as Farnsworth storms in and tosses surveillance photographs of him and Kathleen entering Sinn Fein headquarters:

Farnsworth: Your career's over.
Harrington: We have a deal in place.
Farnsworth: It's not a deal, it's surrender.
Harrington: I warn you I have strong support.
Farnsworth: You'll be lucky to get a pension. Get out. Now!

Farnsworth concocts a watered down compromise granting "privileges" instead of "rights." Boyle angrily rejects this deal. Kathleen goes to her son's bedside and signs the release, taking him off hunger strike as Frankie dies in the next cell. When Kathleen breaks the news she ended Gerard's hunger strike, Annie is not angry but states quietly, "Somebody had to."

The final credits lists the names, death dates, and ages of the ten hunger strikers, noting that the strike ended "after several mothers intervened to save their sons" and the British government conceded to the prisoners' demands.

Some Mother's Son does not take sides in the conflict as much as it condemns the self-righteous cynicism of British conservatives and the IRA, whose adherence to ideological purity will not allow them to compromise, and heralds the sensible humanity of Kathleen Quigley and Harrison, who can rise above their political differences to save lives.

HUNGER (2008)

Steve McQueen's award-winning *Hunger* (Blast! Films) focuses on Bobby Sands (Michael Fassbender) within a very defined and at times existential framework. Unlike *Some Mother's Son*, the wider political and social conflict is not represented.

The film, shot without a soundtrack and containing extensive wordless scenes, opens with a brief prologue showing a nighttime street with a woman bashing a trashcan lid on the street, symbolizing the reaction following Sands' death. The film then follows prison guard Raymond Lohan (Stuart Graham) through his morning routine of soaking his injured hands, dressing, having breakfast, and checking under his car for bombs before turning the ignition. Driving to work, he listens to news reports commenting on the prisoners' demands for political status. In an extended shot, Lohan stands silently against a brick wall, smoking and watching the snow fall. Close-ups reveal his bloodied knuckles. The soaking of his hands is repeated. He winces as he plunges his bloody hand into cold water after beating prisoners.

Bobby Sands first appears twenty minutes into the film, being forcibly bathed and groomed, his bathwater turning red with blood. Sands and Lohan are both shown in long silent scenes staring into space, lost in contemplation, the prison taking a toll on both.

Issued civilian-style uniforms, the prisoners riot, smashing up their cells. Prison guards in black riot gear with helmets and shields are sent in to restore order. Beating their shields with batons like Roman soldiers, the faceless guards form a phalanx of black, depersonalized authority figures against the frailty of their naked prisoners. With little dialogue, the conflict is universalized so the prison drama could just as easily be taking place in Argentina or Iran.

In a following scene Lohan takes flowers to his senile mother in a nursing home. As he kneels beside his unresponsive mother, trying to communicate, an IRA gunman enters the room and shoots Lohan in the back of the head. He pitches forward into the blood-soaked lap of his mother, who remains expressionless, unaware of what has happened.

Michael Fassbender as Bobby Sands (left) and Liam Cunningham as Father Moran in *Hunger* (2008).

This is followed by a twenty-three-minute uninterrupted scene, seventeen minutes of which are shot from a single angle, between Bobby Sands and Father Moran (Liam Cunningham) which serves as a one-act play within the film. After some friendly banter, Bobby Sands and the priest debate the proposed hunger strike. Father Moran is a Republican who supported a previous hunger strike because it was a "protest."

That strike, Sands explains, failed because it was "flawed," and became "emotional," because seven men started at the same time. "They all got weak and couldn't let the weakest ones die," which made them "susceptible" to British machinations. This time, he states, the IRA will stage a series of consecutive hunger strikes, with each prisoner going on fast two weeks apart. When one man dies, he will be replaced by another. Sands tells Father Moran that seventy-five Republicans have volunteered.

The priest is appalled at the prospect of serial suicides:

Father Moran: So what makes this protest different is that you are set to die, Bobby?
Bobby Sands: It may well come to that.
Father Moran: You start a hunger strike to protest for what you believe in. You don't start already determined to die, or am I missing something here?
Bobby Sands: It's in their hands. Our message is clear. They are seeing our determination...
Father Moran: You are going head to head with the British government ... who are unshakable and can easily live with the deaths of what they call terrorists...
Bobby Sands: I know that.
Father Moran: And if you're not even willing to negotiate, you're looking for them to capitulate. Is that it?
Bobby Sands: Right.
Father Moran: So failure means many dead men, families torn apart, and the whole Republican movement demoralized?
Bobby Sands: Aye ... but short term. Out of the ashes, guaranteed, there will be a new generation of men and women even more resilient, more determined.... There is a war going on.... I have my belief. And In all its simplicity that is the powerful thing.

The priest asks Sands if he is seeking martyrdom and a chance to "write his name large for the history books." Father Moran argues that Sands has "lost all sense of reality" in prison and has "no appreciation of life." True "freedom fighters," he tells Sands, are "men and women out there working in the community," not people determined to take their lives in a wasted gesture.

Sands states he loves freedom, and that his life means everything to him. But he will not be dissuaded:

This is one of these times when we've come to a pause. It's a time to keep your beliefs pure. I believe that a united Ireland is right and just.... But having respect for my life, a desire for freedom, an unyielding love for that belief means I can see past any doubts I may have. Putting my life on the line is not just the only thing I can do, it's the right thing.

Sands concludes their meeting with a story from his childhood. On a sports outing in Donegal, he and some other boys found a badly injured foal lying in a stream. Although a priest told him to leave the animal alone, Sands held its head under water to drown the foal and end its suffering. Though he was punished for this act, he knew he had done the right thing. Realizing Sands will not reconsider his plan, Father Moran leaves, saying, "I don't think I'm going to see you again, Bobby."

In the next scene a prison janitor sweeps a dimly-lit prison corridor, with the voice of Margaret Thatcher presenting the British response to the hunger strike:

Faced now with the failure of their discredited cause, the men of violence have chosen in recent months to play what may well be their last card. They have turned their violence against themselves through the prison hunger strike to death. They seek to work on the most basic of human emotions, pity, as a means of creating tension and stoking the fires of bitterness and hatred.

A physician then details to Bobby Sands' parents the effects of starvation, the degeneration and failure of vital organs, and the slow breakdown of his body, culminating in cardiac failure.

A ten-minute wordless sequence chronicles Sands deterioration as he becomes thinner and weaker. Michael Fassbender's drastic weight loss is shocking, evoking images of Auschwitz. As he loses weight, his skin breaks down and erupts with sores that are gently treated by nameless prison staffers.

The image of an emaciated young man covered in sores is remicient of films of the late Eighties about AIDS patients. But unlike the patient dying of disease, Bobby Sands' suffering is self-inflicted and can easily be remedied. In a time-lapse sequence, meal after meal is placed beside his bed — nourishment he ignores. Eventually unable to stand, he is carried from a bath tub. Long sequences are silent, with Sands dreaming of his boyhood or absently watching the flickering of a fluorescent light. Visited by fellow inmates, their voices are muted, as he is unable to hear. The dying Sands dreams of cross-country running as a boy.

Sands' dead body is covered and wheeled down a prison corridor. The doors close, and a series of titles place his death in a wider context, noting his election to Parliament, the deaths of nine other hunger strikers, the killing of sixteen prison officers, and the eventual unofficial concession to inmate demands.

Hunger received numerous awards at film festivals in Stockholm, Sydney, Chicago, Montreal, Toronto, and Cannes, where it prompted walk-outs. It won numerous nominations in Britain, including a BAFTA Award, a Best Film Award from the Evening Standard Film Awards, and a London Critics Circle Film Award. Critics acclaimed the film for its "stagecraft," "painterly purity" and "power." Ty Burr of *The Boston Globe* viewed the subject of the film as "the dangerous, necessary hunger to break one's bonds: Northern Ireland from Britain, the prisoners from their cells, Bobby from life."[37] Writing in *The New York Times*, A. O. Scott declared that "the real subject" of *Hunger* was "dignity, more than any political strategy or ideological principle."[38]

Any film about Bobby Sands was destined to ignite controversy. David Cox of *The Guardian* stated that "far from being shocked at seeing the inmates roughed up a bit, I found myself wishing they'd been properly tortured, preferably savagely, imaginatively and continuously."[39] He admitted that his responses to "this beautifully made film" were "uncharitable" and "indeed reprehensible."[40] He defended his reactions by focusing not on the cinematic Sands but the historical Sands and his fellow hunger strikers. "The men heroized in *Hunger* chose to murder my fellow citizens, on their own island and mine, indiscriminately and brutally, in pursuit of a cause I consider unimpressive. What do you expect me to feel?"[41] Chris Tookey titled his review "More Pro-Terrorist Propaganda," deriding *Hunger* as a "preposterously over-praised" film that "worship[s] at the shrine of terrorism." [42] Tookey was highly critical of the movie's "implication" that Sands and "others like him were imprisoned for their political beliefs" and not criminal offenses involving firearms. Bobby Sands is willing to die for his "unyielding love" of his belief, but as Tookey notes, "There is, of course, no mention of his determination to shoot and bomb the Northern Ireland majority into a Socialist republic, whether they voted for it or not."[43] By invoking images of the Crucifixion and the Holocaust in displaying Sands' emaciated body, "the filmmakers' sympathies throughout are with terrorists," Tookey reasons and not with "their tens of thousands of victims, who, unlike Bobby Sands, were not granted the choice to live or die."[44]

Thirty years after his death, Bobby Sands remains an iconic figure and symbol of the Troubles, whose protracted death is interpreted either as a heroic sacrifice or a histrionic suicide distracting attention from countless nameless victims. Ten men had died on hunger strike; sixty-one others had been killed in retaliation.[45]

Into the Nineties

The Troubles continued. In 1982 IRA bombs killed eleven soldiers in London. A year later five people were killed by a bomb in Harrods department store. In March 1984 Gerry Adams and several others were wounded when Loyalists fired upon their car. The gunmen were arrested on the spot by British security who had advance warning of the assassination attempt but let it proceed after they had tampered with the ammunition to lessen the impact of the bullets.[46] In October an IRA bomb exploded in a hotel in Brighton hosting a Conservative party conference, killing five. In the late 1980s the IRA received weapons from Libya; Loyalists imported arms from South Africa. In 1991 the IRA fired mortar shells on No. 10 Downing Street. In 1993 the IRA detonated a massive bomb in the financial district of London that caused $1.45 billion in damage — more than had been inflicted in Northern Ireland since the start of the conflict in 1969.[47]

THE CRYING GAME (1992)

Written and directed by Neil Jordan, *The Crying Game* (Palace Pictures/Channel Four Films) did poorly on its initial release in Ireland and Britain, where many objected to a British character using the word "soldier" to describe an IRA man. In distributing the film in the United States, Miramax capitalized on the transgender "secret" of the plot. The political element became a mere background to a psychological sexual thriller that became a "sleeper hit." The famous "reveal" scene became much parodied, most notably reenacted by Leslie Nielson and Anna Nicole Smith in *Naked Gun 33⅓: The Final Insult*.

In the opening scene of *The Crying Game*, blonde IRA volunteer Jude (Miranda Richardson) lures an off-duty British soldier named Jody (Forest Whitaker) into being kidnapped by her male comrades. The unit, led by Peter Maguire (Adrian Dunbar), intends to hold Jody hostage for a prisoner exchange. If their demands are not met within three days, the IRA will execute their prisoner. While guarding Jody in a deserted barn, Fergus (Stephen Rea) develops a bond with his captive, who asks him to look up his lover Dil in London if he is killed. When the deadline passes, Fergus leads Jody outside to be shot. Jody breaks away, and Fergus gives chase. Jody runs into a road and is ironically run over by a British Saracen. Soldiers emerge from the vehicle, and Fergus escapes while a helicopter rakes the IRA farmhouse with machine-gun fire.

Disillusioned, Fergus travels to England and finds a job, using the name Jimmy. Though troubled by Jody's death, Fergus becomes romantically involved with Dil (Jaye Davidson). Though nauseated when he discovers Dil to be a transsexual, Fergus remains attracted to her. Wrestling with his feelings, he returns home to find Jude, now transformed from an easygoing blonde to a severe, mannish-looking woman with dark red hair and leather gloves. She informs Fergus that he had been court-martialed *in absentia* for desertion and that she pleaded clemency until his case could be heard. The fact Fergus had become a "Mr. Nobody" in London made him an asset to the IRA, now plotting to assassinate a British judge. "We'll need a Mr. Nobody," Jude tells Fergus, who announces that he wants out of the IRA. Reminding Fergus of the IRA policy, she tells him, "You're never out." To prompt Fergus to cooperate, Jude threatens Dil and begins to shadow the couple, following them from a restaurant to a bar. She forces Fergus into a car, where Maguire outlines their plot. Fergus is to shoot a judge as he leaves a brothel. Given that two armed bodyguards will be waiting outside, Fergus recognizes it will be a suicide mission.

Fergus tries to protect Dil by cutting her hair and transforming her into a boy. While Fergus sleeps, Dil ties him to the bed. Waking and fearing he will be late for the assassination, he begs Dil to free him. Waiting in a car near the brothel, Maguire and Jude realize Fergus has failed to appear. Impatient, Maguire seizes a small machine gun and runs across the street, shooting the judge and a bodyguard before being killed. Jude races from the scene and enters Dil's apartment, enraged that Fergus has failed a second time. Armed with Fergus' gun, Dil shoots Jude several times, jealous that she had seduced Jody. Fergus urges Dil to leave, remaining behind to wipe the gun clean, then placing his own fingerprints on it before the police arrive. In the final scene, Dil, restored to her female persona, visits Fergus in prison to declare her love for the man who saved her.

The film received six Academy Award nominations, winning one for Best Original Screenplay. It became a "sleeper hit" in the era of other edgy thrillers such as *Basic Instinct*. Costing less than five million dollars to make, the film grossed over $60 million in the U.S. alone. Perhaps the most widely seen film about the Troubles in the United States, *The Crying*

Forest Whitaker (left) and Stephen Rea in *The Crying Game* (1992).

Game portrayed the IRA as methodical, organized, and ruthless. Operating under orders, conducting courts martial and considering clemency pleas, the Irish Republican Army is depicted as a government-in-exile rather than a terrorist gang.

Response to Terror

Britain's ongoing struggle with the IRA generated several motion pictures and television movies that examined the nation's response to terrorism, generally focusing on police and judicial abuses. British-made productions generally provoked less criticism than an Irish film that in many ways was milder in its indictment of the British legal system.

HIDDEN AGENDA (1990)

Set in Belfast in the 1980s, Ken Loach's *Hidden Agenda* (Helmdale Film) is inspired by the Stalker inquiry of RUC abuses. In 1983 John Stalker, then Detective Chief Superintendent of the Manchester Police, headed an investigation into the alleged "shoot-to-kill" policy of IRA suspects in Northern Ireland.* Before his findings could be presented, Stalker was suspended, based on allegations later proved to be false. His dismissal caused a political and media controversy in Britain, with accusations of conspiracies and official cover-ups.

Loach's film expands the Stalker controversy from a cover-up of rogue cops into an Oliver Stone–like conspiracy at the highest levels of British government. Assigned to investigate the questionable shooting of an American human rights attorney, Paul Sullivan (Brad Dourif), outside Belfast, Deputy Kerrigan (Brian Cox) arrives from Britain and promises Sullivan's grieving fiancée, Ingrid Jessner (Frances McDormand), that he will follow all leads in the case. Ingrid informs Kerrigan that Sullivan had been killed on his way to meet a Captain Harris.

Kerrigan discovers inconsistencies in the official police story and compiles evidence of an illegal shooting and a cover-up. Pressed by Kerrigan about the suspicious shooting, RUC Chief Brodie responds, "The RUC do run covert operations, but so do the IRA! If you want to bring home the bacon, you first have to kill the pig."

In Loach's film it is the RUC and British intelligence that conduct illegal surveillance, kill without legal reason, and terrorize journalists threatening to expose them. Violence by the IRA is referenced in dialogue but never shown. The Republican position is articulated in song and dialogue.

In a highly staged scene, Kerrigan accompanies Ingrid to a Republican club to meet Harris. They sit through a rebel folk song containing the line "And you dare call me a terrorist while you look down your gun." They are joined by Liam Philbin (Jim McAllister) of Sinn Fein, who briefs the pair on Republican ideology, quoting James Connolly's claim that "England has no more moral right to administer Irish affairs than it has to administer the affairs of America or Japan." The answer to the conflict, in his view, is simple: "British withdrawal." When Ingrid mentions the death of innocent people, Liam agrees but argues that violence is necessary for occupied nations to achieve liberation. "George Washington," Liam asserts, "was called a terrorist in his time.... Unfortunately, colonies appear to have to fight for their freedom. It is never granted willingly. They must struggle for it."

After this polemic setup, Liam leads the pair to a back room where Captain Harris

---

The alleged RUC policy was also the subject of Peter Kosminsky's 1990 Yorkshire TV movie Shoot to Kill, *with Jack Shepherd playing John Stalker.*

(Maurice Roëves), now under IRA protection, waits to meet them. Harris explains that he conducted psychological warfare against the IRA, printing bogus Republican documents to discredit the organization. As a British army officer he had no reservations about using these tactics against terrorists. During the election of 1974, however, the Conservative Party, disillusioned with Heath, sought a "new leader from the hard right" and used Harris' unit to circulate rumors about Heath's private life to remove him from power, to be replaced by Margaret Thatcher. Fearing that another Labour government would be opposed to NATO and nuclear weapons, a group of military and business leaders engaged in treason. Working with the CIA, the Conservatives used illegal tactics to undermine Harold Wilson and ensure a Thatcher victory. Harris claims that he secretly taped the conspirators, including Alec Nevin, a principal Conservative spokesman and close advisor to the Prime Minister. He offers to provide a copy of the tape to Ingrid the following day in Dublin.

Kerrigan, who doubts Harris' story, is summoned to a meeting with Conservative leaders Alec Nevin and Sir Robert Neil, who not only verify Harris' allegations but justify their actions. Britain in the 1970s was not only threatened by IRA bombs, but by strikes, inflation, and a loss of prestige in Europe. "A few of us got together to do something about it," Kerrigan is told. When he calls their actions a conspiracy, Kerrigan is lectured somewhat patronizingly by Sir Robert, "My dear chap, politics is a conspiracy." Illegal methods were used in the election of 1974, the Conservatives admit, but the conspirators were "wrong for the right reason." To release the tape now would endanger the state and empower its enemies. Kerrigan is warned by Sir Robert to back off and let "historians discover it in fifty years' time."

Sir Robert proposes that Kerrigan limit his investigation to the illegal shooting of Sullivan and forget Harris' tape. He concludes their encounter by commenting on the pleasant weather, joking that "Ireland would be a lovely place if it wasn't for the Irish." To assure Kerrigan's cooperation, Sir Robert hands Kerrigan photos showing him with Ingrid at the Republican club, hinting that they not only suggest a link to terrorism but provide evidence of an extra-marital affair.

After giving Ingrid a copy of the tape, Harris is kidnapped, kneecapped, and killed by British intelligence, his murder blamed on the IRA. Having heard the tape, Ingrid asks Kerrigan if he is going to do anything about the Conservatives who "committed murder and treason," but Kerrigan demurs, saying he can do nothing. Insisting that British intelligence assassinated Harris, she demands Kerrigan take action. "You can't win against these people," he explains, prompting Ingrid to accuse him of being a puppet in a "police state." Enraged at Kerrigan's cowardice, she claims, "That's how fascism starts." Kerrigan tells Ingrid to return to America because she is in danger in Ulster. As Kerrigan leaves in the last shot, a title rolls up the screen:

> It is like layers of an onion, and the more you peel them away, the more you feel like crying. There are two laws running this country: one for the security services and one for the rest of us.

In Loach's film the IRA are idealistic nationalists fighting a war of liberation. The oppressive British, corrupted by their use of violence against "terrorism," have turned their counter-insurgency tactics against themselves, destroying the democratic values they claim to uphold.

Innocent Until Proven Irish

Two films recount parallel cases of wrongful convictions of Irish suspects for IRA bombings carried out in Britain in the fall of 1974. The bombings, trials, and appeal campaigns received wide publicity in Britain and Ireland, raising questions about police brutality and the British government's steadfast refusal to release people they knew were innocent.

The Guildford Four and the Maguire Seven

On Saturday evening, October 5, 1974, a bomb exploded in the Horse and Groom pub in Guildford, England. A half hour later a bomb exploded in the nearby Seven Stars pub. Both bars were crowded with off-duty British soldiers. The massive explosions destroyed the front walls of the buildings and shattered windows in neighboring shops. Five people were killed and scores were injured, many of them permanently maimed. The bombings caused a national outrage, leading David Howell, former Minister for Northern Ireland, to declare, "It's quite clear that we must hunt down the maniacs and animals who would do this kind of thing."[48]

Four people, soon known as the Guildford Four, were arrested and charged with the bombings: Paul Hill, Gerard Conlon, Patrick Armstrong, and Carole Richardson. All four signed confessions. Subsequently, seven others, including Conlon's father and aunt, were arrested and charged with handling explosives: Patrick "Giuseppe" Conlon, Anne Maguire, Patrick Maguire, Patrick Maguire, Jr., Vincent Maguire, Sean Smith, and Patrick O'Neill. The Guilford Four were convicted largely on the basis of their confessions. No eyewitnesses could place them at the pub, and no substantive circumstantial evidence was presented. All four were given life sentences. The "Maguire Seven" were convicted on the basis of forensic evidence and received sentences ranging from four to fourteen years.

An appeal campaign challenged the convictions, alleging that the defendants were subjected to mental and physical abuse, and coerced into confessing, and that prosecutors ignored exculpatory evidence and alibi witnesses. The appeal movement gained credibility following a spectacular admission of guilt by the "real bombers."

In December 1975 Britain was captivated by a six-day standoff with the IRA in London that was followed by millions on television. The event, known as the Balcombe Street Siege, began when four IRA men fired shots into a London restaurant. Chased by police, they entered a flat on Balcombe Street and held two people hostage. Declaring themselves to be members of the IRA, the four demanded a plane to fly them and their hostages to Ireland. After intense negotiations, the four surrendered. At their trial, the defense announced it would call no witnesses. Instead, one of the defendants, Joe O'Connell, would make a statement from the dock. Addressing the court, O'Connell admitted to the Guildford bombings:

> We have instructed our lawyers to draw attention to the fact that four totally innocent people ... are serving massive sentences for ... bombings, which three of us and another man now imprisoned have admitted that we did. The Director of Public Prosecutions was made aware of these admissions in December 1975 and has chosen to do nothing.[49]

The British government resisted re-opening the case. A mounting campaign, supported by a variety of Irish and British organizations and individuals, finally pressured authorities to examine allegations of both torture and the suppression of evidence favorable to the defense.

On October 18, 1989, the convictions of the Guildford Four were "declared a gross miscarriage of justice and quashed by the Court of Appeal."[50]

The Birmingham Six

On November 21, 1974, bombs exploded in two pubs in central Birmingham, killing twenty-one and injuring a hundred-and-sixty-two people. Six local residents, all born in Northern Ireland, were arrested. Five of the men had left Birmingham shortly before the explosions to attend the Belfast funeral of an IRA volunteer accidentally killed while planting a bomb in Coventry. Forensic tests indicated two of the suspects had handled explosives. All six defendants were convicted in 1975 and sentenced to life terms.

As in the Guildford case, the defendants — Hugh Callaghan, Patrick Hill, Gerard Hunter, Richard McIlkenny, William Power, and John Walker — were largely convicted on the basis of statements made to the police. Like the Guildford defendants, the Birmingham Six retracted their statements, alleging they had been extracted after brutal interrogations. Their first appeal was denied in 1976.

Chris Mullen, a journalist for the Granada television program *World in Action*, investigated the case, producing several programs that cast doubts about the guilt of the six men. In 1986 he published a book, *Error of Judgment—The Truth About the Birmingham Pub Bombings*, outlining a case for the men's innocence. In his book, Mullen claimed to have met those actually responsible for the bombings. A second appeal upheld the original conviction.

Mullen's work and that of other journalists and attorneys led to a third appeal in 1991. Evidence of police fabrication and suppression of evidence was presented. The forensic evidence was challenged. The convictions were overturned in 1991, and the defendants were released from prison.

WHO BOMBED BIRMINGHAM?/THE INVESTIGATION:
INSIDE A TERRORIST BOMBING (1990)

"A television programme alters nothing. We do not have trial by television here." —*Margaret Thatcher*

"It remains an unhappy fact that a victim of a miscarriage of justice is far more likely to overturn a conviction successfully if he or she can first attract the attention of a television company, rather than a lawyer." —*Chris Mullen*

Written by Rob Ritchie and directed by Mike Beckam, *Who Bombed Birmingham?* (Granada) is a dramatic "reconstruction" of the investigation by the journalists behind the *World in Action* broadcasts that publicized the case of the Birmingham Six and were widely credited for their eventual release. Opening titles announce that the six men remain in prison (at the time of airing).

The film flashes back and forth between reenactments of the 1974 bombings and the investigation started in 1985 by Chris Mullen (John Hurt), Ian McBride (Martin Shaw), and Charles Tremayne (Roger Allam). The journalists examine the evidence, interview the Birmingham Six, question police officers, and review the forensic testing. In 1974 Dr. Frank Skuse administers a Greiss test for explosives on samples taken from the hands of the suspects, claiming positive results for Hill and Power. A decade later independent chemists demonstrate that positive results could have been produced because the men had been playing cards. Flashbacks depict the Six being beaten and water tortured. Police photographs taken in 1974 show their faces covered in cuts and bruises.*

In Ken Loach's Hidden Agenda *(Helmdale Film, 1990) Sir Alec Nevin tells Kerrigan that the police "kicked the hell out of the murdering swine" to obtain confessions of the Birmingham Six.*

Tremayne points out that the confessions contain incorrect and conflicting accounts about the locations of the bombs. Mullen raises the point that "at the end of the day it's not where the bombs were planted but who put them there." To be convincing, their program must not only question the evidence used to convict the Six but identify the actual bombers.

Warned by one of the Six that if "you start messing around with the IRA, you're going to end up in a ditch," Mullen travels to Dublin, tracking down the IRA unit responsible for the bombing. An IRA contact arranges for him to meet with one of the bombers, who insists on remaining nameless. The IRA in Dublin is divided, Mullen discovers, between the leadership of the 1980s seeking a political settlement and the older volunteers of the 1970s who still view the conflict as an armed struggle. The unnamed IRA man expresses little sympathy for the Birmingham Six he knows to be innocent, stating, "There's a war going on. Innocent people get hurt." He supplies Mullen with information of how the IRA operates, discrediting the government's version of events. Questioned about the loss of life, the anonymous bomber blames the police for failing to clear the scene.

Joe Cahill, former Belfast Commander and Chief of Staff of the IRA, goes on camera to declare the Birmingham Six innocent but claims not to know the names of the actual bombers. A first *World in Action* program presents the Cahill interview, along with statements by chemists questioning the accuracy of the 1974 tests. The program, Mullen admits, "weakens the case" but does not exonerate the Six. Three days after the broadcast, Dr. Skuse suddenly retires at the age of fifty, raising questions about his forensic tests. Mullen continues his investigation, interviewing IRA volunteers who were threatened with prosecution for the pub bombings after the conviction of the Six. Following leads, he identifies the actual bombers.

Mullen's book *Error in Judgment* is published, generating more speculation about the case, leading MPs to raise questions in Parliament. In 1986 Mullen meets with representatives of the Home Office, who assure him the government is willing to "own up" to its mistakes. A second *World in Action* program about the case is aired.

In 1987 the government announces that the Court of Appeals will take up the case of the Birmingham Six based on new evidence presented by the two *World in Action* programs and Mullen's book.

During the second appeal Mullen meets with another IRA bomber and establishes the sequence of events of the Birmingham attacks, proving the innocence of the Six, who could never accurately state where the bombs had been placed.

The court dismisses the second appeal. Chris Mullen, now a Labor MP, challenges Margaret Thatcher in Parliament, arguing, "Nothing discredits our system of justice so much as the widespread notion that some mistakes are too big to own up to." In response, Thatcher defends the dismissal of the second appeal.

The film ends with credits listing the names and locations of the actual bombers, including Michael Christopher Anthony Hayes, who is credited with further acts of terrorism. Not only did the botched case convict innocent men, it allowed the guilty to continue bombing.

Who Bombed Birmingham? helped intensify public support for the Birmingham Six that led to their successful 1991 appeal and eventual release.

IN THE NAME OF THE FATHER (1993)

Jim Sheridan's *In the Name of the Father* (Hells Kitchen Productions) was one of the most anticipated and highly acclaimed motion pictures about the Troubles. It would ultimately receive nominations for seven Academy Awards and two BAFTA awards. Based on Gerry Conlon's autobiography *Proved Innocent*, the film, written by Jim Sheridan and Terry George, narrates the plight of the Guildford Four. Because the actual case aroused controversy and media attention, any motion picture based on the Conlon book, especially one produced by the Irish, was presumed to be an indictment of the British legal system and an apologia to the IRA.

As Ruth Barton chronicles in her book about Jim Sheridan, the British press condemned the film, in some instances before its release. Critics cited numerous inaccuracies — Gerry and Guiseppe did not share a prison cell as depicted, the Guildford Four and the Maguire family were not tried together, the alibi witness was not met in a park but at a hostel. The conflation of scenes and composite characters led some to compare the film to Oliver Stone's *JFK*. In addition to the script departing from the facts of the Conlon case, it offered, critics argued, a biased and simplistic view of the conflict in Northern Ireland, the opening Belfast scenes depicting an "occupied Ireland." The *Mail on Sunday* ran a column condemning the film unseen, predicting it would bring "a cash bonanza" to the IRA, especially from naïve Americans.[51]

The hostility towards Sheridan's film in contrast to *Who Bombed Birmingham?* is notable. At the time of the broadcast of the Grenada TV movie, the Birmingham Six were still in prison, the British courts having rejected their second appeal. By the time Sheridan produced his film, the Guildford Four had been released, so that even the British government validated his conclusions about his protagonists' innocence.

Sheridan's film tells two stories, one Irish, one British. The Irish story is familial; the British story is political. The Irish characters are naïve, apolitical victims of the British, humanized by their devotion to faith and family. The British characters depict the internal struggle of a state confronting terrorism.

In the opening scene two young British couples enter a pub, wave to friends and are blown up. The first principal character audiences see is Gareth Peirce (Emma Thompson), an English lawyer challenging the Conlons' wrongful convictions. The person who takes on injustice and ultimately wins is English, not Irish.

The triumph at the film's end is both a vindication for the Irish victims and the British system of justice. The crowds cheering for the freed Guilford Four are British, not Irish. Britain, audiences see, is capable of reform and redemption. The fact that no police officials were convicted for their actions is reserved for titles in the ending credits.

The IRA, however, is depicted throughout the film as brutal, cold, and sadistic. During the opening riot sequence an IRA leader stands atop a roof, surveying the confusion in the streets. He gives orders to "grab" Conlon and Danny. The IRA threaten to kneecap them, until Guiseppe intervenes. The family's support for Gerry's decision to emigrate to London is motivated more by a fear of the IRA than the British army. Gerry's friend Danny, who remains in Belfast, is shot in the knee and eventually executed by the IRA for committing crimes the occupying Brits would punish with a prison sentence.

The Conlons' innocence is demonstrated to viewers by a scene in which IRA leader Joe McAndrews (Don Baker) orders the pub bombed without warning. Arrested, he takes responsibility for the Guilford explosion. In contrast to the shiftless, drug-taking Gerry Conlon, McAndrews enters the prison with icy determination, leading a Jamaican prisoner to call him "the real thing."

Unlike the Conlons, who eat in their cells to avoid contact with hostile British inmates, McAndrews establishes himself by immediately confronting them head on. He assumes the

Pete Postlethwaite (left) as Giusseppe Conlon and Daniel Day-Lewis as Gerry Conlon in *In the Name of the Father* (1992).

role of protector, offering to help the Conlons. He explains that although he confessed to the bombing, the British cannot "afford to face" the truth of their wrongful conviction. "It's a war. You're one of its innocent victims," he tells Guiseppe. McAndrews shows no remorse for the bombing, arguing, "It was a military target, a soldier's pub."

Taking Gerry under his tutelage, McAndrews indoctrinates him in Republican ideology, explaining "how the Brits never left anywhere without a fight, how they had to be beaten out of every country they occupied." The prison, McAndrews argues, is "an extension of their system." The symbol of the system is the chief prison officer, Barker (John Benfield), who, though authoritarian, shows compassion to the ailing Guiseppe, bantering with him about his name and commenting about his campaign for release. In order to confront Barker, McAndrews needs to gain the support, or at least non-interference, of the British inmates. He earns the grudging cooperation of their leader, Ronnie Smalls (Frank Harper), by threatening to have his house blown up if any harm comes to any Irish prisoner. McAndrews leads all the prisoners in a protest, making demands. When Guiseppe warns that his actions will lead to violence, McAndrews agrees, claiming, "It's all they understand."

In a horrific scene, McAndrews sets Barker on fire. Transformed into a screaming torch, Barker's burning body illuminates the darkened prison. As Barker lies quivering on the floor, McAndrews watches with the cold detachment of a psychopath and orders the prisoners to stand their ground behind him. Led by Gerry Conlon, each prisoner rejects the IRA leader and returns to his cell.

In Sheridan's film, the Irish, wrongly convicted for IRA crimes, are brutalized and mistreated. The British, who wrongly convict them, are exposed and disgraced and shaken with guilt. The Ulster detective (Gerard McSorley) who coerced Gerry to confess by threatening to shoot Guiseppe is clearly distressed when he learns the Conlons are innocent. The IRA, however, show no remorse to anyone, British or Irish, who fail to accept their ideology. The Brits jail thieves; the IRA execute them. The Brits place murderous McAndrews in solitary confinement; the IRA set a benign prison official on fire. There is violence on both sides in Sheridan's film, and it is asymmetrical. The British arrest, mistreat, and imprison innocent Irish "suspects"; the IRA blow up and maim innocent Brits on general principle.

RUN OF THE COUNTRY (1995)

"Say nothing till you hear more."

Peter Yates' *Run of the Country* (Castle Rock Entertainment) depicts the IRA as an ongoing feature of Irish life operating with such secrecy that even local residents are unaware of their identity. The film relates a standard coming of age story about a teenager named Danny (Matt Keeslar) grappling with leaving home, an uncertain future, and a girlfriend's unintended pregnancy. Troubled by his mother's recent death and increasingly frustrated by his overbearing father (Albert Finney), Danny moves in with Coco Prunty (Anthony Brophy), a scruffy, long-haired ne'er-do-well. Prunty exudes the earthy clowning charm of a perpetual adolescent, living with his mother, dodging responsibility, engaging in petty crime, drinking, and making smutty remarks about sex.

When Danny discovers a map in a barn, Prunty tells him it is evidence that the SAS has the place under surveillance. Danny asks if they should tell anyone, but Prunty urges him to replace the map and keep quiet. "Say nothing till you hear more," he tells Danny. "Around here that's what you got to do."

Danny faces choices about his future — emigrating to America or attending university. Growing up on the border, Danny also speculates about joining the IRA, the way British teens might consider enlisting in the navy:

Danny: Did you ever think of joining the IRA?
Prunty: There are two kinds of men, fighters and talkers. I think I know the kind you are. Have a dream you can live for, lad. Not one that will put you in the grave.

When the barn later explodes, killing two British soldiers, the event is treated as a surprising but not unexpected aspect of life on the border. After Prunty is killed in a tractor accident, Danny goes to the wake and is stunned to find two masked IRA men in berets, dark glasses, and field jackets standing as an honor guard. When Danny expresses his surprise that Prunty was in the IRA, he is told, "Say nothing till you hear more."

Along with the audience, Danny realizes that Prunty's border antics were an elaborate deception, and that he was most likely responsible for the bombing. The IRA is so entrenched in border life that the least likely inhabitants are among its members.

The IRA Saves the Royals

In pointed contrast to the attack on Lord Holmes in *Patriot Games* (Paramount, 1992), two films — one American, the other British — depict the IRA operating parallel investigations with British intelligence to thwart an assassination plot against the royal family.

HENNESSY (1975)

"You have a friend, and you have a cause; which comes first?"

Don Sharp's *Hennessy* (American International) portrays the Irish Republican Army as sensible radicals. The title character, Niall Hennessy (Rod Steiger), is a World War II British Army veteran who operates a demolitions firm in Belfast. When his long-time friend, IRA commandant Sean Tobin (Eric Porter), asks him to supply gelignite for a "big job," Hennessy declines, claiming that he does not believe in violence. Tobin insists he only wants Niall to provide material, not participate in the organization. "Our support is growing," he tells Hennessy. "We'll get the British out of Ireland, but we have to keep up the pressure. Now, we need that stuff." Hennessy still refuses, claiming that he puts his wife and daughter first. Tobin remarks that for him, Ireland comes first.

Passing a demonstration, Hennessy's wife and daughter are accidentally gunned down by a British soldier. Tobin visits a grief-stricken Hennessy, assuring him that the IRA has the names of the soldiers involved in the shooting. Standing over the coffins of Hennessy's wife and daughter, Sean promises Niall justice: "A British life for every Irish martyr." His response is measured; he will execute the soldiers who killed an innocent mother and child.

In contrast to Tobin's "eye for an eye" retribution, a distraught Hennessy plots a mass murder-suicide to decapitate the British government. Wearing a high-explosive vest, he will enter the House of Lords during the opening ceremony and blow himself up, along with the Queen and Parliament.

The following day Hennessy flies to London. Informed that Niall left Belfast after inquiring about the opening of Parliament, Tobin suspects that Hennessy is plotting his own act of retaliation. He arranges for two IRA gunmen to meet Niall at the airport and demand to know his intentions. In a scuffle, Hennessy kills one gunman, forces the other out of the car, and escapes in their vehicle. In London, Hennessy stays with Kate Brooke (Lee Remick), widow of a childhood friend involved in the IRA.

Alarmed that Hennessy purchased a one-way ticket from Belfast, Special Branch Commander Rice (Trevor Howard) sees Niall as a potential threat. As Hennessy tours the House of Lords, examining the location of the opening ceremony, British investigators track down leads, beating suspects to no avail.

IRA Commandant Sean Tobin also wants to stop Hennessy's presumed plot, telling a young volunteer, "We're trying to get the British out of Ireland. Hennessy tries to kill the Queen of England, we'll have the whole bloody world on our backs, whether he's a member of the IRA or not. It will set us back fifty years." Tobin learns that Inspector Hollis, someone he fought in Belfast, is leading the hunt for Hennessy in London. Realizing that they must not only stop but "get rid of" Hennessy, senior IRA members ask Tobin, "You have a friend, and you have a cause; which comes first?" Recalling his words that he placed Ireland above everything else, Tobin orders that Hennessy must be "killed immediately on sight."

Pressuring an IRA cabbie in London, Hollis learns that Tobin has ordered his close friend to be killed, evidence that Hennessy is planning something serious enough to cause massive political fallout.

Tobin arrives in London, his IRA men spreading out in search of Hennessy. Tobin confronts Hollis, informing him that Hennessy intends to blow up Parliament and denying IRA involvement, stating, "If you don't find a way to stop him, we will." Hollis tells Rice he believes Tobin's story because he is "political" and can appreciate the consequences of an attack on the royal family.

The IRA and Special Branch carry out parallel manhunts for Hennessy. The IRA, however, are far more successful than Scotland Yard. They stake out Kate Brooke's flat, hoping to catch Hennessy, but he escapes in a shootout that kills one of Tobin's men.

Both Tobin and Hollis independently discover evidence of Hennessy's plan to impersonate MP Burgess to gain entrance to the ceremony. Though intent on killing him, Tobin admires Hennessy's scheme to go "behind enemy lines." He calls the Burgess home, and when Hennessy answers the phone, Tobin tells him to surrender to the IRA by leaving the house. He promises to take him back to Belfast peacefully. If he fails to surrender, they will "come in shooting." Hanging up the phone, Hennessy discovers Hollis being ushered into his room by a servant. Keeping his back to Hollis, Hennessy, assuming Burgess' identity, tells him that he has just been threatened by the IRA and needs police protection and an escort to the opening of Parliament in the morning. Leaving Burgess, Hollis spots the IRA arriving. Not realizing that Hennessy is impersonating Burgess, the Special Branch open fire on the Irishmen, who escape. Tobin assigns a sniper to take up position outside Parliament to fire on Hennessy. The next morning Hollis realizes that Tobin is targeting Burgess because he is, in fact, Hennessy. Hollis rushes to the Burgess home and finds the real MP bound and gagged.

Disguised as Burgess, Hennessy enters Parliament. As the Queen delivers her speech, Hennessy prepares to detonate his suicide vest.* Hollis edges through the crowd and immobilizes Hennessy with a karate chop. Hennessy is carried out but makes a break. Pursued by Hollis, Hennessy races outside, where an IRA man shoots him in the leg. Hollis fires a second shot, and Hennessy blows up in a mushroom cloud. The monarchy and Parliament are saved by the joint efforts of Special Branch and the Irish Republican Army.

MIDNIGHT MAN (1995)

"Peace. Of course I want peace. Just depends on whose terms."

Based on a novel by Jack Higgins, *Midnight Man* (VisionView/Carousel/Telescene) is a sequel to *On Dangerous Ground* (VisionView/Carousel/Telescene, 1996), which brings ex–IRA enforcer Sean Dillon (Rob Lowe) out of retirement in Luxembourg to assist British intelligence in locating his former comrade John Engel (Hannes Jaenicke).† General Ferguson (Kenneth Cranham) and Chief Inspector Hannah Bernstein (Deborah Moore) ask Dillon to help foil a royal assassination plot. Engel is involved, and Dillon understands why the British want his help, noting, "I'm the only one who thinks like him." He declines the request — until Ferguson reminds him, "I've got files on you that will keep you tied up in the courts or worse for years."

Engel has been hired by Mr. Tayi (Michael Sarrazin) to launch terrorist attacks that will "change British history" and "shake the world." Russian and Syrian conspirators will pay for a high level assassination they intend to blame on the IRA.

Engel persuades IRA armaments expert Danny Farmer to come out of retirement to create a special long-range rifle. Farmer, who promised the IRA never to work for outsiders, breaks his pledge to obtain money for his disabled daughter. Farmer devises a foolproof

*Hennessy *was little seen in England. The Parliament scenes included newsreel footage from the actual ceremony that was so carefully edited that it appeared the Queen was acting in a movie. The British review board rejected the film until a disclaimer was added at the beginning, announcing that the Royal Family did not participate in the production of the motion picture. Even with the change, major distributors chose to boycott the film.*
†*The film offers no explanation why IRA men would have American, let alone German, accents.*

rifle that uses a homing mechanism that will plant "the fingerprints of the IRA all over the hit."

To locate Farmer, Dillon contacts his old IRA comrade Frank Doyle (Oengus Mac-Namara). Dillon convinces trench-coated Doyle that the IRA will be blamed for the Syrian assassination of Prince Charles. Doyle has his men eliminate Farmer and informs Dillon that Engel will be using a long-range rifle. Engel's actual target is not Prince Charles but his sons, who will be awarded specially designed silver medals (secretly modified to act as homing devices for Engel's bullets) as part of a children's peace celebration.

Dressed in a police uniform, Engel takes his position on a rooftop overlooking the event. Princess Diana and the sons (never mentioned by name in the film) arrive at the ceremony. British security, in the form of armed police officers, surround the park. Now realizing that the target is not Prince Charles but his sons, Dillon takes charge. He orders a British squad to rush to the children's ceremony and calls Frank Doyle, telling him to get his men to the ceremony, promising him, "You will have no problems with the police." Dillon tells Ferguson to remind the police that Doyle is "on our side."

As Engel prepares to assassinate the royal sons, IRA men pour out of a van and take up positions. Spotting Engel atop a roof and realizing the peace dove medallions are homing devices, Doyle races to the ceremony. Barging past British security, he snatches the medals off the boys' lapels and holds them to his trench-coated chest as Engel fires, taking a bullet for the royal children.

The message of these films, if any, seems to echo that of *The Gentle Gunman* (Ealing Studios, 1952). The Irish Republican Army, no matter how violent, is at heart an organization that respects limits and, in a pinch, would protect British royalty against a murderous psychopath or alien conspiracy. Doyle's men will kill Farmer, but they will not allow alien terrorists to blame them for a royal assassination.

Moving Toward Peace

> The national territory consists of the whole island of Ireland, its islands and the territorial seas. — *Irish Constitution, 1937*

> ... A united Ireland shall be brought about only by peaceful means with the consent of a majority of the people, democratically expressed, in both jurisdictions of the island. — *Irish Constitution, 1998*

Early in the conflict, both the IRA and British intelligence realized one thing: They could not win. The IRA recognized that Britain was not going to abandon Northern Ireland, no matter how much damage they inflicted. The British recognized, in Peter Taylor's words, that "a military defeat in strict military terms of the Provisional IRA was simply not in the cards."[52] The IRA needed only a few hundred volunteers to wage a guerrilla war. No matter how many were incarcerated or killed, there were other Republicans willing to take their place.

Starting in the earliest days of the conflict, the IRA and British intelligence conducted secret meetings that would continue for over twenty-five years. In 1972 Gerry Adams met with Frank Steele of MI6. Adams and the IRA leadership attended clandestine talks in London. Throughout these discussions, the British tried to convince the IRA that it could not achieve its goal through violence, and that it should abandon the armed struggle for a political one. Again and again they challenged the IRA narrative about Northern Ireland. The conflict, London reiterated, was not between Republicans and the British but between Republicans and their fellow Irishmen, the Unionists. Beginning in 1975, MI6 met with the IRA Army Council, repeatedly telling the Republicans that Britain had no "selfish, strategic, or economic interest" in Northern Ireland. But as a democracy Britain could not abandon Ulster as long as the majority of its residents wished to maintain the Union.[53]

After years of torturous negotiations and ceasefires broken by acts of violence, the major parties in the conflict — Sinn Fein, Loyalists, Britain, and Ireland — reached a settlement. The Good Friday Agreement (also called the Belfast Agreement), signed on April 10, 1998, was not a traditional treaty in which adversaries accept a final resolution but an agreement to a process, leaving the future of Northern Ireland open. The main provision was that a change in the status of Northern Ireland would only occur following a majority vote in both Northern Ireland and the Republic, and that all parties would use "peaceful and democratic means" to pursue their goals. A Northern Ireland Assembly would be created with a power-sharing arrangement that would apportion ministries to the main political parties. Sinn Fein would now be part of the government of the Province. The IRA and Loyalist paramilitaries agreed to decommission their arms. The United Kingdom repealed its 1920 Government of Ireland Act; the Irish Republic revised its 1937 constitution, removing its claim to Northern Ireland. The Agreement was ratified by referendums in both Northern Ireland and the Irish Republic on May 23, 1998.

The IRA had fought for unification for thirty years but finally accepted that its armed struggle could not continue. Gabriel Megahey, who served seven years for attempting to buy American missiles for the IRA, told Peter Taylor he realized there was no other way forward but through a political process:

> Looking back on it, we were never going to beat the Brits entirely, ever.... We have to move politically to make it work. The Brits are never going to sail away into the sunlight like we all hoped. It's never going to happen. The facts of life are ... there is a Loyalist community, and there is a nationalist community. We've got to learn to live together. There is no way we're going to get a united Ireland overnight.... We have got to come to the middle and work out some solution.[54]

Not everyone in the Provos shared this point of view, and Adams had to delicately guide, cajole, and pressure volunteers to compromise and recast the armed struggled into an electoral one.

Although greeted by the mainstream press and much of the public as a grateful termination of a thirty-year conflict, the Agreement was not universally accepted. Traditional Republicans denounced it as a surrender, a death, a "crucifixion." For Anthony McIntyre, a former IRA member, the talks reminded him of the final passage in Orwell's *Animal Farm* in which the betrayed creatures looked from pig to man and back again, unable to tell them apart.[55] More pointedly, Bernadette Sands-McKevitt, spokesperson for the 32 County Sovereignty Movement, reminded Republicans what her brother Bobby Sands had died for:

> Bobby did not die for cross-border bodies with executive powers. He did not die for Nationalists to be equal British citizens within the Northern Ireland state. Bobby did not die for peace: he died for independence.[56]

Almost immediately, splinter IRA groups formed, dedicated to continuing the armed struggle until victory was achieved.

For staunch Loyalists the Agreement rewarded terrorism, granting political power and legitimacy to the killers of soldiers, police officers, and civilians. Kevin Myers condemned the Agreement as a "moral abyss" that legitimized terrorism:

> Sinn Fein–IRA was brought, bought and feted into the peace process ... while their rivals in the Catholic population, the constitutional SDLP, were all but frozen out.... No tea and biscuits for peaceful nationalists; only those who had blown the heart out of London, who had tortured people to death, who had been responsible for starting and continuing a savage war, got the hospitality, and in due course, a place in the power-sharing Executive.[57]

In 2010 a Real IRA arms cache was discovered in County Louth. Garda Commissioner Fachtna Murphy stated, "We continue to work closely with our colleagues in the PSNI [formerly the RUC] and in the security service to thwart the intent of a small group of people who want to inflict violence and pain on communities."[58]

THE BOXER (1997)

"What do you mean, innocent people?"

Although shot in Dublin, Jim Sheridan's *The Boxer* (Universal) recreates the ubiquitous features of Belfast — the omnipresent British soldiers, security cameras, surveillance helicopters, olive drab armored cars, dreary concrete public housing blocks, sandbagged checkpoints, and the Berlin Wall–like "peace line." The underground nature of the IRA in West Belfast is illustrated when its leader, Joe Hamill (Brian Cox), attends a wedding party held at a pub. To avoid surveillance helicopters monitoring the streets he enters an apartment and walks thorough a passageway cut through the walls of connecting units, allowing him to enter the bar unnoticed.

Arriving at the festivities, Hamill is applauded as a community leader, who bestows money on the bride of an imprisoned Republican. Hamill's leadership, however, is challenged by those who object to abandoning the armed struggle for political negotiations. Hamill is prepared to accept the terms of a ceasefire, a decision that does not sit well with one of his followers, Harry (Gerard McSorley), who orchestrates a violent car bombing in front of a butcher shop that inflicts only civilian casualties.

The conflict between Hamill and Harry becomes personal when Hamill's daughter Maggie (Emily Watson) takes up with her former boyfriend Danny Flynn (Daniel Day-Lewis). Danny, a former prizefighter, has been released from prison after serving fourteen years for IRA activities. Once free, Danny shuns contact with Republicans, arousing suspicion. Joe Hamill orders him to leave Belfast, but Flynn states he is determined to remain in his home town. He returns to the gym where he trained as a youth and discovers it transformed into a community center. His former trainer, Ike Weir (Ken Stott), disenchanted by the deaths of so many of his young protégés, is now an alcoholic. Danny wants to rebuild the boxing program and works with Ike to create a non-sectarian endeavor where Protestants and Catholics can engage in sports. Discovering a stockpile of explosives in a locked cabinet at the community center, Danny carries the gear through a night landscape of patrols and helicopters and throws it in the river, disposing of his IRA past. When the Semtex under the stage is found missing, Danny is in trouble and is warned by Maggie.

> Danny: I found some stuff. Semtex.
> Maggie: Where is it now?
> Danny: In the river.
> Maggie: Well, why didn't you give it back to my father?

Moving toward peace. Daniel Day-Lewis in *The Boxer* (1997).

Danny: So they can kill more innocent people?
Maggie: What do you mean, innocent people?

Harry is angered by the boxing club's nonsectarian status. Before a fight, Ike asks the audience for a moment of silence as he reads off the names and dates of death of young athletes killed in the Troubles. Ike introduces the parents of a dead Protestant boxer and asks the audience to welcome them back. People applaud, leading Harry to dismiss Ike as a "sentimental shite."

The RUC attempt to exploit Ike's diplomatic gesture by donating boxing supplies, an event filmed by the media. Danny warns Ike that they cannot accept gifts from the police, but Ike argues they need the equipment. TV reports of a police community relations officer handing out boxing gloves to poor Catholic boys inflame militant Republicans. Harry tells Joe Hamill that Danny is spreading dissent because his non-sectarian club is an affront to those who died and suffered for the Cause. In turn, Hamill accuses Harry of causing conflict:

Harry: I'm trying to hold it together in a district full of junkies, thieves and losers, while all he's trying to say is that everything will be all right if the Catholics and Protestants will hold hands together....
Joe: You know we're going to have to live with them sometime.
Harry: Who's "them"?
Joe: The Protestants, Harry. The other half of the population.
Harry: You're never going to be treated as an equal, Joe.
Joe: Not if we keep bombin' 'em, no.

Joe Hamill struggles to make peace with the British but has trouble obtaining concessions on the prisoner issue. Hamill confides to Maggie the challenges he faces trying to hold the IRA together. Harry, he tells her, insists on continuing the armed campaign because he feels "the only thing they respond to is violence." He wonders aloud if the British refuse to compromise on the prisoner issue because they want the ceasefire to fail.

Harry and his militants kill the RUC community relations officer with a car bomb outside a boxing match, causing a riot, instigating a return to violence and hatred, with children tossing petrol bombs. Maggie's son Liam burns the donated sporting equipment, setting the gym on fire.

Hamill is furious with Harry's violation of the ceasefire:

Joe: I'm in the middle of negotiations, and you let off this fuckin' bomb. What did you achieve by it? You achieved zero.
Harry: Zero?
Joe: Grow up. Stop livin' in the past and get your head into the future. You can keep goin.' You can split this organization in two. But you're gonna have to accept the consequences.
Harry: What consequences?
Joe: You know what fuckin' consequences.
Harry: You don't have all the guns, Joe. A lot of the active servicemen won't accept this peace bullshit anymore.
Joe: Are you threatening me?
Harry: You're going soft, Joe.... You had men in prison who starved themselves to death for you, Joe. Ten of them. Now you have Danny Boy Flynn wanderin' around the place making a mockery of everything you stood for, and you don't even see it. But a child can see it. A wee innocent child can see the truth.... Why don't you ask Liam why he burnt down the gym.

Aware of his tentative hold over the IRA, Hamill warns Maggie to leave Danny because he will be unable to protect him. Any illicit relationship in Hamill's family will jeopardize his standing in the Republican community.

Distressed by the loss of his gym, a drunken Ike Weir confronts Harry and his crew. "I know you, Harry!" he cries. "You're only interested in hurting people. That's your only pleasure." He charges that fourteen years ago Harry ran away and "left Danny to take the blame.... You killed this district, Harry! You killed the one thing you loved." Ike accuses Harry of killing his own son because "you filled his head full of shit! And you sent him out to die."

Ike is found dead, presumably murdered by Harry. Driving from Ike's funeral, Danny, Maggie, and Liam are stopped by Harry and his thugs. Danny is grabbed, bundled into a van, and taken to an underpass to be executed. An IRA gunman aims at Danny, then at the last moment turns and shoots Harry in the head. Like Lenihan at the end of Anderson's *Shake Hands with the Devil* (Pennebaker Productions/Troy Films, 1959), Harry, the hard man, must be killed by the peacemakers to end violence for violence's sake. Driving away, Maggie and Danny are stopped by police and asked their destination. Maggie says simply, "We're going home."

In this film, unlike Dermot and Neeve in *The Nightfighters*, the couple does not have to leave Ireland to find a new life. With Harry gone and peace on the horizon, the Catholic couple can build a future in West Belfast.

The Comedies

Beginning in the 1990s a number of comedies included IRA characters. With the decrease of violence, the IRA again became a feature of Irish life that could be held up to ridicule, used to provide a villain, or simply appear as part of the social landscape. In *Divorcing Jack* (Scala, 1998), newspaper reporter Dan Starkey (David Thewlis), chased by paramilitaries and the police, takes refuge with a nurse and part-time stripper, Lee Cooper (Rachel Griffiths). The violence of Northern Ireland becomes part of their post-coital banter:

> Lee: Did you hear the IRA have shot two Mormons in Derry?
> Starkey: Morons?
> Lee: Mormons. Apparently they were mistaken for plainclothes police. It's the short hair and superior smiles.

AN EVERLASTING PIECE (2000)

Barry Levinson's *An Everlasting Piece* (Dreamworks) takes place in Belfast "sometime in the '80s," showing streets patrolled by army Land Rovers and the peace walls separating Catholic and Protestant houses, one of which is enmeshed in a giant cage to shield against fire bombs. A Catholic barber, Colm (Barry McEvoy), gets a job in a mental institution working alongside a Protestant hairdresser named George (Brian F. O'Byrne). Among the deranged inmates is "the Scalper" (Billy Connolly), the only hairpiece merchant in Northern Ireland, who went mad and scalped four of his customers.

With the "baldies" of Northern Ireland lacking a source of wigs, Colm and George see an opportunity and form a hairpiece company called The Piece People. When a rival firm, Toupee or Not Toupee, opens up, the supplier establishes a contest to determine which business will receive an exclusive contract.

In their search for clients, Colm and George become lost on a country road. Stopping to study a map, their car is surrounded by an IRA patrol. The bald leader takes a wig in tribute, which he loses during a bombing attempt.

Arrested by the RUC, Colm and George are interrogated about the wig found at the crime scene. They identify the wig as a sample that is not supposed to be sold. Asked where their sample toupee is, they claim it has been misplaced. The police inspector decides to locate the bald IRA man and orders a round-up of anyone who might have purchased a wig. "We will unleash a wrath on the bald of this troubled land," he promises his officers. When he finds the bald man who matches the wig, he will have his IRA suspect.

Eager to shield their bald members from arrest, the IRA approach Colm, stating they want to purchase thirty hairpieces, supplying him with a list of dimensions and style orders. Sensitive to his Protestant partner, Colm does not wish to be the official wig purveyor to the IRA and makes a moral distinction. He will sell toupees to individuals but "not to an army." His girlfriend, Bronagh (Anna Friel), however, does not accept his compromise, seeing it as a betrayal of George. Colm argues, "There's two types of Catholics: the ones who support the RA and the ones who make excuses," and accuses her of being a Brit.

In the end the Piece People win the competition because Bronagh learns that the British army has a sensitive issue it is trying to hide from the public. Large numbers of young soldiers are losing their hair from stress. George and Colm get a government contract to provide wigs for the stricken servicemen. As a Catholic, Colm rationalizes the transaction as a gesture of forgiveness "to stop the cycle." He does, however, plan to charge the Brits double.

BREAKFAST ON PLUTO (2005)

Neil Jordan's *Breakfast on Pluto* (Pathe Pictures International) is a playful autobiographical film shot in thirty-six brief, titled chapters dramatizing the metamorphosis of

Patrick Braden (Cillian Murphy) from effeminate boy in Ireland to transsexual Patricia, or "Kitten" Braden, in London. The film opens and closes with a commentary by a pair of robins, their chirpings subtitled.

Abandoned as an infant, Patrick is estranged from his foster family, preferring to indulge in a rich fantasy life and explore his growing fascination with women's clothing and makeup. By his teens, Kitten is a swishy, curly-haired boy-girl in tight slacks and lipstick. Preoccupied with his sexual identity, glamour, men, and his long-lost mother, Kitten has no political awareness. The Troubles remain present in the background. In childhood, his friends play rebel with toy guns and a tricolor, pretending to execute a blindfolded playmate. Years later a boyhood friend, Irwin (Laurence Kinlan), marches in an IRA parade and later acts as a getaway driver for IRA gunmen who execute a Loyalist bomb maker.

Kitten falls in love with Billy Hatchett (Gavin Friday), who heads the band Billy Hatchett and the Mohawks. When the band crosses the border, a British soldier, referencing Bloody Sunday, remarks they have "thirteen less to deal with." After performing for a Republican Prisoners Welfare Association (where they are harassed offstage when Kitten appears as a squaw), Hatchett takes Kitten to a shabby trailer, which a gushing Kitten sees as "a house of dreams and longing." In cleaning the "house of dreams," Kitten discovers a weapons cache Hatchett keeps for the IRA.

After a bomb kills a retarded friend, Kitten returns from the funeral and decides it is time for "serious spring cleaning" and tosses the guns into a pond. When he finds the weapons missing, Billy is worried and tells Kitten, "You don't know what you're dealing with." Hatchett runs away, fearful of paramilitary retribution.

In a chapter titled "In Which I Get Out of My League," two IRA men arrive at the trailer to collect their weapons. Blaming Kitten for the lost arms, they prepare to execute him, then decide the "mental nancy boy" is not worth killing.

In London to search for his mother, Kitten becomes increasingly feminine, resorting to prostitution to earn a living. Irwin arrives in London with his pregnant girlfriend Charlie (Ruth Negga), who suspects her boyfriend is "up to something" that involves "secrets" and "revolution." Dressed in full drag, Kitten dances in a nightclub full of soldiers back from a tour in Northern Ireland. A bomb explodes, killing eleven patrons and wounding Kitten. Discovered to be both male and Irish, Kitten is immediately suspected as the bomber. London tabloids carry headlines about the "Killer Queen" and "Cross-dressing Killer." Convinced he planted the bomb, the police beat Kitten, who speaks incoherently about Pluto and the Milky Way. Enduring six days of interrogation, Kitten finds security with the police and is reluctant to leave when they release him. Working as a peep show girl, Kitten is visited by the priest who took her in. In a parody of the confession booth, Father Liam (Liam Neeson) tells Kitten where to find his mother. Dressing conservatively, Kitten now moves from drag queen to woman, and, posing as a survey taker, calls on his mother and learns about her new life and family. Charlie writes Kitten that she was arrested on a drug charge. To win her release, Irwin informed on the IRA and was executed in reprisal. Kitten returns to Ireland to stay with Father Liam, who has taken in the grieving Charlie. Offended by the odd couple staying with Father Liam, townspeople burn the church. Kitten and Charlie decide to return to the "welfare state" of Britain. With the robins fluttering over them and quoting Oscar Wilde, Kitten and Charlie leave the hospital, pushing the pram holding their newborn.

Kitten can transform herself from male to female and leave Ireland for Britain, but can never escape the influence of the IRA.

Bookends: The Docudramas

A pair of television movies explore in-depth two of the most notorious incidents of the Troubles: the controversial killing of thirteen demonstrators by British paratroopers in 1972 and the Real IRA bombing in Omagh in 1998 that killed twenty-nine civilians. Paul Greengrass, who wrote both films, conducted extensive research to create historically accurate dramas.

BLOODY SUNDAY (2002)
"We've got to teach these people a lesson."

Paul Greengrass' *Bloody Sunday* (Granada Films) recounts the events of January 30, 1972. Shot with handheld cameras and natural lighting, with long blackouts between scenes, the film has the choppy look of a documentary assembled from newsreel footage. The lighting is dark, so that action is sometimes obscured. The camera jerks awkwardly, often missing dramatic events, which are blocked by buildings and people. Action sequences were filmed by cameramen on the run. When gunfire erupts, the camera ducks behind barricades or buildings. The death of victims is shot at a distance, without close-ups. In many scenes background conversations and ringing telephones render the dialogue indistinct. The result is an urgent realism that captures the chaos of battle.

The film cuts back and forth between Ivan Cooper (James Nesbitt), a Protestant Member of Parliament who insists on staging a banned civil rights march, and British officers and paratroopers intent on arresting "hooligans." Cooper urges people to protest against internment without trial while dissuading them from engaging in violence. Moving through the streets and passing out handbills, he breaks up confrontations between soldiers and young Catholics, repeatedly cautioning young men to "walk away." At the outset of the march Cooper tells a supporter he feels "like Martin Luther King."

As the marchers assemble, Cooper discovers the IRA "sniffing about" on the edge of the crowd. Restless young men are shown moving around, directed by middle-aged handlers sitting in a car. When Cooper asks one of the leaders if they are "keeping the guns away," he is told, "That's no concern of yours." Cooper pleads that he only wants a peaceful march for civil rights, but the IRA view him with contempt, their leader telling him, "Ivan, it's all very well for you sitting pretty with your wee Westminster paycheck every week. Marching's not going to solve this thing." In response, Cooper retorts, "Watch us."

As Cooper's march proceeds, the British Army outlines a plan to lift two hundred "hooligans." Expecting an IRA "contribution" to the protest, they anticipate using force. While Cooper directs the demonstration to turn right at an intersection, young marchers break off and throw stones at British troops. As Cooper tries to maintain order, events spin out of control. Water cannons and tear gas are loosed on the crowd. Soldiers shoot rubber bullets, then begin firing live rounds. In the confusion of gunshots, British paratroopers snipe at "terrorists," reporting to headquarters that they are engaged in a "fire fight." The film balances claims made by both sides after the event. Paratroopers are shown taking aim at unarmed civilians fleeing the march, in one case standing over and firing at a wounded victim lying on the ground. In one scene a Catholic brandishes a rifle, but it is taken away from him. In another a civilian fires a few shots from a handgun before being stopped by fellow Catholics. Provos remove weapons from the trunk of a car and duck into a building. The overall impression is confusion rather than brutality, showing the tragic consequences

Docudrama of the Troubles: *Bloody Sunday* (2002).

of assigning soldiers trained for combat the job of containing a civil disturbance with automatic weapons.

After the demonstration, an emotionally drained Cooper visits a hospital crowded with wounded and is shaken when he discovers six bodies left lying in a blood-smeared hallway. Cooper moves throughout a waiting room, embracing weeping family members of the victims. Reenacting an actual interview from 1972, an army officer tells a reporter the hooligans fired first, and paratroopers fired a total of three rounds in response. Behind the scenes, panicked soldiers scramble to "get their stories straight." Officers at the scene are shocked at the number of army rounds fired and become frustrated when a search reveals no dropped weapons or spent shell casings to indicate that the paratroopers had been fired at. At British army headquarters Major General Ford (Tim Pigott-Smith) congratulates his staff for behaving with "restraint and great professionalism," promising them that "the war against the IRA will go on."

The film ends with a distressed Cooper conducting an impromptu press conference. Addressing reporters, he announces that twenty-seven people had been shot and thirteen killed. He calls the day's events a "moment of truth and a moment of shame," then bitterly addresses the British government:

> I just want to say this to the British government. You know what you've just done, don't ya? You've destroyed the civil rights movement. And you've given the IRA the biggest victory it will ever have. All over this city tonight, young men ... boys will be joining the IRA, and you will reap a whirlwind.

Asked by a reporter what message he would give to those young volunteers, Cooper sadly admits, "I feel very ill-equipped to give any preaching to them after today."

Though produced as a Granada TV movie, *Bloody Sunday* was shown at the Sundance Film Festival, winning an Audience Award and gaining international attention. The film, James Nesbitt, and Paul Greengrass received several awards and nominations from film festivals in Stockholm, Ghent, Rio de Janeiro, and Berlin. The movie was nominated for several BAFTA TV Awards, winning one for photography and lighting. James Nesbitt and David Greengrass received British Independent Film Awards.

Bloody Sunday overshadowed a TV movie aired days later on Channel 4. *Sunday* (Sunday Productions) juxtaposed reactions of the British military and the Derry community to the day's events. Greengrass's film was criticized for diminishing the victims by showing them as anonymous forms lying on the ground, in contrast to its heroic portrayal of Ivan Cooper. Jimmy McGovern's *Sunday* focused on the families, with no actor credited for playing Ivan Cooper.

OMAGH (2004)

"We will not go away. We will not be quiet. We will not be forgotten."

As he was completing *Bloody Sunday*, Paul Greengrass contacted Michael Gallagher, chair of the Omagh Support and Self Help Group, to make a film about the organization's struggle for justice following the August 15, 1998, bombing that killed twenty-nine people. "It was important for me, having made the first film, to bookend the conflict with his one," Greengrass stated. The filmmakers worked with the families, allowing them to read the scripts to see how they would be portrayed. Filming was conducted in Dublin in 2003. Greengrass believed that shooting in Omagh just five years after the bombing would be insensitive, particularly any recreation of the fatal explosion. The town of Navan, outside Dublin, was used for exterior scenes. Speaking of the film, Michael Gallagher stated, "I would like to think *Omagh* shows that in the midst of evil and wickedness, ordinary people from a wide variety of backgrounds have come together in the fight for truth and justice."[59] *Omagh* (Channel 4) was written by Paul Greengrass and directed by Pete Travis. Gerard McSorley* was cast as Michael Gallagher, a garage owner who emerges as head of a family support group after his son is killed in the IRA bombing.

Omagh opens with the Real IRA assembling a bomb and placing it in the trunk of an automobile. The next scene depicts the shops opening on Market Street in the town of Omagh. Michael Gallagher and his son Aidan (Paul Kelly) work on a car in their garage. Aidan leaves to run an errand in town. The Real IRA park their car on a crowded street and telephone an inaccurate warning. The police mistakenly clear the wrong area, unknowingly directing shoppers toward the car bomb.

Following the explosion, Gallagher frantically looks for his son among the survivors and the injured. The hospital scenes of confusion, bloodied victims, and anxious relatives mirror those of *Bloody Sunday*. Gallagher moves through a crowded waiting room, asking doctors and nurses, and checking lists in an agonizing search until he learns that Aidan has been killed.

Two months later Gallagher attends a meeting of family members who are frustrated by the lack of police action. Thirty-eight suspects have been arrested and released. The gathering degenerates into a shouting match until Gallagher rises and, speaking with a soft, awkward dignity, reminds the families that the room contains Catholics, Protestants, Pres-

*McSorley was born in Omagh, County Tyrone, in 1950.

(Left to right) Pauline Hutton, Gerard McSorley and Michele Forbes in *Omagh* (2004).

byterians, and a Mormon. "We're not going to get anywhere," he tells the families, "unless we do it together."

Elected chairman of the group, Gallagher meets with officials who promise they are making progress on the investigation. Dissatisfied with their officious assurances, Gallagher begins a campaign to demand greater police effort on the case. The families, lacking political experience and contacts, are unsure which avenue to pursue. Taking note of the O. J. Simpson civil suit, an English member of the group, Victor Barker (Stuart Graham) recommends they sue the Real IRA for damages because they have "money coming in from America." A break in their case comes when an anonymous caller provides Gallagher with the names of the men involved in the bombing.

Gallagher meets with Gerry Adams (Jonathan Ryan), who condemns the bombing as a "dreadful and appalling atrocity," assuring Gallagher that the Real IRA "are as much our enemies as they are yours." He extends his sympathies and offers to help "if it's possible," but he will not admit knowing anyone on the list of names Gallagher shows him. Urged to help the police by the families, Adams declines because any cooperation with the RUC would be unacceptable to rank and file Republicans. Focusing on the fragility of the peace process, Adams urges the group "to put the past behind us." Speaking quietly, Gallagher challenges Adams' suggestion:

> Mr. Adams, my brother was murdered by an IRA gunman in 1984. No witnesses came forward for that either. So they got away. So I agree with you — let's put the past behind us. That was my brother then. But this is my son now. The war is supposed to be over. You say you want to build a new Northern Ireland. A peaceful Northern Ireland. But how can we build a peaceful Northern Ireland unless you help bring his killers to justice?

Adams expresses his sympathies but argues that assisting the RUC will "alienate hard-liners in our community — the very people we have got to keep on board.... This is the reality we face." Adams simply cannot or will not cooperate with the investigation.

Gallagher is equally disappointed by the British, who fail to respond to Victor Barker's pleas to Tony Blair. He becomes the point man for the group's frustration, fielding phone calls and dealing with the press. Gallagher is bewildered and angered at the lack of government action. The RUC, the IRA, the Garda, and the British government appear uniformly determined to look the other way and allow the Omagh bombers to remain free to avoid jeopardizing the peace process.

After a British television program claims that police on both sides of the border know the identities of the bombers but decline to press charges, Gallagher starts his own investigation. He meets with Kevin Fulton, a thirteen year veteran of the IRA, who recognizes the list of names as former Provos who left the organization after the Good Friday Agreement to form the Real IRA and continue the armed struggle. Fulton tells Gallagher he is asking the wrong question. Fulton admits that he had been a mole working for the RUC and the British and that he had given them advance warning about the Omagh bombing. Yet there were no checkpoints around the city or soldiers on the streets to indicate the government took any action to prevent the attack. Fulton gives Gallagher a contact in the Republic who arranges a meeting with John White (Brendan Coyle) of the Garda's National Surveillance Unit. White tells Gallagher he had a source in the Real IRA and knew that a car with a bomb was going to cross the border into the North. His superiors, he tells Gallagher, decided to "let it go." Gallagher is incredulous, asking why the Garda would deliberately allow the IRA to proceed with a bombing. White presumes they wanted to protect an informant or believed a large bomb would discredit the Real IRA. They did not think, he tells Gallagher, that anyone would be killed. "Maybe," he admits, "they didn't think it through." White tells him there will not be any prosecutions. The government, he believes, made a deal with the Real IRA not to charge anyone for the Omagh bombing in return for a ceasefire. "You're in the way of the Peace Process, Michael. And nothing ... nothing is going to be allowed to do that."

The RUC Chief Constable briefs the families, discounting allegations made in the press, assuring the support group that Fulton was simply making up stories for money. Six months later the Police Ombudsman delivers a report on the Omagh investigation, detailing the missed warnings and the failure to take precautions and concluding that the families have been let down by "defective leadership, poor judgment, and a lack of urgency" so that any chance of prosecuting the bombers has been "significantly reduced."

Leaving the meeting, Gallagher addresses the media. Speaking on behalf of all victims of terrorism, he tells reporters, "We will not go away. We will not be quiet. We will not be forgotten."

In 2011, Ronan Kerr, a twenty-five-year-old Roman Catholic police officer, was killed after a bomb exploded under his car outside his home in Omagh. The killing was condemned by Peter King, Gerry Adams, Martin McGuinness, and Hillary Clinton. Taoiseach Enda Kenny and Northern Ireland First Minister Peter Robinson attended his funeral. The presence of the Protestant Robinson at a Catholic service was seen as a "significant step in the dismantling of community barriers."[60] Gerry Adams urged Catholics to continue to join the police force, once viewed as the intractable enemy of the IRA.

5

The Classics

The Informer and *Odd Man Out*

The two classic films most commonly associated with the Irish Republican Army—John Ford's *The Informer* (RKO, 1935) and Carol Reed's *Odd Man Out* (Two Cities Films, 1947)—do not actually name the IRA and only casually touch on the underlying conflict. Both are largely apolitical melodramas that use the backdrop of the Irish "Troubles" to present allegorical morality tales that avoid controversy and achieve universal appeal. Both are based on popular novels, which themselves present jaundiced views of Irish nationalism and its adherents. In essence, both movies are dark crime thrillers that follow the last hours of an impaired and isolated hero hunted down in the cold wet streets of a city at night. Ford's Gypo, wanted for betraying a murderer to the police, goes on a drunken romp through Dublin that could just as easily occur in Prohibition-era Chicago. Reed's Johnny, wounded during a robbery, endures an anguished journey through the alleys of Belfast that visually presages Harry Lime's shadowy flight through the sewers of Vienna in his 1949 film *The Third Man*.

Both protagonists make poor advocates for ideological causes. Gypo is a loutish drunk whose motivations are animalistic—money, liquor, food, warmth, and sex. He informs on a comrade simply for the money. His goal of rejoining the unnamed organization is wholly personal and apolitical. He hungers to be reinstated to regain security, status, and a sense of belonging. Johnny, a rebel leader, is so weakened by the loss of blood that he becomes disoriented and delirious. Incapable of articulating any arguments, he becomes an abstract Everyman figure suffering an existential conflict pitting the survival of a hunted, alienated individual against the uniformed forces of impersonal authority. To further depoliticize the films, both open with titles that shift the focus away from social conflict to personal tragedy and end with their dying protagonists assuming Christ-like poses. The final scenes in both films are dramatic portrayals of lapsed Catholics rediscovering their lost faith.

The popularity of these films, one American and the other British, lay in their ability to appeal to an international audience. *The Informer*, shot in seventeen days for less than a quarter million dollars, became RKO's highest grossing film in 1935.[1] *The New York Times* praised Ford's film as a masterpiece. Nominated for six Academy Awards in 1936, *The Informer* received awards for Best Actor, Best Director, Best Screenplay, and Best Musical Score.[2] It also earned a New York Film Critics Circle Award for Best Film and Best Director. *Odd Man Out* was well-received in Britain and the United States and became one of the most successful motion pictures ever shown in South America. Named as the best British film of 1947 by the *British Film Yearbook*, *Odd Man Out* received the British Academy Film Award for Best British Film and was nominated for an Academy Award for editing.

The *Daily Express* chose James Mason as the best actor of the year based on his performance. The film earned Carol Reed a Golden Lion nomination at the Venice Film Festival
in 1947.[3]*

Both these films portray the IRA (called only the "Organization" in the scripts) as
barely more than an underworld gang whose principal activities are robbery, murder, and
vigilante reprisals. The cause of Irish nationalism is largely absent, particularly in *Odd Man
Out*. The films' avoidance of politics was greatly influenced not only by a studio desire to
achieve universality but to circumvent controversy and pass the censors.

In the 1930s and 1940s the British Board of Film Censors controlled film distribution
in the lucrative British and Commonwealth markets, and Hollywood was sensitive to its
concerns, often submitting shooting scripts with British themes to identify and forestall
potential objections that might jeopardize a film's acceptance in much of the English speaking
world.[4] Joseph Breen, head of the Motion Picture Producers and Distributors of America,
supplied British censors with the script of *The Informer*. The British Board of Film Censors
requested numerous changes to excise references to the Anglo-Irish conflict. Again and
again the word "Ireland" itself was marked for deletion.[5] With an eye to the American market, British censors contacted Joseph Breen a decade later, who identified potentially offensive
dialogue in *Odd Man Out* and pointed out that the novel's final scene, involving a murder-
suicide, violated Hollywood's Production Code.[6] The symbiotic relationship between British
and American censors ensured that major motion pictures about Ireland would avoid politics.
Their reception in Ireland itself, a nation of four million, was of little importance to filmmakers in either Britain or Hollywood.

In both films Ireland is depicted as a troubled island where the possibility of freedom
and happiness for the protagonist lies not in revolution, negotiation, political reform, or
an end to foreign occupation, but emigration. Both films differ from the original novels by
including the theme of escape by ship. In O'Flaherty's and Green's stories, the wounded
protagonists remain trapped in a tightening maze with no possibility of flight. Both films,
however, include a female character seeking to rescue the hunted protagonist and take him
away from Ireland to build a new life overseas. In these films romance, no matter how
tainted, transcends politics.

THE INFORMER (1935)

"I didn't know what I was doing."—*Gypo Nolan*

The Informer (RKO) is based on the Liam O'Flaherty novel published a decade earlier.
Set in Dublin in the early 1920s, O'Flaherty's story follows the fate of Gypo Nolan, a boorish
and impoverished outcast who betrays Francis McPhillip, a fellow member of an unnamed
"revolutionary organization," for a twenty pound reward. Gypo's motives are purely self-
serving. He is destitute, hungry, friendless, and despondent, having been ousted from the
organization for failing to carry out an execution. Armed with Gypo's information, the
police corner McPhillip in his father's house and kill him as he attempts to flee. Confused,
guilt-stricken, fearful, and unable to assemble a plan of action, Gypo lumbers through the
back streets of Dublin with his sudden bounty, drinking and spending wildly. He gives a

---

*The universality of the film is demonstrated by The Lost Man, *a 1969 remake in which Sidney Poitier plays
a black militant hiding from the police after being wounded in a robbery to seize money to aid imprisoned comrades.*

pound note to a blind man and treats a crowd to fish and chips. Visiting a brothel, he gives three pounds to an Englishwoman seeking to return to Britain. Suspicious of Nolan's behavior, the organization seizes Gypo and places him on trial. He childishly attempts to cast blame on another and rationalize his unexplained wealth. Convicted and sentenced to death, Gypo is placed in a cell. Gypo escapes but is gunned down by the organization. He stumbles into a church where he discovers McPhillip's grieving mother sitting in a pew. The dying Nolan confesses to her that he informed on her son and begs her forgiveness. McPhillip's grieving mother forgives Gypo, telling him, "Ye didn't know what ye were doin'."[7]

The novel ends with Gypo Nolan achieving final peace and salvation:

> He stood up straight, in all the majesty of his giant stature, towering over all, erect and majestic, with his limbs like pillars, looking toward the altar.
> He cried out in a loud voice:
> "Frankie, yer mother has forgiven me."
> Then with a gurgling sound he fell forward on his face. His hat rolled off. Blood gushed from his mouth. He stretched out his limbs in the shape of a cross. He shivered and lay still.[8]

In 1934 Liam O'Flaherty arrived in New York for a national speaking tour. That July he was in Hollywood where he secured a two-week writing assignment at Paramount studios.[9] Although *The Informer* had been the subject of a silent film shot in Britain in 1929, the major Hollywood studios were uninterested in producing an American version. John Ford cautioned O'Flaherty that the project would face opposition because of the content of the book. In addition to the political elements that might limit the movie's marketability, the novel contained scenes of brothels and included the character of Katie Fox, a drug-addicted prostitute that would be challenging to film in an era of intensified censorship. Paramount, Fox, MGM, and Warner Brothers all rejected *The Informer*.[10]

John Ford, however, was determined to make the picture. Born John Feeney, the son of an Irish immigrant, he felt a deep personal connection to O'Flaherty's story. In 1921 Ford had traveled to Ireland to learn about the Irish revolution first-hand. The ship from New York landed in Liverpool, and the young director found himself sailing across the Irish Sea on the same boat as Michael Collins and Arthur Griffith, returning with British offers to Dail Eireann. Ford traveled to his ancestral hometown in Galway, recording his observations in letters to his wife:

> Spiddal is all shot to pieces. Most of the houses have been burned down by the Black and Tans and all the young men had been hiding in the hills.... Tell Dad that the Thornton house is entirely burned down and old Mrs. Thornton was living with Uncle Ned's widow while his sons were away..."[11]

This trip had a profound impact on Ford, who connected with both his family and the nation of Ireland in its struggle for independence. His cousin Martin Feeney was an IRA leader wanted by the Black and Tans. Like the character Francis McPhillip in O'Flaherty's novel, Martin Feeney was a man with a price on his head. According to Feeney, his American cousin was repeatedly stopped by the Black and Tans and once badly roughed up. Eager to rid themselves of a Hollywood moviemaker, the British detained John Ford, placed him on a ship bound for England, and warned him that he would be imprisoned if he returned to Ireland.[12]

Film rights for *The Informer* were eventually purchased by RKO for the modest sum of $2,500.[13] With a limited budget that excluded major stars, large sets, or location shooting, Ford decided to focus on the "look" and "feel" of a more intimate film. Great attention was paid to lighting, camera angles, and double exposures. Fog, according to Ford's grandson, would be a critical image in the film, serving "as a visual metaphor for both the city and for the psychological fog inside Gypo Nolan's head."[14] Ford labored on the script with Dudley Nichols, dictating scenes, correcting drafts, and continually hectoring Nichols for his lack of understanding of the Irish.[15]

The final script, the fog, low camera angles, and Max Steiner's haunting score worked to make *The Informer* a memorable film. Ford's plot deletes much of the book's political commentary, focusing on developing the character of Gypo Nolan. Like O'Flaherty's character, the film's Gypo is a simplistic man-child, his limited intelligence dulled by drink. He is a brainless giant. In the fish and chips scene Victor McLaglen stands heads and shoulders over the crowd on the pavement and is so tall that his head strikes a low-hanging sign. McLaglen contorts his face in exaggerated childlike expressions of confusion, guilt, and surprise. Trapped in lies or inconsistencies during his trial, he snaps his fingers and says, "I jes' remembered" and lamely invents improbable tales and excuses. Not only is he incapable of formulating a plan, he is unable to avoid immediate gratifications, leading him to betray himself by openly squandering his money. Like Steinbeck's Lenny Small, Ford's Gypo evokes sympathy because of his limitations.

The Informer opens with the hulking silhouette of flat-capped Gypo Nolan, hands in pockets, lurching through fogbound streets as Black and Tans march past with rifles. Two titles appear, the first establishing the time and place of the drama:

> A certain night
> in strife-torn
> Dublin — 1922

The second indicates the direction of the film, framing the plot in moral rather political terms:

> "Then Judas repented
> himself— and cast down
> the thirty pieces of
> silver — and departed"

Gypo Nolan (Victor McLaglen) strolls down a street pasted with torn posters and discovers one announcing that Francis McPhillip is wanted for murder. A brief flashback shows Nolan and McPhillip, dressed in IRA trench coats with rifles slung over their shoulders, drinking in a pub. Nolan is fixated on the headline announcing the twenty pound reward. He tears the poster from the wall and throws it into the street. The windblown poster follows him, clinging to his leg as if to show Gypo's inability to dismiss temptation. Spotting the streetwalker Katie leaning against a lamp post, Gypo tosses aside a potential customer. This act of protective gallantry is met with exasperation by an exhausted Katie, who explains she is hungry and cannot pay her room rent. She calls Gypo her "only one" and mourns their inability to "escape." Looking at a large sign advertising a steamship company's ten pound fare to America, Katie muses, "Twenty pounds and the world is ours." The mention of "twenty pounds" enrages Gypo, who grabs her, asking why she mentioned that amount. Katie leaves in a huff, seeking a man who can provide her money for a room.

When Frankie meets Gypo in an eating house, Gypo visualizes the figure of £20 as a subtitle under his face. Famished, Gypo sits with knife and fork in his heavy fists, complaining that he is an impoverished outcast without prospects. Frankie reminds Gypo they had once been an active team in the organization, with Gypo providing the muscle while

Victor McLaglen in *The Informer* (1935).

he supplied the intelligence. "Man alive," he tells Gypo, "I'm your brain." After Frankie leaves for his father's house, Gypo recalls the £20 wanted poster and the sign advertising £10 tickets to America.

Gypo enters a police station and tells the officers where they can find Frankie McPhillip. Once word reaches the police station that McPhillip is dead, an officer slides the twenty pounds across the table to Gypo with a stick. After taking the tainted money, Gypo feels cursed. As he leaves the rear of the police station, he spots a potential witness and seizes him, only to discover that the man is blind. Haunted by memories of the wanted poster, Gypo stops for a drink, paying the barman with a pound note, immediately arousing suspicion. Sitting in the pub, he whispers to himself, "I've got to have a plan." But having betrayed McPhillip, his brain, Gypo is lost, left with only his apelike strength and mounting guilt. Spotting Gypo through the window, Katie enters the pub and declares her love for him. Gypo mutters that he "did it for her," hinting at escape to America. When the barman hands Gypo his change, Katie asks the agitated Gypo where he got so much money. At first he says he robbed a church, then changes his story, stating that he rolled a drunken sailor from an American ship. When Katie says she will keep his secret, Gypo panics when she mentions the word "informer."

As Katie leads Gypo from the pub, the blind man passes them and Gypo hands him a pound note. Remembering that he should pay his respects to his fallen comrade, Gypo leaves Katie and goes to the McPhillip home. Encountering Frankie's grieving mother, he blurts out condolences so loudly that he arouses suspicion. Rising to his feet, he drops a number of coins. As members of the organization watch, Gypo gathers his money from the floor and leaves.

At the unnamed organization's headquarters, Gypo professes his loyalty to commandant Dan Gallagher (Preston Foster) and complains, "I got no clothes. I got no money. I got nothing!" Gallagher offers Gypo a "fair deal," promising to reinstate him if he discovers the man who betrayed Frankie McPhillip. Gypo becomes excited, pours several drinks in celebration, then names Mulligan as the informer, boozily concocting a lame story involving Frankie and Mulligan's sister. Gypo claims he spotted Mulligan entering the headquarters of the Black and Tans at half past six. After Gypo leaves, Gallagher expresses doubts about the Mulligan story and is determined to identify McPhillip's informer, stating, "One traitor can destroy an army." He assigns Bartly Mulholland (Joe Sawyer) to follow Gypo. As in the rest of the film, there is no explanation for Gallagher's army or its purpose.

Elated at the prospect of regaining his status in the organization, Gypo goes on a spree, drinking and engaging in horseplay, knocking down a policeman with one punch. He buys fish and chips for a crowd, paying with a pair of pound notes, savoring his status as benefactor of the poor. Soon he boasts he will be "the cock of the walk." Through a window, Bartly watches Gypo's largesse with suspicion.

Gypo stumbles off with a chum, seeking Katie. Passing the sign announcing tickets to America, he looks through the window at a model ship and imagines himself and Katie in evening dress on the deck of an ocean liner. Clutching his dwindling bundle of pound notes, Gypo enters a brothel full of well-dressed men. Buying a round of drinks, Gypo tosses pound notes in celebration, reducing the funds needed to reach America. He gives a prostitute seeking passage back to Britain five pounds. When the madam demands additional money for her board and lodging, Gypo pays her four pounds.

Bartly continues to shadow Gypo, adding up the money he has been spending and enters the brothel to escort him to the commandant Gallagher. En route they are stopped by Katie. A drunken Gypo repeatedly mentions the phrase "twenty pounds" and hands her the remainder of his money before being led away.

Brought to a dungeon-like cellar to stand trial, Gypo is drunk, wild, and incoherent. Seated next to an ailing Mulligan, Gypo greets him and tells him he is so sick he should be in bed, forgetting that he had named the frail man as McPhillip's informer. Blaming his lapse of memory on drink, Gypo rises, points an accusing finger at the quaking Mulligan, and denounces him as the informer. Mulligan provides a convincing alibi, stating that the sister McPhillip had supposedly got into trouble has been living in Boston for twenty-eight years.

Trapped in a lie, Gypo blabbers, "I don't know what I'm doing." Gallagher presses him to account for his actions and his sudden wealth, counting out each unexplained pound, starting with one given to the blind man. Where, Gallagher asks, did he obtain the twenty pounds? Gypo covers his face with his hands and repeatedly states, "I didn't know what I was doing." Crying, he turns to his accusers, asking them, "Tell me why I did it?"

Gypo is led to an improvised cell to await execution. Using his brute strength, he crashes through the ceiling and races outside into streets patrolled by Black and Tans. Haunted by memories of Frankie's wanted poster, Gypo runs to Katie's room and confesses that he informed on Frankie for her.

After Gypo falls asleep before her fireplace, Katie goes to Gallagher and begs him to spare Gypo's life. She blames herself for putting the idea into his head. Gypo, she claims, "did not know what he was doing." Gallagher sees Gypo as a threat to the organization that must be eliminated. When Gallagher leaves to find Gypo, Katie again begs for Gypo's life, asserting once more that he did not know what he was doing.

Hearing whispers outside Katie's door, Gypo rises and tackles the men trying to capture him and races outside where Bartly shoots him several times. Stumbling across the street, he enters a church, encounters Frankie's grieving mother, and quietly tells her that he informed on her son. As in the novel, Frankie's mother forgives Gypo, twice telling him, "You didn't know what you were doing." Standing up before a life size crucifix, Gypo stretches out with arms in a Christ-like position and cries, "Frankie, Frankie, your mother forgives me!" and collapses out of sight.

For all its drama and attention to detail, *The Informer* provides audiences with no understanding of the Irish Troubles or the goal of the unnamed organization. Gallagher justifies eradicating Gypo because he is a threat to the army and endangers the lives of many others, but there is no explanation of what the organization is attempting to accomplish. The group has more in common with a criminal mob. The wanted poster announces that McPhillip is "wanted for murder," not treason or even terrorism. Gypo is gunned down in the streets not unlike a character in an American gangster film.

The success of *The Informer* lay in part in the fact that, though set in Dublin in 1922, its gray images of poverty, hunger, and desperation resonated deeply with Depression-era audiences. Gypo's blind ignorance, his inability to justify or explain his actions at the end, becomes an excuse and a sign of innocence. He is the large powerful man trapped by forces he cannot understand, driven by circumstances to commit acts he cannot comprehend.

ODD MAN OUT (1947)

"I believe in everything we're trying to do, but this violence isn't getting us anywhere."
—*Johnny McQueen*

Set in 1922, *The Informer* presented the Troubles as a background, with images of military patrols, checkpoints, sandbag barricades, and barbed wire, even if the nature of the underlying conflict went unexplained. Taking place in postwar Belfast, Carol Reed's *Odd Man Out* is far more depoliticized. The film offers no visual images of political conflict or any discussion of social or economic problems.

The protagonist, Johnny McQueen, is more mob boss than revolutionary. He gives no speeches to crowds. He issues no proclamations. He never confronts or even identifies the opposition. Nowhere does he inspire his followers with a vision of what their activities will achieve or articulate the injustices he seeks to remedy. He is simply the leader of a gang planning a robbery, suggesting that the "illegal" organization is criminal rather than political. The man he kills is not a government official or uniformed representative of an oppressive regime or occupying army, but a civilian employee of a linen mill. The crime that puts the entire film in motion could just as easily have happened in Newark or Naples. He is chased not by soldiers but policemen, wanted not as a rebel threatening to overthrow a regime but as a common felon.

Carol Reed based his movie on the 1945 novel by F. L. Green. An Englishman born in Portsmouth in 1902, Frederick Laurence Green married an Irishwoman and moved to Belfast in 1932. Green's novel suggests in several places that the men in the unnamed "revolutionary organization" are driven not by political ideology or social injustice, but by a lack of vision and experience. Living on an island, they have a crabbed, small-minded view of the world that leads them to engage in violence for a futile cause:

A train's whistle blew for several seconds, and ... from the docks came the slow, majestic note of a ship's siren. The three men standing irresolutely in the windswept, empty street heard it. Momentarily, it lifted their sordid lives to the contemplation of life beyond the streets which their own bitter purposes had made deadly. It proclaimed the oceans and wide lands, and rendered small and trivial by comparison the meager territory and the unrelenting civil strife which were all that these three outlaws had known from earliest infancy. Hatred, fanaticism, and murder, within a tiny island beyond which they had never ventured, and outside of which their stunted imagination could not extend.[16]

The novel characterizes the cause of Irish nationalism as a symptom of the country's isolation from the wider world its narrow-minded inhabitants are unable to comprehend. This view of the "political unrest" is voiced by Father Tom, who tells Agnes (called Kathleen in the film):

You are one of them, my child! I know it. It is in your eyes. You are obsessed with the dream, as they are. You are one of those who see the rivers and mountains of the the land and assert that they belong to you and your friends, and that amidst them you will have a nation segregated from the rest of the nations. What stupidity! The Divine Creator made this world for all mankind, not for a few of you to parcel into wretched fields upon rocks behind which you think you will resurrect a silly dream. To live as you and your friends would have men live is a bitter, evil thing![17]

Carol Reed was impressed with the novel and wanted to create a film that, like the book, would eschew politics for a wider discussion of human experience. Reed consulted with Green in Belfast. Although he had no experience writing films, Green was selected to coauthor the script with R. C. Sheriff, best known for his 1928 play *Journey's End*.[18]

Reed made other decisions that would make his film a remarkable blend of reality and symbolism. Unlike many movies of the era, *Odd Man Out* made use of extensive location shootings. The transition from Belfast-shot exteriors to studio interiors was so seamless that tourists still visit The Crown Bar in Belfast believing it served as The Four Winds saloon that appears in the film. In fact, a detailed copy of the pub was recreated on an English soundstage.[19] To further enhance a sense of reality, Green did not use standard movie sound effects but recorded the actual drum of mill machinery and the echo of hoof beats on a city street banked by high buildings.[20] The narrowness of Johnny's world is represented by scenes shot in small rooms, tunnel-like alleys, and a series of enclosed spaces — a brick air raid shelter, the back of a cab, a pub crib — all creating a sense of stifling claustrophobia.

These touches of reality blend with a pattern of symbolic sights and sounds. The Albert Memorial Clock, an imposing four-faced clock tower, is omnipresent in the film.* It is seen in the background in key scenes, sometimes through a window or over a character's shoulder. In contrast to the great clock marking down the last hours of the protagonist's life, a ship offers the chance of escape and continued life. It, too, appears in the background in several shots. The themes of time passing and the opportunity of escape are represented by sounds as well — ticking clocks, chimes, bells, and a ship's horn. Clock tower and ship appear in the opening scene and combine to become powerful contrasting symbols in the finale. The clock tower signals the beginning and conclusion of the narrative, its face filling the screen to show four o'clock as Johnny plans the robbery, and ending with the clock tolling midnight after his death.

Carol Reed's film opens with an aerial view of a large city and a disclaimer:

*The 113-foot clock tower was damaged by an IRA bombing in January 1992.

James Mason and Kathleen Ryan, with the Albert Memorial Clock in the background, in *Odd Man Out* (1947).

> This story is told against a background of political unrest in a city in Northern Ireland.
> It is not concerned with the struggle between the law and an illegal organization, but only with the conflict in the hearts of the people when they become unexpectedly involved.

The camera sweeps over an airfield, highways, a river, ships, and docks to focus on a tall stone clock tower striking four as a ship in the background sounds its horn, merging the two symbols of the movie. The opening aerial sequence underscores the enclosed environments featured in the rest of the film and symbolizes the greater world and wider consciousness that Johnny and his compatriots are unable to experience or understand.

The disclaimer is hardly necessary because the film deals only with politics by faint association. The motives of the "illegal organization" are never delineated. Only passing references to a "headquarters" and an "organization" distinguish the mill robbers from common gangsters. One of the conspirators refers to a share of the expected haul as "a slice of the party cake." But the characters never voice their grievances, discuss the goal of their struggle, or even name their opposition. The words "Ireland," "Irish," "England," "independence," "unity," or "partition" are never spoken. Instead, the "revolutionaries" discuss only their immediate goal, the robbery of a mill and the reliability of the stolen getaway car.

The action starts with the camera following a lone figure from the base of the clock tower down a narrow street into a small row house and upstairs to a crowded room where Johnny McQueen (James Mason), the chief of an unnamed organization, rehearses the robbery of a mill in order to fund their activities. Johnny sits with his back to the window, with the clock tower visible on the horizon. According to his plan, he and three comrades, dressed as businessmen, will take a stolen car to a linen mill and rob the payroll.

Johnny's second-in-command, Dennis (Robert Beatty), questions his leader's commitment to the cause and his fitness to lead the raid. "Your heart's not in this job, Johnny," Dennis tells him, offering to take charge of the raid.

"I believe in everything we are trying to do," Johnny insists, "but this violence isn't getting us anywhere." Reminded that he had been sentenced to seventeen years for bringing arms and ammunition into the city, Johnny notes, "In prison you have time to think. If only we could throw the guns away and make our cause in the Parliaments instead of in the back streets." Johnny's misgivings about violence and his warning to Pat (Cyril Cusack) to avoid gunplay hint at inner doubts, but these are never expressed.

Kathleen (Kathleen Ryan), the daughter of the homeowner, serves the men tea. In love with Johnny, she urges him not to go on the raid. Her infatuation with Johnny is not returned. Johnny refers to her only as a "great friend." When she asks him if he will ever be free, it is unclear what she refers to — free from oppression or free from the organization that consumes his attention.

The stolen car carrying Johnny and his gang passes both ships and the clock tower on the way to the mill. The motion of the car makes Johnny dizzy. Passing buildings and the city street are shown in a disorienting blur, indicating that Johnny, accustomed to his prison cell and cramped bedroom, is unable to function in the wider world.

An office clock reads 4:35 as the men slip into the mill, hold the employees at bay with revolvers, stuff their briefcases with cash, and exit. With the burglar alarm clanging, the thieves race to the getaway car. Descending the steps, Johnny becomes faint and falls behind. An armed cashier confronts Johnny, and the two struggle, falling to the steps. The employee shoots Johnny, who returns fire, killing the cashier.

Panicked, Pat drives off as Nolan (Dan O'Herlihy) and Murphy attempt to pull Johnny into the back seat. Refusing to slow down, Pat makes a sharp turn, and Johnny falls to the street. Believing Johnny to be dead, Pat hesitates to drive back. When Johnny stumbles to his feet and lurches down an alley, Pat drives around the corner hoping to catch up with Johnny at the other end of the alley but loses him and returns to Kathleen's house.

Panting and in pain, Johnny takes refuge in a small brick air raid shelter. The shelter becomes the first of several enclosed environments where Johnny spends the last hours of his life.

The film cuts to a series of short scenes dramatizing a city-wide manhunt. Police check identity cards of people leaving the city on planes, trains, and ships. A large hand draws a heavy circle around a map of Belfast, further limiting Johnny's range of motion on the island nation.

A wounded Johnny stirs when a small girl enters the shelter chasing after a soccer ball. Delusional from loss of blood, Johnny mistakes the brick enclosure for his prison cell and the child for a prison guard. Confusing reality with hallucination, Johnny speaks to the imaginary prison guard:

> Oh, Donald, what a dream I had. Oh, what an outing! I dreamt I had escaped from prison. I dreamt I was on a raid robbing a mill — funds for the organization.... After we'd done the job, there was a fight, and I shot a man.... Yes, I dreamt I shot a man. And I couldn't get onto the car ... somehow I couldn't get onto it ... that's right, I was wounded ... in the left arm ... and I came to an air raid shelter, slumped down ... must have passed out.

With the mention the air raid shelter, Johnny is brought back to the present and the realization that he has killed a man. The child runs off, leaving Johnny alone.

At Kathleen's house Dennis plans to help Johnny by posing as a decoy. Knowing the police will be looking for a wounded man, he asks Kathleen to bandage his hand. He intends to head to the street where Johnny was last seen and draw off the police, giving him a chance to escape. Kathleen asks to accompany Dennis, telling him, "Sooner or later the police will get him, let me have him until then." Dennis insists she cannot claim Johnny because "as long as he lives he will belong to the organization."

Locating Johnny in the shelter, Dennis tells him he will create a diversion and run from the police. When he has drawn the police away from the shelter he will fire three shots as a signal for Johnny to make his break. Johnny is more concerned about the man he shot, twice asking Dennis if he killed the clerk. Dennis does not answer and runs off toward the police, rolling up his sleeve to reveal a bandaged arm. As the police give chase, Dennis climbs up the scaffolding of a building. Reaching the rooftop, the illuminated face of the clock tower is visible behind him.

Hearing three shots, Johnny slowly leaves the shelter and painfully makes his way down a street. Johnny collapses as a truck drives past him. Thinking he has been struck by the truck, two sisters help him to their home. Trained to give first aid during the war, Maudie (Beryl Measor) and Rosie (Fay Compton) tend to his injuries. Helping Johnny take off his coat, Rosie sees the bullet wound and finds his gun and recognizes that their accident victim is the wounded "chief of the organization" wanted by the police. As she discusses with Maudie what they should do with Johnny, the cuckoo clock on the wall reads 7:15. Despite a thousand pound reward announced in the newspaper, Rosie cannot bring herself to turn over a wounded man. Again Johnny asks if he killed the man but receives no answer.

Rosie's husband Tom arrives home and, noticing the gun, recognizes the wounded man in his parlor as Johnny McQueen. As Rosie argues with her husband whether to turn him in, Johnny overhears that he has killed the clerk. Tom states that he "respects the law," but Rosie insists it would be "cruel" to punish a dying man. Johnny rises from the sofa and makes his way to the door, telling them he will not trouble them further. In a gesture of compassion, Tom offers Johnny a drink as he passes through the door into the windswept street.

Disoriented and weak, Johnny leans against a horse-drawn cab. Two passing British soldiers smell alcohol on Johnny's breath and, assuming he is drunk, help him into the back of the cab. As the cabbie Gin Jimmy (Joseph Tomelty) climbs aboard his cab and drives off, a clock shows 7:30. Unaware he has a passenger, Gin Jimmy passes through a police cordon, ironically joking that he has Johnny McQueen as a passenger.

The clock in Kathleen's house reads 7:40 as the police question her about Johnny. After the officers depart, Kathleen takes a gun and leaves.

When Gin Jimmy finds Johnny in his cab, he tells his wounded passenger, "Listen, I'm not for you, I'm not against you, but I can't afford to get mixed up in this." Gin takes the cab down an alley to a cluster of abandoned sheds. In the distance the clock tower reads 7:50. Gin Jimmy carries Johnny from the cab to a shed and dumps him into an old tin bathtub. Returning to his carriage, he encounters a tramp named Shell (F. J. McCormick) who tells Gin Jimmy he saw what he did.

As the clock tower strikes eight o'clock Kathleen reaches the docks and asks a sailor to help her smuggle Johnny out of the city. The sailor tells her the ship sails just after eleven and promises to leave the gate near the clock tower open for them.

Seeking Johnny, Kathleen visits Father Tom (W. G. Fay) who already has a visitor. Shell sits with a caged bird on his lap, explaining that he has a bird named Johnny that escaped from his cage and now has a hurt left wing. As Kathleen listens to Shell's metaphorical tale, she stands at the window, where the clock tower is shown striking eight-thirty. Kathleen becomes angered as Shell remains elusive about Johnny's whereabouts and mentions the reward money. The priest offers to get Shell something for his efforts. Shell wants money. Instead, the priest tells him, "Bring back Johnny, and I'll show you the way to real riches." As Shell leaves to find Johnny, a clock is shown on the priest's mantle.

Alone with Father Tom, Kathleen asks him to give Johnny to her. Father Tom explains that Johnny is not his to give away. He wishes only to hear his confession then persuade him to surrender to the police. Kathleen asks to take Johnny away to hide and protect him. Told by Father Tom that Johnny has committed murder and must pay the penalty, Kathleen vows to kill Johnny herself then end her own life. The law, she asserts, wants to kill Johnny for revenge but she would do it out of pity. She tells the priest she could not endure Johnny's trial, execution, and the loneliness that would follow. In murder-suicide he would not die alone and she would be able to protect him. Father Tom urges her to consider her faith and realize she has no right to take his life or her own.

With the tower clock overhead, Johnny wakes in the shed as snow begins to fall. He climbs out of the tub and journeys down the street, the clock face glowing behind him. He stumbles through the doors of the Four Winds bar and shuts himself into a snug and passes out. A waiter encourages him to leave, then, realizing Johnny is too exhausted to walk, locks the door, planning to get rid of him after closing time.

Searching for Johnny, Shell discovers a bandage on the street and enters the Four Winds. Noting the locked snug, he surmises Johnny is hiding in the corner. At 10:50 Lukey (Robert Newton), a wide-eyed, wild-haired failed artist, enters the bar. Claiming that he is not afraid of Johnny, the police, or the organization, Lukey tells the men at the bar he wants to paint the dying killer because "the truth of life and death" will be in his eyes. At that moment Johnny lets out a loud, pained moan that is heard throughout the pub. Turning, Lukey spots Shell and attacks him, chasing him around the bar, smashing bottles. The barman moves the hand of the clock past eleven and shouts closing time.

Surveying the damage, the barman demands twenty-five pounds from Lukey, who is unable to pay. The barman threatens Lukey with jail but offers to let the matter drop if he removes Johnny from the premises. Excited at the prospect of painting the dying man's eyes, Lukey stuffs his coat pockets with bottles and bundles Johnny into a cab.

Lukey takes Johnny to his studio in a decaying mansion he shares with Shell and Tober (Elwyn Brook-Jones). Lukey props Johnny in a chair to paint his portrait as the tower clock chimes. Tober, a failed medical student, begins to dress Johnny's wound. Inexplicably, the clock tower appears both through the window behind Lukey painting the dying Johnny and the window behind Tober treating Johnny's wound. Lukey frantically tries to capture Johnny on canvas, telling Tober, "Look at him, Tober.... He's near death. He sees it.... Wonderful thoughts in his eyes!"

When Tober announces he will take Johnny to a hospital as soon as he finishes bandaging his wound, Lukey tells him he is only patching up a man destined to be tried and executed. "There is more to be considered than the body, Tober. That may be dying, but the soul is still alive," he declares. In Johnny's doomed eyes, Lukey states, he can see "the truth about us all." Tober dismisses Lukey, soberly noting as he works to save Johnny's life, "We're all dying."

A police inspector arrives at Father Tom's church as the clock tower over Kathleen's shoulder shows 11:45 and the ship horn sounds. As the clock strikes, the inspector enters and tells the priest he knows Kathleen has come to him searching for Johnny. "That's a crime?" Father Tom asks the officer, setting up a debate between law and faith:

Inspector: A serious one, Father.
Father Tom: Tell me this. From your experience of men and women, would you say they're all bad?
Inspector: In my profession, Father, there is neither good nor bad; there is innocence and guilt, that's all.
Father Tom: I have seen the bad in them. And we condemn that, and rightly, too, but what do we do when we find something that is good in them? Shouldn't we recognize that? ...
Inspector: Father, I have my duty to do. Where is this man McQueen?
Father Tom (beckoning to the window): Out there somewhere amidst the storm of the city...
Inspector: I am sorry, Father, but it is our duty to bring this man to justice.
Father Tom: That's the duty of all of us.

Kathleen slips from the church and goes to the ship, asking the seaman not to sail until she can find Johnny. He warns her that with the water quickly dropping, the ship must put to sea by midnight.

In the studio Tober prepares to take Johnny to the hospital for a transfusion. Lukey objects, wanting to complete his portrait. As the two men debate which is more important, the body or the soul, Johnny begins to hallucinate, imagining that he sees Father Tom speaking wordlessly among the collection of Lukey's garish portraits. Leaning forward, trying to discern the priest over the voices of Tober and Lukey, Johnny mourns his lost Catholic education. He confesses to Father Tom that as a boy he never listened to his teachings, but only "repeated the words without thinking what they meant." Johnny recalls a Bible lesson from his childhood, "...when I was a child — I spoke as a child.... I thought as a child.... I understood as a child.... But when I became a man I put away childish things..."

As Tober and Lukey watch, Johnny rises from his chair, raises his arm and recites from 1 Corinthians Chapter 13:

Though I speak with tongues of men and of angels and have not charity, I am become a sounding brass or a tinkling cymbal. Though I have the gift of prophecy and understand all mysteries and all knowledge, and though I have all faiths so that I can remove mountains and have not charity, I am nothing!

Lukey sees this outburst as a sign of madness, but Tober dismisses it as mere delirium, a symptom of his blood loss. Lukey insists on completing his portrait as Tober leaves to get an ambulance. Mediating between the two, Shell guides Johnny out of the room to find Father Tom. Lukey moves to the window to examine his painting. With the clock tower now appearing in his window, Lukey studies his failed painting with disappointment and throws it to the floor. In despair, he grabs for a bottle. Discovering it empty, he tosses it away, turns his face to the clock, and weeps.

Shell guides the weakened and delirious Johnny past police patrols until Johnny collapses. Shell runs to fetch Father Tom. Reviving, Johnny stumbles closer to the clock tower, now reading 11:55. Kathleen finds him resting against the rails of an iron fence. She tries to guide him to the ship, but he is too weak to continue. With his arms outstretched in a crucifixion pose, he tells Kathleen to abandon him and "go back to life."

The ship horn sounds as Kathleen tries to guide Johnny across the square. The ship is shown gliding down the river as the headlights of police cars and flashlights of officers approach them. Falling against the fence, Johnny is unable to go farther. Realizing their hope of escape is lost, Kathleen assures Johnny, "We are going away together," and fires two shots at the police, who return fire, killing both of them in a volley of bullets.

The departing ship sounds its horn as midnight chimes. Father Tom guides Shell from the square, and the face of the clock, showing midnight, fills the final frame.

Odd Man Out was presented to American audiences as a romance and crime thriller. The ads appearing in *The New York Times* avoided political and Irish references, and distorted the theme of unrequited love to transform the film into a gangster classic: "A killer on the loose ... hiding in the shadows ... seeking desperately to claw his way to the arms of the woman he loves ... the woman who sticks by him while an angry city screams for his blood."[21] Significantly, *Odd Man Out*'s alternative title was *Gang War*.

In a 1947 interview, Carol Reed defended his decision to steer the film away from politics, stating, "What counts is the story value and characterization.... I believe that a director has no right to inflict his amateur politics and opinions on an audience."[22] But as Radu Davidescu argues, the decision to depoliticize the story "constitutes a politicization in itself."[23] Stripping away the historical background of Northern Ireland and rationalization for the militant organization, the film presents Johnny only as a misguided lost soul. Revolutionary politics appear as fruitless as Lukey's art or Shell's obsession with birds.

Audiences are given a deeply metaphorical tale, laden with symbolism and full of thought-provoking debates on a range of subjects. But the actions of the unnamed organization and the conflict that created it remain unexplored. DeFelice asks, "Is Johnny McQueen's odyssey through the streets of Belfast more or less meaningful because Reed is not concerned with the cause for which he gives his life?"[24]

Both *The Informer* and *Odd Man Out* illustrate Malachi O'Doherty's observation about the current condition in Ireland that "Northern Ireland's story is not its own" but one told by foreign filmmakers who "can use the IRA simply as a backdrop to a great morality drama in which the issue is more compelling than the detail."[25]

6

American Angles

In Ireland we regard America as the next parish after Galway.—*Conor O'Clery*

You don't have to be Muslim, or poor, or an extremist, to feel the romantic pull of terrorism. You can be a middle-class American and a lapsed Catholic whose grandmother happened to come from Dongeal.—*Anne Applebaum*

George Washington was called a terrorist in his time.—*Hidden Agenda*

Americans played dominant roles both in creating the Irish Republican Army and shaping its celluloid image. The influx of over a million Irish Catholics following the Famine meant the United States would be home to a sizeable population with ties to Ireland and with an animus towards Great Britain. In contrast to other immigrants who focused on building new lives in a new land, the Irish maintained a sentimental attachment to their "Emerald Isle." Nostalgic folk songs, poems, and stories lamented a loss of home and perpetuated grievances against a foreign occupation. Early Irish-American novels relived the horrors of the Hunger with melodramatic scenes of starvation, eviction, forced emigration, and family separation. A common narrative was that of the exile who achieves money and success in America and returns to Ireland to buy back his homestead.[1] Unlike other European immigrants, no language barrier would separate subsequent generations from their homeland. Second and third generation Irish-Americans could easily follow events in Ireland. Visiting Irish nationalists were able to address American rallies in their native language. Rebels facing arrest and imprisonment for revolutionary activities in Ireland could operate freely in the United States, amassing money and weapons, often with the support of Irish-American politicians and patrons. Collectors for "skirmish funds" became fixtures in Irish-American communities for decades. Recalling his Milwaukee childhood, actor Pat O'Brien described boyhood friends who married their high school sweethearts and "raised up their broods as good Americans (who spared a dollar for the I.R.A. and 'the trouble' in Ireland)."[2]

For a century and a half America remained a source of arms, money, and recruits for "the Cause."

The Fenians

In 1858 James Stephens founded the Irish Revolutionary Brotherhood (later called the Irish Republican Brotherhood), a precursor to the IRA, in Dublin. That same year John O'Mahony established a parallel organization in New York named the Fenians* after ancient

Though the name of a specific nineteenth-century Irish-American movement, "Fenian" became a generic term for Irish Republicans, now used contemptuously by Unionists and the British.

Gaelic warriors known as the Fianna.[3] As Andrew Greeley notes, the Fenians saw themselves as a government-in-exile rather than simply a nationalist organization, establishing a "pseu-dostate with a president, a congress, ambassadors, and all the paraphernalia of government."[4] Declaring an Irish Republic in New York, the Fenians issued bonds to finance their activities, published a weekly newspaper, and raised money to support a rebellion in Ireland. Like other Irish nationalist organizations, the Fenians disagreed over tactics and leadership and broke into diverse factions.

The American Civil War had a profound effect on the Fenians, temporarily interrupting operations but transforming it from a political organization into a military force. Both Con-federate and Union armies had Irish brigades, many of them going into battle carrying green flags bearing distinctly Celtic symbols of harps and shamrocks. O'Mahony became a Union colonel, forming a Fenian regiment of the New York National Guard.[5]

At a convention in Cincinnati in January 1865, O'Mahony declared that the Fenians were "virtually at war with the oligarchy of Great Britain."[6] Once the Civil War ended, Irish veterans of both armies united to exploit their combat experience and available stocks of war material to free Ireland of English rule. The United States government turned a blind eye to Fenian military preparations, selling the Irishmen surplus weapons at discount prices. Still displeased by its support for the Confederacy, Washington hoped to use the Fenian threat to pressure London to pay reparations for damages caused by the *Alabama*, a British-built Confederate blockade runner.[7]

In a venture that would be replicated many times in the twentieth century, the Fenians shipped arms to Ireland. The *Jacknell Packet* left New York with thirty-eight officers and five thousand rifles. Once at sea, the Fenians raised a green flag and renamed the ship *Erin's Hope*. As in many later attempts, the arms shipment never reached the rebels. Unable to find a secure port, the officers, running low on provisions, left the ship and were soon arrested.[8]

While some Fenians sought to fight the British in Ireland, others planned attacks closer to home. In April 1866 a thousand Fenians assembled in Maine to launch an invasion of Campobello Island. Poor planning and an intercepted telegram alerted the Canadians. British sailors drove the raiding Fenians off the island without losses, though the Irishmen managed to burn a few buildings and steal a Union Jack. Undaunted, the Fenians staged another attack. On June 1, General John O'Neill led over eight hundred men across the Niagara River to capture Fort Erie. Though nineteenth-century paintings depict the Fenians dressed in matching green jackets, most wore civilian clothing or remnants of their Union and Confederate uniforms. A few units went into battle bearing flags reading Irish Repub-lican Army, and some soldiers wore coat buttons stamped with the letters IRA, marking the first public use of the term. The Fenians skirmished with Canadian troops, with the loss of a dozen men. His reinforcements and supplies cut off by American troops, O'Neill was forced to retreat to Buffalo. A few days later, 1,800 Fenians, under the command of Samuel Spiers, attacked from Vermont with the goal of capturing Montreal. They occupied two border villages and waited for additional support, which never arrived. After looting the captured towns, the Fenians retreated. Another attempt to occupy Montreal was staged four years later, with similar results. Fenian agitation along the Canadian border continued for several years, extending as far west as British Columbia.[9]

Having received reparations from Britain, Washington terminated its support for the Fenians. Although the federal government interdicted their raids, retributions were not taken against the Fenians themselves. Captured Irishmen were quickly released, given their weapons back, and sent home with free train tickets.[10] Some Fenian officers returned to the ranks of the U.S. Army. The Fenian president, William Randall Roberts, served two terms in Congress in the 1870s and was appointed an envoy to Chile by President Grover Cleveland in 1885.[11]

One of the more inventive Fenian endeavors was worthy of Jules Verne. Unable to interest the U.S. Navy in his experimental submarines in 1875, Irish-born inventor John Holland turned to the Fenians. Having failed to seize Canada, Irish nationalists were seeking new strategies to attack Britain. After demonstrating a fourteen-foot prototype, Holland received $60,000 from "skirmishing funds" to construct a larger boat. Equipped with a conning tower and diving planes, Holland's second vessel could fully submerge and travel underwater. The thirty-one-foot cigar-shaped submarine, operated by a crew of three, included a pneumatic gun. Holland made several test runs in New York Harbor in 1883, firing both underwater and aerial projectiles. Dubbed the *Fenian Ram* by a reporter, Holland's submarine was designed to attack the British navy. Given the sub's limited operational range, the Fenians planned to stow the submarine aboard a conventional steamship that would approach British warships at anchor. The *Ram* would be secretly launched through a "sea door" to attack its unsuspecting prey from underwater, much like Captain Nemo's *Nautilus*, then return to the "mother ship."[12] Holland's novel weapon never saw action. After a dispute over financing, Fenians stole the *Ram* and towed it to Connecticut. Discovering they were unable to operate the futuristic submarine without its inventor, they abandoned the project, and the *Fenian Ram* was warehoused.[13]*

The Clan

By the 1880s the Fenian movement was largely supplanted by the secret American organization the Clan na Gael, founded in 1867. The Clan worked closely with the Irish Republican Brotherhood in Ireland, advocating armed conflict, including terrorism, as a way of achieving Irish independence.[14] Members of the Clan continued Fenian-style attacks. In the 1880s they planted bombs throughout England, including Scotland Yard and the House of Commons.[15] A Clan leader, Luke Dillon, attempted to blow up the Welland Canal locks in Ontario to disrupt British supply lines during the Boer War.[16] The Irish Republican John Devoy emigrated to America and became a leading figure in the Clan, raising money to assist Parnell and later the Republicans. British authorities considered Devoy the most dangerous person in the Irish Republican movement.[17]

At the outbreak of the First World War, Clan leaders met with the German ambassador to the United States and later sent envoys to Berlin to discuss how Irish nationalism could aid German war aims. The Clan played a significant role in planning the Easter Rising in 1916. Three of the sixteen men executed spent time in the United States. Padraig Pearse visited America to raise money for the Irish Volunteers. James Connolly lived in the United States for seven years, involving himself in American Socialist organizations. Thomas Clarke spent nearly a decade in the United States. Active in the Clan na Gael, he became an American citizen in 1905.[18] Their executions following the Easter Rising angered Irish-Americans, and a relief fund raised a hundred thousand dollars to send to Ireland.[19]

*The Fenian Ram *was displayed in Madison Square Garden in 1916 as an attraction for a fund-raising drive to aid victims of the Easter Rising. The sub is now on exhibit at the Patterson Museum in Patterson, New Jersey. In 1900 Holland sold the U.S. Navy its first practical submarine, the USS* Holland, *commissioned as SS-1.*

Even in his seventies Devoy remained a dominant figure in the Republican movement, powerful enough to feud with de Valera, the Republic's acknowledged president. Irish-American nationalists were not complacent benefactors of the Cause but active strategists who often disagreed with Irish Republicans actively fighting the British. De Valera viewed America as critical, both in securing funds for the Republic and in gaining diplomatic leverage against Britain. The Dail, which allocated one million dollars for the armed conflict against the English, devoted a million and half for de Valera's efforts to gain American recognition of the Republic. Half a million was set aside to influence the 1920 American presidential election.[20] De Valera attended both political conventions with so much publicity that commentators joked he was running for president.

During the Anglo-Irish War, Irish-Americans sent money and weapons to the IRA. Michael Collins was impressed with the new Thompson submachine gun supplied by the Clan. Dubbed the "trench broom" by its inventor, General John Thompson, the light machine gun, developed too late for use in World War I, became the infamous "chopper" favored by Twenties gangsters.[21] The Clan purchased a large stock of tommy guns, most of which were seized by customs before they could reach Ireland. A few dozen did get through, and two Irish-American war veterans arrived from Chicago to train the IRA in their use.[22]

The Clan na Gael, like the IRA itself, split into two factions over the Treaty. John Devoy accepted the Treaty and supported the Free State, rationalizing it as a first step toward Republican aims.[23] A more militant faction in the Clan, headed by Joseph McGarrity, a prominent leader and donor in many Irish-American organizations, broke with Devoy. McGarrity supported the anti–Treaty IRA members and declared de Valera's 1927 entrance into the Dail "an act of treason." He continued to support the IRA after the organization was outlawed in 1936, approving of Sean Russell's 1939 bombing campaign. McGarrity visited Ireland that year but was ordered to leave the country. Returning to America by way of Germany, he met with Herman Goering to discuss Nazi assistance for the IRA. With McGarrity's death the following year, the Clan ceased to play a major role in supporting the IRA.[24]

In April 1939 Sean Russell, chief of staff of the IRA, made a fund-raising tour of the United States. In his speeches (now attended by German-American Nazis) he openly took credit for the bombing campaign, promising it would continue until the British withdrew from Northern Ireland and released Irish political prisoners.[25] Though Russell could raise little money, the protest by Irish-American Congressmen following his arrest in Michigan demonstrated a strong residual support for the Cause.

The Second World War dampened Irish-American support for the Irish Republican Army. Marginalized by its association with Nazi Germany, the IRA lost its propaganda war against Britain, which was now viewed not as an "Empire" but a tiny embattled island made famous during the Blitz by Edward R. Murrow's broadcasts celebrating England as the lone country standing against Hitler. Churchill's association with Black and Tan thuggery was eclipsed as he emerged as a beacon of hope in democracy's darkest hour. A younger generation of Irish-Americans, many of them stationed in England, harbored less antipathy towards the British than their parents.

The border campaign of the Fifties did not attract major attention in the United States, though a few self-described "Minute Men" protested outside the British Consulate in New York in 1958 over the trial and alleged ill-treatment of two Irishmen accused of killing an RUC sergeant.[26]

Armalites and Stingers

The Troubles of the 1970s rekindled American interest in the unresolved Irish conflict. Four IRA veterans founded Irish Northern Aid (NORAID) in New York in 1970.[27] It soon became the most prominent American organization supporting the Provisionals — raising money for families of internees, advocating the Republican cause through petitions and protests, and helping IRA fugitives find new identities in the United States.[28]

Support for Irish nationalists played to diverse audiences in America: working class Irish Catholics who continued to see themselves as an oppressed minority, leftists who championed indigenous people fighting imperialism, and civil rights advocates opposed to institutionalized discrimination. Though often at cross-purposes, and with highly different values and agendas, sympathizers could be counted on to share the nationalist narrative, even if they did not countenance Republican methods. Though they paid less attention to the conflict than politically active Irish-Americans, most Americans generally accepted the view that Northern Ireland was "occupied by the British." Evening news reports showing mobs stoning armored vehicles and military patrols bolstered this conception. Relying on Tory support from Britain, Unionists never established parallel organizations in the United States. Loyalist clergyman, like Ian Paisley, who denounced Papists found little sympathy from American Protestants.

With few weapons available in Ireland or Britain, America became the prime source for arms.[29] At first, the guns shipped to Northern Ireland were odd lots of handguns and army surplus M-1s. After seeing a magazine article about the American semi-automatic AR-15, the IRA's Belfast Brigade determined this could be the weapon that might "win the war."[30] Weighing just seven pounds and equipped with a folding stock, the accurate semi-automatic rifle fired a .223 that tumbled in the air like a dum-dum bullet. Gerry Adams was impressed with the weapon and directed Brendan Hughes to travel to New York to obtain the guns.[31] The AR-15, known in Ireland as the Armalite after its manufacturer, became the IRA's weapon of choice throughout the Seventies.*

Gun-runners like George Harrison provided the IRA with weapons, including highly favored Armalites. "I sent thousands of guns to Ireland," Harrison later recalled, "and I'd do it again tomorrow. I'm only sorry I didn't send more."[32] Two hundred Armalites were smuggled across the Atlantic aboard the *QE2*. One group of IRA members was called "the M60 gang" because they were armed with heavy machine guns stolen from the U.S. military and smuggled into Ireland.[33]

In 1971 security forces in Northern Ireland recovered 700 weapons and two tons of explosives, most of which came from the United States.[34] By the end of the decade, the British government reported that 80 percent of the IRA's weapons originated in the United States.[35] In 1984 Irish authorities seized seven tons of arms aboard the trawler *Marita Ann* off the Irish coast. The weapons, intended for the IRA, had come from America. According to some reports, members of the Boston police department assisted the project, providing bodyguards and helping the gun-runners with customs.[36]

Initially, American authorities, focused on Soviet espionage and campus radicals, devoted little attention to middle-aged Irishmen running guns. In the late Seventies Britain pressured the United States to take action. Margaret Thatcher was effective in prompting

---

The popularity of the automatic weapon inspired the Irish rebel song "Me Little Armalite." Accompanied by sounds of gunfire, the bouncy lyrics also celebrate the use of armor-piercing bullets.

the Reagan administration to suppress American support for the IRA. Donations to NORAID were monitored, and gun-runners like Harrison were arrested.[37] Facing a loss of weapons from the United States, the IRA looked to new sources of supplies — namely, Libya.

The ultimate weapon sought by the IRA was the Stinger missile, which could down British helicopters and was thought to be the weapon that would "win the war." The appeal of the weapon made it a perfect lure for an FBI sting operation. In 1990 undercover FBI agents offered to sell a missile to three Florida IRA supporters, who handed over money, took possession of the Stinger, and were then arrested. Tracing the origin of the money, agents staged raids in New York and Arizona, making additional arrests.[38] These cases led a prominent lawyer to decry the arrests as a "witch-hunt against Irish-American business-men."[39]

The amount of the money, which often totaled only a few hundred thousand a year, was less important than the "idea of the money." Support from America was never as great as the IRA hoped or as vast as the British feared. Its mere existence, however modest, emboldened IRA morale, reassuring Republicans that their struggle was legitimate, recognized, and destined to win. The idea of the money also exasperated the British, who blamed American support for the terrorism. The Irish problem remained a sore in the special relationship. For the British, the face of the IRA was that of dead and maimed civilians killed in terrorist attacks. In America, it was the smiling innocent face of hunger-striker Bobby Sands depicted on posters, T-shirts, and buttons circulated in Irish bars and college campuses.

Kennedy and King

Unionists and the British were troubled not only by organizations like NORAID but the actions of American politicians, many of them Irish Catholics, who were accused of providing moral support to the IRA. Sympathy for Irish nationalism was bipartisan. In 1972, Democratic senator Ted Kennedy and Conservative senator James Buckley, in separate statements, called on the United States government to pressure Britain to withdraw from Northern Ireland.[40] The year before, Kennedy had joined Abraham Ribicoff to introduce a Senate resolution urging President Nixon to call for a removal of British troops. Speaking in support of the resolution, Kennedy argued that "Ulster is becoming Britain's Vietnam," a statement that infuriated British Tories at a time when American forces were using napalm and B-52s.[41] In 1978 Kennedy persuaded President Carter to ban arms sales to the RUC, a measure traditionally reserved for military and police forces of Third World dictatorships.[42] In the 1990s, Kennedy urged President Clinton to grant a visa to Gerry Adams, allowing the Sinn Fein leader to visit the United States. Adams' American media blitz angered the British but was later seen by many as an important step in pulling the Republicans towards a political process. Through his contacts with Adams and Hume, Kennedy was seen as a man whose views on Ireland matured over time. Though Senator George Mitchell played a more active role in helping move nationalists to the Good Friday Agreements, Kennedy's support was widely recognized by Irish and British commentators. Graham Walker, a political science professor at Queen's University in Belfast, credited Kennedy as being a "moderating influence" whose role was "keeping the wilder voices of Irish America in check."[43]

Gordon Brown's 2009 announcement before a joint session of Congress that Senator Kennedy, then dying of cancer, was to be awarded an honorary knighthood ignited a storm of protest. Conservative columnist Simon Heffer saw the decision as an "insult to those husbands, wives and children who were blown up in shopping centers by the IRA."[44] Writing in the *Daily Mail*, Andrew Roberts called it "absurd" for Gordon Brown to award a man who "did his damnedest to poison U.S.–U.K. relations over Ulster." For Roberts, Kennedy's antipathy to Britain stemmed from a historical grievance. The Kennedy family "has nursed a deep resentment against the country that they blame for forcing them out of County Wexford during the Great Potato Famine." Accusing Kennedy of using "weasel words" to condemn violence, Roberts told readers, "For the Queen to be obliged to honour this man is nothing less than an obscenity."[45]

While *The Belfast Telegraph* headlined its announcement of Kennedy's death with "Farewell to a Peacemaker," conservative commentators reminded readers of Chappaquiddick and Kennedy's early bellicose statement that Ulster Protestants who objected to a unified Ireland "should be given a decent opportunity to go back to Britain."[46]

Republican congressman Peter King of New York had more direct links with the IRA throughout the 1980s and 1990s, speaking at NORAID rallies and denouncing British "imperialism." King made frequent trips to Northern Ireland, where he was seen as a direct supporter of the IRA. A Belfast judge ejected King from a courtroom during the trial of IRA volunteers, labeling the American congressman "an obvious collaborator with the IRA."[47] While in Northern Ireland, King associated with IRA veterans, drinking at clubs like the Felons, which limited membership to former IRA prisoners. King, who called the IRA "the legitimate voice of occupied Ireland," was banned from the BBC.[48] He was grand marshal of New York's St. Patrick's Day Parade, a celebration derided by British conservatives as that "great festival of plastic patriotism and falseness."[49] To Unionists, Representative King, more than Kennedy, represented the tribal nature of Irish-Americans. King, a conservative pro-life attorney and son of a police officer, seemed an unlikely supporter for the neo-Marxist, pro-choice revolutionary movement that aligned itself with Columbian rebels and assassinated policemen and judges. Irishness, it seemed to British commentators, trumped any rational ideology, so that conservative Irish-Americans who championed law and order at home would support a rebel organization it would never tolerate on its own shores.

Moving to Peace

Just as Gerry Adams had to move Republicans away from the armed struggle at home, he had to bring along the Irish Diaspora. Granted a visa to visit the United States by President Clinton, Adams gave a speech in New York in which he spoke of "peace." No one from NORAID was allowed on stage, a clear signal that he was distancing himself and Sinn Fein from the armed struggle. Adams' trip to America and his appearance on *Larry King* angered many in Britain. Clinton's overture to Adams, however, was later credited as being a constructive intercession that gave legitimacy to the peace process while dampening Irish-American support for terrorism.

The 9/11 Effect

> September 11 was terrible, but if one re-examines the history of the I.R.A., what happened in the United States wasn't so bad…. Many people died; two prominent buildings fell, but it was neither as terrible nor so extraordinary as they think. — *Doris Lessing*

The terror attacks on September 11, 2001, had unintended but profound consequences for the IRA. Stunned by the carnage and the images of Arabs dancing in the streets, Irish-Americans lost any ability to rationalize or minimize terrorism. The romance of the gunman — or especially the bomber — evaporated. The deaths of so many Irish police officers and fire fighters at Ground Zero was noted by British commentators, who responded with smug satisfaction. As Ed West stated on the death of Ted Kennedy, "It's not often said aloud but many British people when they first saw United 175 hit the World Trade Center felt, alongside shock, pity, and a sense of solidarity with the American people, also a feeling of 'now you know what terrorism is like, will you stop funding the murder of our people?'"[50] Simon Heffer offered a similar view on the announcement of Kennedy's honorary knighthood, noting, "Since some nasty people flew airliners into a few buildings in 2001 the Americans have stopped seeing the glamour of terrorism. Until then, however, Fenian murderers were routinely feted on St. Patrick's Day, and no American welcomed them more warmly than Ted."[51] The events of 9/11 had an effect on Peter King, who stopped visiting Ireland, distressed at the anti–American protests staged in Ireland following the U.S. invasion of Iraq. In 2005 he called for the IRA to disband.[52]

The IRA-American angle was invoked again by British commentators when Americans criticized the 2009 release of Libyan "Lockerbie bomber" Abdelbesset al-Megrahi. Given America's record of supporting terrorism, any American "outrage" over the release of a man who did serve time behind bars seemed naïve and hypocritical. Writing in the *Spectator*, Rod Liddle pointed out that the year before the Lockerbie incident the IRA had killed twenty people:

> That campaign of terror, waged against British citizens for more than 30 years, was bankrolled by donations from the USA — and in those 30 years not a single terrorist was extradited from the U.S. to face charges here, despite our repeated requests. Both federal and local U.S. courts refused extradition requests almost as policy, while the funding of the IRA continued without interruption....
>
> The truth is, Britain has been more successful in appealing to Libya to extradite alleged terrorists than it has been in appealing to our ally, that country with which we enjoy a "special relationship." ... We remember faux–Irish U.S. politicians giving succor to the Provos; we remember the imperviousness of every U.S. regime, Democrat and Republican, to our pleas for justice. So see how you like it now.[53]

The Irish-American angle of the Troubles was the subject of Richard Bean's 2010 play *The Big Fellah*. Set in an IRA safe house in the Bronx, the play chronicles the lives of IRA supporters over a thirty year period, from Bloody Sunday in 1972 to the World Trade Center attacks in 2001. In Bean's drama, Irish-Americans, including a Protestant fireman, provide shelter to a gunman on the run, raise money, and maintain support for the Cause until 9/11 shatters their consciences and challenges their perceptions about terrorism.[54]

The IRA-American Film

Numerous IRA films feature the American angle, depicting Irish-Americans going to Ireland to join the IRA, wanted IRA men taking refuge in America, or the IRA conducting highly improbable operations in the United States. The IRA even makes a brief appearance in John Ford's iconic romantic comedy *The Quiet Man* (Argosy/Republic, 1952) when volunteers inspect Sean Thornton's luggage on his arrival in Ireland.

MICHAEL COLLINS, WE ARE HERE: THE VOLUNTEERS

"I came here to contribute what I can for the Cause."—*The Outsider*

Several films depict Irish-Americans volunteering to join the Cause. In *The Day They Robbed the Bank of England* (Summit Film Productions, 1960) Irish-American Norgate (Aldo Ray) arrives in London to exploit his expertise in mining to help Irish nationalists tunnel into underground vaults to seize gold for the movement and strike a propaganda blow against Britain. Irish-American Kerry O'Shea (Don Murray) is drawn into the conflict during the War of Independence in *Shake Hands with the Devil* (Pennebaker Productions/Troy Films, 1959). Initially refusing to join the squad protecting him until he can return to the United States, O'Shea takes part in IRA actions until the Treaty is announced. Charming Southern horsewoman Monica Moore (Shelly Hack) participates in an IRA-Libyan gun-running operation in the Frederick Forsyth thriller *A Casualty of War* (IFS Productions, 1990).

Two films relate parallel narratives about a young idealistic Irish-American going to Ireland to fight for the Cause, only to be cynically manipulated by both the IRA and the British. Both Americans are unknowingly set up by the IRA but escape Belfast and certain death by fleeing to Scotland with the aid of a sympathetic woman.

THE OUTSIDER (1979)

"This isn't your war."

Tony Luraschi's *The Outsider* (Cinematic Arts BV) depicts the IRA as a mercilessly Machiavellian organization that exploits the idealism of an American volunteer and "uses up" its own Irish soldiers. Michael Flaherty (Craig Wesson), though disillusioned by his service in Vietnam ("I thought I'd be fighting for my country"), remains inspired by his grandfather's exploits in the Anglo-Irish War. Six months after his discharge from the army in 1973, Flaherty leaves his upscale Detroit family to join the IRA in Ireland. Serving with a unit based in County Monaghan in the Republic, he participates in border operations, blowing up a British army checkpoint under construction, planting roadside bombs, and executing a British magistrate.

Flaherty's value to the IRA is raised at an Army Council meeting when the need to "keep the momentum going" and desire for "an opportunity to collect funds" lead to a discussion about the advantage of having an American volunteer killed by the British. Of the four "Yanks" serving in the IRA, Flaherty is the likeliest candidate, the other three having blown up a courthouse in America. Flaherty's father is dismissed as a rich American "who thinks he's Irish" but who sent so much money they could not reject his son as a volunteer. The decision is made to send Flaherty to Belfast where he can "be more exposed" to risk. A councilman muses, "If he were killed or wounded, look at the publicity we'd get. It would help with all the American Irish.... We'd get coverage on the television networks. We could get interviews."

John Russell, an Irish caterer and liaison between the Army Council and the Belfast unit, drives Flaherty across the border to Northern Ireland. As an American, Flaherty is out of his element in Belfast, which appears as bomb-scarred as wartime Berlin. At one point he is beaten by residents suspicious of outsiders. Russell promises to introduce Flaherty to the Farmer, the local commander. Chafing to get into action, Flaherty is frustrated by waiting in a small house where Irish Catholics urge him to "go home to America" after he expresses his desire to help the Cause.

The Farmer directs a young volunteer, Tony Coyle (Frank Grimes), to obtain a British weapon so that an English bullet can be "dug out of" Flaherty when needed. Tony befriends Flaherty, though he becomes jealous when Flaherty begins sleeping with Siobhan (Patricia Quinn). Though attracted to Flaherty, she is highly critical of his politics, telling him that Ireland does not need more gunmen.

The British Army has a well-placed informer who alerts them to Flaherty's presence in Belfast. Major Nigel Percival (David Collings) tells his colonel that Flaherty is an "idealist who's found a cause that fits him," presuming that he is "making up for something he didn't feel in Vietnam." Colonel Wyndham (Geoffrey Palmer) urges caution in handling Flaherty, noting, "We can't afford a situation which would give the Irish-American press just what they need to triple the IRA's funds."

Percival, anxious to protect an IRA informer, sees a way to make double use of Flaherty. The IRA, he tells Wyndham, know they have a leak. In order to throw suspicion off their actual informer, Percival suggests setting up Flaherty, leading the IRA to suspect him instead, providing the British with a propaganda coup. He posits the benefits of his solution: "An Irish-American executed by the IRA? If the matter were correctly handled by the press?"

Wyndham considers the proposal, warning Percival to be careful. "We're getting enough problems from America as it is," he observes. Potential reaction to the death of an American volunteer would make any operation against Flaherty delicate. "If you think you can get the IRA to kill him, which is fine," the colonel advises, "but if they thought the British Army killed one of their citizens that would make it difficult."

Both the IRA and the British are presented as methodically cruel and cynical. The IRA deliberately expose Flaherty to risk and plan to "use him up" if needed for propaganda purposes. The British plan a parallel scenario. Their elaborate scheme fails when the man set up to overhear Percival praise Flaherty's cooperation unmasks John Russell as the true informer.

The Farmer orders Tony to kill Flaherty with the British rifle. Troubled by Tony's actions in a recent bombing, the Farmer determines this will be Tony's last mission. After he kills Flaherty, he himself will be eliminated. Tony leads Flaherty on an operation. Once secluded in an alley, Tony aims the British rifle at him, telling Michael, "You're more use to us dead. Public relations." The rifle jams, giving Flaherty time to shoot Tony with a handgun.

Siobhan warns Flaherty not to attempt crossing the border into the Republic and leads him to a ferry sailing to Scotland.

Back in his upper middle class home in the Detroit suburbs, Flaherty visits his dying grandfather Seamus (Sterling Hayden). At first his grandfather greets him by asking, "Did you kill lots of those British bastards for me?" Eager to please his dying grandfather, Flaherty lies about his experiences, saying the fight in Ireland was just like he told him it would be. He falsely states that his grandfather is remembered in Ireland by his old comrades who celebrate his bravery. Seamus smiles, musing, "I fooled them all, everybody ... you." Puzzled at first, Michael is stunned when his beloved grandfather confesses that he was an informer. Captured by British and threatened with death, he agreed to help, betraying his friends, who were executed. Seamus admits he sided with Michael Collins, accepting the Treaty as a "stepping stone," telling his grandson, "You can't fight forever."

Realizing that his role model is false, Michael explodes in rage, shouting, "I always

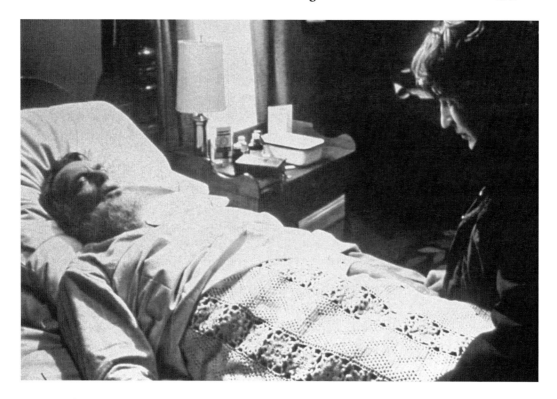

Sterling Hayden (left) and the American volunteer, Craig Wesson, in *The Outsider* (1979).

wanted to be just like you! I thought you were a great man!" He asks his grandfather why he lied to him as a boy. "I owed," Seamus explains, "and I didn't want to die owing." Guilty over his betrayal of the IRA in the 1920s, the exiled gunman felt obligated to commit his grandson to the Cause a half century later. Michael is incredulous at his grandfather's self-serving betrayal, asking, "You owed my life?"

Shaken, Michael is next seen walking through a Detroit slum, its boarded-up shops and graffiti reminiscent of Belfast. He attempts to call Siobhan from a pay phone, but the operator tells him all the circuits to Belfast are busy. When he tries to exit the phone booth, he finds himself trapped, sealed in a glass box. Infuriated, he punches out the windows, smashes through the door, and begins kicking the phone booth as the screen goes black.

Flaherty finds his idealism betrayed and exploited a second time, the Cause in Ireland and his beloved grandfather even more disheartening than the war in Vietnam.

PATRIOTS (1994)

Patriots (Boston Pictures) opens with a brief prologue in which IRA soldier Sean McGinnis (Mark Newell) is ordered to recruit an American volunteer while on a gun-running mission to Boston. The Army Council, Sean is told, has decided to use an outsider to unknowingly carry a bomb into UFF headquarters. This scene is followed by the opening credits and a written preface:

> Inspired by true events, the following recounts Boston native Alexis Shannon's two week ordeal in Northern Ireland during February of 1993. The contents of an audio tape she returned with have never been made public and she has since disappeared.

The plot unfolds in flashback. In March 1993 Alexis Shannon (Linda Amendola) summarizes her experiences during an interview with federal authorities in Boston after her return from Belfast. She explains that she always had a "keen interest in Irish affairs," believing in the cause for a united Ireland and seeing the IRA as "just and noble."

She recalls her encounter with Sean McGinnis in a Southie pub the month before. Discussing the troubles in Belfast, the IRA gunrunner ridicules the Boston Irish sitting around them who are content to sing rebel songs, "talking their mighty worthless talk." None of them, he declares, are willing to risk their lives for a united Ireland.

Alexis becomes infatuated with the bearded revolutionary. Like Michael Flaherty, she grew up listening to her grandfather's stories of fighting the Black and Tans. "I admired what he did," she tells Sean. A graduate student in Irish studies, she admits she is only "studying the past" rather than "shaping the future." Sean asks her to return to Ireland with him the next morning. Inspired by this handsome, poetic IRA soldier, she abandons her university work and joins Sean at a warehouse where he takes delivery of hundreds of weapons. The warehouse is raided by the ATF, but Sean and Alexis escape to the boat.

In Belfast the unit leader Paddy McClure (Dermot Petty) immediately suspects Alexis because IRA sources in London alerted them that the British penetrated the Boston gunrunning operation with a female agent. Determined to eliminate a possible security risk and exploit Alexis's potential as an outsider, McClure decides to turn her into a human bomb. She is given a video camera and told to enter UFF headquarters posing as an American journalist to conduct a surveillance operation. She is directed to tape as much as she can and memorize the layout. Unbeknownst to her, the camera is packed with plastic explosives set to detonate when it is switched on.

Just before she enters the headquarters, McGinnis takes her aside, warning her not to turn the camera on and to leave the building immediately. Introducing herself as a journalist, Alexis sets up her equipment to conduct her interview. Guarded by masked gunmen, the leather-jacketed UFF leader threatens to punish anyone who supports the IRA, even organizations in the United States. After assembling the camera tripod, Alexis asks to use the restroom, then flees. Seeing her running out the door, an IRA man triggers the bomb with a remote device and fires at wounded Loyalists as they stumble outside. British soldiers arrive on the scene and a firefight erupts, during which Alexis is captured.

Alexis is interrogated by an SAS major who warns her that membership in the IRA is punishable by a sentence of seven years. She denies involvement in the IRA, but the British major knows all about the "hapless recruit from America" tricked into a suicide mission by the IRA. Like Flaherty, she is seen as a "misguided" patriot, a pawn to be used by both sides. Drugged, she is cast adrift by the British to blindly wander the streets of Belfast, wanted by the Loyalists for planting the bomb and hunted by the IRA for being a spy. Making her way into a pub, she is rescued by the owner, Belle McCreesh (Carmel O'Reilly), who hides her. Recognizing her as the American girl who planted the bomb, Belle tells her she is Protestant but has long believed in a united Ireland, though she adamantly resents "being bombed into it."

As with Michael Flaherty, the British attempt to engineer her execution by the IRA, tipping off the Provos about her location. When the IRA fail to find her in the pub, the SAS major orders to tip them off again so they "can get it right."

Told that "the mick" is waiting in his office, the SAS major meets with the IRA informer — Sean McGinnis — who demands that Alexis be located and put on a plane to Boston and given federal protection on her arrival. That, he insists, was a condition of their agreement. The SAS major claims the situation has changed and that "it would have been better for everyone if you'd let her blow herself up." He reminds McGinnis the girl was brought in to provide cover for him. The plan "worked beautifully," and the IRA "swallowed everything we gave them," he states, but now Alexis is a liability because "as long as that girl is alive, the truth can be found out." She could reveal that British intelligence knew about the UFF bombing and let it proceed. "How would that reflect on our government?" the major asks Sean. The truth would cause "unrest" in Northern Ireland and "backlash" in Britain. "In the grand scheme of things," the major tells Sean, "...the young lady doesn't count for very much. Now, just let the local paramilitaries take care of this, and no one will be the wiser."

Belle dyes and cuts Alexis's hair, and, like Siobhan in *The Outsider*, helps the American volunteer flee Belfast by taking a ship to Scotland. Belle tells Alexis the war has been lost politically, militarily, and morally. As Alexis looks on, the IRA kills Belle when she visits the grave of her husband. Alexis flees to the waterfront but is captured by the IRA.

Alexis is next seen in a basement room, naked and hooded, forced to lean against the wall, her arms and back covered with welts. Two IRA women whip her as Paddy repeatedly orders her to confess that she is a British agent. With almost Islamic piety, Paddy keeps his back turned to her nudity until he covers her with a Union Jack.

Paddy orders McGinnis to kill Alexis. As in *The Outsider*, the IRA plans a chain of executions. McGinnis will kill Alexis, Damien will kill McGinnis, and another gunman will kill Damien. At the execution site, the SAS major shoots Damien, giving Sean a chance to help Alexis flee Northern Ireland.

At the dock, Sean plays a tape of his conversation with the SAS major, revealing that British intelligence knew about the bombing and wanted Alexis dead. Stunned, Alexis asks Sean, "Who are you?" McGinnis reveals that he is a mercenary chameleon, answering, "Who do you want me to be? You need a mole? I'm your man. You need a gunrunner, I can do that, too. Makes no difference. I can play it both ways, so long as it pays." Like Flaherty, Alexis is shocked and dismayed that she has been lied to and used. Sean acknowledges his betrayal but assures her he will try to protect her by working things out with the Loyalists and Paddy McClure. The only problem, he tells her, will be the SAS. He gives her the tape for insurance, telling her "as long as this survives, so will you." He tells her to deliver the tape to John Hicks, an ATF agent "who will know what to do."

In Boston, Alexis tells Hicks that Sean was "a man as complicated and confused as the country itself," declaring she now realizes that "a cause that first seemed noble and romantic was in truth only sad and utterly insane." Her IRA adventure "was just a mad game after all, because no one wins."

The film ends with a casualty list of the Troubles and the comment, "And so it continues." Alexis Shannon, viewers are told, has subsequently disappeared, raising the possibility that the madness of Belfast followed her to Boston.

Both *The Outsider* and *Patriots* reveal the "mad game" of the Troubles that maliciously consumes naïve American volunteers seeking to serve a romantic and noble Cause that is only vicious and ugly.

The IRA Comes to America

The 1990s saw a number of major motion pictures featuring IRA characters coming to American shores. In the decade between the end of the Cold War and 9/11 screenwriters and directors needed new adversaries for suspense and action films. The violence of Belfast could be transplanted to the United States, providing American agents and action heroes with new challenges.

PATRIOT GAMES (1992)

Phillip Noyce's *Patriot Games* (Paramount), based on the Tom Clancy novel, presents a mural of IRA current events — terrorist attacks in London, training camps in Libya, and fundraising American-Irish bars — as background to a family-in-peril drama. At its heart, the plot is no more ideological than *Cape Fear*. A strong, all–American father defends his household from a murderous villain seeking revenge. As in other movies of the era, the IRA is mentioned in media reports of a terrorist attack within the film, and its name is invoked by several characters, though the script clearly identifies the terrorists as belonging to a "fringe" or "renegade group." Accompanied by Annette (Polly Walker) and Sean Miller (Sean Bean), Kevin O'Donnell (Patrick Bergin) launches an unauthorized attack on a car carrying Lord Holmes (James Fox), the Minister of State for Northern Ireland and cousin of the Queen Mother, as it leaves Buckingham Palace.

The assassination attempt is thwarted when ex–Marine, former CIA analyst, family man, and professor John Patrick Ryan (Harrison Ford), enters the fray and kills the younger brother of Sean Miller. The operation is condemned by the official IRA, represented by Jimmy O'Reardon (Jonathan Ryan), who argues that attacking the royal family turns the public against them. Insisting that "in its heart and soul, England is still a monarchy,"

The Fenian comes to America: Sean Bean in *Patriot Games* (1992).

O'Donnell reasons they must strike the "royals and the ruling class." O'Donnell has O'Reardon killed and sends his team to rescue Sean Miller, who was captured in the aborted attack.

The film depicts a fringe IRA group having an unlikely range of resources, including an English spy working in Buckingham Palace who supplies the team with intelligence about the unscheduled trips of royal officials and the route of a van transporting Sean Miller to prison.

The central plot quickly moves from the political to the personal, with an escaped Sean Miller vowing revenge against Jack Ryan who killed his baby brother. Miller, denounced as a "Fenian bastard" by a British interrogator, is the exact opposite of Ryan. Forever glaring, narrowing his eyes, and spouting vengeance, he is animalistic, driven by a wholly tribal vendetta that supersedes ideology. Ruthless and without pity, Miller kills a priest during confession, executes unarmed men in cold blood, dispatches an IRA operative who outlived his usefulness, and shoots up a car carrying Ryan's wife and young daughter in retribution for "my baby brother." While O'Donnell and Annette want to complete their mission against Lord Holmes, Miller only wants revenge against Ryan, arguing that getting Holmes "is not my mission." The enemy is no longer Great Britain but the man who killed his brother. Similarly, Ryan wants back in the CIA not to fight Irish terrorism but to go "after the man who tried to kill my family."

Ryan, solely interested in getting Miller, approaches a Sinn Fein spokesman and fundraiser, Paddy O'Neil (Richard Harris), in an Irish pub and demands to know the whereabouts of Sean Miller. Though O'Neil condemns the terrorist attacks and denies IRA responsibility, he refuses to inform on his fellow Irishmen, stating, "The day that I sell out my countrymen will be the day that I put a bullet through my own head." Ryan threatens to use his injured daughter to bring public pressure against IRA fundraising in the United States, vowing, "I will put such a stranglehold on your gun money, you'll be out in the street throwing rocks. I will fucking destroy you. I will make it my mission in life." O'Neil supplies him information about Annette, who, conveniently and inexplicably, is English, not Irish, allowing the Sinn Fein bagman to maintain his ethnic code of honor while assisting Ryan. Given Annette's identity, Ryan backs off on his threat, telling a CIA official, "Paddy O'Neil can sleep at night." Presumably, O'Neil is left free to raise gun money for the IRA in Belfast because Ryan is concerned only with the safety of his family in America.

After training in North Africa, the O'Donnell team, tipped off by their English informer, descends on the Ryan home on the evening Lord Holmes arrives to award Ryan a medal for bravery. While O'Donnell and Annette focus on capturing Holmes, Miller pursues his personal mission to avenge "me baby brother." In the final scene, Miller kills O'Donnell and Annette, who demand he target Holmes and not Ryan. Reduced to a fringe group of one, Miller battles Ryan, who ultimately kills the "Fenian bastard."

Critics found the film unconvincing, with *Variety* denouncing it as "mindless, morally repugnant and ineptly directed," and a "shoddy" sequel to *The Hunt for Red October*. "By painting the IRA faction as monsters," *Variety* declared, *Patriot Games* is "sentimentally loaded" and "blatantly anti–Irish."[55]

Patriot Games celebrates the Anglo-American "special relationship," with British and American agents cooperating to destroy the ruthless terrorists who threaten a pair of respectable fathers and their families. As "anti–Irish" as it might appear to critics, the film nevertheless gave audiences a largely Republican narrative of the Troubles. In the only Belfast scene, an IRA hideout is stormed by heavily armed British security forces. Though the men making bombs are hardly depicted as heroic, the scene does leave viewers with a *Battle of*

Algiers impression that the conflict is one between an oppressed people using terrorism against foreign occupation. As in countless other films, Irish Unionists are distinctly noticeable by their absence.

BLOWN AWAY (1994)

Released two years after *Patriot Games*, Stephen Hopkins' *Blown Away* (MGM) presents another "Fenian bastard" in the form of Ryan Gaerity (Tommy Lee Jones) who, like Sean Miller, stalks an American authority figure on his home turf in a parallel terrorist-come-to-America story. In *Patriot Games* John Ryan is a former CIA analyst; in *Blown Away* Jimmy Dove (Jeff Bridges) is a Boston bomb disposal officer. John Ryan has a wife and young daughter; Jimmy Dove has a new wife and young step-daughter. Ryan foils an assassination attempt; Dove foils a Belfast bombing. A revenge-driven terrorist stalks Ryan's family; a revenge-driven bomber stalks Dove's family. Both films end with the Fenian monster dead and the all–American family saved.

Blown Away opens on a dark and stormy night in Castle Gleigh Prison, Northern Ireland, with a long-haired, Irish-speaking Ryan Gaerity reading in a book-lined cell. After lights out, he smothers his cellmate, assembles a bomb, and blows a hole through the wall of the prison, and escapes.

The film cuts to Boston where Jimmy Dove attends a child's birthday party. An all–American Irish cop, he rides a motorcycle, owns a dog, and lives in a house decorated with an American flag imposed on a shamrock. Called from the party to handle an emergency at MIT, Dove demonstrates his expertise at disarming a bomb. While "shutting down" the device, Dove experiences black-and-white flashbacks to a Belfast bombing. Audiences learn that in disarming bombs in Boston, Jimmy is doing "penance" for his Republican past.

Gaerity, now hiding in Boston, sees a television news report about the MIT incident and recognizes Jimmy Dove as Liam McGivney from Belfast. Blaming him for disrupting a bombing that led to his imprisonment, Gaerity begins a campaign of revenge, planting bombs that kill Boston cops. Gaerity phones Dove/McGivney, blaming him for his twenty years of imprisonment and the death of his Republican comrades, including his own sweetheart. Dove contends he was trying to stop Gariety from detonating a bomb that would kill civilians. "We were at war," Gaerity retorts, and "your conscience caused the death of your own.... Whilst you've been prancing around the streets of bloody America playing hero, I've been a man without a country. I spent the last twenty years of life in jail or on the run because of you!" Cackling fiendishly and bouncing on a bed with childish delight, he announces he is not a destroyer but a "creator." When Dove insists he not a creator but a "sick freak," Gaerity ominously states, "I have come here to create a new country for you called chaos and a new government called anarchy." When Gaerity condemns him because he "betrayed the Cause," Dove insists, "You never gave a damn about the Cause! The only thing that turned you on were your goddamn bombs!" Gaerity then threatens Jimmy's new wife and daughter.

Dove races home to find his dog dead. Burying his pet in the back yard, he tells his wife his true identity, revealing that he was "born and raised in Belfast" and involved in the Troubles.* "We were at war," he explains. "I was just a kid. They recruited me off the playground.... My whole life I was taught to hate the English, get 'em out of Ireland." When

---

Though born and bred in Belfast, Dove has no detectable Irish accent, so that his new bride is shocked that he is not a Boston native.

The mad bomber in Boston: Tommy Lee Jones in *Blown Away* (1994).

his wife mentions the IRA, Dove denies membership, saying Gaerity "was too crazy for that."

Like Sean Miller, Gaerity is driven solely by personal revenge, not politics. He terrorizes Dove's family and fellow cops, planting elaborate Rube Goldberg explosives and sending authorities psychotic videos featuring a Liam doll.

In another parallel to *Patriot Games*, the IRA assists in identifying the terrorist. Jimmy's uncle (Lloyd Bridges), a retired police officer, tells a Boston IRA fundraiser that if he has been "feeding a wayward brother just new here in town" he has "done the Cause a huge big harm." The bagman is moved only when he learns that Ryan Gaerity killed an Irishman in escaping prison. Like Paddy O'Neil, the Boston bagman informs on the non–IRA terrorist.

As in *Patriot Games*, the films concludes with a brutal, deadly battle between hero and terrorist, followed by a scene of the victorious all–American father embracing his wife and daughter.

In *Blown Away* the Cause remains unquestioned, as does the IRA, which has nothing to do with the "sick freak" who is motivated by violence alone. A fellow police officer (Forest Whittaker) questions Dove's true identity, but in the end he lets him go, telling him to "go back to his wife and his kid." For a Boston cop, Dove's participation in terror for the Cause is forgivable, and whatever sins he committed in Ireland can be overlooked.

THE DEVIL'S OWN (1997)

Alan Pakula's *The Devil's Own* (Columbia Pictures) makes a lyrical departure from the terrorist-in-America theme. Instead of a vengeful psychopath bent on a personal vendetta, the Irish rebel is boyishly charming Frankie McGuire (Brad Pitt) who comes to America to acquire weapons for the Cause at home. Unlike Sean Miller, who participates in an attack on unarmed family members, or Gaerity, who intends to bomb civilians, McGuire targets British troops and armed officers. He appears as an urban guerrilla, a revolutionary soldier, not a "terrorist" bent on killing non-combatants. In addition, his goal is political, not personal. While Miller and Gaerity target a wife and mother for personal vengeance, Frankie attacks military targets, not to defeat an enemy but drive his adversaries to the peace table. His motivation is both ideological and pragmatic.

More importantly, a rationale, if not a justification, is provided for Frankie's actions. Unlike Sean Miller or Gaerity, he is given an emotionally wrenching backstory. A prologue set in 1972 depicts a young Francis McGuire living peacefully with his fisherman father, mother, and young sister in a seaside stone cottage. While the family is saying grace at the dinner table, a masked Loyalist storms through the door and shoots the father dead for being "a Republican sympathizer."

The film then fast-forwards to 1992 Belfast where Harry Sloan, a British intelligence officer, conducts a briefing about Frankie McGuire, who is responsible for the deaths of eleven British soldiers, seven RUC officers, and "countless numbers of Loyalist paras." An attempt to capture Frankie triggers an improbably intense firefight, with masked IRA men firing automatic weapons from a house as British troops storm out of armored vehicles.

Frankie escapes to a remote hideout where a confederate tells him that while the cabinet was talking peace, the SAS was preparing to eradicate them. Frankie agrees, noting, "They say the word 'peace' ... but at the end of the day all they want is surrender." Hearing a helicopter overhead, Frankie muses, "If we could take them out, they would have to listen."

The heroic volunteer, Brad Pitt, in *The Devil's Own* (1997).

His comrade agrees, sending him to America to acquire Stinger missiles so that "maybe then they'll talk peace."

A clean-cut Frankie arrives at Newark Airport in 1993 under the name Rory Devaney. He is picked up by a New York state judge who collects money for the IRA and states the barrier to fundraising is that people don't know what is going on in Northern Ireland. The judge provides Frankie/Rory with money, a cover job, and a safe house — the home of Tom O'Merea (Harrison Ford), an unsuspecting New York police officer and family man. The film builds on the irony the British find both puzzling and distasteful. Tough on crime at home, American police officers and judges embrace and celebrate those who kill police officers and judges in Britain. Frankie receives a satchel of money from the judge to purchase missiles from arms dealer Billy Burke (Treat Williams) and begins restoring a ship to transport the arms to Ireland.

Staying with O'Merea, the fatherless Frankie develops a father-son relationship with the American cop, who only has daughters. The two males bond over drinks and games of pool. In a moment of stress after a police shooting, a stricken O'Merea is driven home by Frankie. In twenty-three years on the police force, he tells Frankie, he has fired his weapon four times. Asked if he ever shot anyone, Frankie answers by telling Tom about the murder of his father.

Accidentally discovering Frankie's cache of money, O'Merea assumes he is running guns for the IRA. Confronted about the money, Frankie offers to leave but insists he needs the funds. O'Merea challenges him, asking, "Why? So other eight-year-olds can watch their fathers gunned down in front of them? If this money leaves here, more people will die. Can you tell me that won't happen?" In response, a tearful Frankie answers the family man with a question: "What if tonight everything you had was burned down around you? What if you and yours were ... spat on? Told you were nothing, you're no good? What if it was one of yours cut down by a plastic bullet, one of yours you had to bury?" Frankie provides a rationale for terrorism, telling the American cop and family man, "We're normal people in an abnormal situation, fighting a disgusting ugly war which you can't understand because you haven't lived it." Tom takes McGuire and the money into custody, but Frankie escapes, killing O'Merea's partner.

The FBI questions O'Merea about his association with McGuire, informing him that "Frankie the Angel" is a unit commander in the Provisional IRA wanted for murdering soldiers and police officers. The FBI agents are accompanied by Harry Sloan, who has a terse interchange with O'Merea:

> Sloan: Exactly what is your relationship to this terrorist, Sergeant O'Merea?
> O'Merea: Who are you?
> Sloan: Harry Sloan, Sergeant. British intelligence. You are Irish?
> O'Merea: So is Cardinal O'Connor.
> Sloan: I've been tracking these murderous bastards for nearly two years. He's the last of them....
> I have been given the authority by both my government and yours to use any means necessary to bring closure to this issue.
> O'Merea: If you want to talk to me again, you read me my rights.

Told by his Irish police chief to cooperate, O'Merea balks, stating, "They're not going to bring him in, they're going to kill him." Unlike *Patriot Games*, no Anglo-American alliance forms between British intelligence and American law enforcement. Frankie may be a terrorist who killed his partner, but O'Merea has no interest in working with Sloan to execute him without trial. Although intent on bringing him to justice, O'Merea expresses empathy for McGuire's actions, telling Frankie's girlfriend, "I understand why he's doing what he's doing. If I had to endure what he's endured. If I was eight years old and saw my father gunned down in front of my family—I'd be carrying a gun, too, and I wouldn't be carrying a badge."

Having obtained the missiles after a shootout with a double-crossing Billy Burke, Frankie prepares to sail to Ireland. Just as he casts off, O'Merea boards the ship and tells Frankie the killing must stop. Frankie shoots O'Merea, who returns fire. Frankie raises his automatic, then stumbles to the deck, bleeding. O'Merea grips the dying Frankie, who tells him that his father had been a fisherman. The cop and cop killer maintain an Irish bond that supplants all other loyalties. "It's not an American story, it's an Irish one," Frankie states. A tearful O'Merea mutters, "We never had a choice," then takes the helm, steering the ship back to shore.

The Devil's Own generated protest in the British tabloids. The mere casting of heart-throb Brad Pitt as an Irish rebel was bound to provoke offense, leading newspapers to condemn the film as IRA propaganda. Commentators were especially incensed with Princess Diana for taking her son to the film.[56]

Patriot Games and *Blown Away* portray the IRA characters as men apart from social norms. While Sean Miller and Ryan Gaerity are psychopaths, the more sympathetic Frankie McGuire describes himself as a "normal person in an abnormal situation."

All three films depict the United States as a source of IRA funds. In *Patriot Games* Paddy O'Neil raises gun money in an Irish pub. In *Blown Away* a stadium hot dog vendor collects money for the Cause, no doubt picking up nominal sums here and there. The judge in *The Devil's Own* hands Frankie a canvas bag stuffed with hundred dollar bills. No amount is mentioned, but from the size of the bag and the merchandise it is to purchase—Stinger missiles—audiences can assume the judge has provided several hundred thousand dollars. The skirmishing collectors of Pat O'Brien's boyhood are shown still at work in the 1990s, raising money for "the trouble back home."

RIOT (1999)

Joseph Merhi's *Riot* (PM Entertainment Group) is a cartoonish action film starring kickboxing champion Gary Daniels and former prizefighter Sugar Ray Leonard. In a plot worthy of a computer game, an SAS superhero rescues a damsel in distress from masked Provos in the middle of a Los Angeles race riot.

After three teenagers are mistakenly shot by the police on Christmas Eve, the city erupts in violence. The opening montage of looted stores, burning police vehicles, and military patrols resembles the Los Angeles riots of 1992. A TV newsman tells viewers he is reporting from a "war zone," referring to the riot area as "ground zero." In the midst of the rioting, black gang members break into a car and abduct Anna Lisa Gray (Paige Rowland), the fashion model daughter of the British Ambassador.

Shane Alcott (Gary Daniels), an SAS officer in the United States training American soldiers, is summoned to the British embassy* with his American sidekick, Major Williams (Sugar Ray Leonard). The ambassador has received a videotaped demand for a two-million-dollar ransom from Shyboy, leader of a black gang. The money, the tape insists, must be delivered by one man.

Shane Alcott is inserted into the burning ghetto by helicopter and forced to run a

---

*Why the British ambassador is located in Los Angeles and not Washington is never explained.

gauntlet of thugs, including a horde of masked hockey players in full team uniform who swarm toward him on roller blades, armed with sticks. He hides one million in a spare tire and presents the briefcase with half the ransom to Shyboy, promising to deliver the rest after the girl's release. At the embassy Major Williams persuades an FBI agent to let him use a helicopter to rescue Shane. Shyboy's gang fires a missile at the chopper, and Williams falls to his death. As Shane and Lisa take cover, they observe the gang meeting with white men in black berets. Shane recognizes their leader as Provo chief Bryan O'Flaherty (Patrick Kilpatrick). The kidnapping, Alcott realizes, was not a random crime of opportunity but part of an IRA plot. O'Flaherty tells Shyboy, "You and I are much more alike than we know.... You have your American oppressors, and I have the British." With that, the IRA open fire on their black confederates for allowing Lisa to escape. "Gentlemen," O'Flaherty tells his Provos, "we've got work to do." Mounting motorcycles, the Provos in black helmets and flak jackets chase after Shane as Anna Lisa tries to run to a police outpost at the edge of the "riot zone." Shane manages to outwit and dispatch the Provos, who, helmeted or masked, remain anonymous robotic adversaries. Alcott discovers Anna Lisa wounded and finds shelter for her in the home of Fred Baker, a black Vietnam veteran protecting his wife and daughter with a shotgun. Displayed on his wall are an American flag and a portrait of Martin Luther King. Baker explains the lack of presents under their humble tree by stating he had been laid off and forced to tell his daughter that Santa Claus would not be coming this Christmas. Shane leaves Anna Lisa with the black family, then sets out to take on the IRA singlehanded.

In a final confrontation, O'Flaherty vows to kills Shane, calling him an "English fuck." Shane replies, "Bryan O'Flaherty, big shot terrorist. Since when has the IRA been operating on American shores? What, even Ireland's not safe for your sick ideology?" Shane and O'Flaherty play out their final battle in a demolition derby in a high-rise parking structure until O'Flaherty's car crashes to the street below.

The film ends with the TV reporter commenting that peace is being restored to the city as people attend church and recall the lessons of that first Christmas, and that "the sword must give way to the ploughshare.... Violence like this must never, never occur again." The Baker daughter discovers a package under their tree containing half the ransom money. As Christmas Day dawns over Los Angeles, Shane Alcott carries Anna Lisa out of the burning ghetto to safety.

In *Riot* the Provos are not only depoliticized but dehumanized into masked, helmeted aliens. They are simply the embodiment of evil — malicious, mendacious, and heartless. In contrast to O'Flaherty's cynical pseudo–Marxist alliance with Shyboy, Shane forms a genuine bond with Baker, both of them fellow veterans protecting vulnerable females.

THE IRA SAVES THE FIRST LADY: *THE JACKAL* (1997)

In *The Devil's Own* Frankie McGuire is given a sympathetic backstory to provide a method to his madness, so that audiences view the IRA man not as an embodiment of evil but a poor misguided youth driven to violence by social injustice. *The Jackal* (Universal) moves beyond empathy to adoration, as an imprisoned IRA man is elevated from convict to action hero. Based loosely on Fred Zinnemann's *The Day of the Jackal* (Universal, 1973), Michael Caton-Jones' version is a post–Cold War thriller which borrows elements from the original Frederick Forsyth plot about a chameleon-like assassin.

When his brother is killed in a joint FBI-MVD operation, Moscow gangster Terek

Murad (David Hayman) plots revenge against the United States and hires an assassin known only as the Jackal (Bruce Willis) to send a "public message" to the Americans and "strike fear into the marrow of their bones" by killing a high-profile personality. The intended victim is identified to the Jackal by a photograph held out of view of the audience. The prominence of the target leads the Jackal to demand $70 million. The MVD learns through a brutal interrogation that Murad has hired the Jackal to kill the director of the FBI.

As the Jackal moves from Helsinki to London to Canada to America, changing disguises and identities while assembling his equipment for the assassination, the FBI and MVD attempt to track him down. The only lead they have is that former Basque terrorist Isabella Zancona (Mathilda May) knew his identity, and the only person believed to know Zancona is Declan Mulqueen (Richard Gere), a former IRA sharpshooter who retired to the United States where he was arrested on old weapons charges and sentenced to fifty years. FBI Deputy Director Carter Preston (Sydney Poitier) and MVD major Valentina Koslova (Diane Venora) visit Mulqueen in a maximum security prison in Massachusetts, offering him a transfer to a minimum security facility for providing information about Isabella. Mulqueen refuses to betray her, even after Preston guarantees her immunity from extradition to Spain. Asked what it will take to get him to cooperate, Mulqueen makes a demand that sets off a brief debate in which he declares himself to be a soldier, not a "terrorist":

> Mulqueen: Then you'd have to let me go. Back to Ireland, free man.
> Preston: Out of the question. Besides gunrunning, you're a known killer of British government personnel.
> FBI agent: Not to mention all the women and children you've probably blown up.
> Mulqueen: ... I was never a bomber.
> Koslova: I don't see the distinction. You still took human lives.
> Mulqueen: The distinction is I killed in war. Now I want to go home.... Look, even in Russia soldiers go home when the treaty's signed, nyet?

Mulqueen moderates his demands, asking simply for Preston's "best efforts" to set him free. When Preston refuses, Mulqueen claims he is the only one who can save the FBI Director because he met the Jackal and knows his methods.

Preston agrees to let Mulqueen out of prison to meet Isabella. At first Mulqueen is handcuffed and placed under close surveillance by agents. Isabella, now living in suburban Virginia with a husband and children, tells Major Koslova, "We were all dangerous people," but the Jackal was "different." Whereas Declan had "fire" and "passion" because "he had a cause," the Jackal "was ice" and without "feeling." In parting, Isabella slips Mulqueen a key to a Greyhound locker containing a passport and ten thousand dollars. She urges him to return to Ireland, but he tells her he has given his word not to escape.

Having established himself as a soldier and man of his word, Mulqueen transforms from jailed terrorist to FBI asset. No longer handcuffed, he meets with the FBI Director as a consultant, outlining the techniques the Jackal will likely employ. As the Jackal moves closer to his target, changing names and appearances, Mulqueen becomes a more constant and reliable character. At one point, while Major Koslova is asleep, he discovers a gun in a desk. True to his word, he makes no attempt to escape and closes the drawer. Spotting him at the desk, Preston orders him to open his shirt to see if he took the weapon. Mulqueen obeys, baring his chest, which is covered in scars he describes as "souvenirs of British hospitality."

In a following scene Mulqueen flies in an FBI jet with Preston and Koslova. He is no longer portrayed as a shackled prisoner but as a professional providing expert advice. After the Jackal kills Koslova, Mulqueen evolves from advisor to planner as he stands at a map, giving FBI agents and U.S. military officers directions on how to capture the Jackal. Mulqueen has a sudden epiphany and realizes that the Jackal's target is not the FBI Director but the First Lady, who is scheduled to appear at the opening of a children's hospital.

On a military helicopter flying to the ceremony, Preston orders a soldier to hand Mulqueen a rifle. Dropped onto a rooftop, the former IRA sniper sights the van containing the Jackal's remote-controlled gun and fires just as the Jackal targets the First Lady. His assassination attempt frustrated, the Jackal sets his weapon to fire wildly into the crowd and flees, with Mulqueen in pursuit.

While the police, FBI, and Secret Service remain clueless, Mulqueen follows the Jackal into the Metro. Needing assistance, Mulqueen calls for backup — not from the FBI or the army, but from Isabella. In a final shootout on a subway platform, the two former terrorists with a cause slay the ice-cold terrorist who kills only for money.

Days later Mulqueen and Preston watch as the Jackal's coffin is lowered into a grave. Preston regrets that Mulqueen has been denied a pardon, although the FBI Director "sends his warmest thanks." Preston confesses to Mulqueen that he knew about the locker key and respects him for not escaping. Now credited for saving the First Lady, Preston muses that he is "untouchable" and could "screw up" without fear of reprimand. Suggesting that with a clean passport and a wad of cash Mulqueen could elude the FBI and get back to Ireland, Preston offers to get him coffee. Smiling, he informs Mulqueen he will be back in half an hour. Turning his back on the IRA hero, Preston allows Mulqueen to casually walk away a free man, the "killer of British government personnel" wholly redeemed by a grateful nation. As with Jimmy Dove in *Blown Away*, Mulqueen's terrorist past is forgettable and forgivable because his victims were English, not American.

IRISH IDENTITIES: THE CIA COMES TO IRELAND
MY BROTHER'S WAR (1997)

James Brolin directed and starred in *My Brother's War* (New Horizons), playing John Hall, a retired Irish-American CIA agent who teams up with IRA volunteer Gerry Fallon (Patrick Foy) to track down his brother Liam Fallon (Salvator Xuereb), a rogue Republican threatening peace negotiations.

In the opening scene the Fallon brothers construct a bomb and plan an attack on a member of the royal family. The importance of the American connection to the "movement" is demonstrated when Liam suggests killing more people to gain publicity. Their IRA leader warns him sternly, "The movement doesn't gain support by blowing up innocent women and children. Our brothers in the States are quite sentimental about the weak and defenseless being victimized." Liam is unmoved by these concerns. Preparing to stage the attack, Gerry notices children in the royal car and attempts to abort the mission. Undeterred, Liam insists that it "doesn't change anything" and proceeds with the plan.

Retired CIA agent John Hall, like Jack Ryan in *Patriot Games*, intervenes when the IRA attacks a royal motorcade. In Northern Ireland for his sister's wedding, Hall spots a sniper in a nearby building and attempts to warn British security. Dismissing Hall's concerns, the agents allow the motorcade to proceed. Despite the presence of the children and civilians, Liam Fallon triggers a bomb that blows up the royal and kills Hall's sister. Liam escapes, leaving a wounded Gerry behind to take the blame. Convicted of twelve murders he did not commit, Gerry Fallon is sentenced to life without parole.

Five years later, as peace talks between Sinn Fein and the British government are announced, the official IRA orders its units to disarm. Liam refuses to abandon the fight, dismissing the Republican leadership as "old withered bastards." He insists, "A good leader knows there is a time to obey orders and a time to stand for what he believes in." Liam rebels against the official policy and leads a renegade group called Brothers in Arms that kills the IRA man attempting to collect their weapons, then robs an armored car, videotaping the execution of its crew to make a political declaration. The Brothers in Arms is dedicated, Liam states, to dismantling the peace process.

Back in the United States, John Hall is shown the armored car video by British and American intelligence officers who are concerned that secret negotiations involving the Secretary of State will be compromised. Hall is told he will be sent to Belfast to meet with Gerry Fallon in prison. Although he states he only wishes to see Gerry Fallon "with my gun in his mouth," Hall accepts the assignment. Gerry Fallon tells Hall he is willing to cooperate to get his brother. But like Declan Mulqueen in *The Jackal*, he insists on being released, claiming to be the only one who can bring down Liam. Though serving life without parole for twelve murders, Gerry Fallon is freed to work unshackled with Hall.

Gerry views Hall as naïve, telling him that Liam is not "some mugger in the streets." To defeat him, he tells Hall, "You got to get inside his head. Think Irish. Feel our pain." These remarks set up an argument about the legitimacy of the Irish-American experience.

Josh Brolin in *My Brother's War* (1997).

Unlike the wholly assimilated Jack Ryan, Hall retains a measure of Irishness and challenges Gerry Fallon's assertions:

> You know when my grandfather immigrated to the U.S. he shortened his name from O'Halloran to Hall because nobody in the city would hire a dirty mick. Does that make me less Irish than you because of the geography? Is that it? Get smart, Gerry boy. Don't ever get being Irish confused with being a damned sociopathic killer. I know that pain. And I've lived in the streets. And I have been poor. But it will never be an excuse for pulling the maniacal sick shit that you've pulled.

Liam assembles his revolutionary band, interviewing recruits and enlisting those with weapons training. When Hall's official attempt to seize Liam fails, Gerry insists that Hall work for him. The CIA agent who once served the British must now take directions from the IRA to achieve his aims. Like Declan Mulqueen, Gerry Fallon moves from inmate to coordinator, helping Hall set up security for talks involving the Secretary of State.

Disguised as caterers, Liam's men enter the country estate where the talks are being held, kill the guards, and demand the release of IRA prisoners. Gerry enters the house and confronts his brother, calling him a murderer. "And what were you?" Liam challenges him. "I thought I was a patriot," Gerry counters.

Spotting Hall outside the door, Gerry wounds him. The brothers flee in a boat, with Liam believing that Gerry has embraced his cause. Telling Liam that he must "take responsibility" for what he has done, Gerry opens his jacket to reveal a suicide belt, then hugs his brother and sets off the device.

Hall survives, and the peace talks continue. As Hall, his arm in a sling, visits Gerry Fallon's grave, a voiceover recites a poem: "Help my brother dry his tears/Help erase these last few years.... But I am here to rescue him/And try to understand his whim.... My baby brother's life is mine/ My heart is his. It is now our time."

American Haven

America often appears as a destination of escape in IRA films. John Ford's informer Gypo Nolan envisions himself sailing to America to start a new life. After a bombing mistakenly blows up a school bus in *A Prayer for the Dying* (The Samuel Goldwyn Company, 1987), Martin Fallon (Mickey Rourke) deserts the IRA and is lured by English gangsters into becoming a hit man in exchange for a passport, money, and passage to America.

Two films depict IRA volunteers trying to build new lives in the United States after fleeing Ireland.

THE BREAK/A FURTHER GESTURE (1997)

Robert Dornheim's *The Break* (Channel Four) follows Sean Dowd (Stephen Rea) as he attempts to find a new life in the United States after participating in a massive prison break in Ireland. His colleague, Richard (Brendan Gleeson), tells Sean that he has two options — to drop out and go abroad or stay with the organization. Sean decides to leave Ireland. In a parting scene overlooking the Atlantic, Richard provides him with a passport and American money, cautioning Sean to avoid the "Irish districts" to evade detection.

In New York City, Sean takes a shabby room and becomes a dishwasher. His Hispanic coworkers question why he works in a kitchen. "Your people can do better than this," Tulio (Alfred Molina) tells him, suggesting he become a carpenter, a job an irate coworker maintains is owned by the Irish. Offering him a drink after work, Tulio asks Sean, "Why aren't you with your own people?" Sean suggests he is fine on his own, but his loneliness is made evident in scenes dramatizing the isolation of his hotel room. Dowd intervenes in a domestic dispute and is stabbed. Afraid of being discovered, he does not go to a hospital. Tulio takes Sean to his apartment, where he and his sister Monica (Rosana Pastor) nurse him back to health. While recuperating, Sean discovers handguns hidden behind some books. He learns that Tulio and his sister intend to assassinate Colonel Ramon, a CIA-backed official who tortured and murdered their father in Guatemala.

Sean calls Ireland to obtain the name of a local contact, a bartender in an Irish pub. New York, Sean tells the barman, is "hotter" than he expected. The police have been looking for him, and he wants a safer location. Sean is told that arrangements can be made because they are "moving" someone else, suggesting that a kind of reverse witness protection program is in place in America, sheltering IRA fugitives from the FBI. Hoping to escape New York with Monica, Sean asks if he can bring someone else.

Realizing he cannot dissuade Monica from assassinating Ramon, Sean reluctantly provides technical advice to keep her from being arrested. Dowd never mentions the IRA, offering the Guatemalans only a vague explanation of his past, stating, "A long time ago I made a decision to get involved with something." Judging their guns to be inadequate "toys," he directs them to acquire money for better weapons and vehicles, establish safe routes, and destroy any forensic evidence after the attack.

After successfully killing Ramon, Sean and Monica stop at an Irish pub. Monica waits in the car as Sean goes inside and runs into Richard, who explains he has been visiting New York off and on, "arranging a few wee things." Leaving the pub, Sean and Richard are surrounded by the FBI. Richard surrenders, but Sean runs off. Encircled by police officers, Dowd pulls out a gun and is shot in a "suicide by cop" finale. Monica rushes toward Sean but is held back by police and told that it's just "some Irish thing."

Lacking other skills, Sean Dowd, like Martin Fallon in *A Prayer for the Dying* (Samuel Goldwyn, 1987), is drawn into an unrelated violent cause which ultimately leads to his death.

DISAPPEARING IN AMERICA (2009)

"This isn't your suburban America. People die for their causes every day."

Rick Rodgers' *Disappearing in America* (String and a Can Productions) is set entirely in San Francisco. Sean (David Polcyn), an IRA volunteer, has fled Ireland to protect his family from retaliation after bombing a Belfast police station. The details of his action remain obscure, with a few references to "bad planning" and the deaths of children.

The film opens with his surreptitious arrival on the San Francisco docks. At the outset Sean is established as an object, referred to as being an "it" and a "package delivered in good condition" that will later be "handed off." Covered in a blanket, he is lifted from the trunk of one car and placed in another and finally deposited in a one-room safe house. The studio apartment is unfinished and unfurnished. He sleeps on a blanket on a concrete floor, surrounded by brick and bare drywall. Isolated, locked in, denied contact with the outside world, he appears more like a hostage in the hands of benevolent kidnappers.

Sean is visited by Mickey (Richard Eden), the leader of a small ODESSA-like organization that prepares new identities in the United States for IRA fugitives. He is accompanied by his daughter's oafish cousin (Michael Morrison) and a nameless bodyguard (Mark Pellegrino), who admits to having made the same transition from Ireland to America. At the outset Mickey tells Sean, "I respect, we respect what you did for the Cause ... but the Cause doesn't fucking matter anymore. And it needs to be forgotten." Sean is given a new name and told never to use his own. Mickey further orders him not to talk about Ireland, visit Irish pubs, or even meet Irish people. His past life, his family, his old profession must be forgotten. Although Mickey later tells Sean it is an "honor" to help him, he warns him that it takes only a single "wag of the tongue" to put them all in jeopardy. Failure to follow the rules could lead Sean to be "tossed in a ditch." Sean is both the honored veteran of the Cause and a toxic agent that must be bottled up and destroyed if needed. Mickey instructs him to "lose that goddamn accent" and strips him of all personal belongings. Sean's handlers seem both protective and threatening, operating like cult deprogrammers and holding out promises of identity papers, a job, and an apartment.

Locked in an empty room, listening to a pictureless TV to practice American pronunciations, Sean exists in a Spartan limbo between past and present. Although Jackie (Devin DiGonno), the American widow of his murdered brother, lives within driving distance of San Francisco, he is barred from seeing or speaking with her. The bodyguard calls Jackie, exhorting her to make a "commitment" to the Cause by sending money. She offers to write another article and suggests Sean would be safer with her, but the bodyguard insists the best thing she can do for him is send fifty thousand dollars. He accuses Jackie of being a "plastic Paddy" who fled Belfast when the trouble started. She reminds him that her IRA husband was murdered and her brother-in-law and his family are in danger. The bodyguard toys with Sean, using him in drug deals, comforting him, then taunting him with suggestions that his family is in peril. He informs Sean that the doctor who delivered his son was shot by the UDF in retaliation for the police station bombing. Departing, he does not lock the door, tempting Sean to break the rules by leaving the safe house to call Ireland. Sean's fate in San Francisco parallels Michael Flaherty's in Belfast in *The Outsider*. He, too, is kept under wraps in a safe house while the IRA determines how best to exploit him.

Each member of Mickey's organization uses Sean. The bodyguard forces him to act as an expendable go-between in drug transactions with an Asian gang. The friendless cousin visits with whiskey and bemoans his fumbling ways, seeking a sympathetic companion. Mickey's daughter Sara (Anna-Marie Wayne) delivers food, offering Sean sympathy and encouraging him to build "a new life here." She speaks of a "second life" and "a new family." When Sean tells her about his wife and six-year-old son, Sara reveals that she has an eight-year-old son from a failed marriage who "desperately needs a good father." She brings her son to visit, suggesting Sean move in with her so she can keep a better eye on him. On her final visit, she has sex with Sean and urges him to live with her and attend her son's soccer games. Agitated, Sean suggests they move to Seattle or Vancouver, but she wants to remain in San Francisco, begging him, "Be patient — for me."

Sara is less concerned about Sean's future than her own needs for a new man and father for her child. Disappointed with his reluctance, she makes a phone call and delivers a cryptic message: "He's not going to do it."

The bodyguard and the cousin storm into the safe room, grab Sean, take him to a precipice overlooking the Golden Gate Bridge and execute him.

The nameless American organization exhibits a duplicitous attitude toward the Cause. At one point the bodyguard asks Sean, "Do you know how much money flows out of here for the IRA?" He speaks of "private funds" for "private causes." Americans are willing to fight for Ireland — from a safe distance. They supply money for the struggle but "let other people die for it." They are willing to help veterans of the Cause — as long as they serve their own interests. The IRA man who believes he is battling for his community in Belfast is a pawn in a much larger, unexplained American game. He is honored and sheltered as long as he meets the self-serving needs of his American keepers. Mickey, who professes to honor the IRA volunteer, also sarcastically notes that Sean "is so fresh he bleeds green."

The leaders of the Cause in San Francisco are just as willing to "use up" a dispensable volunteer as their counterparts in the backrooms of Belfast.

The Hapless American

Americans have been depicted as innocent victims of the Troubles who are either wholly oblivious to the danger around them or naïvely confident in their sense of security.

THE RAILWAY STATION MAN (1992)

Michael Whyte's *The Railway Station Man* (BBC Films) was written by Shelagh Delaney, based on a novel by Jennifer Johnston about a midlife romance between two damaged recluses, a Northern Irish widow and a disabled American. Helen Cuffe (Julie Christie) leaves Londonderry with her young son Jack after her husband is mistakenly killed by paramilitaries.

Settling in a remote home in County Donegal in the Republic, Helen builds a new life as an artist. She becomes intrigued with Roger Hawthorne (Donald Sutherland) who has come to Ireland to restore a disused railway station. Once renovated, the station can serve no useful function. There are no trains and no tracks, merely a few stone buildings too far from any town to serve as a museum. Nevertheless, Hawthorne is committed to the project and hires Damian Sweeney (John Lynch), a village local, to rebuild the signal boxes. Interested solely in trains, Hawthorne is unconcerned when Helen tells him that Sweeney is rumored to be a member of a "violent illegal organization."

Jack Cuffe (Frank MacCusker), now a college student, has become committed to Republican politics and assists IRA leader Manus Dempsey (Mark Tandy), who needs temporary storage for a weapons shipment. Manus dismisses Helen's artwork as ephemeral and useless to the Cause, telling her, "You have to destroy in order to create."

He views Hawthorne as a pathetic eccentric playing with a "glorified train set." Jack's mother and her disabled lover, he states, are "fiddling while Rome burns." The American's railway station, however, interests Manus because it contains an empty warehouse perfect for his purpose.

Helen is apprehensive about her son's growing association with the IRA, but Damien assures her that Jack is "only on the edge of it," working as a "messenger boy" who "would never use a gun."

Dempsey has a truck deliver weapons to the railway station, confident that Hawthorne is preoccupied with Jack's mother. When a tipsy Hawthorne leaves the Cuffe cottage and drives off, Jack follows, honking his horn and flashing his high beams, hoping to alert Dempsey. Unaware of what is happening, Hawthorne pulls into the station yard and slams into the arms truck. The resulting explosion kills IRA men, Hawthorne, and Jack Cuffe.

Helen is left alone with her paintings, the Troubles having claimed her husband, her son, and her hapless American lover.

HIDDEN AGENDA (1990)

Ken Loach's *Hidden Agenda* (Helmdale Film Corporation) presents a pair of well-intentioned Americans trapped in a murderous British conspiracy. Paul Sullivan (Brad Dourif), a human rights attorney, and his fiancée Ingrid Jessner (Francis McDormand) arrive in Northern Ireland to investigate accusations of RUC brutality against Republican suspects. They present their findings at a press conference in which Sullivan naively states that Britain is respected the world over as a democracy, telling reporters that he is "sure" the British government will respond to the abuse allegations. Scheduled to depart the following day, Ingrid says she is glad to leave Belfast because the "killings, torture, and intrigue" remind her of Chile. Sullivan reassures her that "what happened in Chile can't happen here."

The following morning Sullivan receives a call from Captain Harris (Maurice Roëves), an AWOL British army officer, now sheltered by the IRA, who tells him they must talk. Agreeing to a meeting outside Belfast, Sullivan is driven by a British Ministry of Defense official, Frank Molloy (now considered "a fringe member of the IRA"). En route to the meeting, they are followed by undercover RUC officers, who open fire on their car, forcing it off the road. When a wounded Sullivan crawls from the wreckage, an undercover policeman rushes forward to deliver the coup de grâce.

Deputy Kerrigan (Brian Cox) flies in from London to head an investigation of the shooting and immediately determines the police story does not match the forensic evidence. A weapon found in the vehicle was clearly planted. Stonewalled by the RUC, Kerrigan consults a retired colleague who tells him that the RUC men who shot Sullivan are SSU, Special Support Unit, an undercover anti-terrorist squad run by Special Branch. SSU, he tells Kerrigan, are "cowboys, not policemen" who are "out of control" and "trigger happy."

Initially assuring Ingrid that he will pursue all leads in the case, Kerrigan backs off after Harris reveals evidence of a wider and greater conspiracy at the highest levels of the British government. Blackmailed by Conservative leaders, Kerrigan prepares to leave Northern Ireland, limiting his investigation to the illegal shooting of Sullivan and Molloy. Confronted by Ingrid at the airport, Kerrigan warns her to get out of Belfast because she is in danger, then boards his plane, leaving the hapless American adrift in a Northern Ireland full of death squads, a place more dangerous than Chile.

Small Screen Republicans

Television writers found Irish Republicans suitable subjects for criminal dramas. IRA characters appeared in a number of long-running American series, including *Hawaii Five-O*, *Columbo*, and *Law and Order*.

FALSE PRIESTS, POETS, AND PATRIOTS

The 1977–1978 television season saw charming and ruthless IRA killers appearing in the guise of a priest and poet in Hawaii and California. *Hawaii Five-O* opened its tenth season with an episode titled "Up the Rebels" (aired September 15, 1977) in which Irish terrorist Sean Rourke (Stephen Boyd) poses as Father Daniel Costigan visiting charitable Catholic organizations in Hawaii as a cover while purchasing a shipment of high-tech plastic explosives hijacked from the U.S. Marine Corps. Naval intelligence informs Hawaii Five-O that the highly lethal material, described as suited for "urban warfare," may be headed to Ireland, leading Steve McGarrett (Jack Lord) to quip "shamrocks among the sugar cane."

Casey Fogarty (Elayne Heilveil), the daughter of a wealthy Irish-American industrialist, arrives from Boston and calls Rourke, using the phrase "the color is green" as a password. She presents Rourke with a suitcase full of cash from her father as "contributions from your American friend." A naïve romantic associated with "causes," Fogarty tries to impress Rourke, telling him she was at Wounded Knee, which he dismisses as a "skirmish," insisting his conflict "is a real war." Rourke mentions to her that he (like Brendan Behan) spent time in a Borstal facility.

Fogarty's arrival on the day of the hijacking arouses McGarrett's suspicions. In questioning her, McGarrett states that her wealthy father has "never made any secret where his sympathies lie." Casey denies involvement in the hijacking, dismissing her father as an "Irish sentimentalist" and noting, "Aside from wearing green on St. Patrick's Day, the only thing my father and I have in common is the family name."

Fogarty becomes smitten with Rourke and expresses a desire to play a larger role than simple courier, asking if there are "women in the movement in Ireland." Rourke is grateful for her father's money but views Casey as an adolescent romantic seeking "a kiss from a soldier of the revolution." When she says that her father would approve of her involvement because "Ireland needs heroes," Rourke responds with bitter remorse. "There are no heroes in Ireland anymore," he tells her, "only desperate men and dead fools. And graves. Too many graves."

Investigating recent arrivals with Irish passports, McGarrett interviews Father Costigan. When asked why he is not working in Northern Ireland, because "children are dying there every day," Rourke answers, "A nation is dying." When Rourke maintains that the people of Northern Ireland are being denied their honor, rights, and dignity, McGarrett tells him, "You sound more like an Irish patriot than a priest." Rourke insists that a man can be both. Recalling Matthew's words that a man cannot serve two masters, McGarrett states, "Many sins have been committed in the name of patriotism, father." When Rourke maintains he is not a rebel but doing "God's work," McGarrett states he does police work and concludes, "Let's both pray the explosives are found before they're turned to the devil's work." His suspicions about Costigan raised, McGarrett keeps the priest under surveillance.

Rourke works with men named Ryan and Foley, whom he kills when they are implicated by the police or attempt to extort money from him. These Irish-Americans have no political agendas, supplying arms solely for the cash. When asked if he is a Loyalist or a Republican, Folely answers, "Neither, I'm a capitalist." Rourke smiles, stating, "I like doing business with professionals. They have no ethics, no principles, and no moral standards." Rourke feels justified in killing them after they serve their purpose, explaining to Casey that "whenever someone becomes a danger to the cause he must be eliminated. There's no room for questions or conscience."

Despite the murders, Casey's affection for the rebel Rourke intensifies. Watching the explosives (ironically labeled "toys") being loaded onto the ship (suitably named *The Halls of Tara*), she tells Rourke she wants to go with him, declaring, "I want you, not your war."

When McGarrett confronts Casey at a warehouse, she admits being in love with Sean Rourke. Asked what the explosives will be used for, she answers with the euphemistic phrase "tactical necessities." McGarrett angrily confronts her with a British newspaper article describing the "tactical necessity" of a school bus bombing in Belfast which killed thirteen children and blinded and wounded others. He tells Casey that the "innocent children maimed in the streets of Belfast" is the work of her "beloved rebels." Fuming, he calls events in Northern Ireland "savagery" and "insanity," with "Catholics killing Protestants. Protestants killing Catholics. That's what your money is going to be used for." Forced to confront the article, Casey points to the *Halls of Tara* in the channel behind them. "Everything you want is on that boat," she confesses.

McGarrett stops the ship and arrests Rourke, who says defiantly, "Up the rebels." To this McGarrett responds, "God help the children."

On May 13, 1978, the original *Columbo* series concluded with a two-hour finale entitled "The Conspirators," with a similar plot involving wealthy Irish-Americans financing a weapons smuggling operation orchestrated by a deceptive rebel. Joe Devlin (Clive Revill) is a Brendan Behan–like poet, singer, raconteur, and reformed terrorist. Like Behan he went to England with explosives as a teenager (presumably during the 1939–1940 bombing campaign) and was imprisoned by the British. Renouncing violence ("nothing was ever solved by guns"), he penned an autobiography, *Up from Ignorance*. Providing the entertainment for an American Friends for Northern Ireland fundraiser, he offers his upscale audience (ironically, a Rolls Royce is shown parked outside the venue) a comic standup version of his arrest, then becomes serious, telling them that he is just "a boy from the back streets of Belfast come to wring your pockets and your consciousnesses" to help "the widows and orphans." Answering the rhetorical question that he was once a terrorist, a somber Joe Devlin disagrees, rationalizing that he was, in fact, "one of their victims." The event, hosted by the wealthy O'Connell family, raises $45,200.

Devlin's charming demeanor and the charitable aims of the Friends for Northern Ireland are a ruse. Devlin is in Los Angeles not only to promote his book but arrange the purchase and shipment of 300 Uzi-like weapons for "hit and run close quarter" fighting in Belfast. When the arms dealer attempts to extort an additional $50,000 from him, Devlin "executes" him with one of his own handguns. Investigating the murder, Lt. Columbo (Peter Falk) connects Devlin to the victim with stereotypical Celtic clues — an Irish whiskey bottle and a copy of *Up from Ignorance* inscribed "Ourselves Alone." As in other episodes, Columbo verbally duels with his suspect, but this time in verse. Sitting in a pub, Devlin and Columbo trade limericks. Finally unmasking the amusing Devlin as both a gun-runner and a murderer, Columbo accuses him of "pretending to raise money to help the Irish victims and all the while you were planning to make more victims." Unmoved, Devlin cynically responds that he has no regrets because "politics makes liars of us all, Lieutenant." The episode's ending is nearly identical with the end of *Hawaii Five-O*'s "Up the Rebels," with the authorities stopping a ship carrying weapons to Ireland before the vessel can put to sea.

The *Columbo* episode appears to support prevailing British assumptions that Irish peace organizations are simply fronts for terrorism and that the IRA is backed by powerful and wealthy Irish-Americans. Devlin's sponsors are Kate O'Connell (Jeanette Nolan), widow of an industrialist, and her son George (Bernard Behrens) who live in a palatial mansion, presiding over a family empire of dams, docks, and skyscrapers. Encountering them, Columbo is impressed, describing a "whole country raised under the O'Connell flag." While professing to reject violence, the elderly, wheelchair-bound Kate O'Connell is, in fact, bankrolling the gun-running to Northern Ireland.

The blood-tie to Ireland is so strong that even Kate's son, who has never set foot in the country, devotes himself to a cause that runs counter to his interests as a capitalist. When he admonishes Devlin for drinking, the poet gun-runner tells George that his only contribution has been "safe cash and a righteous tongue." Like Rourke in the *Hawaii Five-O* episode, Devlin expresses a degree of contempt for his wealthy Irish-American benefactors. Both rebels appear to view Americans as naïve and malleable, people easily charmed for expediency.

Above all, the episode reinforces the image of the beguiling terrorist who entertains naïve Irish-Americans, book sellers, and talk show hosts while cynically using his charm to camouflage murder and mayhem.

The first season of NBC's long-running drama *Law & Order* included an episode called "The Troubles," featuring a Joseph Doherty–like figure. Ian O'Connell (Anthony Heald) is described as having been held in federal custody for five years awaiting extradition to Britain on terrorism charges. A federal judge has blocked his extradition, ruling that "whatever he had done was not common crime but was related to the IRA's political goal of a unified Ireland." Ordered deported, O'Connell applied for political asylum. Subpoenaed to appear in New York as a witness against six Westies, described as "nice altar boys" who "make the sign of the cross as they slit your throat," he arrives in a prison van shackled to two other federal prisoners. Opening the door to the van, detectives discover O'Connell seated with a Cuban drug dealer named Montez and a strangled Lebanese inmate named Mustafa.

Investigating the two federal prisoners as suspects, Mike Logan (Chris Noth) and Max Greevy (George Dzundza) meet with Ian O'Connell, who immediately inquires about their Irish lineage. Greevy remains coolly distant from O'Connell. Asked if he hails from County Mayo, Greevy cites Hells Kitchen as his home. Normally cynical, Logan bonds with O'Connell. When he tells Greevy that he and O'Connell both had grandparents from the same town in Ireland, Greevy dismisses the ethnic connection as "blarneystone crap." Greevy views O'Connell as a terrorist, but Logan insists that he "never killed anybody," arguing "the man's a thinker, he's an organizer, he's a patriot."

After Montez is found hanged in his cell, the detectives concentrate on O'Connell and check an O'Connell fundraiser at an Irish pub, where a barmaid informs them, "The IRA is everywhere. It's in the prisons. On the streets. Maybe even in your own precinct. The Provos, the Sinn Fein, they're all the same bloody thugs." At the fundraiser, McCarter, a young prison guard, is celebrating his birthday. Recognizing him as the same guard who discovered Montez' body, the detectives arrest him for murder. McCarter is defended by an Irish attorney, Daniel Mallahan (Donal Donnelly), paid by the Friends of Sinn Fein, who initially refuses to accept a plea bargain until his questionable conflict of interest is challenged. McCarter, it is discovered, is a former sanitation employee fired for petty larceny. He could only be hired as a guard with the intervention of an Irish-American political official, suggesting influential Americans helped plant an IRA operative in a federal prison.

Explaining the prison guard's reluctance to testify that he killed Montez on orders from O'Connell and the IRA, Ben Stone (Michael Moriarty) tells DA Adam Schiff (Steven Hill) that McCarter "thinks of himself as a soldier, a loyal member of a long-standing army that has been under arms ... since the Battle of the Boyne." Asked if he has researched the subject, Stone says he did not have to, having had it "spoon-fed" to him by an Irish grandmother who considered the struggle a "holy war" and recited the names of Michael Collins and Robert Emmet "like they were saints in heaven." But Stone now sees O'Connell and McCarter as nothing more than "thugs" and "Nazis with brogues."

Unable to make a connection between O'Connell and Mustafa, Stone admits he cannot establish a motive. Schiff calls the British Consulate for assistance in the case. Fenwick, an English official, explains the nexus between Lebanon, Syria, and the IRA. The Syrians fund terrorism with drug money, supplying the IRA with plastic explosives and surface-to-air missiles. For the British, O'Connell is a dangerous international terrorist who must be imprisoned.

In contrast, the American federal official Axelrod wants to get the O'Connell case "off page one" by granting him political asylum, despite his apparent involvement in two murders. He tells an assistant DA to look at the "big picture" because "there are forty-three million Irish-Americans in this country, some of whom wield enormous political weight." Washington would prefer to overlook the murder of an Arab drug dealer and allow O'Connell to go free to avoid a "political hand grenade."

Arrested for the murder of Mustafa, O'Connell is defended by an Irish-American lawyer who asserts that his client is a political prisoner held without charge or trial because "the British government is afraid to have the truth come out." O'Connell, he tells jurors, is a patriot.

McCarter testifies he killed Montez on orders from O'Connell because the Cuban had witnessed the murder of Mustafa, who had cheated the IRA in an arms deal. On the stand, O'Connell admits membership to Sinn Fein, described as the legal, non-violent wing of the IRA, but denies any connection with the Provos. He denounces the use of violence but admits that he "understands it." He denies dealings with Mustafa, claiming to abhor drug dealing.

Sensing the defense is making a strong case, Fenwick offers to help Stone by providing a witness who can refute O'Connell's claim to be non-violent. In court, Stone asks O'Connell what the political wing of the army thinks when the "other wing blows up a busload of school children." O'Connell states the IRA has always given warnings before "a device is activated" but admits "there's always the risk of human error."

At one point O'Connell asks Stone how, "with the map of Donegal on your mug, did you ever end up with a name like Stone?" Irritated, Stone responds, "Happenstance, sir. Same way you ended up with the name of a real Irish patriot."

The British-supplied rebuttal witness identifies O'Connell as a man who left a satchel beside a police van. When her husband picked up the briefcase to chase after O'Connell, it exploded, killing him and their two children. "Take a good look," Ben Stone tells O'Connell. "There's your human error." O'Connell is sentenced to twenty-five years to life.

These television programs all offer a similar image of Irish Republicans. Whether posing as a priest, poet, or patriot, the charming and persuasive rebel is unmasked as a cold, cynical terrorist who has the ability to elicit the knowing or unknowing support from wealthy and politically powerful Irish-Americans.

Hawaii Five-O implies Irish-Americans looking for a cause are easily duped by duplicitous rebels who exploit ethnic allegiances to support terrorism. *Columbo* depicts wealthy Irish-Americans contributing to front organizations that finance terrorism, operations run not by young scruffy rebels but staid middle-aged moguls managing capitalist empires. *Law and Order* insinuates that the IRA is well-entrenched in American society and aided by politically influential Irish-Americans. It also suggests the federal government, sensitive to the Irish American influence, can be soft on terrorism. While the British official Fenwick is determined to keep O'Connell behind bars somewhere ("your jail, our jail"), the American Axelrod is willing to see a terrorist achieve political asylum to get him off page one.

Save for McGarrett's comments about "Catholics killing Protestants and Protestants killing Catholics," indicating a civil conflict, the other dramas portray the Troubles as a struggle between rebels and occupiers.

BURN NOTICE

Premiering in 2007 on the USA Network, the espionage series *Burn Notice* features the character of Fiona Glenanne (Gabrielle Anwar) as the hero's former girlfriend and valued sidekick. She is described as having been "affiliated with the IRA for fourteen years, but ran afoul of her old organization because she didn't like being told what to do." Characterized by her creators as "definitely a shoot first and ask questions later kind of gal," Fiona uses her expertise in explosives and her "fearless nature" to assist her former lover.[57]

BOARDWALK EMPIRE (2011)

The second season of the HBO series *Boardwalk Empire* contained a subplot linking Atlantic City's Prohibition-era kingpin Enoch "Nucky" Thompson (Steve Buscemi) with the IRA. The episode "Ourselves Alone" introduces the character of John McGarrigle (Ted Rooney), a lean bespectacled Irish Republican who bears a striking resemblance to Eamon de Valera. Touring America to collect funds for the Cause, McGarrigle calls upon a beleaguered Thompson, who meets the Fenian with a sense of weary obligation. Aloof and officious, McGarrigle demonstrates a clear disdain for both Atlantic City and the man he petitions for support:

> McGarrigle: Mr. Thompson, the Irish people are at war against a barbaric foe. The English murder us in our homes. They fire into crowds. Last month they put the torch to Cork City and shot the firemen come to fight the blaze. We need guns and the money to buy them. Mr. Moran tells me you are a loyal son of Erin. I call upon that loyalty now.
>
> Thompson: What would you consider sufficient?
>
> McGarrigle: What do you have?

Nucky writes out a check for an undisclosed sum to the Ancient Order of Celts. McGarrigle, who states he prefers cash, pockets the donation and mentions that he is heading to New York then back to Ireland. He leaves his advance man Owen Slater (Charlie Cox) behind, ostensibly because the youth is seeking an escape from the Troubles at home. Slater becomes part of Nucky's entourage, though Thompson suspects he remains an IRA operative.

Hard-pressed by rivals and the authorities, Nucky is short of cash and contemplates the loss of political power and a forced retirement from bootlegging. Noticing crates of surplus Thompson submachine guns being stored in the Atlantic City armory, Nucky sees a way to capitalize on his IRA connection to secure a new source of alcohol and reverse his fortunes. He directs Slater to set up a meeting in Belfast with McGarrigle to discuss a proposition.

In a subsequent episode, "Battle of the Century," Nucky uses the death of his father as a subterfuge to smuggle weapons to Ireland. Accompanied by Owen Slater, Thompson arrives in Belfast with a coffin, supposedly to bury his father in the land of his birth. Summoned to a mortuary, McGarrigle expresses his condolences to Thompson, who reveals that the casket holds a dozen submachine guns. Slater assures his IRA chief that "one of these can finish off an entire platoon in the time it takes to fry an egg." Nucky calls the shipment "my donation to the rebellion." Musing that "a hundred might make a difference," McGarrigle is stunned when Nucky informs him he has three thousand guns in Atlantic City. The austere McGarrigle is noticeably put off, however, when he asks what Nucky wants in return. Told he will exchange the guns for "Irish whisky, all I can get," McGarrigle shoots a glance at Slater, stating, "And that's the kind of man you bring me." He promises to present Nucky's offer to "the leadership" for discussion. When Nucky asks to meet "the man in charge," McGarrigle brusquely rebukes him, stating, "We'll tend to our affairs in our own way, if it's all the same to you."

Undaunted, Nucky has Owen demonstrate the "trench broom" to a group of flat-capped IRA volunteers. Impressed with the weapon, a Republican declares, "A few thousand of these, and we'd blaze a path to Buckingham Palace!" Asked if he is the inventor of the Thompson submachine gun, Nucky calls the name "just a happy coincidence." McGarrigle arrives on the scene announcing that the English have offered a truce and that de Valera is traveling to London to negotiate for a free state. The news sparks a discussion among the volunteers presaging the schism leading to the Civil War. While some insist on full independence, recalling their oath to fight "to the bitter end," others see talks as a sign of progress. John McGarrigle, whose youngest son was killed the month before, asserts that enough blood has been shed, proclaiming, "I'll keep fighting if I must and make peace if it's wise."

After McGarrigle departs, a Republican volunteer offers Nucky a drink. Pouring whiskey in the warehouse of his distillery, Daniel Fitzgerald tells Thompson he once produced two million gallons a year. Studying a wall of whiskey cases, Nucky asks if the rebellion had blocked exports to England. Fitzgerald agrees, adding that the collapse of the local economy also hurt his business. But the "final nail," he claims, was American Prohibition. The United States, he tells Nucky, once accounted for eighty percent of his foreign sales. Thompson proposes taking ten thousand cases on consignment, an offer Fitzgerald politely declines. With a truce on the horizon, he believes he will soon be back in business. In addition, he will not betray McGarrigle. "I'll not go against John," Fitzgerald declares, "he's brought us this far and paid for it with his own blood along the way." Nucky sadly realizes that Fitzgerald has a warehouse full of whiskey but "no use for machine guns."

Dining with McGarrigle, Thompson continues to press for an exchange of liquor and arms. Now intent on seeking a peaceful resolution, McGarrigle dismisses the "arms for whiskey" arrangement, leading Nucky to argue his case more forcefully:

Thompson: Can you really afford to send me back empty-handed? ... Has Britain released any of your imprisoned men? Stopped seizing your guns and ammunition? Did they not just land another fifteen thousand troops on your soil and threaten martial law? Mr. McGarrigle, what have the British offered you in the form of good faith?
McGarrigle: This is the pinch of the game. If the fighting's to stop, one must take the lead.
Thompson: That strategy might put your people at risk.
McGarrigle: A risk I'm willing to take.
Thompson: You came to me in your time of need. I helped you without hesitation. I'm asking you to do the same.
McGarrigle: And what's our cause to you, sir?
Thompson: I beg your pardon?
McGarrigle: Will you think on the thousands that'll die, cut down by the Thompson guns you'll put in our hands? Or will you laze about your cabin as you sail back across the sea. Climb into your berth and count yourself to sleep?
Thompson: Let's not lie to each other, Mr. McGarrigle. Whenever men like you need to win, you'll turn to men like me.

After the meeting, McGarrigle questions Owen about his relationship with Thompson. Claiming to be working for the Cause in America, Owen professes loyalty to his IRA chief. McGarrigle warns him that Thompson is "out for nothing but himself." Slater remarks that

Nucky has "his own war" in America over "a great pile" of money, leading the somber McGarrigle to sigh, "Is that all they fight for?" He directs Owen to remain in Ireland and aid in the peace process, telling him, "Every battle ends, boy. You'll have to understand that." Asked for his help, Owen promises to serve as needed.

Preparing to return to America empty-handed, Thompson bids farewell to his Irish hosts. McGarrigle assures Nucky he will land on his feet back in the States and directs one of his men to see him safely to the port. As their car pulls away, an IRA volunteer shoots McGarrigle in the back. While Thompson flinches in shock, his hard-faced escort coldly states, "You'll deal with me now. A thousand machine guns for ten thousand cases of whiskey."

Nucky returns to Atlantic City with a new source of alcohol and suspicions about Owen who betrayed the IRA boss he claimed to serve.

Boardwalk Empire echoes the main theme of *Shake Hands with the Devil* (Pennebaker Productions/Troy Films, 1959). Pro-truce Republicans are presented as sensible rebels willing to compromise to avoid bloodshed. Those vowing to fight "to the bitter end" are violent, pitiless fanatics willing to murder comrades and ally themselves with gangsters. Overall, the Irish are portrayed as a race apart, duplicitous, charming, and ruthless.

THE 9/11 EFFECT: *CRACKER: A NEW TERROR* (2006)

The 9/11 Effect on American attitudes toward terrorism is the focus of a British TV movie aired at the height of the Iraq War. Robbie Coltrane reprises his role as the abrasive but brilliant police psychologist Dr. Edward "Fitz" Fitzgerald from the Nineties television series *Cracker*. In this two-hour "final episode," Fitz returns to Manchester after a seven-year hiatus in Australia to attend his daughter's wedding and becomes involved in a murder investigation. Throughout the movie images of Belfast and the War in Iraq are juxtaposed, along with pointed comments about terrorism and American attitudes. The IRA is mentioned by a cab driver as Fitzgerald and his wife pass the Arndale Centre, site of a massive 1998 bombing.

News about British soldiers being killed in Iraq has triggered post-traumatic flashbacks in Manchester police officer Kenny Archer (Anthony Flanagan), who has painful memories from three tours of duty in Northern Ireland. He is haunted by the death of two comrades and resentful that their sacrifice has been forgotten. Visiting a memorial for soldiers killed in Northern Ireland, he finds the site neglected and closed because of a lack of funding. Drinking heavily, he calls a helpline, bitterly complaining that British soldiers had to fight terrorism with one arm behind their backs until Americans were hit. Asked if he feels suicidal, Archer says he has thought about killing himself because he knows if he does not, he will kill others. He hangs up the phone and goes out drinking. Sitting in a nightclub, he watches an American standup comic crack jokes about Osama bin Laden. When a patron mentions Gerry Adams, the comic quips, "You call that terrorism?"

Enraged, Archer follows the American to the men's room and breaks his neck. At the police station he is present when the comic's mother, Jean Molloy (Lisa Eichhorn), and her son's friend, Harry Peters (Demetri Goritsas), discuss the murder. Peters, an American living in Britain for a decade, derides the British police, calling Archer and his partner "Laurel and Hardy."

In a scene entitled "Chickens Home to Roost," Archer breaks into Peters' home, demanding "revenge for every British soldier killed in Northern Ireland":

> Every bullet that hit every British soldier bought with American dollars. Every bomb bought with American dollars.... You funded terrorism for years, then, hallelujah, you get what's coming to you. 9/11. Then suddenly you don't like terrorism one little bit. I call that hypocrisy.

Referencing the war in Iraq, Archer calls Americans cowards because they like to kill "from thirty thousand feet." Peters characteristically pleads for his life with offers of money. Archer is unimpressed, calling America a "land of hypocrites and cowards" before snapping the American's neck.

Assigned to protect the comic's mother, Archer is angered when she uses the term "the Troubles" to describe the conflict in Northern Ireland. "We don't call them troubles," he explains bitterly. "Troubles is leprechauns, shamrocks, Danny Boy, filling the buckets full of dollars for the boys back home standing up to those nasty Brits.... It's war, Mrs. Malloy." He makes a move to kill her but leaves when a hotel employee enters the room.

As the images of Belfast and Iraq conflate in Archer's mind, Fitz interviews the troubled officer because he fits the killer's profile. To establish a connection, Fitz baits Archer's anti–Americanism, telling him that thirty years of conflict in Northern Ireland has been over-shadowed by 9/11 so that his mates died for nothing. Asked about his experiences in Ulster, Kenny relives the death of his mates. In the flashback sequence the American national anthem plays as an IRA sniper kills one British soldier and another is blown up by a booby trap.

Drinking heavily and acting irrationally, a despondent Archer brandishes a revolver and locks his wife out of their home. Fearful for her children, she calls the police, who sur-round the house. Kenny allows Fitz to enter, and the two men drink whisky and talk. Speaking of his murder of the Americans, Archer tells Fitz that everything he did was "per-fectly understandable." Fitz agrees, up to a point. Though "understandable," Kenny's actions, he explains, were not "justified." Having vented his anger and not wanting to be taken alive, Kenny arranges a "suicide by cop" incident. Knowing that there is a marksman in the street, Kenny stands in front of the window and fires in Fitz's direction. Shot by a fellow officer, Archer falls to the floor amid a rush of flashbacks of British soldiers dying in Belfast.

For Cracker, the killing of Americans following 9/11, though not "justified," is "perfectly understandable."

7

International Intrigue

The sole *raison d'être* of the Irish Republican Army is the creation of a thirty-two county Irish Republic wholly independent from Great Britain. It has no global agenda, though at times its anti-imperialist philosophy has linked it to similar organizations throughout the world. It has relied on aid from Irish-Americans and sought assistance from Britain's adversaries, whether Germany during the Second World War or Libya in the 1980s.

The IRA has carried out highly publicized operations outside the British Isles on several occasions. A three-hundred-pound car bomb exploded outside a British officers' mess in West Germany in 1987, injuring thirty-one. The following year, two IRA men and an IRA woman were shot by the SAS in Gibraltar, and Belgian police found an IRA bomb intended for the British foreign secretary in Brussels.[1] Three years later two Australian tourists, mistaken for off-duty British soldiers, were killed in Holland.[2] On August 11, 2001, three IRA operatives were arrested in Bogota, Colombia, having spent time in the FARC-controlled regions of the country.[3] The possibility of a link between the IRA and narco-terrorists in South America weakened American support for the Republican movement, leading to added pressure from the United States for the IRA to decommission its weapons. The 9/11 attacks exactly a month later further diminished Irish-American support for an armed struggle in Northern Ireland.

The IRA's foreign dealings have been largely low-level and of modest success. Money from America usually amounted to only a few hundred thousand dollars annually. Libya may have supplied the IRA with $3.5 million over three years.[4] Americans delivered Armalites but never the Stingers that could have taken the conflict to a new level of intensity. Libya supplied millions of rounds of surplus ammunition, much of it useless from age.[5] Through all its international efforts, the IRA was unable to obtain the high-tech weaponry that could have challenged British military supremacy in Northern Ireland or supported major actions in England that might have forced a favorable political outcome. Informants and poor planning led to many arms shipments being interdicted or discovered before they could be put to use. Britain's adversaries saw the IRA as a tool of harassment rather than a strategic weapon.

Following the model of *The Man Who Never Was* (Sumar Film Productions, Ltd., 1956), two British television films depict the IRA working with Arab terrorists to carry out operations on British soil. In marked contrast, another British television movie portrays a former IRA enforcer as Her Majesty's ablest secret agent.

ATTACKING ZION: *THE GLORY BOYS* (1984)

The Glory Boys (Yorkshire Television) is a four-part British TV mini-series depicting an IRA/PLO plot to assassinate Israeli nuclear scientist David Sokarev (Rod Steiger) during a London speaking engagement. The film opens with the Israelis capturing an Arab fighter in Southern Lebanon who mentions the word "kima" ("mushroom") during a harsh interrogation. In the next scene police chase a trio of Arab terrorists in northern France, but one escapes and makes his way to London. British intelligence detects an Irish voice on a wiretap of an Arab embassy. Kieran McCoy (Aaron Harris) of the IRA arrives in London to meet Abdel El-Famy, graduate of a Palestinian training camp. British intelligence reports that the IRA and Arabs have "been in harness before" because "sometimes the IRA wants weapons, sometimes the Arabs want help, so they will share a bed." The British then face the prospect of "an Irishman and an Arab, probably both terrorists, joining forces on our London streets." The crisis is serious enough to draw an alcoholic agent out of retirement. Jimmy (Anthony Perkins), though cynical and unconventional, retains his investigative skills and tracks leads.

Kieran McCoy, a four-year veteran of the IRA suspected of killing two RUC police officers and a British paratrooper, is judged to have "high leadership capabilities." El-Famy is a novice full of jihadist zeal willing to die for his cause, but as an outsider to Britain is ill-suited to operate in London. He does not, for instance, even know how to drive a car. McCoy's original assignment was to supply three assassins with hardware and a safe house. He sees his role as being the "quartermaster," with the Arabs serving as the "sharp end" of the mission. When El-Famy arrives alone, McCoy wants to call the operation off. His IRA leadership insists, however, that he carry out his orders. He is directed to "assess the situation" and help plan the assassination for El-Famy.

McCoy becomes El-Famy's mentor, teaching him how to conduct surveillance, dodge the police, and blend into the public. McCoy and El-Famy are forced to go into hiding after El-Famy kills a girl he catches stealing in the safe house. Kieran's fingerprints are found in the house, and witnesses provide a description of El-famy. With their identities known, the pair goes underground, waiting for Sokarev to arrive and rehearsing their assassination plot.

While Sokarev is giving a speech, El-Famy fires several shots and tosses a grenade. An Israeli intelligence officer throws himself on the grenade, sparing the scientist's life. With McCoy wounded, the assassins flee, unsure whether they succeeded in killing Sokarev.

Wounded again by Jimmy, McCoy takes his girlfriend's family hostage, giving his partner a chance to head to the airport to kill Sokarev before he can leave Britain. El-Famy makes a second assassination attempt on the tarmac but is wounded then executed by Jimmy in front of the public. Unharmed, the nuclear scientist observes that both the protectors and assassins lead to the "same thing, murder." Touching the flag-draped coffin of the dead Israeli agent, he wonders, "What is it that is in us that leads us to murder? Are we animals?"

The film ends with Jimmy drinking in a bar, then breaking into laughter when a TV news report announces that Sokarev, who survived two assassination attempts, died of a heart attack on the flight to Tel Aviv.

Certain Animals: *A Casualty of War* (1990)

A Casualty of War (IFS Productions) opens with a film clip of Ronald Reagan's 1986 speech announcing an air strike against Colonel Ghaddafi in Libya. After a montage of Cold War imagery — the Kremlin, the Berlin Wall, the White House — Frederick Forsyth appears, walking along the Thames, to introduce the film adaptation of his novella. Ghaddafi, he tells viewers, survived the bombing and vowed revenge, not just against America but Britain because it allowed U.S. aircraft to use its bases. "The conduit he chose for his revenge," explains Forsyth, "was the Provisional IRA. And the method? A massive gift of weapons to the terrorists."

Learning of the plan, British intelligence, personified by Sam McCready (Alan Howard), selects Tom Rowse (David Threlfall), a writer and former agent, to locate the arms shipment.

Rowse is uninterested in coming out of retirement until he is shown a photograph of the IRA man involved in the plot. Recognizing Terrence Mahony (Vinny Murphy), Rowse has a flashback to his SAS service in Northern Ireland when, escaping capture, Mahony seized a car and threw a child to her death. Mentioning that he still writes the little girl's mother, Rowse is told that Sinn Fein wrote her as well to express their "regret."

Agreeing to help, Rowse follows leads to Hamburg, where he accompanies a contact to an IRA nightclub. Rowse is recognized, and his contact is later beaten to death. A Soviet official tells Rowse to see a Libyan intelligence official named Jaloud. Denied entry into Libya, Rowse meets Jaloud in Cyprus, who tells him his Hamburg friend was killed by "certain animals" who "deal in heroin and cocaine, but their principal hobby is planting bombs in crowded places and failing in elaborate schemes to assassinate your British leaders." While in Cyprus, Rowse becomes romantically involved with the charming American horse buyer Monica Browne (Shelly Hack).

British intelligence informs Rowse that the IRA has received a "huge arms and explosives gift from Ghaddafi," who "fondly imagines it will be used to arm the Republican population and start an uprising in the Six Counties." Ghaddafi's price for the shipload of arms is an attack on the American ambassador in London to avenge the Reagan air strike. Rowse argues, "The IRA needs U.S. support, they wouldn't dream of it." But Mahony has subcontracted the assignment so a European group "will take the blame," and as a result, "U.S.-U.K. relations go down the tube."

Back in London, Rowse dines with Sam McCready, who notices they are being watched by a young couple. They leave the restaurant and drive off, with the couple following on a motorcycle. McCready spins his car to a sudden halt, causing the motorcycle to crash, throwing the bikers to the road. Sam coldly approaches one and shoots him through the helmet. The other struggles to pull a gun and is shot by Rowse in self-defense. Shaken, Rowse asks McCready, "How can you justify ... two murders?" McCready readily defends killing anyone associated with the IRA, stating, "We're talking misery to the power whatever you like, old women and wee boys torn limb from limb to satisfy some ... psychos whose only cause is the cause of ego-tripping power at the point of a gun." Rowse asks him, "If you and I had been born on the Falls Road, Sam, which side would we be on?" Sam answers, "I was, and I'm on the side of humanity, heaven help me." In this film the IRA do not deserve to be arrested but shot on sight.

Monica Browne is spotted aboard the ship carrying the arms, and Rowse realizes that the soft-spoken American girl is an IRA agent. Storming aboard the ship, he encounters his former lover brandishing a gun and shoots her. Distraught, Rowse asks, "Who was she?" The captured IRA leader responds, "A casualty of war, sir, just like yourself."

In Forsyth's story the IRA are child-killing, drug-dealing terrorists with no other cause than violence who will betray their American sympathizers to achieve their goals.

THE PROVO JAMES BOND:
ON DANGEROUS GROUND (1996)

Jack Higgins' Provo turned international agent for hire stands in marked contrast with the IRA "psychos" in Frederick Forsyth's drama. In the British TV movie version of the

Higgins novel *On Dangerous Ground* (VisionView/Carousel/Telescene), Rob Lowe stars as Sean Dillon, a former Provisional IRA "enforcer" who has quit "the grand Cause" to assist British intelligence. A skilled pilot, scuba diver, and sky diver, Dillon (whose American accent is never explained) is a Bond-like action hero — brash, independent, charming, and often at odds with his superior, General Charles Ferguson (Kenneth Cranham). Ferguson explains to his assistant, Hannah Bernstein (Deborah Moore), that he interrogated Dillon in the Maze prison after an IRA "atrocity." All the other IRA prisoners confessed under duress ("one man [was] sprayed with a fire hose for forty-eight hours"), but Dillon "never broke," leading Ferguson to admit, "I've wanted him on my side ever since." Blackmailed into assisting Ferguson, Dillon is a petulant but heroically reliable freelancer. In addition to helping the British, Dillon is credited with sinking PLO boats off Beirut for the Israelis and working for the KGB.

When British intelligence learns of an assassination plot on the President of the United States during a visit to Britain to meet the Chinese Foreign Minister, Ferguson calls upon Dillon. In Higgins' story, the "psycho" Irish assassins plotting with Islamic terrorists (Iran's Army of God) are renegade Loyalists. Dillon saves the President, then realizes the attack was a diversion from the terrorists' real target, the Chinese minister. Dillon foils the second assassination attempt when he discovers a bomb during a tree-planting ceremony.

Dillon is then drawn into a convoluted drama involving Mao Tse-Tung, Lord Mount-batten,* a lost document, and the Sicilian mafia. In New York a dying Scotsman tells his hospice physician that while serving in China in 1944 he witnessed Mao sign "The Chungking Covenant" that promised to extend the British lease over Hong Kong for another hundred years in return for military assistance. The secret document vanished after the war, but the dying Scotsman had seen an officer place it in a Bible for safe keeping. After the man's death, the doctor phones mafia relatives in Sicily who have interests in Hong Kong.

The movie hop-scotches around the globe, from London to New York to Palermo to Scotland, as the Chinese, the British, and the mafia scramble to locate the missing covenant. With the future of Hong Kong at stake, Ferguson never calls upon the SAS or MI6 for help but relies solely on the former Provo.

Dillon recovers the covenant from the wreckage of an airplane discovered at the bottom of a Scottish loch. In the final scene, as Ferguson hands the long-lost document to a Hong Kong official, the paper is blown away by the wind and sucked into a jet engine.

Sean Dillon, ex–Provo, hands the Crown an invaluable prize — control over Hong Kong for a century — only to have it fumbled away by British intelligence.

NIGHTHAWKS (1981)

The American action film *Nighthawks* (Universal) pits two New York cops (Sylvester Stallone and Billy Dee Williams) against the international terrorist-for-hire Wulfgar (Rutger Hauer). The film opens with a smiling Wulfgar entering a London department store. Posing as a customer, he flirts with a sales girl, then slides his shoulder bag under the counter. He leaves the store and heads to a phone booth as the building explodes behind him. Calmly professional, Wulfgar calls the United Press to announce that he has just struck a blow against "British colonialism."

His IRA employers, however, are dissatisfied with his actions. An Irish contact tells Wulfgar the job was "overdone" and "will hurt the movement" because several children were

---

An ironic inclusion, even in a brief flashback, given Mountbatten's murder at the hands of Provos in 1979.

killed. Believing the IRA contact led the police to him, Wulfgar shoots his way out, pausing to kill the Irishman. He travels to New York to launch a one-man campaign of terror to demonstrate his skills. Proclaiming himself to be a liberator of the oppressed, Wulfgar uses and kills women, takes hostages, and murders civilians, with his only cause being to advance his freelance career. In contrast, the Irish Republican Army appears almost reasonable, using limited violence to achieve a political goal.

Being more skilled at dealing with terrorists, the British provide training to New York's Finest, who object to their methods, claiming, "You're training us to be nothing more than assassins. The only difference between him and us will be the badge." In response, the cops are told, "To combat violence you need greater violence. To defeat a violent people you have to be trained to react in a given situation with ruthless cold-blooded violence as well."

In *Nighthawks* the IRA appear as rational terrorists whose rules of engagement are violated by a psychotic hired gun who sabotages their movement and turns on them, claiming his handler as one of his numerous victims.

THE IRA IN MEXICO:
A FISTFUL OF DYNAMITE (1971)

"When I started using dynamite, I believed in many things. Finally, I believe only in dynamite."

Filmed in Spain, Sergio Leone's *A Fistful of Dynamite* (Rafran Cinematografica), originally released in the United States under the title *Duck, You Sucker!*, is a typical spaghetti Western, with two American stars backed by a largely Italian cast. Rod Steiger portrays the Mexican bandit Juan Miranda, and James Coburn plays Sean (John) Mallory, an Irish rebel on the run from the British government. Set in 1913, three years before the Easter Rising, the main plot line predates many of the flashback sequences set in Ireland a decade before. The flashbacks are wordless, their action accompanied only by music, obscuring any historical or political commentary. Mallory never discusses his past in any detail, referring only to having participated in "a revolution" viewers presume failed.

Juan Miranda leads a band of outlaws intent on robbing a bank. He encounters a motorcycle-riding Sean Mallory, who demonstrates his skill in using explosives. Searching through Mallory's belongings, Miranda discovers a green flag bearing the letters IRA and an announcement in the *United Irishman* that the British government is offering a £300 reward for the "Irish terrorist" Sean Mallory. Miranda sees Sean as an important asset for the bank raid.

Mallory also attracts the attention of Dr. Valli (Romolo Valli), a revolutionary leader who also sees the Irish bomber as "an asset" to his cause. Asked if is he is taking part in the Mexican revolution, Mallory responds, "No, one was enough for me." Throughout the film, events in Mexico trigger a series of wordless flashbacks. A younger, well-dressed Mallory appears riding in a luxury car and romancing a young lady. Nolan (David Warbeck), an Irish nationalist, is shown distributing leaflets to young men in a pub. In a subsequent flashback, a beaten Nolan in police custody informs on Mallory, who turns and shoots the officers and his former comrade. Mallory, the disillusioned idealist, finds himself caught up in a new revolution which Miranda passionately denounces:

Revolution? Please, don't try to tell me about revolution. I know all about the revolutions and how they start.... The people who read the books go to the people who can't read the books —

The IRA in Mexico: James Coburn in *A Fistful of Dynamite* (1971).

the poor people — and say we have to have a change. So the poor people make the change. And then the people who read the books, they all sit around the big polished table and they talk and talk and talk, and eat and eat and eat. But what has happened to the poor people. They're dead! That's your revolution!

Afterwards, Mallory tosses his copy of Bakunin's *The Patriotism* into the mud. Nevertheless, he tricks Juan into joining a revolutionary battle. Mortally wounded, Mallory recalls his failed revolution in Ireland and an unexplained lost love.

Even in Mexico, the defeated Irish nationalist cannot escape the romance of the Cause.

8

The Gangster Film
Criminalizing the IRA

The Irish Republican Army has long been implicated in criminal activity — typically robberies, protection rackets, money laundering, and kidnappings — to obtain funds to purchase arms, finance operations, provide support for prisoners' families, and pay pensions to its veterans. Republican supporters rationalize that as a revolutionary underground organization, the IRA is forced to engage in "expropriations," generally aimed at the rich or state enterprises. Like violence, the securing of funds by extralegal methods is justified as a means to achieve a political goal. Unlike crimes committed for personal gain, IRA operations are considered strategic attacks against an oppressive state and an iniquitous economic system.

The IRA conducted an estimated one thousand armed robberies in Northern Ireland during the Troubles, small post offices being a favorite target.[1] In West Belfast the IRA extracted protection money from building contractors, driving many of them bankrupt.[2] For several years the IRA staged kidnappings, both in Northern Ireland and the Republic, abducting the children of bank managers and visiting millionaires.[3]

However necessary they were to sustain a secret army, these actions, many of them staged with theatrical daring, provided opponents with an additional avenue of attack. Actions taken against the IRA could be separated from politics. They were not assaults against Catholics, nationalists, or even the concept of Republicanism, but strikes against crime. Roy Mason, who became Northern Ireland Secretary in 1976, routinely referred to IRA leaders as "godfathers" as part of a deliberate policy "to change perceptions of the conflict from the colonial war of Republican propaganda to that of a campaign against criminal gangs."[4] Throughout the Troubles British tabloids and Unionists denounced the IRA as a "murder gang" comprised of sociopathic thugs and psychotic hit men.

The need for IRA capital did not end with the Good Friday Agreement. To maintain discipline in the ranks and persuade hardliners to accept an unpalatable compromise, funds were needed to compensate veterans, assist volunteers' transition to a postwar life, fund political candidates, and placate recalcitrants threatening to form splinter organizations. With disarmament, the IRA transformed from a secret army to an underground conglomerate. By 2005 *The Times* claimed the IRA had become "the biggest crime gang in Europe," obtaining millions of pounds a year from illicit distilling, cigarette smuggling, sales of pirated DVDs, and expanded protection and extortion rackets in Belfast and Dublin. The most spectacular crime attributed to the IRA by Special Branch was the theft of £26 million from the Northern Bank in December 2004. The IRA is now believed to control a "portfolio" of nightclubs, taxi companies, gas stations, office complexes, and nursing homes.[5] British and Irish investigators estimate that IRA rackets generate $20 million annually and place the organization's total assets at $400 million.[6] At a party conference in 2005 Gerry Adams declared that Sinn Fein would "refuse to criminalize those who break the law in pursuit of legitimate political objectives."[7]

Filmmakers have made the IRA-crime link for dramatic as well as political reasons. *Odd Man Out* (Two Cities Films, 1947) devotes more running time to the unnamed organization's mill robbery and its aftermath than to the obscure political motivations behind it. Though Johnny McQueen speaks a few lines about the cause, the bulk of the film differs little from a Hollywood gangster movie. Joseph Merhi's *Riot* (PM Entertainment Group, 1999) depicts the IRA conspiring with a black LA street gang to kidnap the British ambassador's daughter for a two-million-dollar ransom. In James Brolin's *My Brother's War* (New Horizons, 1997) a renegade IRA group robs an armored car and executes its crew. In Pat O'Connor's *Cal* (Enigma Productions, 1984) the IRA conducts a holdup. *Some Mother's Son* (Castle Rock Entertainment, 1996) mentions a bank being robbed four times by the IRA.

In several films IRA characters appear primarily as criminal conspirators, their ideology providing little more than a colorful backstory.

THE DAY THEY ROBBED THE BANK OF ENGLAND (1960)

> "Robbing grocers' tills and blowing up public lavatories will not make a nation out of Ireland."

Released the same year as Basil Deardon's *The League of Gentlemen* (Allied Film Makers, 1960), John Guillermin's *The Day They Robbed the Bank of England* (Summit Film Productions) is a similar heist adventure with an IRA theme. Produced in Britain during the waning days of the Border Campaign, it has a tone and style that would be unthinkable a decade later. Although often identified as an IRA film, it is set at the turn of the twentieth century, at least a decade before the organization was officially formed. The film makes a strong Irish-American connection in the opening prologue:

> On a summer's day early in this century when Ireland was still struggling against the might of England for independence, a certain Irish-American presented himself at the cashier's desk at the bank. It was the beginning of a strange and daring venture.

The Irish-American is Norgate (Aldo Ray), a mining engineer paid by "friends in New York" to assist O'Shea (Hugh Griffith) in robbing the Bank of England to secure funds for "the movement." O'Shea rejects an initial plot to steal a gold shipment worth £160,000, conspiring instead to steal a million pounds. "A hundred and sixty thousand pounds," he notes, "is a matter for the police, a million is a political offensive." The movement had staged bombings, but small bombings, O'Shea argues, might kill a few Englishmen but have little effect because they "breed like rabbits." Instead, he seeks to strike a major blow at British imperialism by securing funds and violating its most respected and secure institution.

With his expertise in mining, Norgate is central to the plan to breach the Bank of England's elaborate security system. But Norgate finds the London Irishmen suspicious of his loyalty to the movement, especially Walsh (Kieron Moore), who becomes his romantic rival for Iris Muldoon (Elizabeth Sellers). Asked what Home Rule means to him, Norgate states, "We may grow up in America, Mr. Walsh, but some of us still have our roots in Ireland."

To obtain information about the bank, Norgate befriends Captain Fitch (Peter

O'Toole), commander of the guards. Learning that architect's drawings of the bank are locked in a museum, Norgate breaks in and traces the blueprints. Posing as an archeologist in search of Roman ruins, he pays an elderly scavenger to obtain details about an abandoned sewer that runs under the bank. As Norgate tunnels toward the vaults, Fitch, growing suspicious, warns that a robbery may be in progress.

Just as the suspense builds between cop and robber, O'Shea arrives at the movement's headquarters announcing the mission must be aborted immediately. The Irish Home Rule Bill is about to be reintroduced in Parliament, and "nothing must be allowed to jeopardize the passing of that bill." For O'Shea, the robbery is a means to a political end, a tactic to be abandoned when a more efficacious strategy appears. If Norgate cannot be stopped, O'Shea insists the movement will "dissociate" itself from the venture. "I am involved in the struggle for the independence of Ireland, I have no other loyalties," says O'Shea, who promises to inform on Norgate if necessary.

Meanwhile, Norgate breaks through into the bullion vault stacked with gold bars. Told to abandon the robbery, Norgate insists on continuing and is caught by Fitch. The film, a typical morality tale, reveals how greed overcomes higher motives and demonstrates that Irish nationalism is entwined with criminality.

THE LONG GOOD FRIDAY (1979)

John Mackenzie's *The Long Good Friday* (Handmade Films) is a gangster/suspense film detailing a series of mysterious events that first threaten, then finally overwhelm a gangster's tightly-run empire in a single day.

Harold Shand (Bob Hoskins) is an enterprising London mobster/entrepreneur overseeing a highly successful criminal organization he calls "the corporation." His staff includes Councilor Harris, who provides political favors, and Parky (Dave King), a police official who supplies intelligence and investigative services. Having appeased lesser gangs, Shand has moved into legitimate business and real estate dealings. Depicted as a kind of Al Capone/Donald Trump, he imagines a major revitalization of London. On Good Friday Shand entertains investors aboard his mammoth yacht, extolling his venture to capitalize on the derelict wharves lining the Thames. London, he announces, is destined to be the capital of Europe, and no other major city has so much prime space available for development. Central to his endeavor is securing capital from Charlie, a visiting American mafioso who arrives with his attorney. Shand proposes a toast celebrating "hands across the ocean."

Shand's Good Friday then starts to go seriously wrong. A phone call informs him that his Rolls Royce has been blown up, along with his chauffeur. Colin, an employee and long-time friend, is murdered during an apparent homosexual encounter at a swimming pool. An unexploded bomb is discovered in Shand's Mayfair casino. Shand puts his corporation into motion, but his team is unable to find any leads. Parky provides no information. A police snitch claims total ignorance. The blows keep coming. Shand invites the Americans to dinner at his pub. As their car pulls up to the entrance, the building explodes.

The only clue to the culprits comes from the pub manager who tells Shand about "two heavy micks" who showed up asking for protection money. Examining the blast damage, Parky begins to suspect that this is not a typical gang war. "If that bomb is Irish," he tells Shand, "it's a different game. Those boyos don't play by the rules."

Still convinced he is dealing with rival criminals trying to shake him down on the eve of a critical business deal, Shand orders his corporate thugs to round up London's gang

The London underworld in turmoil: Bob Hoskins (foreground, in black trench coat) in *The Long Good Friday* (1979).

lords. Hung upside down on meat hooks, the mobsters are swung into a slaughter house where Shand explodes in rage, demanding to know who is responsible for the attacks he compares to "Belfast on a bad night." The mob bosses claim loyalty to London's supreme gangster. Parky arrives to alert Shand that he is not dealing with a gang war but something larger and more menacing, which has him frightened. The unexploded bomb was the type used by the IRA:

> Shand: What're the Irish got to do with me? Just a bunch of hoods trying to muscle in.
> Parky: For Christ's sake Harold, they're not just gangsters. They run half of Londonderry.... Could be London next.
> Shand: Oh no, I run London!
> Parky: Not now, Harold. They're taking it away from you. It's Special Branch now, and I'm getting out.

In Mackenzie's script, the IRA is a super-mafia spreading from Northern Ireland to conquer London. Shand learns from his assistant that Colin had gone to Belfast to make a delivery to the IRA from Councilor Harris, who was being extorted. With a hundred "micks on his labor force," Harris' construction projects would be paralyzed by strikes unless he paid protection to the Republicans. Colin, however, withheld £5,000 for himself, setting off an IRA revenge attack. The night Colin delivered his lightened payment, three top IRA men were murdered, and the Republicans assume Shand was responsible.

Shand vows to destroy the "mick terrorist scum," promising to "annihilate" the IRA and "crush them like beetles." Jeff, his assistant, argues, "Never ... you can't wipe them out.... Kill ten, kill twenty ... bring out the tanks and flamethrowers.... Work with them.... They can take over whenever they want." Infuriated by this suggestion, Shand kills Jeff in a burst of rage.

Pressured by the Americans to resolve the crisis within twenty-four hours, Shand is determined to eliminate the Irish threat. Accompanied by Harris, he meets the IRA men with a payment of £60,000. The offer, however, is a trap. As the IRA men examine the pound notes, Shand's corporate gunmen storm in and kill the blackmailing Provos, along with Harris.

Arriving at the Savoy Hotel, Shand tells the Americans that "all the troubles are over." But Charlie and his attorney are packing for New York. Disturbed by the bombings and killings, Charlie compares the day's events to a "bad night in Vietnam." Judging London to be a worse investment than Cuba, the mafia men are leaving. Shand calls the Americans "wankers" who lack British "vitality" and "the Dunkirk spirit." He is looking for "someone who can contribute to what England has given to the world — culture, sophistication, genius. A little bit more than a hot dog." His Anglo-American alliance over, Shand looks to Europe. "We're in the Common Market now!" he tells the Americans, announcing plans to work with "the krauts," who have "ambition" and "know how."

Dismissing the mafia, Shand marches out of the hotel and climbs into the back of his Jaguar, which lurches forward with IRA men in the front seat. Held at gunpoint by a smiling Irishman (Pierce Brosnan), Shand is driven off as the film ends, leaving the IRA the new godfathers of London.

ANGEL (1982)

"Hating is easy."

Neil Jordan's debut film, *Angel* (Film Four), is an apolitical crime drama. The conflict between unnamed paramilitary organizations over protection money differs little from an American mob film. Danny (Stephen Rea) is a saxophone player who witnesses the murder of a club owner by masked men accusing him of making payments, apparently to the IRA. Danny notices that one of the masked men wears an orthopedic shoe and tracks him down. Breaking into his home, he finds an automatic weapon. When the man returns, Danny kills him.

The politics of Northern Ireland are only hinted at in Jordan's film. In a police station an officer named Bloom shows Danny a stack of files:

Bloom: We can show you every face in the country, if it will help you. Catholic or Protestant. By the way, in case you're wondering, I'm Jewish.

Danny: Are you a Catholic Jew or a Protestant Jew? (looking at photos) They can't all have done something.

Bloom: Oh yes they can.... Nowadays, here, everybody's guilty.... But it's deep. It's everywhere, and it's nowhere.

Danny: What is?

Bloom: Evil.

Danny tracks down and kills the two other men from the nightclub murder and shoots an IRA collector taking a payment from his new manager. Although his motives are personal and not political, Danny's evolution from musician to killer illustrates the ease with which normal people can take to violence. Preparing to execute Danny, a detective involved with a Loyalist gang indicates his gun, saying, "It's a lot easier to play than a saxophone, eh? You only have the one tune." Before he can shoot Danny, Bloom appears and kills the renegade detective. When Danny asks Bloom why he never told him about the corrupt detective, Bloom answers absently, "I didn't know." As in an LA film noir drama, evil in Northern

Ireland is omnipresent and infectious, the murky politics of Republican and Loyalist gunmen providing only a thin camouflage for greed and violence.

A Prayer for the Dying (1987)

A Prayer for the Dying (Samuel Goldwyn) follows IRA deserter Martin Fallon's (Mickey Rourke) transformation from disillusioned volunteer to gang hit man. Running from both the authorities and the IRA, he is offered a chance to escape to America by London gangsters. An English mobster will provide money and a passport if Fallon eliminates a rival. Fallon initially refuses the offer, stating that he "never killed for money." The gangsters mock his dedication to the "glorious Cause" and encourage him to kill just "one more." Wanted for his part in blowing up a school bus in Northern Ireland, Fallon to them is simply a cold-blooded murderer. They do not understand his insistence on distinguishing between killing for a cause and killing for money. Seeing no other way of moving on, Fallon agrees and becomes a mob hit man, though his latent Catholicism will not allow himself to kill a priest who witnesses the murder.

The General (1998)

John Boorman's *The General* (Merlin Films) is a biopic tracing the rise and fall of Martin Cahill (1949–1994), one of Ireland's most famous and colorful gangsters, known as much for his public antics as his daring crimes. The film opens in August 1994 with Cahill (Brendan Gleeson) leaving his two-storey brick home in Rathmines, getting into his car, and being shot by an assailant. The film cuts to Garda headquarters where officers break into a cheer at the news. When Inspector Ned Kenny (Jon Voight) arrives at the scene, reporters tell him that the IRA has claimed responsibility.* Given the lack of Garda presence at Cahill's home, allegations of police–IRA collusion are raised.

The film flashes back to Cahill's impoverished boyhood and evolution from juvenile delinquent and petty housebreaker to criminal mastermind, who shows up at a Garda station to establish an alibi while his crew robs a bank. When he announces their next target will be O'Connor's, a Dublin jewelry firm holding two million pounds in gold and diamonds, his men are skeptical, with one stating, "The IRA cased O'Connor's, and even with their firepower they walked away from it." After robbing O'Connor's, Cahill is approached by the IRA, people he distrusts because "they are not proper criminals." When they demand half the loot, Cahill refuses to give the IRA a penny, shouting, "There's nothing as low as robbing a robber." To retaliate, the IRA whips up public opinion against Cahill by accusing his crew of dealing drugs. In Boorman's film there is no mention of the IRA's ideological agenda, so that it appears simply as a rival mafia family demanding a share of a big score.

Martin, known as the General, is wholly apolitical. Like Tony Soprano, his loyalties lie with his family, his crew, and his community. He distributes goods and cash to the poor, which he calls his "way of paying taxes." When a drunken crew member molests his own daughter, Cahill urges the girl not to be a "tout" and testify, telling her grandmother he will provide the girl with a home and some money. Problems are to be handled within the family, not in court.

---

*Veronica Guerin *(Touchstone, 2003) includes a police press conference announcing that the IRA has claimed "responsibility for the murder of Martin Cahill," which leads a reporter to ask, "Why is progress never made in cases involving the IRA?"*

Though Catholic, Cahill has no problem doing business with the UVF. After stealing thirty million pounds worth of paintings from Russborough House,* Cahill finds himself stalked so relentlessly by Garda that a gang member urges him to turn in the artwork to claim the reward money and end the constant surveillance. Cahill tells him he has received an offer for the stolen art from the UVF, which plans to fence the paintings to pay for arms from South Africa. When told to avoid the Loyalist group, the General scoffs that he does not "give a fuck for them or the IRA." In meeting with the UVF, Cahill outlines his political ideology:

> UVF Leader: Are you a Republican, Cahill?
> Cahill: Criminal. What are you?
> UVF Leader: Loyalists.
> Cahill: I'm all for loyalty. Who youse loyal to?
> UVF Leader: The Queen.
> Cahill: Great. I identify with her. Her ancestors tortured and murdered and grabbed what they
>   wanted and she don't pay no taxes. She's my hero.

The IRA, infuriated by his antics and dealings with the UVF, shoot Cahill. In *The General* both the IRA and UVF are depicted as rival gangs willing to cooperate with or extort from more successful mobsters.

RONIN (1998)

John Frankenheimer's *Ronin* (United Artists) takes its title from a Japanese term designating warriors whose lords have been killed. Shamed by their failure to protect their masters, these unemployed men of arms were no longer considered *Samurai* but *Ronin*, rogue fighters "forced to wander the land, looking for work as hired swords or bandits."

The Ronin in Frankenheimer's tale are Cold War castoffs — ex CIA, KGB, and SAS men in Paris who, needing money, are hired by Irish-accented Deirdre (Natascha McElhone) to obtain a mysterious metal suitcase also wanted by the Russians. Lacking enough money to buy the case, Deirdre directs Sam (Robert De Niro), Vincent (Jean Reno), Spence (Sean Bean), and Gregor (Stellan Skarsgard) to steal it. The contents of the case are never disclosed, nor are the motives of Deirdre, who takes orders from Seamus O'Rourke (Jonathan Pryce).

The film launches into a gangster action thriller with numerous car chases and shootouts in the South of France. At the climax of the film, O'Rourke, who is gripping the case, is killed by Vincent. Only after the death of O'Rourke is a connection made to the IRA. At the end of the film an audio montage of British, French, and American news broadcasts announces that "after almost thirty years of bloody and seemingly intractable civil conflict in Northern Ireland ... a peace agreement has been reached." The agreement, CNN reports, was made possible following the "apprehension and slaying in France of the Irish terrorist Seamus O'Rourke" who "had been earlier denounced by the IRA ... as a rogue breakaway operative."

The movie ends with a saddened Sam and Vincent going their separate ways. With a peace agreement in Northern Ireland ending a source of employment, the Ronin are left seeking new lords.

In 1974 an IRA gang, which included British heiress Rose Dugdale, broke into Russborough House and stole £8 million in paintings, demanding that prisoners held in London be transferred to a Belfast prison. Gardai recovered the artwork eleven days later in a raid. Some of the recovered art was stolen in Cahill's 1986 robbery.

Natascha McElhone in *Ronin* (1998).

Divorcing Jack (1998)

In David Caffrey's black comedy *Divorcing Jack* (Scala Productions) the IRA character Patrick "Cow Pat" Keegan (Jason Isaacs) is a pure gangster figure. Known for robbing thirty-three banks for the IRA, he dresses like a Hollywood mafioso, with short, styled hair, a designer suit, and jewelry. Seeking an incriminating audiotape, he threatens the luckless hero, Dan Starkey, kidnapping his wife and killing a visiting American reporter to make a statement. The script by Colin Bateman, based on his novel, never mentions any political motives for Keegan's robberies. He appears simply as a murderous thug, braced by sneering gunmen. In the climactic scene, reminiscent of many mob films, the incriminating tape is exchanged for a briefcase full of cash. Both items are booby trapped, so that the mobster and the corrupt politician he blackmailed are blown up, leaving Starkey untouched.

Shergar (1999)

Written and directed by Dennis C. Lewiston, *Shergar* (Blue Rider Pictures) is a boy and horse drama based on the 1983 kidnapping of famed racehorse Shergar from an Irish stud farm. The thieves demanded millions in ransom from Shergar's owner, the Aga Khan. He refused to pay, and the horse was never recovered. Although the IRA never claimed responsibility, a number of authors and journalists, relying on police reports and informants, have reconstructed a general narrative. Seeking funds, the IRA planned to steal the famed racehorse. Named European Horse of the Year in 1981, Shergar was valued at thirty million pounds. Masked men raided the stable, loaded Shergar into a horse van, and drove off. The horse, according to some sources, became agitated and injured a leg. Believing the horse to be seriously lamed, the IRA put it down. According to one account, the IRA men had no experience euthanizing horses and killed Shergar with a machine gun. Shergar's body was never located, and no arrests were ever made. For the IRA, the affair was an economic failure and a public relations disaster.*

The film starts with a fairly accurate recreation of the events of the February 1983 operation in County Kildare. Masked figures with flashlights and guns rush toward the gates of the farm. Gavin O'Rourke (Mickey Rourke) shoots guard dogs with a gun equipped with a silencer. His team breaks into the stable, leads a horse into a van, and drives off into the night. The truck travels a hundred miles to a farm owned by Garrity (David Warner) who is ordered to hide the horse in his barn and take care of their "walking goldmine." Given the sophistication of the operation and the lack of fingerprints and other clues, investigators presume the horse, valued at fifteen to twenty million pounds, has been taken by the Provisional IRA.

Lewiston's narrative introduces the wholly fictional character of Kevin (Tom Walsh), a boy abandoned by his mother who works on the farm. Not allowed in the Garrity home and verbally abused, he sleeps in the barn and bonds with the horse. Garrity watches television reports about the missing horse and an announced reward of a hundred thousand pounds. Garrity's wife (Virginia Cole) urges him to take the reward money and start a new life in England or America, arguing that the IRA has done nothing for him. Garrity refuses to consider his wife's suggestion, telling her, "They find us, then it's a bullet in the head."

While Garda search Garrity's farm without success, British officials meet in London. An intelligence officer states the operation was staged by a splinter group of the Provisionals calling itself Freedom 1290, which threatens to kill Shergar unless paid five million pounds ransom. The intelligence officer warns that such a sum given to terrorists would "buy enough to blow up Belfast and London." Not wishing to support terrorism, the horse owners refuse to pay the ransom. The British government offers to compensate the owners for losses up to twenty-five million pounds. With no ability to obtain money, the IRA will be forced to release the horse or kill it, suffering a humiliation in either case.

Hearing the news, O'Rourke orders Shergar to be shot and his head sent to the *Belfast Telegraph* as a publicity stunt. Learning that the IRA intends to kill Shergar, Kevin saddles the horse and rides off during a rainstorm. Breaking into teams, IRA men give chase, with orders to kill both boy and horse.

Taking refuge in an abandoned barn on the edge of a village, Kevin disguises Shegar with hair dye. As the IRA close in, Shergar bolts. Kevin chases after him through a forest and finds the horse with Joseph Maguire (Ian Holm), a poetry-reciting traveler (Irish gypsy). Lonely and troubled, Kevin finds a father figure in Maguire, who clings to the iconoclastic life of a social outcast. Joining him and his granddaughter, Kevin eludes the IRA, who, spotting their horse-drawn caravan, assume they are just "tinkers."

O'Rourke is killed in a shootout at a checkpoint. Undaunted, the remainder of the splinter group continues to search for Kevin and Shergar. Spotting Kevin at a county race, the IRA chase him and Shergar in Land Rovers, cornering the pair on the edge of a steep cliff. Shergar rears and jumps into the sea. Believing that both horse and boy have been

---

Months later another kidnapping ended in a public relations debacle when the IRA kidnapped Don Tidey, an English-born supermarket executive, in Dublin. Tidey was freed after a shootout in which a Garda recruit and an Irish soldier were killed, inflaming animosity toward the IRA in the Republic.

killed, the IRA men depart. Maguire's granddaughter spots Kevin in the sea and pulls his apparently lifeless body to shore. Magically, Shergar appears atop the cliff, and Kevin comes back to life. A year later Kevin and Shergar, now with the Maguires, are shown riding unnoticed through a rural town.

In Lewiston's family-friendly film, the troubled boy and his horse finds peace and security. The murderous IRA men in leather jackets, disconnected from any political motivations, are presented as stereotypical Hollywood gangsters — brutish, emotionless, and evil.

The IRA as Law Enforcement

Considering itself the legitimate government of Ireland, the IRA has dissuaded Catholics in Northern Ireland from cooperating with or even seeking assistance from the RUC or British authorities. Catholics whose cars were stolen, for example, often contacted Sinn Fein, sensing the police would do little to aid them. If Sinn Fein identified the car thief, an IRA punishment squad would force the culprit to make restitution or administer a crippling beating.[8] Repeat offenders were kneecapped and occasionally executed. Thieves, sex offenders, and particularly drug dealers were viewed as a social scourge and a threat to IRA operations. A continual fear was that criminals arrested by the police would inform on the IRA to escape prosecution or bargain for lesser sentences.

Law enforcement duties distracted the IRA from its main objective — fighting British "occupation" — but Sinn Fein felt compelled to respond to Catholic victims to keep them from turning to the authorities. "Acceptance of the police," John Conroy noted in *Belfast Diary*, "would ultimately result in rejection of the IRA, as people who talked to the RUC about delinquents would eventually talk to them about where the weapons were stored and who would likely use them."[9]

The hallmark punishment of the IRA was kneecapping, a crippling gunshot wound to the knee intended to create "limping examples for those who would stray from the straight and narrow."[10] Belfast orthopedic surgeons became knee wound experts, treating over a thousand victims between 1973 and 1985. British tabloids often cited kneecappings as evidence of the IRA's psychotic viciousness, but IRA punishments were not random and followed an established protocol. According to Sinn Fein spokesman Richard McCauley, women were never kneecapped. Boys under sixteen were beaten with hurly sticks but not shot. When a kneecapping was ordered, the punishment squad would inflict a flesh wound for a minor transgression or aim at the joint, shattering bones and destroying tendons and major arteries for more severe offenses. Some victims received multiple joint wounds.[11]

The IRA not only punished criminals but disciplined residents whose behavior compromised their political struggle. When unemployed Catholics helped themselves to television sets from a hijacked truck, armed IRA men intervened, telling them, "That's looting. We are a disciplined military organization, not a bunch of criminals thieving anything we can lay our hands on."[12] The IRA mounted house-to-house searches for stolen goods, seizing the TVs and smashing them in the streets. Martin McGartland recalled the impression this had on him, "I watched all this with a certain envy and admiration, but also with fear. I had no intention of crossing these strong men who would brook no argument, demanding that their orders be obeyed without question."[13]

In several films the IRA are depicted as vigilantes, enforcing ruthless justice in the name of community security. In *In the Name of the Father* (Hell's Kitchen Productions,

1992) the IRA threatens Gerry Colon for petty stealing, prompting his move to Britain. His friend, who remains in Belfast, is first kneecapped then executed by the IRA for being a habitual thief. In *The Informant* (Hallmark Entertainment, 1997) Gingy's wife reminds her husband, "It's not the police that keeps people safe around here. It's the organization that protects us." In *Fifty Dead Men Walking* (Handmade International, 2008) the IRA kneecap a teenager suspected of stealing and dealing drugs as a menace to the community.

WHEN THE SKY FALLS (2000)

In *When the Sky Falls* (Icon Entertainment) Sinead Hamilton (*Joan Allen*) plays an investigative journalist (clearly based on Veronica Guerin) tracking down the leaders of the Dublin drug trade. Her investigations lead her to a Martin Cahill–type gangster called Martin Shaughnessy (Pete Postlethwaite) who is killed by the IRA for colluding with Loyalists. At an anti-drug protest march she speaks with a former addict and dealer who limps after being beaten with a baseball bat. When Hamilton asks who assaulted him, he gestures toward a trio of leather-jacketed men overlooking the demonstration. "They look weird enough to be the IRA, am I right?" she asks the dealer. He agrees, noting that they use demonstrations to recruit volunteers. As Hamilton's articles build pressure on the drug lords, one of them complains he has "the pigs, the IRA, and media" after him.

In one scene IRA men enter a poolroom and smash the fingers of a gang member to destroy "the apparatus" he uses to roll joints. A Garda investigator, Mackey (Patrick Bergin), tells Hamilton he has no political loyalties to Sinn Fein or the IRA but sees them running a parallel fight against narcotics. He arranges for Hamilton to meet with the IRA in a remote lighthouse. An IRA leader, Paul McCarling (Frank Grimes), congratulates Hamilton for never printing allegations that Sinn Fein or the IRA had connections with drug dealing. "I have never found any evidence of it," she tells him, then states that she is not "dazzled" by the IRA or its motives. McCarling hands her a taped IRA interrogation of a small-time hood, who, with a gun to his head, implicated the crime lord Dave Hackett in narcotics. McCarling offers to provide Hamilton with a tape to eradicate drugs from Dublin:

> McCarling: The cesspit needs to be cleaned up.
> Hamilton: With your vigilantes acting as judge and jury?
> McCarling: What do you call a trial by journalism?
> Hamilton: That doesn't get people killed.
> McCarling: I wouldn't be too sure about that. Our methods may be different, but the goal is the same.
> Hamilton: Our goal is not the same. I'll use this anyway, thank you.

Like Mackey, who is willing to bend the law and use brutal methods, to go after drug lords, the journalist heroine claims not to approve of the IRA or its methods but will use evidence it obtained through coercion. In this Dublin gangster film, the puritanical IRA takes on criminals out of ideological virtue and notions of Irish purity, apparently wanting no share of their loot.

9

Themes and Characters

Whether produced in Ireland, Britain, or the United States, films about the Irish Republican Army contain recurring themes, common references, and archetypal characters. Many are based on historical events and personalities, while others are the inventions of screenwriters and directors seeking to either make or avoid political statements.

Not the IRA

A consistent feature of many IRA motion pictures is that they are explicitly *not* about the IRA. Early films such as *The Informer* (RKO, 1935) and *Odd Man Out* (Two Cities Films, 1947) refer only to an unnamed "organization" but give visual clues, such as trench coats or portraits of Republican heroes, to lead audiences to associate characters with the Irish Republican Army. Later films allude to the IRA in advertisements and reviews, often mentioning the organization by name in headlines and media reports within the plot. The audience, however, is informed at some point that the characters, especially those presented as terrorists, actually belong to a "fringe" or "splinter" group, often at odds with the "official IRA." This allows filmmakers to exploit the public's fascination with the IRA while clearly stating that their scripts are not depictions of an actual organization, much less a political commentary. Their storylines are not to be seen as endorsements or condemnations of any ideological position but dramas about lone renegades who are often repudiated by the "real IRA."

Avoiding politics, however, does make a political statement, granting a cloak of legitimacy to the IRA by blaming violence and extremism on lone malcontents. Thus, *Hawaii Five-O*'s Jack Lord fights not the IRA but "a rebel splinter group." In *Patriot Games* (Paramount, 1992) Jack Ryan battles "renegade" terrorists who kill Provos and are betrayed by an IRA bagman. The terrorist bomber from Belfast in *Blown Away* (MGM, 1994) is deemed "too crazy" to be in the IRA. The Irishmen in *Shergar* (Blue Rider Pictures, 1999) who kidnap a racehorse and pursue the boy trying to save him belong to a splinter group. In *Ronin* (*FGM Entertainment, United Artists Corporation,* 1998) the Irish trying to secure a mysterious suitcase turn out to be headed by a "terrorist" who is "denounced by the IRA" as "a rogue breakaway operative." In *Hennessy* (American International, 1975) the IRA comes to the rescue, working parallel to British intelligence to stop a suicide bomber from blowing up Parliament and the royal family. In *My Brother's War* (New Horizons, 1997) a CIA agent works with a former IRA member to track down a Republican dissident threatening peace negotiations.

215

The Cause

Throughout the films dealing with the IRA, the organization's philosophy, ideology, and goals are encapsulated into one word: the Cause. In *Shake Hands with the Devil* (Pennebaker Productions/Troy Films, 1959), a young prostitute begs IRA commandant Lenihan (James Cagney) for understanding because her brother died "for the Cause." When the retired cop Max tracks down the psychotic bomber Ryan Gaerity in *Blown Away*, he warns a Boston IRA operative that in assisting the renegade he is doing "the Cause a huge big harm." Tony Luraschi's *The Outsider* (Cinematic Arts B.V, 1979) features a Vietnam veteran who travels to Belfast to do what he can "for the Cause." In *Disappearing in America* (String and a Can Productions, 2009) the IRA fugitive hiding in San Francisco is honored for his service to "the Cause," something he must forget to start a new life.

For IRA characters, the Cause is sacred and held above concerns for individuals. The gunrunner revolutionary in "Up the Rebels" tells an infatuated admirer that anyone who endangers the Cause must be eliminated. The club-footed commandant in *The Night Fighters* (D.R.M. Productions, 1960) argues against rescuing a captured volunteer, stating, "You can't put the Cause in danger for the sake of one man."

In American films the cause of Irish nationalism is not condemned, only the violence of renegades who are usually shown to be psychopaths working to avenge a personal grievance rather than achieve a political objective. In *Patriot Games* Sean Miller shoots at the family of the man who killed his baby brother; the protagonist in Don Sharp's *Hennessy* plans to blow himself up along with the royal family (and much of the House of Lords) to avenge the shooting of his wife and daughter. Other films, such as *The Devil's Own* (Columbia Pictures, 1997), only question the means and never the goal of the IRA.

British films are more likely to denounce the Cause, implying that it is Republicanism itself that leads to terror, not merely its maladjusted adherents. Films from the 1940s and 1950s suggest the nationalist cause is simply outmoded and misguided, perpetuated by ancient and irrelevant grievances. In *I See a Dark Stranger* (Individual Pictures, 1946) the pro–Treaty museum director tries to convince the would-be IRA recruit Bridie Quilty that Ireland is at peace with England, and that "constitutional" means can resolve partition. *The Gentle Gunman* (Ealing Studios, 1952) includes repeated speeches by Terry, who tries to dissuade his younger brother from becoming a Republican gunman, arguing that the narrow nationalist identity represented by the Cause is outmoded in the modern world.

Films made after the Troubles of the 1970s and 1980s contain more strident rejections of the cause of Irish unity. In *Belfast Assassin* (Yorkshire Television, 1982) Mrs. Rennie derides the "great movement" that amounts to "killing people in their homes." The SAS officer Shane Alcott in *Riot* (PM Entertainment Group, 1999) mocks the Provo leader's "sick ideology." For Sam McCready in Frederick Forsyth's *A Casualty of War* (IFS Productions, 1990) the IRA are "psychos whose only cause is the cause of ego-tripping power at the point of a gun."

The Heritage

"1169. Eight hundred years. That's how long we've been fighting for independence. Sword, famine, burning, hanging, shooting, transportation. We've had it all."— *Hidden Agenda*

Closely related to the Cause is the concept of a nationalist legacy stretching back to the Norman invasion. The IRA views itself as the modern revolutionary embodiment of that ancient struggle. Confronting a British officer in *The Wind That Shakes the Barley*, Damien O'Donovan mentions seven hundred years of British occupation. In *Shake Hands with the Devil*, the General (Michael Redgrave) pleads with the hard-line Republican Sean Lenihan to accept the Treaty because it will mean "we'll be ruling ourselves at last, after seven hundred years." *Michael Collins* (Warner Brothers, 1996) includes the quip contrasting Collins being "seven minutes" late with "seven centuries" of British occupation. The prologue of Max Kimmich's *The Fox of Glenarvon* tells German audiences that Ireland has suffered "eight centuries of fraud and deceit, plunder, murder and arson" at the hands of the British. Eager to join the IRA, Bridie Quilty in *I See a Dark Stranger* refers to Ireland's "private war that's been going on for the last seven hundred years." In Loach's *Hidden Agenda* (Helmdale Film, 1990), the centuries-long struggle is invoked to justify the IRA's armed campaign of the 1980s. An irate Republican supporter in *Titanic Town* (BBC Films, 1998) berates British soldiers searching her West Belfast home, shouting, "We've been fighting you for eight hundred years." She launches into a tirade of historical abuses, leading a bored neighbor to comment, "When she gets to the Famine, call me." When Father Brendan in *Boxed* (Fireproof Films, 2002) objects to an IRA squad's plan to kill an RUC officer, its leader, Ann, asserts, "We've been asking nicely for eight hundred years to have our country back. They answered us with starvation and the gun. But now we have the gun."

Soldiers Not Terrorists

Central to the tenets of the Irish Republican Army is that it is an "army," a legitimate nationalist organization seeking the right of self-determination and a unified Ireland. Its 1956 *Handbook for Volunteers* declares the IRA to be a guerrilla army with traditions going back to the fourteenth century.[1] The guerrilla fighter, the handbook states, must be able to "fight alone with the weapons at his disposal."[2] Volunteers must rely on the elements of surprise and lethality to "exhaust the enemy by constant harassment."[3]

Sensitive to the accusation of terrorism, IRA volunteers defend their actions by stressing the soundness of their cause and the oppressive weaponry of their occupiers. Acting in retaliation with limited means, the IRA cannot be condemned for not fighting like a conventional army.

De Valera's comparison of stone walls and armored cars is dramatized in a scene in *The Treaty* (Merlin Films, 1991) in which de Valera and a British colonel watch soldiers carry a flag-draped coffin:

> Colonel: That is one of my young officers. Two days ago he went for a drive in the Dublin mountains with two lady friends. He was murdered in full view of them.
> De Valera: Many young men die in war.
> Colonel: You call shooting from behind hedges and stone walls war?
> De Valera (pointing to an armored car): Isn't that just as good a protection as hedges and stone walls? How can you hide behind that and fire on the Irish people?

A similar defense of guerrilla tactics appears in John Ford's *The Plough and the Stars* (RKO, 1936) when Jack Clitheroe and Fluther Good argue with an English sergeant who condemns the IRA's use of snipers during the Easter Rising:

> Sergeant: Private Taylor got it right through the chest he did. Gang of Assassins. Potting at us from behind roofs.
> Clitheroe: Assassins! What kind of artillery you have on us?
> Sergeant: They're not playing the game. Why don't they come out in the open and fight fair?
> Fluther: Fight fair! A coupla' hundred scrawls of fellas with rosary beads and shotguns against a hundred thousand armed men with horse, foot, and artillery. And he wants us to come out and fight fair?
> Clitheroe: Do you want us to come out in our bare skins and throw stones?

In *The Informant* (Hallmark Entertainment, 1997) an IRA attorney denounces the "violence of the British army, the Royal Ulster Constabulary, Special Air Service, Protestant paramilitary assassination squads." Asked if he opposes the violence of the IRA, the lawyer muses, "Ah but with all the violence thrown at our poor Catholic minority, it's small wonder they turn to their own army for protection."

When Father Da Costa questions his blind niece's infatuation with the IRA killer Martin Fallon (Mickey Rourke) in *A Prayer for the Dying* (Samuel Goldwyn, 1987), she reminds her uncle of his previous service in the SAS, equating the IRA and British special forces:

> Father Da Costa: Anna, that man has lived by violence for years.
> Anna: And what did you live by? ... You said you enjoyed the army, the action. But you became a priest, you gave it up. And so has Martin Fallon.... Don't you see how alike you two are?

In the following scene the priest speaks with Fallon in the church. Mounting the pulpit, the IRA deserter explains why he renounced violence, "I destroyed people. For what? Somebody's victory? Two sides want total victory, Father, and I took one side. In war nobody wants to give or talk. I didn't. I destroyed lives. And I realize that every time I pulled the trigger I was only destroying myself." Fallon is disillusioned with the IRA's "war," not terrorism. It remains a "war" with two, presumably equivalent, sides.

In *Boxed* an IRA volunteer tells a priest he feels no guilt for killing a former comrade wrongly suspected of being an informer, "The fact that he was the wrong man doesn't matter. After all, what's the official line? This is a war. Innocent people get killed in a war. And I didn't start this one." He views himself as an enlisted man following orders, with no personal responsibility for the loss of lives. "See the likes of me don't get a say," he states, "Swimming upstream. If you don't keep going, you get swallowed up. And I'm in there, just another casualty."

Imprisoned in Massachusetts for gunrunning, Declan McQueen (Richard Gere) in *The Jackal* (Universal, 1997) argues that he should be allowed to return to Ireland because he was fighting in a war and that after the treaty is signed, soldiers go home. In *Who Bombed Birmingham?* (Grenada, 1990) when an IRA man responsible for the deaths of twenty-one civilians is asked how he feels about the casualties, he responds coldly, "I'm a soldier."

George Washington is mentioned in two films as a defense against the accusation of terrorism. The Sinn Fein representative Liam Philbin in Ken Loach's *Hidden Agenda* and renegade IRA member Liam Fallon in James Brolin's *My Brother's War*, both argue that Washington was called a "terrorist in his time."

Courts-Martial

Military trials form a recurring theme in IRA movies. The court-martial gives the organization legitimacy, refuting British tabloid characterizations of the IRA as a "murder gang" composed of psychotics. *The Informer, The Gentle Gunman, A Terrible Beauty, A Prayer for the Dying*, and *The Crying Game* include scenes or references to IRA trials passing judgment on suspected informers or deserters.

Disillusioned Patriots and Reformed Rebels

The theme of the disillusioned patriot and the reformed rebel runs throughout IRA films, allowing directors to explore the organization without endorsing its goals or tactics. Numerous Irish, American, and British films feature IRA protagonists who have abandoned the Cause or rejected violence in pursuit of its goals.

In *Young Cassidy* (Metro-Goldwyn-Mayer, 1965) John Cassidy follows his brother's advice and abandons the clownish rebels to inspire people through his writing rather than politics. In *The Boxer* (Universal/Hell's Kitchen Films, 1997) Danny Flynn leaves the IRA after serving fourteen years in prison to resolve community grievances through a non-sectarian boxing club.

In many films disillusioned patriots not only leave the IRA but emigrate to find new lives. Refusing to "make war on the innocent," Dermot O'Neill in *The Night Fighters* leaves neutral Ireland with his girlfriend to find work in wartime England. IRA protagonists in Mike Hodges' *A Prayer for the Dying*, Neil Jordan's *The Crying Game*, and Mark Hammond's *Johnny Was* go to London to escape the reaches of the organization.

The theme of the disillusioned patriot dominates *A Prayer for the Dying*. After his road-side bomb detonates under a van of schoolgirls instead of a convoy of British army vehicles in Northern Ireland, IRA volunteer Michael Fallon flees to England with plans to escape to America. Liam (Liam Neeson) arrives in Britain with instructions from an IRA court of inquiry to bring the deserter back to Ireland or execute him as a potential security risk. Fallon, however, refuses to accompany Liam, telling him he is finished with killing:

Liam: Tell me, why did you leave? Why did you pack everything in?
Fallon: I don't want to keep waking up every night hearing the screams of young children. I lost something a long time ago.... Everything got black, like dried blood.
Liam: Martin, we all have to live with it.
Fallon: I can't.

British films depict not only disillusionment but reformation and conversion. In two wartime films, IRA characters come to see the armed struggle as futile and recognize the English as people they should work with rather than fight against. The IRA volunteer Terry Sullivan in *The Gentle Gunman* argues that planting bombs in Britain serves no purpose. Having lived among the English, he sees them as counterparts to the Irish — working people trying to provide for their families. Bridie Quilty in *I See a Dark Stranger* experiences an epiphany when she realizes that spying for the Nazis will lead to the deaths of British and Irish soldiers on the beaches of Normandy. Abandoning her work for the Cause, she cooperates with and eventually marries a British officer.

The ultimate conversion character is Jack Higgins' Sean Dillon (Rob Lowe), an IRA enforcer tortured but never broken in Long Kesh, who is recruited to assist British intelligence. In *Midnight Man* (VisionView/Carousel/Telescene, 1995) Dillon foils an assassination attempt, and in *On Dangerous Ground* (VisionView/Carousel/Telescene, 1996) he single-handedly disrupts a plot against British interests in Hong Kong.

American films depict former IRA men doing a form of rehabilitative penance. Former IRA volunteer Jimmy Dove in *Blown Away* works as a bomb disposal officer in Boston. In *The Jackal*, the FBI frees the IRA sniper Declan Mulqueen from prison to outwit a hit man intent on assassinating the First Lady. Both men, presumably wanted by the English, are allowed to remain at large when U.S. authorities look the other way. Because their victims were British and not American, they are not held to account.

The Hard Men

> Flynn: Where were you in '72 when the Brits were bustin' down our doors?
> Michael: I wasn't born yet.
> Flynn: That's no excuse.—*Johnny Was*

The villain in many IRA films is the Republican fanatic, the "hard man" who views compromise as surrender, denounces negotiation as treason, places abstractions above people, and ruthlessly uses violence to not only attack enemies but anyone within the organization who fails to follow his rigid standards. For the hard man, the Cause is an absolute not to be violated by conciliation or weakened by personal considerations.

In *Shake Hands with the Devil*, physician/IRA commandant Sean Lenihan exudes a cold disregard for humanity, urging a volunteer, "Forget pity and mercy, those are peacetime words used to soften and weaken us." He is opposed to any concession with Britain, vowing to fight on when the rest of his squad is willing to accept the Treaty. Lenihan's stubborn refusal to compromise in the 1920s is echoed by Harry (Gerard McSorley) in *The Boxer* during the peace talks of the 1990s. While the IRA leadership is negotiating with the Unionists, Harry plants bombs and opposes a non-sectarian boxing club as a threat to the Cause. After the Good Friday Agreement, Flynn (Patrick Bergin) in *Johnny Was* breaks with the Army Council's decision to stop the armed campaign and is eager to set off bombs to "get started again."

Viewing himself as a soldier fighting a war, Flynn has little concern for innocent victims he dismisses as "collateral damage." Harry sets off a car bomb in front of a butcher shop that kills civilians. In *The Gentle Gunman* Shinto disregards the presence of children when he lobs grenades at a prison van. Similarly, Liam Fallon in *My Brother's War* ignores his brother's concern about children to launch an attack on a royal motorcade.

For the hard man the willingness to take life is a distinction to be treasured. Manus, the IRA leader in *The Railway Station Man* (BBC Films, 1992), views himself as superior to a potential recruit. Arrogant and aloof, he claims to be one of the few who has "the clear eye and steady hand" needed in the struggle. He belittles Jack Cuffe, telling him he lacks "imagination" and is one of those who "faint at the sight of blood."

For the fanatic, comradeship is based on immediate practicality. In *The Day They Robbed the Bank of England* (Summit Film Productions, 1960), O'Shea is willing to betray the once invaluable Norgate out of political expediency, arguing that he owes him nothing. "I am involved in the struggle for the independence of Ireland," he explains. "I have no other loyalties." In *Hennessy*, the IRA commandant Sean tells his friend Niall Hennessey that he is "for Ireland first" above everything else, including family. That loyalty to Ireland,

The Hard Man: Gerard McSorley (left) and Brian Cox (right) in *The Boxer* (1997).

ironically, leads him to cooperate with British intelligence to thwart Hennessy's assassination attempt against the Queen, ordering his men to shoot his friend on sight.

The denial of personal loyalties is also expressed in an icy celibacy or abnormal sexuality. Shinto, Lenihan, and Liam Fallon are depicted without references to wives or girlfriends. When an infatuated girl asks *Hawaii Five-O*'s Rourke if he has a wife or girlfriend, the dissident Republican answers soberly, "Ireland is what I have."

Lenihan maintains a puritanical misogyny akin to a Taliban commander. Encountering a pimp and prostitute in a Dublin tenement, he chases the thug away with a gun, then examines the made-up girl with obvious disgust and tears off her necklace, ordering her not to keep her appointment. When she pleads poverty, Lenihan sternly orders her to find another way to support her family, arguing, "We're fighting to keep Ireland a fit place to live in."

Discovering the barmaid Kitty (Glynis Johns) at an IRA hideout, Lenihan is outraged that his oath-bound volunteers have anything to do with "her kind." For Lenihan, Kitty represents not only a distraction and possible security threat but a toxic element endangering the purity of men dedicated to the Cause. When Kitty tells Mrs. Curtis (Dana Wynter) that she is hated by Lenihan, the Englishwoman is puzzled, asking, "I don't understand, you're both on the same side, aren't you?" Kitty reveals that her Irishness is no shield against the commandant's vicious misogyny. "That one's on no woman's side," she explains. "There are things about that one, deep things."

Noticing Lenihan watching her on the beach, Kitty challenges his facade of chastity, "Don't you think I see you looking at me with your hot eyes wanting to put your hands on me? Isn't that the truth now?" Infuriated, Lenihan orders Kitty to leave the squad and throws her to the ground. Spotting her at the site of an ambush and assuming she is an informer, Lenihan shoots Kitty, deriving grim satisfaction from killing a woman he finds sexually appealing. The only female he respects is the elderly Lady Fitzhugh, whom he calls "a fine old woman willing to die for her beliefs." After her death while on a hunger strike, Lenihan insists on executing their English hostage in revenge, even though a truce has been declared. His persistence in executing Mrs. Curtis seems driven as much by her sexuality as her nationality.

Liam Fallon rejects sexual advances made by fellow IRA soldier Sinead (Emma O'Neill), claiming he wants to "stay focused." Grabbing his pants, she taunts him, asking if he is a virgin. He angrily knocks her to the floor and storms from the room. Later, he refuses to enter a pub with his brother, vowing he must "keep the temple pure" the night before an IRA operation. During the attack, he shoots his brother for trying to abort their mission and kills Sinead in a rage. Willing to murder children, his brother, and a potential lover, Liam reserves his compassion for stray animals.

A variant to the asexual Hard Man figure is Don McGinnis, the lame IRA commandant in *The Night Fighters* who burns with sexual frustration and hopes his military status will overshadow his disability and make him desirable to a local flirt.

Shake Hands with the Devil, The Boxer, My Brother's War, and *Johnny Was* end with the Hard Man being killed by a fellow volunteer to achieve or maintain peace. Like the renegade terrorist denounced by the IRA, the Hard Man executed by more sensible volunteers presents the regular Irish Republican Army as being a legitimate and rational organization.

Informers

> On the blood stage of Irish history, the informer is the villain, a cultural bogeyman who has played his part in the downfall of endless fine and noble patriots.— *Kevin Toolis*

> "Any of ye who've read Irish history will know that movements like ours have always been destroyed by paid spies and informers. And I want to set up an outfit that will rectify that."— *Michael Collins*

> "A good informer is worth his weight in gold. But a bad one is a disaster."— *Omagh*

The informer, paid or unpaid, volunteer or victim, has been a dominant figure in Irish history. Wolfe Tone was betrayed by a spy in 1798. A century later James Carey informed on the Invincibles after the Phoenix Park killings. Carey was tracked down and killed aboard the *Melrose* off the coast of South Africa. His killer was arrested and hanged but achieved his goal — the eradication of a hated informer.[4]

Through his own spies in Dublin Castle, Michael Collins exposed the extensive network of Irish informers who passed information to the British, often for surprisingly low sums. For Collins, the war for independence was largely a war against informers, spies, and agents. After the Civil War, the Free State government depended on informers to monitor the activities of dissident Republicans. With the onset of the Troubles in the 1970s, the RUC and British security services made extensive use of informers in Northern Ireland to gather intelligence, disrupt operations, weaken morale, and sow dissent within the IRA.

"For Republicans," Kevin Toolis notes, "'touting' (informing), for whatever reason, remains the ultimate crime."[5] Informers in Ireland, he points out, could not be compared to traditional spies. Because IRA men grew up in close communities with strong family ties, the British and RUC could not easily "insert" outsiders. Tactics like supplying an agent with a uniform, false identity, fake papers, and a cover story that could be used in Nazi-occupied Europe could not work in Northern Ireland, where even IRA men from the next county were greeted with suspicion. With no way of penetrating this close-knit "web of social and extended family relationships," British intelligence relied on generating informers "from within."[6]

British security services and the RUC employed a variety of strategies to identify prospective informers. The Force Research Unit (FRU) was established by the British Army to develop human intelligence in Northern Ireland. FRU "handlers" researched potential assets carefully, concentrating on people who had access to information and a motivation to assist authorities. A "target" trying to sell a home might be offered "£120,000 for a house worth £85,000" as an inducement to inform.[7] With high unemployment in Republican neighborhoods, jobs and money were the most successful lure.[8] Having less access to cash, RUC handlers focused on criminals, granting amnesty or reduced sentences to drunk drivers, drug dealers, or burglars in exchange for information about the IRA.

Matthew Teague documented the case of Freddie Scappaticci for an article in *The Atlantic* in 2006. The son of Italian immigrants, "Scap," as he became known, grew up in Catholic Belfast, joining his Irish peers in throwing bricks at British patrols and clashing with Protestants. Rounded up with other suspects and interned in Long Kesh, Scap became a "hard-shelled IRA man."[9] However, according to Teague, the once-committed Republican became disenchanted with the IRA as he noticed its leaders growing rich on money extorted from Catholic merchants and sending younger men into harm's way while they drank in pubs. Beaten by fellow IRA men after a policy dispute in 1978, Scap became embittered and agreed to work for British intelligence.[10]

Still viewed trustworthy by fellow volunteers, Scap graduated to the IRA's Nutting Squad charged with dispatching traitors. Under his command, at least a dozen men were executed. Operating under the mistaken belief that the British would never use a known killer as an agent, the IRA never suspected that the man shooting informers was an informer himself. With knowledge of arms dumps, planned operations, and tactics, Scap was able to help the British disrupt numerous IRA plots. As head of the Nutting Squad, he could cover his betrayals by implicating and executing others for his own security leaks. Scap informed on the IRA for over a decade before fleeing Ireland in 2003.[11]

Their organization undermined from within, Republicans became increasingly fearful about being deceived by informers or falsely accused of spying by double agents or jealous rivals. In a thirty year period the IRA executed 71 alleged informers.[12] To lessen the threat posed by traitors, the IRA altered its structure, abandoning traditional military-style brigades that could be compromised by the turning of a single volunteer for the cellular system used by other underground organizations.[13]

The informer is an archetypal figure in IRA films, beginning with John Ford's Gypo who becomes a hunted outcast, doomed because he turned in a wanted murderer for twenty pounds. The publican in *Ryan's Daughter* (MGM, 1970) proclaims nationalist sympathies but betrays the gun-running rebel O'Leary and cowardly stands by while the townspeople blame his daughter and shear her hair in revenge. In *The Wind That Shakes the Barley*, Damien, the young doctor, is emotionally torn when he learns a childhood friend informed on the IRA. He feels compelled to shoot him, then tells his mother and accompanies her to his grave. In the comedy *Breakfast on Pluto* a young volunteer is executed after working with police to have drug charges against his girlfriend dropped. In *The Outsider* (Cinematic Arts B.V, 1979) and *Patriots* (Boston Pictures, 1994) the British plan to eliminate American volunteers and score a propaganda coup by setting them up to be shot as traitors by the IRA.

The Outsider, in particular, builds on the informer theme. Michael Flaherty, the idealist volunteer from Detroit, is betrayed by John Russell, the IRA leader who transports him to Belfast, then provides the British with news of his arrival. The British try to provide cover for Russell by implicating Flaherty, setting him up for execution. Escaping Belfast, Flaherty returns to his revered grandfather, who confesses on his deathbed that he was an informer.

THE INFORMANT (1997)

"People have got to learn there is no future in touting."

Jim McBride's *The Informant* (Hallmark Entertainment, 1997) dramatizes the plight of a Provo turned informer and the IRA's obsessive fear of betrayal.

Set in 1983, the film opens with two IRA volunteers traveling to the Irish Republic to bring Jon "Gingy" McAnally (Anthony Brophy) out of exile for a special mission. Having served five years in Long Kesh, Gingy claims to have done "his bit" for the Cause and is reluctant to rejoin the IRA because it is "riddled with touts." Frankie Conroy (Sean McGinley) reminds Gingy of his "oath for life" and his family in Belfast. When Gingy hesitates to accompany them, his visitors explain they will not leave without him.

Once home, Gingy is pressured by his wife Roisin (Maria Lennon) to "do the right thing" and fight for the IRA. "I don't mind helping," he tells her but resists undertaking an operation he calls "fucking kamikaze."

The IRA Chief (John Kavanagh) orders Gingy to carry out an assassination because he is the only man who knows how to operate the unit's sole remaining rocket launcher. Gingy fires the projectile into a Jaguar, killing a judge and two constables. Recognized by a British officer as he flees the scene, Gingy is arrested. Suspecting a fourteen-year-old boy of betraying Gingy, the Chief vows revenge, "We're here to get the Brits out of Ireland; touts destroy us." The innocent boy is burned with cigarettes, then crippled with a gunshot to the knee.

Chief Detective Inspector Rennie (Timothy Dalton) tells Gingy that he had been betrayed. Now facing a minimum of twenty-five years in prison for three murders and feeling no loyalty to the IRA, Gingy offers to cooperate in exchange for immunity from prosecution. Rennie casually disregards Gingy's suggestions until he promises to testify against the IRA leadership — the quarter master, intelligence head, and Chief of the Belfast Brigade.

Based on Gingy's information, armored vehicles sweep across Belfast, rounding up the IRA high command. Only Frankie Conroy and a few volunteers escape arrest. Frankie vows that Gingy will not live to testify, stating, "First, I want him cringing, then I want him screaming, then I want him dead."

After Gingy agrees to talk, his family is taken to a British army compound for protection. Roisin is incensed by her husband's betrayal, declaring, "We never had a tout in our family before." As part of the agreement, Gingy and his family are offered money and new identities in a British enclave, such as Gibraltar or Cyprus. For Roisin, witness protection is treason. The house they are assigned is larger and better furnished than their own, but the Union Jack flying overhead and the presence of British handlers are intolerable for her. She calls her mother, revealing her location to Frankie, who is listening in. Roisin leaves

Gingy, preferring to face the hostility of her Catholic neighbors than stay with a husband working for the British.

Drinking heavily with handlers and bodyguards, Gingy recounts his past service to the IRA to Rennie, who reminds him he no longer has any mates, only his former enemies seeking to exploit him and a suspicious wife who has left him. By informing, Gingy hoped to avoid prison to maintain his family but now watches his family disintegrate. Frank Conroy launches a campaign of harassment against Gingy, tossing a bomb at his safe house and cursing at him through a loudspeaker. Spotting Roisin on the street, Conroy abducts her, drives her to a remote location, and brutally rapes her.

In the final scene, Gingy enters the courtroom and is pelted with refuse by a crowd denouncing him as a tout. With the entire Catholic community standing against him, Gingy is asked by the court if he is prepared to give evidence. Gingy takes a breath and prepares to speak. There is a close-up of his open mouth, then the screen goes black, the audience never knowing his response.

FIFTY DEAD MEN WALKING (2009)

"Information is as powerful as bullets."

Kari Skogland's *Fifty Dead Men Walking* (Future Films) is based on the book by Martin McGartland, who served as "Agent Carol" for the British government spying on the IRA from within. McGartland was among hundreds of informers for the RUC who, once exposed, were relocated and given new homes, jobs, and identities. Born in 1970, McGartland, a Belfast Catholic, grew up a child of the Troubles. He joined the IRA as a teenager, eventually becoming an intelligence officer. He passed information on to the RUC, tipping them off about intended targets, planned attacks, personnel, and weapon caches. He was credited with saving fifty lives. In 1991 the IRA discovered he was informing. During his interrogation he escaped by crashing through a third floor window, saving himself from inevitable torture and execution. After recovering from his injuries, he was relocated and given a new identity. In 1999 two gunmen tracked him down in England and shot him six times. McGartland survived and later that year published his memoir, *Fifty Dead Men Walking*.

Skogland's film of the same title departs sufficiently from McGartland's narrative that an opening credit states the film is "inspired by" rather than "based on" his story. The first scene reconstructs McGartland's 1999 shooting, depicting him being attacked by a masked gunman "somewhere in Canada."* The film then flashes back eleven years to a teenage Martin trying to earn a living as a door-to-door salesman in Belfast, his background explained in a voiceover provided by RUC handler Fergus (Ben Kingsley).

A petty hustler peddling stolen lingerie in Catholic Belfast, Martin McGartland (Jim Sturgess) attracts the attention of a Special Branch officer. Sitting at a bank of television screens beaming images from surveillance cameras, Fergus (a code name) follows Martin's movements, sensing the streetwise teenager could prove useful if he could be persuaded to work for the police.

Taken into custody for dodging an army checkpoint, McGartland is interrogated by Special Branch, who offer to give him cash and overlook his petty crimes — provided he supply information about the IRA. Though McGartland turns down their initial overtures, Fergus remains interested in his potential recruit.

---

*Canada was selected for the film both as a nod to Canadian investors and to dramatize the reach of the IRA.

Fergus is not the only adult male who takes an interest in the brash teen. When Martin attempts to prevent the IRA from kneecapping a young thief, he is grabbed and taken to see the unit leader, Mickey Johnson. Like Fergus, Johnson admires McGartland for being a "go-getter." He offers him a "job" with "a future" and the chance to be "part of something bigger" and "defend his community." Like Special Branch, the IRA lures him with the promise of money and a car.

Fifty Dead Men Walking presents a pair of middle-aged handlers who use similar techniques to induce young men to do their bidding. Too easily recognized, and unwilling to face physical danger themselves, both Fergus and Johnson rely on naïve, disposable recruits to carry out their operations.

Following the meeting with Mickey Johnson, Fergus arranges a confrontation as an excuse to pull Martin in for another interview. Like Johnson, Fergus offers Martin money, a car, and a job he "can feel good about." The IRA, he tells Martin, will "offer you a job that will likely get you killed." Fergus appeals to his patriotism, telling Martin, "It's harder to live for your country than die for it." He dismisses the IRA as "terrorists" and "killers who found a cause to kill for." He hands Martin money and keys to a free car, saying he can trust him because "murder isn't in you."

Mickey Johnson also trusts Martin, assigning him to work as a driver for an IRA bomber. Witnessing the results of a fatal explosion, Martin calls Fergus, offering to inform. Though he is appalled by the violence, he is troubled by betraying people from his own community, especially his friend Sean. Fergus takes Martin to a mortuary to show him the remains of a "tout" who had been tortured by the IRA for seven days, noting, "He saved at least thirty lives, probably more. He's a goddamn hero."

Martin continues to work for the IRA while passing information on to Fergus. The RUC and IRA give him parallel warnings about capture and interrogation. Martin watches Donovan Murphy (David Pearce), an IRA Security Officer, torture a suspected tout until he confesses. Murphy orders Martin to shoot the traitor, but his friend Sean fires first. Although he did not pull the trigger, Martin is shaken. Meeting with Fergus, he tells him he never knew it would come to this. Fergus admits that he misled his recruit, "I lied. We all have murder in us.... The price of a conscience is death. None of us can afford it." Mickey Johnson also comforts Martin about the need for violence, telling him, "It's all about saving lives ... it's got to be done. I dream of one day we'll walk as free men in our own country." He reminds Martin of Bobby Sands, who repeated Lenin's quote that "an ounce of resentment is worth a pound of votes."

Martin is formally sworn into the IRA and sent to collect an arms delivery from Libya. In alerting Fergus about the shipment, he cautions that the lookout is harmless, merely someone's "kid brother" who can be easily bypassed. As Martin watches, British agents gun down the naïve teenager rather than subdue him. Martin, who knows the boy's family, is enraged because he agreed to inform to save lives, not have them taken. In response, Fergus tells Martin he must learn to play by "big boys' rules."

The IRA also plays by "big boys' rules." In the next scene Martin drives two volunteers, who kill a man in front of his seven-year-old daughter. McGartland comes to realize that for both the RUC and the IRA the ends justify the means, even murder. The stress of the violence and complications with his girlfriend and new baby begin to take a toll. Adding to Martin's discomfort is his sense that the IRA is beginning to suspect him. While assembling a bomb, Sean (Kevin Zegers) casually remarks to Martin, "Seems like whenever you're around nothing blows up."

Finally exposed, Martin is seized by the IRA and tortured by Donovan Murphy until he manages to escape by jumping through a window. After failing to kill the informer, Donovan has an alley rendezvous with the head of Special Branch, who demands to know why Martin is still living. Killing the tout, the Special Branch officer explains to the IRA enforcer, "was a simple request."

Fergus, realizing that Martin will not be safe in the hospital, takes him to his own home and negotiates a "deal with Scotland Yard" to get Martin out of Northern Ireland. Unwilling to expose his girlfriend and child to risk, Martin goes into hiding without them.

The film ends with a replay of the 1999 shooting and final written epilogue:

> In 2003 the Stevens Report concluded there was collusion between Loyalist and British interests that led to the murder of innocent people in the 1970s and 1980s.
>
> Later that same year it was revealed that a high ranking member of the IRA, who is implicated in the murder of over 40 people, was working for the British during the height of his IRA activity. Martin is still on the run.

Unlike John Ford's Nolan, who informs solely for money, Gingy and Martin cooperate for higher motives. Gingy talks to avoid prison to stay with his family; Martin spies to stem the violence poisoning his community. Both are exploited by self-serving handlers who, like narcotics officers in police dramas, often become morally indistinguishable from the criminals they are pursuing.

Filmmakers use the informer character not only to explore the nature of the IRA but reveal the cynical machinations of governments who conspire with the paramilitaries they claim to abhor.

Odd Women Out

Films about the IRA reflect general cultural shifts in their cinematic depiction of women, with female characters moving from traditional dramatic roles as romantic heroines and victims to become action figures.

WOMEN AS PEACEMAKERS

"It's a woman's nature to love, just as it's a man's nature to fight."—*The Plough and the Stars*

Many IRA films portray women as emotionally-driven individuals who operate on a value system apart from the male-dominated political struggle. While men, particularly IRA volunteers, view the world in black and white terms of race and nationality, women place personal and family concerns above ideology.

In *Young Cassidy*, Mrs. Cassidy (Flora Robson) views the proposed transport strike as "the savage banging of the hotheads together," warning, "Don't boast going into a strike. Wait for that until you come out of one." When Johnny trains with the Volunteers in the hills, his mother questions the tactics of the rebels, "What good will it do, Johnny? All this drilling and shooting at targets? ... No man and no people can ever be made free by such goings on." Though concerned about her family's poverty, she rejects revolutionary politics as a solution.

In *Beloved Enemy*, an IRA widow overcomes her hatred of the British to help the daughter of an English diplomat plea for peace. Cathleen O'Brien (Karen Morley) helps Lady Helen Drummond (Merle Oberon) enter IRA headquarters to beg for the life of her lover, Dennis Riordan (Brian Aherne), accused of treason for supporting a peace treaty.

The Nightfighters' male characters view Britain as the enemy, while females appear apolitical, seeing England as a potential provider. Dermot's father listens to German broadcasts and celebrates the sinking of a British cruiser, chirping, "Oh, lovely, lovely, lovely! The English can't build them that fast." Dermot's mother, however, considers the casualties, bitterly noting, "And great news for the mothers of them that stays in the sea." While Dermot attacks British soldiers on an IRA raid, his girlfriend urges him to seek employment in England so they can afford to marry.

Titanic Town and *Some Mother's Son* feature mothers who become politically active in order to end violence in Northern Ireland. Bernie McPhelimy launches a peace petition, which brings her into conflict with the IRA; Kathleen Quigley works with a liberal British official to broker an agreement with the IRA to end the hunger strike.

THE TOXIC MISTRESS

"Ireland is greater than a wife." — *The Plough and the Stars*

Female peacemakers are often viewed as a threat to the Cause and a toxic agent capable of weakening the resolve of Republican fighters. In some films Ireland is feminized into a rival lover. In *Beloved Enemy*, Dennis Riordan, who was once accused by the widow of a slain comrade as "being married to a cause," falls for the English Lady Helen, telling her "Ireland was the only woman I ever knew. Ireland was my mother and my sister and my wife." In John Ford's *The Plough and the Stars*, newlywed Nora Clitheroe begs her husband Jack not to heed the call to join the Easter Rising:

Nora: Did you marry me or the Citizen Army?
Jack: Ah, Nora you talk like a child. I have a duty. Ireland is my country, and when she calls
    I must go.
Nora: I'm your wife, and you have a duty to me, too.
Jack: I'm ashamed of you, Nora. A man must fight.
Nora: Aye. You'll do the fighting. But the weeping will be for the women.

For the dedicated volunteer, a wife can act more like a mistress, leading him to betray his commitment to the Cause.

SIRENS AND CHEERLEADERS

Several films include female supporters of the IRA who lure men into taking up arms or staying true to the Cause. The easy barmaid Kitty Brady in *Shake Hands with the Devil* offers her sexual favors to local rebels, telling the ascetic Lenihan, "I've taken no oath, but it's better than tea and three cheers Kitty Brady will be givin' for any brave boy who has." She admits being attracted to young men "marked for an early grave." Dark-lipped Maureen Fagan (Elizabeth Sellars) in *The Gentle Gunman* is accused by her mother of seeking a "cheap thrill" by enticing young lads to become IRA gunmen, telling her, "I'm thinking it's death you're in love with."

For the sirens and cheerleaders, masculinity is equated with armed conflict. Maureen

Woman as peacemaker: Anne Heywood and Robert Mitchum in *The Night Fighters* (1960).

derives a voyeuristic thrill watching men handle guns, and loses interest in Terry when he "goes soft" by rejecting violence. She urges him to change his mind and join his brother in a suicidal mission, asking him if it wouldn't be better "to go out like Matt ... and give your warm blood without fear in a great cause?" In *The Informant*, Gingy's wife connotes her husband's manhood with Republicanism, so that his decision to cooperate with the British to avoid prosecution leads her to denounce him as a "yellow bastard" who "does not have the balls" to face prison.

Maeve O'Brien (Anna Dammann), the long-suffering widow and mother in Max Kimmich's *Mein Leben für Ireland* (Tobis, 1941), blends maternal instincts for family with Irish nationalism. Widowed on her wedding day when her rebel husband is executed, she supports the IRA, sheltering a wounded leader. Jailed for her activities in the film's finale, she cradles the dying Patrick O'Connor in her arms. For Maeve, familial love and patriotism are linked in a common cause that demands sacrifice.

THE PRISONER'S WIFE

With large numbers of IRA men serving lengthy prison sentences, their wives played a special role in maintaining family and community ties, raising funds for prisoners' dependents, promoting the Cause, and serving as their husband's political surrogates.

Maureen, a prisoner's wife, assists the men conducting the mill robbery in *Odd Man Out*. Several scenes in *The Boxer* include prisoners' wives, who are celebrated and cheered in pubs and whose loyalty to their husbands is both honored and enforced.

As Danny Flynn is released from prison, he passes an inmate's wedding. The celibate bride is later feted at a reception. Marriage and family loyalty are Catholic, tribal, and ethnic values that build a sense of community and provide emotional support for the men inside. When a young man dances too closely with a prisoner's wife, he is taken aside and threatened with a kneecapping by IRA men, while the young wife is rebuked by her mother. The prisoner's wife is a symbol of solidarity, sacrifice, and loyalty. The enforced fidelity, monitored by IRA hard men, is presented as a necessity to sustain prisoner morale and social cohesion against a background of unemployment, drug abuse, alcoholism, and emigration.

Maggie Hammil, daughter of an IRA leader, is a prisoner's wife. When Danny emerges from prison after serving fourteen years, she is confronted with the choice of reestablishing a relationship with the man she loved as a girl or continuing her nun-like status as a prisoner's wife. Her father honors the memory of his dead wife, who stood by him while he served time in prison. Maggie, who feels that her marriage ended before her husband was incarcerated, wishes to move on, representing a younger generation of women less willing to be objectified and sacrificed for the Cause.

ACTIVE VOLUNTEERS

The Irish Republican Army, though male dominated, has included female volunteers since its inception. The women's Republican organization Cumann na mBan was founded in 1913 and became an auxiliary to the Irish Republican Army. By 1916 the organization consisted of forty-six units. Dedicated to the creation of an Irish Republic, the Cumann na mBan supported the Easter Rising and was active during the Anglo-Irish War. The organization was led by Countess Constance Markievicz, who served as an officer in Connolly's Citizen's Army. She was condemned to death for her role in the Easter Rising, but her sentence was commuted. Markievicz, along with the majority of the women auxiliaries, bitterly denounced the Treaty. Urging the male delegates in the Dail to vote against the agreement, she claimed, "I say that Ireland's freedom is worth blood, and worth my blood, and I will willingly give it for it, and I appeal to the men of Dail to stand true."[14] An opponent to the Free State, she supported the dissident IRA during the Irish Civil War. The Cumann na mBan was associated with radical Republican causes into the late 1920s. In the late 1970s an IRA staff report proposed dissolving the Cumann na mBan, allowing women to serve in regular IRA cells.[15]

The Wind That Shakes the Barley includes scenes of female volunteers delivering messages, transporting weapons, and conducting Republican courts wearing Cumann na mBan uniforms. John Ford's *The Rising of the Moon* (Warner Brothers, 1957) consists of three separate vignettes, including "1921," based on Lady Gregory's play. Two Republican women enter a prison dressed as nuns to visit a jailed volunteer. One of the nuns gives her habit to the inmate (Donal Donnelly), allowing him to walk past the guards in disguise. Discovering the switch, the British are further frustrated when they discover the faux nun left in his place is Irish-American and less likely to be prosecuted. In *The Break* (Channel Four, 1997) women slip weapons to IRA prisoners in a visiting room, hiding parts of handguns between their legs, adding a sexual element as their partners' hands are shown sliding between their thighs under the table.

No character better illustrates the changing role of the Republican female as Jude (Miranda Richardson) in *The Crying Game*. In the beginning of the film she operates as a blonde femme fatale, luring the British soldier Jody (Forest Whit-

The Hard Woman: Stephen Rea and Miranda Richardson in *The Crying Game* (1992).

aker) into an IRA kidnapping. She appears later in London with dark hair and a "tougher look," blending a mannish sexuality with overt violence. She directs Fergus to take part in an assassination, and races to his apartment to execute him when he fails to obey.

HARD WOMEN

Recent IRA films include active female volunteers who, like the Hard Men, place the Cause above human considerations. In many films the Hard Woman appears deadlier than the male, capable of cold-blooded violence that appalls male protagonists.

In *Boxed*, Ann (Catherine Cusack) is the unquestioned leader of an IRA squad preparing to execute a traitor. Ordering her male subordinates, she is resolute in her purpose. Her dedication to the Cause is so unshakable that even her priest cannot persuade her to reconsider her decision to kill. Siobhan (Alison Doody) accompanies Liam in *A Prayer for the Dying* to either kill or bring back deserter Martin Fallon, who fled to London. As cover, they pose as a married couple while they track their prey. When Liam jokes about "conjugal rights," she humorlessly refuses. Though Liam cannot bring himself to execute Fallon, Siobhan does not hesitate to kill her partner when he fails to obey orders. She coldly enters their hotel room, shoots Liam in the head, then leaves, pausing to switch off the television.

Unlike the chaste Hard Man, the Hard Woman often uses her sexuality as a coercive tool to achieve her aims. In *Patriot Games* Annette (Polly Walker) trains in Libya, acts as a courier, seduces and kills an IRA rival, participates in an assassination attempt, and takes part in the final assault on Jack Ryan's home. Though English, she voices the most hostility toward Lord Holmes, at one point saying, "Post him back to Whitehall in little pieces if that's what it takes to free every Irish political prisoner."

Fifty Dead Men Walking includes the character Grace Sterrin (Rose McGowan), an IRA intelligence officer whose cunning and sexuality lead her to be called Mata Hari. She participates in a dry run attack on a soldiers' pub. Seeing her as a deadly terrorist, Martin McGartland provides her with a disabled weapon. Discovering she cannot fire her gun, she becomes enraged, vowing revenge. While cheerleaders like Maureen Fagan enjoy a voyeuristic thrill watching men handle weapons, the Hard Woman sees the gun as a tool and an extension of her sexuality and power.

THE INFORMER

James Marsh's 2012 film *Shadow Dancer* (BBC Films) features a female volunteer who becomes an informer to avoid a 25-year prison sentence and separation from her young son. Like Frankie McGuire in *The Devil's Own* (Columbia Pictures, 1997), Collette McVeigh (Andrea Riseborough) is a product of the Troubles, emotionally scarred and politically radicalized by a childhood trauma in the 1970s. A flashback shows a young Collette preoccupied with stringing a beaded necklace. Asked by her father to buy cigarettes, she passes the errand to her younger brother Sean, who runs into a crossfire and is killed, presumably by the British. Stricken with grief and guilt, Collette grows up embittered.

In 1993 McVeigh, now a single mother and Republican militant, is arrested trying to plant a bomb in a London subway. Initially defiant, she refuses to cooperate with her interrogators. But as she contemplates spending decades in prison apart from her child, her political convictions waver. Shown evidence indicating that Sean was killed by an IRA bullet and now responsible for another young boy (her son), Collette agrees to return to Northern Ireland to spy on the IRA and her family. Like her male counterparts in other films, McVeigh endures the double agent's constant fear of discovery and the emotional turmoil of betraying one loyalty to serve another. And like Fergus in *Fifty Dead Men Walking*, her British handler (Clive Owen) develops a protective relationship toward his tormented operative that his superiors dismiss as a disposable pawn in a much larger Machiavellian game.

Shadow Dancer differs from most other IRA films by casting a female not as a supporting or peripheral character but as the protagonist at the center of a conflict traditionally depicted in an almost exclusively male terms.

Priests

The Catholic Church, historically opposed to oath-bound organizations, always viewed the IRA with suspicion. The organization's use of violence and Marxist pronouncements led clergy to preach against its activities, using mass excommunication of anti–Treaty volunteers during the Civil War to discourage armed resistance against the newly formed Republic. The Republican custom of firing shots over the coffins of fallen comrades led to churches banning IRA funerals. Individual priests, however, were known to be sympathetic, offering communion to members before going into action and hearing perfunctory confessions afterwards.

Priests have been depicted in IRA films as supporters, apolitical moralists, and vocal opponents. In *The Wind That Shakes the Barley* priests give volunteers a lift on the road and bless them before they go into action. During the Civil War, a priest urges his parish to accept the Treaty, leading dissident IRA volunteers to rise up, denounce the priest as a traitor, and storm out of the church. *The Informant* also presents conflicting roles of the clergy. Early in the film the young son of a volunteer is troubled because his priest tells him the IRA "spits on Jesus." Later, at a goodwill party for Catholics hosted by the British army, a priest tells an officer to "go home ... and take your tanks, and your bombs, and your concentration camps with you," echoing a standard Republican line. In contrast, the priest in the *Nightfighters* reads a letter from the bishops that declares, "It is a mortal sin for a Catholic to bear arms illegally or to fight against lawful authority."

Priests are often viewed with suspicion by the IRA because they encourage their parishioners to follow an apolitical moral code that challenges the supremacy of the nationalist Cause. Father Tom chides Kathleen for her involvement with the illegal organization in *Odd Man Out.* The priest in *Broken Harvest* counsels villagers to put the animosities of the Civil War behind them and abandon lingering Republican loyalties. In *Some Mother's Son*, a priest officiating at the funeral of a hunger striker asks mourners to also consider the deaths of prison officials slain by the IRA. As in *The Wind That Shakes the Barley*, Republicans rebuke the priest, denouncing him as a tool of British imperialism and marching out in protest.

A Prayer for the Dying (1987)

In Mike Hodges' *A Prayer for the Dying* (Samuel Goldwyn, 1987) the IRA deserter Martin Fallon takes confession from the priest (Bob Hoskins) who witnessed him kill a man. He cynically uses the priest's vow of secrecy to silence a potential witness. Resentful about being tricked, the priest does not give up on Fallon, urging him to save his soul. Though a former SAS officer, the priest refuses to violate his vows to cooperate with the police.

The disillusioned patriot confesses: Mickey Rourke in *A Prayer for the Dying* (1997).

BOXED (2002)

"Innocent? How can an RUC man be innocent?"

Marion Comer wrote and directed *Boxed* (Fireproof Films), which explores the ethical dilemmas faced by "tame priests" who provide last rites to Catholics before being executed by the IRA. Viewing itself as a legitimate army punishing people guilty of treason, the IRA provides its Catholic victims the services of a chaplain, a clergyman often coerced or abducted to perform last rites. In the opening scene an older priest, Father Moran (Jim Morton), receives a telephone call and agrees to an assignment, but IRA volunteers mistakenly lift a younger priest, Father Brendan (Tom Murphy), and drive him to a remote house where an informer awaits execution. Masked IRA volunteers brandishing guns guide Father Brendan into a room to hear the confession of their bloodied prisoner. Father Brendan refuses to acquiesce to the IRA ritual, telling the volunteers to go home and avoid committing the mortal sin of murder. He insists they will have to kill him as well, and the IRA is faced with an "uncooperative priest."

For Father Brendan, protecting the informer's life at the expense of his own is a culmination of his priesthood. While the volunteers debate what to do, a lookout spots a man outside the house and knocks out William Hamilton of the RUC and drags him inside. Listening at the door, Father Brendan recognizes the voice of one of his parishioners, Ann (Catherine Cusack), who insists, "We are at war here." For some of the volunteers the use of the priest is simply "company policy." Others see it as a useless gesture, arguing that in wars priests are not called every time soldiers kill in battle. Regaining consciousness, the RUC man, bound and blindfolded, accuses them of using their faith to assure themselves they are morally justified in killing. Asked if he thinks God is on his side when he beats a Catholic, the police officer answers that he works for the state and that "people voted for the powers I work for."

When the informer collapses, Father Brendan calls the IRA volunteers for help, who passively watch as their prisoner dies on the floor. Father Brendan gives the man last rights. Ann asks Father Brendan how he feels about sacrificing himself for a dead man. One of the volunteers tells the priest he is a good Catholic, stating the informer deserved his fate, "He sold out the RA. He sold out his country, and he sold out his friends." The priest asks the volunteer, "Where would any us be if we all got what we deserved?" He confronts Ann, asking her how she feels. "This is a war. You've picked a side, and it's not my side," she tells her priest. Father Brendan insists that "there are no sides, there is just us." The priest, the volunteers realize, is not "tame" and might identify them. The "good Catholic" assists another volunteer in dragging the RUC man into the next room and drowning him in a bathtub.

A senior IRA official arrives at the church and tells Father Moran that he doubts he can release Father Brendan because the volunteers fear he will identify them. Father Moran points out that all that is needed to guarantee the priest's silence is that he hear a single confession. Father Moran calls Father Brendan, ordering him to "pull yourself together, hear a confession, and get yourself out of there." In response, Father Brendan accuses him of being a tame priest, an enabler of IRA violence. By giving last rites to their victims, he tells Father Moran, "We only make them feel better about what they are doing."

Moran arrives at the house to inform Father Brendan that the area is surrounded by British troops who know about the dead RUC man and have no intention of taking prisoners. The authorities have promised Father Moran safe passage to escort his young priest to safety before moving in. Father Moran asks Father Brendan to help him "limit the damage."

Father Brendan removes his collar to stay with the volunteers to be killed, allowing an IRA leader to assume his identity and walk away with Father Moran. Father Brendan serves as a chaplain for Ann's unit, leading them in prayer as shots are fired and a helicopter circles overhead. After Father Brendan leaves the house to surrender, the IRA execute the real informer and the British soldiers open fire. Walking away disguised as a priest, the IRA leader expresses little compassion for the man who gave up his life so he could escape, telling Father Moran, "He brought this on himself."

The Missing Unionist

The most intriguing figure in IRA-related motion pictures is conspicuous by his or her absence. Most films portray the Troubles of Northern Ireland along largely Republican lines. The background narrative is that the Irish Republican Army, however depicted, is battling the British to free the Six Counties and unify the island. The IRA's implacable adversary, the Unionist or Loyalist, is present in only a few films and generally marginalized. A lone Unionist briefly appears in *Michael Collins* and is promptly blown up. In *The Boxer* Joe Hamill (Brian Cox) refers to Protestants as being "the other half of the population," when, in fact, they represent two-thirds of the people of Northern Ireland. The complexities of Irish identity are generally overlooked in motion pictures to reduce the plot to a two-party conflict: terrorist against a lawful society, or patriot against a foreign occupation.

10

Post Troubles?

Films made in the first decade of the twenty-first century began examining a post–Agreement Northern Ireland. Oliver Hirschbiegel's *Five Minutes of Heaven* (Big Fish Films, 2009) presents the Troubles as a past event, its opening title announcing a final casualty list: "An estimated 3720 people were killed as a result of the conflict in Northern Ireland." It is, however, presented as a past event with lingering consequences, as the following title indicates: "This film is a fiction inspired by two men who bear the legacy of one of these killings."

Partially based on Alistair Little's memoir, *Give a Boy a Gun: One Man's Journey from Killing to Peace-Making*, Guy Hibbert's script concerns Loyalist rather than Republican paramilitaries. Fifty-year-old Alistair Little (Liam Neeson) is haunted by the murder of a Catholic he committed as a seventeen-year-old member of the UVF in 1975. After serving twelve years in prison, he renounced violence and became an internationally recognized peace advocate, baring his soul in an ongoing redemptive tour, traveling to South Africa and Kosovo to resolve conflicts. A television program called *One on One* arranges for him to meet Joe Griffin (James Nesbitt), the younger brother of the man he killed, for an on-air reconciliation. The reality TV show, the ubiquitous cell phones, Asian punks on a Belfast train, Little's reference to working with young Muslims, and the TV crew's Russian immigrant indicate that Northern Ireland has moved beyond its bitter Protestant/Catholic sectarianism and become globalized like the rest of Britain. Unlike other films set in Belfast that create a sense of claustrophobia with scenes of narrow streets, cramped row houses, walls, and alleys, *Five Minutes of Heaven* shows Alistair Little walking through large, open squares. Trains and jet planes appear in the distance, suggesting an openness to the rest of the world. Much of the film takes place in two sedans, with shots cutting back and forth between Griffin and Little being chauffeured to the broadcast site. Their cars speed along an expressway that could be a German autobahn or an American turnpike. Belfast is no longer an enclosed, embattled city of barricades and checkpoints patrolled by soldiers and armored vehicles but a busy European capital populated with consumers and commuters.

While Little is prepared to reconcile and seek forgiveness, Griffin, seething with resentment and anger, wants revenge and intends to stab Little on television to earn his "five minutes of heaven." He is angered that Little has achieved fame and money by murder. Any reconciliation, he reasons, will only provide Little with "twenty years of paychecks" and another dramatic story to augment his speaking tours. The television confrontation never occurs, and after a knock-down drag-out fight that leaves both middle-aged men battered and exhausted, Little tells Griffin that he is not worth hating. He urges Griffin to "get rid of me" so he can think of his daughters instead. After attending a group therapy meeting,

Liam Neeson as Alistair Little in *Five Minutes of Heaven* (2009).

Griffin calls Little and states simply, "We're finished." Little is left walking in a large plaza, directionless. There is an end to the Troubles and a tentative closure that terminates the violence but does not bring its survivors peace or reconciliation.

Films that deal with the IRA, however, are less likely to portray the Troubles as finished. For Loyalists, the peace process concluded the conflict largely on their terms. Northern Ireland remains part of Britain; the Protestant majority shares power but remains dominant. For Republicans the Good Friday Agreement, much like the Anglo-Irish Treaty in 1921, represents a compromise that its militant members consider a surrender. Characters in these films echo the debate and disillusionment expressed in the films set in the Fifties and early Sixties, such as *Broken Harvest* (Destiny Films, 1994) and *Amongst Women* (BBC Northern Ireland, 1998). Those disarmed militants with political savvy find jobs in the new Republic or the power-sharing government of a reformed Northern Ireland. Those without, the rank and file volunteers who sacrificed the most, are left to fend for themselves, often jobless and robbed of the romance and camaraderie of the Cause.

FORTY-EIGHT ANGELS (2006)

Written and directed by Marion Comer, *Forty-Eight Angels* (Fantastic Films) follows a dying child on his journey to meet God "before God meets me." Learning that his chemotherapy has failed, Seamus (Ciaran Flynn) decides to imitate St. Columcille by climbing into a rowboat, tossing out the oars, and letting the wind and water carry him to God. Landing on an island, Seamus encounters fifteen-year-old James (John Travers), the Protestant son of a murdered policeman. Together they come across an unconscious man. Noticing his beard, bloodied forehead, and wounded side, Seamus assumes the man to be Jesus.

Seamus' Christ is Darry (Shane Brolly), an IRA man on the run. Chased by the police, he has "come home" after seven years in prison. Feeling betrayed by the IRA, he planted a bomb in their headquarters, injuring himself in the process. Recovering from his wounds, Darry, aided by the boys, ventures on a journey to confront Billy, his former leader. He reaches out to a former friend, Matthew, who reveals to police where the fugitive is hiding.

Leaving with the boys before a police raid, Darry confronts Matthew in a pub, accusing him of informing. Matthew tries to convince Darry that things have changed, arguing, "I can't turn back the clock." He explains that in Darry's absence the struggle has taken a different course:

> Matthew: No one sold us out except the Brits.... Billy seen it coming and he wants to get the best deal he can for us.
> Darby: Right, I forgot. The man who taught me how to kill is now playing politician.
> Matthew: Look around you. Things aren't what they used to be. Things have moved on.

Darry, who went to prison in Billy's place, feels deceived, his sacrifice for the Cause invalidated by what he views as a self-serving capitulation. Matthew insists the nature of the struggle has been transformed into a political process:

> You went inside because you believed in what you were doing. All I'm saying is that we have to do things different now. The guns have had their time.

Darry insists on meeting Billy, threatening to kill Seamus and James and place the blame on his former leader. He kneecaps Matthew and declares, "I'm not giving up what's ours. This is our country."

In their eventual confrontation, Billy recognizes that his once loyal lieutenant has become a troublesome "loose end" left over from the armed struggle. He shoots Darry, who falls onto the fishing boat drifting out to sea with the boys.

Darry's refusal to accept change is in marked contrast to the former prisoner James encounters earlier in the film. Offered a ride, James notices the driver's tattoos spelling out "No Surrender." The ex-paramilitary proclaims, "That's all behind me now." The tattoos serve only as a reminder of a past life of "anger and hate," which he abandoned after encountering Christ in his cell in Long Kesh. Jesus, he tells James, "showed him the way." Listening to gospel music, with a Bible on his dashboard, a cross dangling from his rear view mirror, he has found a new cause, leaving the Troubles behind him. James tricks him and steals his car. Left stranded on the road, the born-again Christian demonstrates no anger or resentment but flashes a wry, knowing smile.

JOHNNY WAS (2006)

Johnny Was (Nordisk Films) opens with a spoken prologue between the lead character, Johnny Doyle (Vinnie Jones), and Ras (Lennox Lewis):

> Johnny: What would you do if you had to make a decision between being loyal to the past or trying to make a future?
> Ras: If a man ain't got no roots, he don't have no future. Ye got to have roots to hold onto.

Johnny's roots lie in the IRA. Now hiding out in London in a Jamaican "squat," he finds himself sandwiched between upstairs neighbor Ras, operator of a pirate radio station, and the drug-dealing gangster Julius below. Living among blacks, far from the Troubles,

Doyle struggles to build a new life and is hopeful for a better future. He tells Rita, a young African-Irish heroin addict, that it is possible for people to improve, reasoning, "They can change for the worst all the time, so I'm sure they can change for the better."

Although preoccupied with surviving in London by working odd jobs, Johnny cannot forget his past. He is haunted by flashbacks of a young woman he failed to save in an IRA bombing gone wrong. Listening to news about the war in Iraq, Johnny hears of a prison break in South London. The escapees are Doyle's former comrade Flynn (Patrick Bergin) and a young volunteer, Michael (Laurence Kinlan), injured during their getaway. Waiting for Johnny Doyle to appear in a market, Flynn outlines his plans for derailing the peace process and reigniting the armed struggle:

> Flynn: Them fuckers went against my orders and voted for disarmament. I wanna see them do that to my face.
> Michael: You said it was orders from the Army Council.
> Flynn: It will be my orders.... What we need is simple. A few strategic bombs to get us started again.

Flynn spots Johnny and coerces him into providing help, pointing to the wounded Michael to gain sympathy. Disillusioned with the Cause, Johnny remarks, "If I thought it would stop him following in our footsteps, I'd break his other ankle." Johnny resents Doyle but agrees to shield him from the police, and hides the wanted pair in his flat. Jimmy (Roger Daltrey), an IRA official, meets Johnny and Flynn in a nightclub, explaining that the organization is upset with both of them. Johnny is viewed as a deserter and security risk. Flynn's unexpected prison break led to two IRA safe houses being discovered during police searches. He tells Johnny he is lucky because "the Army Council is fighting bigger things than deserters like you."

While working with Julius to secure funds, Flynn continues to try to enlist Johnny in his plans:

> Flynn (wistfully): I was gonna restart the war against the Brits and the cops....
> Johnny: ... Who are you really fighting for?
> Flynn: I do it for myself and for the craic. I can't let the Jews, Pakies and fuckin' Yanks have all the fun and glory. I do it — I wanna be the last man standing. I do it for myself.
> Johnny: Funny that.... That's what I've been trying to get away from. Do you remember the girl ... before the bomb? She looked up and smiled straight in my eyes.
> Flynn: I don't remember that girl. It pays not to think in this game. That's why I always come out on top.
> Johnny: It wasn't just her, anyway. It was all of them. All the ones before. All the ones after. All the ones on their side. All the ones on our side. Don't you feel it?
> Flynn: Feel? Feel what?
> Johnny: All that weight. All those wasted lives. For what? That's why it's gotta stop.... End of the line, Flynn.

Johnny hands Flynn a bag he thinks contains drug money. Flynn opens it as a timer flashes down to zero, detonating a bomb that blows them both up.

I.R.A. King of Nothing (2006)

I think I accomplished exactly what I wanted to accomplish, which was making a very small film with a big heart.— *Damian Chapa*

Damian Chapa began work on *I.R.A. King of Nothing* (BBI Films/Latin Lion Pictures) before the Provos officially disarmed. Although he altered his film to reflect ongoing developments in the peace process, Chapa remained adamant about his political message. In an interview he stated:

> The Queen is responsible for murder, and has never had to answer to it because "she's the Queen." Well, in this movie we pretty much tell the Queen what we think about it. And that's why I think Americans will like this film — because they believe in the same spirit of freedom, of not being ruled by a monarchy or a dictatorship.[1]

Chapa's film opens with the first of five flashbacks that trace the IRA career of Bobby Flynn O'Brien (Damian Chapa), a Belfast cabbie. In the first sequence, dated 1970, twelve-year-old Bobby kills a British soldier who shot his mother as she was throwing a petrol bomb. Later flashbacks show him joining the IRA in 1979, training with a unit in the hills in 1981, leading a raid the following year, and finally being imprisoned in London in 1986.

The main narrative, set in 2006, depicts a disillusioned and frustrated Bobby Flynn driving a taxi and bemoaning the decommissioning of arms. "Bobby Sands," he tells his friend Mic, "died for a free Ireland, a united Ireland.... Is that not British soldiers out on our streets still? Where's their decommissioning?" A drunken Mic tells Bobby that "things have changed" and people "are sick" of the conflict and "want to live."

When his former lover Maggie mentions a Republican meeting, Bobby views it as pointless. Referring to the IRA disarmament, he tells her, "We give up all our chips. How can you play poker," he asks her, "with no chips?"

Bobby and Mic confront Loyalists, who kill Mic and his wife Louise in revenge. Bobby is captured and tortured but escapes, killing several Loyalists. Seamus (Joe Estevez), his former IRA leader, orders him to leave Northern Ireland because one of the men he killed was the son of Ian Wilson, a Loyalist leader. Bobby's violent behavior, Seamus warns, is endangering the peace process. Bobby dismisses Seamus as a "politician," telling him that "it's still a war for me." Bobby detests the former IRA men who now "ride in limos" wearing "three piece suits" and "selling books." Seamus remains obstinate, ordering Bobby to leave the country.

In the Republic, Bobby's hotel room blows up, and he is lured to a house where Wilson and another Loyalist lie in wait. Bobby manages to kill both men and flee, convinced he was set up as a "political bargaining chip" by the IRA to keep peace. Maggie travels south to meet Bobby, and their conversation about the Agreement echoes debates over the original Treaty. Maggie speaks for peace and compromise, while Bobby insists on continuing the war until victory is achieved:

> Bobby: I just don't understand. I don't get it. The Cause has changed so fucking much.
> Maggie: Bobby, there is no Cause anymore.... We did it. We fought and we achieved. We've grown Bobby. You have to grow with us. We don't want our children bombs going off where they're playing in the streets.... We want peace.
> Bobby: I don't want those horrible, terrible things, either. But this is a war. There's a foreign army occupying the North.... What happened to you, Maggie?
> Maggie: What happened? I grew up. We grew up.... Only when necessary, that's when we move.... In the boys' minds you're the most dangerous enemy they have.
> Bobby: And why is that?
> Maggie: Because you won't stop fighting.
> Bobby: ...The British flag still flies in Belfast. Bobby Flynn doesn't stop 'till them is leave.

Maggie urges him to "open your heart to peace" and go to America, but Bobby clings to a "chance for freedom, a chance for a united Ireland."

Leaving Maggie, Bobby is taken at gunpoint by a member of the Continuity IRA

(CIRA), who challenges him by asking, "Do you want to continue what was started?" Bobby agrees and is handed a folder containing a photograph of a British businessman staying in Dublin. Backed by MI5, "the Brit" is part of a covert operation to purchase land in the South, giving Britain control over Ireland by having "military power in the North, real estate power in the South." Bobby is promised that if he assassinates "the Brit" he can return to Belfast under CIRA protection. In parting, the gunman tells him, "Tiocfaidh ar Lá!" ("Our day will come").

Bobby takes the assignment, and, after shooting three of the Brit's bodyguards, he confronts the malicious land buyer. Seamus arrives, telling him the Brit has two million in a safe that the boys in Belfast want. Recalling Bobby Sands, Flynn asks Seamus, "Did he die in vain?"

Shot by a wounded bodyguard, Bobby Flynn delivers a protracted dying speech, asking Seamus, "Since when did it become a business? All those people getting shot in the street? All those years? ... We want our Six Counties back! ... I love my country. I love my people. I love Ireland."

Bobby Flynn's body is returned to Belfast for burial. As the flag-draped coffin is about to be loaded into a hearse, an IRA leader drives up and reminds Seamus not to allow any provocative display that will incite Loyalists and endanger the peace process. Seamus consents, promising he won't give the press "anything to look at."

Maggie demands Bobby will "get respect" and that "he will be honored." Learning that there will be no military funeral, she disappears into the house and returns wearing a ski mask. Firing a handgun over the casket, Maggie shouts, "Tiocfaidh ar Lá!"

The film ends with a shot of a Union Jack and the title:

> The British flag
> still flies in Belfast,
> Ireland.

The top two lines slowly vanish, and the screen fades to black, leaving the one word "Ireland," followed by a dedication to Bobby Sands.

The Troubles, audiences are led to presume, are simply in hiatus, the disarmed secret army temporarily at peace, waiting until it "is necessary to move."

Filmed before the crippling recession of 2008, *I.R.A. King of Nothing* depicts Britain launching a two-pronged strategy of "military power in the North, real estate power in the South" to control Ireland. In a 2010 editorial opening with the phrase "Tiocfaidh ar Lar!" Kevin Toolis described Sinn Fein's plan to assume power in Ireland with a two-pronged strategy to "extract political and financial concessions from the compliant Brits" in the North then "using the power of the IRA's hidden financial empire" to "spend their way into power in the South." With anger over unemployment and budget cuts leading voters to reject the long-dominant Fianna Fail party, Toolis predicted "the Irish are returning to the ... politics of small-nationalism." Toolis ended his article warning that with Sinn Fein gaining power, "the politics of the Irish Republic will change forever. A terrible new Irish future is about to be born."[2]

In the 2011 elections, Fianna Fail suffered its greatest defeat in eighty-five years, losing fifty-seven of it seventy-seven seats in the Dail. The main beneficiary was Fine Gael, the party tracing its roots to Michael Collins. Winning 76 seats, it became the largest party in Dail for the first time in its 78-year history. Sinn Fein came in fourth, winning fourteen seats.

Conclusion

Critics have long decried the public's tendency to confuse film and fact. Motion pictures have influenced popular perceptions about history so that actors are more recognizable than the people they portray, fictional scenes are presumed to reenact actual events, and lines from movies are mistaken for historical quotations. George C. Scott's film performance has become the default biography of General Patton, whose photograph is largely unidentifiable to postwar generations. People who have never seen a copy of the Warren Commission Report doubt its veracity because of Oliver Stone's *JFK*.

This blending of Hollywood and history has even greater impact in shaping views about the Irish Republican Army, especially for audiences outside of Ireland less familiar with actual events and personalities. While a movie audience generally recognizes that a spy thriller bears little relation to genuine espionage during the Cold War, or that a drama like *Fail-Safe* is wholly fictional, it is easier for viewers to accept fiction as fact in lesser known conflicts in foreign countries. A single evening of American cable programming may offer three IRA-related films for viewers who have never seen an interview with Gerry Adams or read a book by Tim Pat Coogan.

Film has largely informed the world about the Irish Republican Army. Although the Troubles lasted thirty years, the numbers of IRA volunteers has always been small and typically silent. Republican veterans have been reluctant to write memoirs or grant interviews. Aside from popularized heroes such as Bobby Sands or Joe Doherty, the general public has few images of the rank and file volunteer. Like cowboys or gangsters, the IRA is best known through cinematic representations.

Collectively, motion pictures, whether produced in Britain, Ireland, or the United States, take a generally pro–Treaty stance regarding the IRA. The Irish Republican Army is presented as a legitimate, if not noble, resistance movement during the War of Independence. *Beloved Enemy* (Samuel Goldwyn Company, 1936), *The Plough and the Stars* (RKO, 1936), *Shake Hands with the Devil* (Pennebaker Productions/Troy Films, 1959), *The Treaty* (Merlin Films, 1991), *Michael Collins* (Warner Brothers, 1996), and *The Wind That Shakes the Barley* (Sixteen Films, 2006) depict Republican militants as brave, rational patriots who use justified and measured violence against a brutal, heavily armed foreign occupier.

Torture and terrorism are ascribed not to the IRA but the universally reviled Black and Tans. In the Big House drama *Fools of Fortune* (Polygram, 1990) it is Black and Tans, not the IRA, who torch a Protestant estate. *The Dawning* (Lawson Productions, 1988) portrays a former British army major conspiring with Irish rebels to kill English officers as a poetic idealist rather than a murderous traitor. In most Anglo-Irish War films Loyalists are either wholly absent or appear in small roles as intractable obstacles to peace, usually more talked about than dramatized. Reasonable Republicans embrace the Treaty and the partial freedom it brings; obdurate hardliners reject it, choosing continuing conflict.

The post–Treaty IRA is characterized differently by British and American films. The British wartime dramas *I See a Dark Stranger* (Individual Pictures, 1946) and *The Gentle Gunman* (Ealing Studios, 1952) present Irish Republicanism as a cultish, tribal ideology out of step with the modern world the protagonists learn to reject. Later films such as *Belfast Assassin* (Yorkshire Television, 1982) and *Riot* (PM Entertainment Group, 1999) denounce Republicanism as a "sick ideology," though the characters' revulsion is directed more toward the use of violence than the goal of uniting Ireland. The Provo-turned-James Bond action hero Sean Dillon presents British TV viewers with a redeemed rebel, the "worst of the worst" transformed into Britain's savior. Dillon, who lives in Luxembourg with an Asian wife, reforms himself by rejecting his Irish past.

In contrast, American motion pictures never criticize "the Cause," only the use of violence, which is usually attributed to renegades or lone terrorists condemned by the IRA. The "not the IRA" approach in films like *Patriot Games* (Paramount, 1992), *Blown Away* (MGM, 1994), and *My Brother's War* (New Horizons, 1997) never questions what Republicans are fighting for, only their means. *The Jackal* (Universal, 1997) features a rebel turned action hero, though, unlike Sean Dillon, Declan Mulqueen serves American intelligence but never abandons his devotion to the Cause (and when allowed to escape, he returns to Ireland).

Irish films offer more domestic insights into the IRA, exposing the organization's role as community protector meting out vigilante justice with a ruthlessness generally not shown in American films. *Cal* (Enigma Productions, 1984), *In the Name of the Father* (Hell's Kitchen Productions, 1992), and *When the Sky Falls* (Icon Entertainment, 2000) show the IRA punishing petty thieves and drug dealers with an excessive cruelty that would never be inflicted by law enforcement.

Although British, American, and Irish films present a darker, more sinister, and often criminal post–Treaty IRA, they generally depict it operating in a landscape that suits a Republican rather than a Unionist vision of Northern Ireland. Most notable about nearly all IRA-related films is their lack of political and demographic proportion. Except for a few films like *Four Days in July* (BBC Films, 1984) or *Nothing Personal* (Channel Four Films, 1994), the Protestant Unionist majority is missing in action. The IRA, whether cast as heroes or villains, is usually opposed by British authorities, which makes sense within the script but misleads foreign audiences. A gangster picture typically focuses on the clash between cops and robbers, with a few civilians cast as victims, family members, or witnesses. The audience, however, intuitively understands that outside the scope of the drama there are millions of law-abiding citizens relying on the police for protection. In film after film the IRA is shown battling police and soldiers in war-torn streets patrolled by armored vehicles and barricaded with sandbagged checkpoints, creating a *Battle of Algiers* illusion that the majority of those living in Northern Ireland belong to an indigenous people resisting an unwanted British occupation. The vast blocks of peaceful Unionist neighborhoods and the Loyalist enclaves bristling with Union Jacks appear in brief glimpses if at all. The fact that a referendum held at any point during the Troubles would overwhelmingly support the Unionist position is lost on film audiences. The tendency to blame violence on renegades or defectors has made the IRA repeatedly appear rational, restrained, and reasonable. The Irish diaspora has led filmmakers to approach the IRA with a level of sensitivity and inherent sympathy they would never express in a movie about Serbian nationalists or Islamist militants. Rather than address controversial or contentious political issues, films use the Troubles as backdrops for personal conflicts or existential dramas exploring universalized themes.

If motion pictures distort the political landscape, they also fail to explain the Irish Republican Army. In the conclusion of his history of the IRA, Richard English identifies three prevailing cinematic archetypes of the IRA volunteer: the "unredeemed psychopath," the "unblemished hero," and the "dilemma-ridden, tortured and solitary individual." Despite their diversity, these images, he maintains, fail to capture the essence of the Irish Republican Army:

> These three images (the justified, political hero-warrior; the evil psychopath; the lost, lonely wanderer) have between them accounted for most cinematic treatments of the IRA persona. The attraction is not difficult to explain, for there is something here for most people in any imagined audience. Those who hate the IRA can see them as psychopaths; those who love them can see them as heroes; and those who do not really want to get involved can think that they are all James Mason. But each of these evocations of the IRA is clearly a distortion. The organization cannot be satisfactorily explained according to any of them, unless one believes in caricatured heroes and villains of implausible simplicity; in an inexplicable and spontaneous outburst of mass psychopathology in the north of Ireland; or in the possibility of one of the world's most durable rebel organizations thriving on doubt-ridden loners.[1]

If filmmakers have failed to capture the true IRA, they have, nevertheless, established a cinematic archetype, an identifiable but mutable icon who can be cast to serve as hero, victim, or villain.

Chronology

1858	Irish Republican Brotherhood founded in Dublin; Fenians founded in New York City.
1866–71	Fenian invasions of Canada with some units designated Irish Republican Army.
1905	Sinn Fein founded.
1913	Irish Volunteers founded.
1916	Easter Rising.
1919	War of Independence begins. Irish Republican Army formed, led by Michael Collins.
1920	Bloody Sunday.
1921	Anglo-Irish Treaty ends war, establishes partition of Irish Free State and British Northern Ireland.
1922	Irish Civil War begins. Michael Collins killed in IRA ambush.
1923	Irish Civil War ends.
1936	Irish Republican Army banned in Irish Free State.
1937	New Irish Constitution changes Free State to Erie, lays claims to Northern Ireland.
1939	IRA begins bombing campaign in Britain.
1940	Sean Russell dies aboard German U-Boat.
1949	Erie officially becomes the Republic of Ireland.
1956–1962	IRA Border Campaign in Northern Ireland.
1969	Protestant and Catholic conflicts erupt in Northern Ireland, renewing "the Troubles." British troops arrive in Northern Ireland. IRA splits into Official and Provisional organizations.
1971	First British soldier killed in Northern Ireland. Internment begins.
1972	Bloody Sunday, thirteen demonstrators killed by British troops. Official IRA declares permanent ceasefire. Northern Ireland parliament suspended, beginning of direct rule. IRA detonates 22 car bombs in Belfast in a single hour.
1974	IRA bombings in Birmingham and Guildford. Prevention of Terrorism Act in Britain.
1975	Convictions of Birmingham Six and Guildford Four.
1981	Bobby Sands and nine others die on hunger strike.

1989   Guildford Four released after convictions are overturned.
1991   Birmingham Six released on third appeal.
1998   Good Friday Agreement.
            Real IRA bomb kills 29 in Omagh.
2005   Provisional IRA formally ends armed campaign.
2011   Irish Catholic police officer killed by dissident Republicans in Omagh.

Filmography

Amongst Women (BBC Northern Ireland, 1998) 219 min. *Director:* Tom Cairns; *Writers:* Adrian Hodges, John McGahern; *Cast:* Tony Doyle, Ger Ryan, Susan Lynch.

Angel (Film Four, 1982) 90 min. *Director:* Neil Jordan; *Writer:* Neil Jordan; *Cast:* Stephen Rea, Veronica Quilligan, Alan Devlin.

Belfast Assassin/Harry's Game (Yorkshire Television, 1982) 180 min. *Director:* Lawrence Gordon Clark; *Writer:* Gerald Seymour; *Cast:* Ray Lonnen, Benjamin Whitrow, Nicholas Day.

Beloved Enemy (Samuel Goldwyn Productions, 1936) 90 min. *Director:* H. C. Potter; *Writer:* Rose Franken; *Cast:* Brian Aherne, Merle Oberon, David Niven.

Bloody Sunday (Hell's Kitchen Films, 2002) 107 min. *Director:* Paul Greengrass; *Writer:* Paul Greengrass; *Cast:* James Nesbitt, Tim Pigott-Smith, Nicholas Farrell.

Blown Away (MGM, 1994) 121 min. *Director:* Stephen Hopkins; *Writers:* John Rice, Joe Batteer; *Cast:* Jeff Bridges, Tommy Lee Jones, Lloyd Bridges.

Borstal Boy (British Screen Productions, 2000) 93 min. *Director:* Peter Sheridan; *Writers:* Nye Heron, Brendan Behan; *Cast:* Shawn Hatosy, Danny Dyer, Lee Ingleby.

Boxed (Fireproof Films, 2002) 80 min. *Director:* Marion Comer; *Writer:* Marion Comer; *Cast:* Tom Murphy, Jim Norton, Catherine Cusack.

The Boxer (Universal/Hell's Kitchen Films, 1997) 114 min. *Director:* Jim Sheridan; *Writers:* Jim Sheridan, Terry George; *Cast:* Daniel Day-Lewis, Emily Watson, Brian Cox, Gerard McSorley.

The Break/A Further Gesture (Channel Four, 1997) 96 min. *Director:* Robert Dornhelm; *Writers:* Ronan Bennett, Stephen Rea; *Cast:* Stephen Rea, Alfred Molina, Rosana Pastor.

Breakfast on Pluto (Pathé Pictures International, 2005) 128 min. *Director:* Neil Jordan; *Writers:* Neil Jordan, Pat McCabe, *Cast:* Cillian Murphy, Morgan Jones, Eva Birthistle.

Broken Harvest (Destiny Films, 1994) 97 min. *Director:* Maurice O'Callaghan; *Writers:* Kate O'Callaghan, Maurice O'Callaghan; *Cast:* Colin Lane, Marian Quinn, Niall O'Brien.

Cal (Enigma Productions, 1984) 102 min. *Director:* Pat O'Connor; *Writer:* Bernard MacLaverty; *Cast:* Helen Mirren, John Lynch, Donal McCann.

A Casualty of War (IFS Productions, 1990) 96 min. *Director:* Tom Clegg; *Writers:* Murray Smith, Frederick Forsyth; *Cast:* Shelley Hack, David Threlfall, Alan Howard.

Caught in a Free State (RTE, 1983) *Director:* Peter Ormrod; *Writer:* Brian Lynch; *Cast:* Götz Burger, Benno Hoffmann, Peter Jankovsky.

Cracker: A New Terror (Granada Television, 2006) 109 min. *Director:* Antonia Bird; *Writer:* Jimmy McGovern; *Cast:* Robbie Coltrane, Anthony Flanagan, Stefanie Wilmore.

The Crying Game (Palace Pictures, Channel Four Films, 1992) 112 min. *Director:* Neil Jordan; *Writer:* Neil Jordan; *Cast:* Stephen Rea, Miranda Richardson, Forest Whitaker.

The Dawning (Lawson Productions, 1988) 97 min. *Director:* Robert Knights; *Writers:* Moira Williams, Jennifer Johnston; *Cast:* Anthony Hopkins, Rebecca Pidgeon, Jean Simmons.

The Day They Robbed the Bank of England (Summit Film Productions, 1960) 85 min. *Director:* John Guillermin; *Writers:* Howard Clewes, John Brophy; *Cast:* Aldo Ray, Hugh Griffith, Peter O'Toole.

The Devil's Own (Columbia Pictures, 1997) 107 min. *Director:* Alan J. Pakula; *Writers:* David Aaron Cohen, Kevin Jarre; *Cast:* Harrison Ford, Brad Pitt, Margaret Colin.

Disappearing in America (String and a Can Productions, 2009) 84 min. *Director:* Erik Rodgers; *Writers:* David Polcyn, Erik Rodgers; *Cast:* Devin DiGonno, Richard Eden, Michael Morrison.

Divorcing Jack (Scala Productions, 1998) 110 min. *Director:* David Caffrey; *Writer:* Colin Bateman; *Cast:* David Thewlis, Rachel Griffiths, Jason Isaacs.

The Eagle Has Landed (Associated General Films, 1976) 135 min. *Director:* John Sturges; *Writers:* Tom Mankiewicz, Jack Higgins; *Cast:* Michael Caine, Donald Sutherland, Robert Duvall.

An Everlasting Piece (Dreamworks, 2000) 103 min. *Director:* Barry Levinson; *Writer:* Barry McEvoy; *Cast:* Barry McEvoy, Brían F. O'Byrne, Anna Friel.

Fifty Dead Men Walking (Handmade International, 2008) 117 min. *Director:* Kari Skogland; *Writers:* Nicholas Davies, Martin McGartland; *Cast:* Jim Sturgess, Ben Kingsley, Natalie Press.

A Fistful of Dynamite (Rafran Cinematografica, 1971) 157 min. *Director:* Sergio Leone; *Writers:* Sergio Leone, Sergio Donati; *Cast:* Rod Steiger, James Coburn, Romolo Valli.

Five Minutes of Heaven (Big Fish Films, 2009) 89 min. *Director:* Oliver Hirschbiegel; *Writer:* Guy Hibbert; *Cast:* Liam Neeson, James Nesbitt, Anamaria Marinca.

Fools of Fortune (Polygram, 1990) 104 min. *Director:* Pat O'Connor; *Writers:* Michael Hirst, William Trevor; *Cast:* Iain Glen, Mary Elizabeth Mastrantonio, Sean T. McClory.

48 Angels (Fantastic Films, 2006) 92 min. *Director:* Marion Comer; *Writers:* Marion Comer, Craig Holland; *Cast:* Shane Brolly, Ciaran Flynn, John Travers.

Four Days in July (BBC Films, 1984) 96 min. *Director:* Mike Leigh; *Writer:* Mike Leigh (deviser); *Cast:* Brid Brennan, Des McAleer, Stephen Rea.

Der Fuchs von Glenarvon (Tobis, 1940) 91 min. German. *Director:* Max W. Kimmich; *Writers:* Hans Bertram, Wolf Neumeister; *Cast:* Olga Tschechowa, Karl Ludwig Diehl, Ferdinand Marian.

The General (J&M/Merlin Films, 1998) 124 min. *Director:* John Boorman; *Writers:* John Boorman, Paul Williams; *Cast:* Brendan Gleeson, Adrian Dunbar, Sean McGinley.

The Gentle Gunman (Ealing Studios, 1952) 86 min. *Director:* Basil Dearden; *Writer:* Roger MacDougall; *Cast:* John Mills, Dirk Bogarde, Robert Beatty.

The Glory Boys (Yorkshire Television, 1984) 139 min. *Director:* Michael Ferguson; *Writer:* Gerald Seymour; *Cast:* Rod Steiger, Anthony Perkins, Aaron Harris.

Hang Up Your Brightest Colours: The Life and Death of Michael Collins (ITC, 1973) 77 min. *Director:* Antony Thomas; *Writer:* Kenneth Griffith; *Narrator:* Kenneth Griffith.

Hennessy (American International, 1975) 103 min. *Director:* Don Sharp; *Writers:* John Gay, Richard Johnson; *Cast:* Rod Steiger, Eric Porter, Trevor Howard.

Hidden Agenda (Helmdale Film, 1990) 108 min. *Director:* Ken Loach; *Writer:* Jim Allen; *Cast:* Brad Dourif, Frances McDormand, Brian Cox.

Hunger (Film 4, 2008) 96 min. *Director:* Steve McQueen; *Writers:* Steve McQueen, Enda Walsh; *Cast:* Michael Fassbender, Stuart Graham.

I See a Dark Stranger (Individual Pictures, 1946) 112 min. *Director:* Frank Launder; *Writers:* Sidney Gilliat, Wolfgang Wilhelm; *Cast:* Deborah Kerr, Trevor Howard, Raymond Huntley.

In the Name of the Father (Hell's Kitchen Productions, 1992) 133 min. *Director:* Jim Sheridan; *Writers:* Terry George, Gerry Conlon; *Cast:* Daniel Day-Lewis, Pete Postlethwaite, Don Baker.

The Informant (Hallmark Entertainment, 1997) 149 min. *Director:* Jim McBride; *Writers:* Nicholas Meyer, Gerald Seymour; *Cast:* Anthony Brophy, Cary Elwes, Timothy Dalton.

The Informer (RKO, 1935) *Director:* John Ford; *Writers:* Dudley Nichols, Liam O'Flaherty; *Cast:* Victor McLaglen, Heather Angel, Preston Foster.

I.R.A. King of Nothing (BBI Entertainment, 2006) *Director:* Damian Chapa; *Writers:* Damian Chapa, Carlton Holder; *Cast:* Damian Chapa, Rachel Hunter, Joe Estevez.

The Jackal (Universal, 1997) 124 min. *Director:* Michael Caton-Jones; *Writers:* Chuck Pfarrer, Kenneth Ross; *Cast:* Bruce Willis, Richard Gere, Sidney Poitier.

Johnny Was (Ben Katz Productions, 2006) 93 min. *Director:* Mark Hammond; *Writer:* Brendan Foley; *Cast:* Vinnie Jones, Patrick Bergin, Eriq La Salle.

The Last September (Matrix/Scala, 1999) 103 min. *Director:* Deborah Warner; *Writers:* John Banville, Elizabeth Bowen; *Cast:* Michael Gambon, Keeley Hawes, Gary Lydon.

League of Gentlemen (Allied Film Makers, 1960) 116 min. *Director:* Basil Dearden; *Writers:* Bryan Forbes, John Boland; *Cast:* Jack Hawkins, Nigel Patrick, Roger Livesey.

The Long Good Friday (Handmade Films, 1979) 114 min. *Director:* John Mackenzie; *Writer:* Barrie Keeffe; *Cast:* Bob Hoskins, Pierce Brosnan, Dave King.

The Man Who Never Was (Sumar Productions, 1956) 103 min. *Director:* Ronald Neame; *Writers:* Nigel Balchin, Ewen Montagu; *Cast:* Clifton Webb, Gloria Grahame, Stephen Boyd.

Mein Leben für Irland (Tobis, 1941) 92 min. German. *Director:* Max W. Kimmich; *Writers:* Franz Baumann, Toni Huppertz; *Cast:* Anna Dammann, Will Quadflieg, Werner Hinz.

Michael Collins (Warner Brothers, 1996) 133 min. *Director:* Neil Jordan; *Writer:* Neil Jordan; *Cast:* Liam Neeson, Aidan Quinn, Julia Roberts.

Midnight Man (VisionView/Carousel/Telescene, 1995) 104 min. *Director:* Lawrence Gordon Clark; *Writers:* Jurgen Wolff, Jack Higgins; *Cast:* Rob Lowe, Kenneth Cranham, Oengus MacNamara.

My Brother's War (New Horizons, 1997) 84 min. *Director:* James Brolin; *Writer:* Alex Simon; *Cast:* James Brolin, Josh Brolin, Jennie Garth, Salvator Xuereb.

The Night Fighters/A Terrible Beauty (D.R.M. Productions, 1960) 90 min. *Director:* Tay Garnett; *Writers:* R. Wright Campbell, Arthur Roth; *Cast:* Robert Mitchum, Richard Harris, Anne Heywood.

Nighthawks (Universal, 1981) 99 min. *Director:* Bruce Malmuth; *Writer:* David Shaber, Paul Sylbert; *Cast:* Sylvester Stallone, Rutger Hauer, Billy Dee Williams.

Nothing Personal (Channel Four Films, 1994) 83 min. *Director:* Thaddeus O'Sullivan; *Writer:* Daniel Mornin; *Cast:* Ian Hart, John Lynch, James Frain.

Odd Man Out (Two Cities Films, 1947) 116 min. *Director:* Carol Reed; *Writers:* F. L. Green, R.C. Sherriff; *Cast:* James Mason, Robert Newton, Cyril Cusack, Kathleen Ryan.

Omagh (Hell's Kitchen International, Channel 4 Television, 2004) 106 min. *Director:* Pete Travis; *Writers:* Paul Greengrass, Guy Hibbert; *Cast:* Gerard McSorley, Michele Forbes, Brenda Fricker.

On Dangerous Ground (VisionView/Carousel/Telescene, 1996) 196 min. *Director:* Lawrence Gordon Clark; *Writers:* Christopher Wicking, Jack Higgins; *Cast:* Rob Lowe, Kenneth Cranham, Deborah Moore.

The Outsider (Cinematic Arts B.V, 1979) 128 min. *Director:* Tony Luraschi; *Writers:* Tony Luraschi, Colin Leinster; *Cast:* Craig Wasson, Sterling Hayden, Patricia Quinn.

Patriot Games (Paramount, 1992) 117 min. *Director:* Phillip Noyce; *Writers:* W. Peter Iliff, Tom Clancy; *Cast:* Harrison Ford, Sean Bean, Polly Walker.

Patriots (Boston Pictures, 1994) 83 min. *Director:* Frank Kerr; *Writer:* Frank Kerr; *Cast:* Linda Amendola, Mark Newell, Aidan Parkinson.

The Plough and the Stars (RKO, 1936) 72 min. *Director:* John Ford; *Writers:* Dudley Nichols, Sean O'Casey; *Cast:* Barbara Stanwyck, Preston Foster, Barry Fitzgerald.

A Prayer for the Dying (The Samuel Goldwyn Company, 1987) 107 min. *Director:* Mike Hodges; *Writers:* Edmund Ward, Jack Higgins; *Cast:* Mickey Rourke, Bob Hoskins, Alan Bates.

The Quiet Man (Argosy/Republic, 1952) 129 min. *Director:* John Ford; *Writer:* Frank S. Nugent, Maurice Walsh; *Cast:* John Wayne, Maureen O'Hara, Victor McLaglen.

The Railway Station Man (BBC Films, 1992). *Director:* Michael Whyte; *Writers:* Shelagh Delaney, Jennifer Johnston; *Cast:* Julie Christie, Donald Sutherland, John Lynch.

Riot (PM Entertainment Group, 1999) 94 min. *Director:* Joseph Merhi; *Writers:* William Applegate Jr., Joseph John Barmettler; *Cast:* Gary Daniels, Sugar Ray Leonard, Patrick Kilpatrick.

The Rising of the Moon (Warner Brothers, 1957) 81 min. *Director:* John Ford; *Writer:* Lady Gregory; *Cast:* Donal Donnelly, Maureen Cusack, Doreen Madden.

Ronin (FGM Entertainment, United Artists Corporation, 1998) 122 min. *Director:* John Frankenheimer; *Writer:* J.D. Zeik; *Cast:* Robert De Niro, Natascha McElhone, Jonathan Pryce.

Run of the Country (Castle Rock Entertainment, 1995) 106 min. *Director:* Peter Yates; *Writer:* Shane Connaughton; *Cast:* Matt Keeslar, Anthony Brophy, Albert Finney.

Ryan's Daughter (Warner Brothers, 1970) 195 min. *Director:* David Lean; *Writer:* Robert Bolt; *Cast:* Robert Mitchum, Barry Foster, Leo McKern.

Shadow Dancer (BBC Films, 2012) 101 min. *Director:* James Marsh; *Writer:* Tom Bradby; *Cast:* Andrea Riseborough, Clive Owen.

The Shadow of Béalnabláth: The Story of Michael Collins (RTE, 1989) 120 min. *Director:* Colm Connolly; *Writer:* Colm Connolly; *Narrator:* Colm Connolly.

Shake Hands with the Devil (Pennebaker Productions/Troy Films, 1959) 111 min. *Director:* Michael Anderson; *Writers:* Marian Spitzer, Rearden Conner; *Cast:* James Cagney, Don Murray, Dana Wynter.

Shergar (Blue Rider Pictures, 1999) 95 min. *Director:* Dennis C. Lewiston; *Writer:* Dennis C. Lewiston; *Cast:* Alan Barker, Billy Boyle, Stephen Brennan.

Some Mother's Son (Castle Rock Entertainment, 1996) 112 min. *Director:* Terry George; *Writers:* Terry George, Jim Sheridan; *Cast:* Helen Mirren, Fionnula Flanagan, John Lynch.

A Terrible Beauty/The Night Fighters (D.R.M. Productions, 1960) 90 min. *Director:* Tay Garnett; *Writers:* R. Wright Campbell, Arthur Roth; *Cast:* Robert Mitchum, Richard Harris, Anne Heywood.

Titanic Town (BBC Films, 1998) 100 min. *Director:* Roger Michell; *Writers:* Anne Devlin, Mary Costello; *Cast:* Julie Walters, Ciarán Hinds, Nuala O'Neill.

The Treaty (Merlin Films, 1991). *Director:* Jonathan Lewis; *Writer:* Brian Phelan; *Cast:* Brendan Gleeson, Barry McGovern, Ian Bannen.

When the Sky Falls (Icon Entertainment, 2000) 107 min. *Director:* John Mackenzie; *Writers:* Ronan Gallagher, Guy Andrews; *Cast:* Joan Allen, Patrick Bergin, Frank Grimes.

Who Bombed Birmingham?/The Investigation: Inside a Terrorist Bombing (Granada TV, 1990) 104 min. *Director:* Mike Beckham; *Writer:* Rob Ritchie; *Cast:* John Hurt, Martin Shaw, Gerard McSorley.

The Wind That Shakes the Barley (Sixteen Films, 2006) 127 min. *Director:* Ken Loach; *Writer:* Paul Laverty; *Cast:* Cillian Murphy, Padraic Delaney, Liam Cunningham.

Young Cassidy (Metro-Goldwyn-Mayer, 1965) 105 min. *Director:* Jack Cardiff, John Ford; *Writers:* John Whiting, Sean O'Casey; *Cast:* Rod Taylor, Julie Christie, Michael Redgrave.

Series Television

"Battle of the Century," ***Boardwalk Empire***, 60 min. Aired: 20 Nov. 2011. *Director:* Brad Anderson; *Writers:* Terrence Winter, Steve Kornacki; *Cast:* Steve Buscemi, Ted Rooney, Charlie Cox

"Ourselves Alone," ***Boardwalk Empire***, 60 min. Aired: 2 Oct. 2011. *Director:* David Petrarca; *Writers:* Terrence Winter, Howard Korder; *Cast:* Steve Buscemi, Ted Rooney, Charlie Cox.

"The Conspirators," ***Columbo***, 100 min. Aired: 13 May 1978. *Director:* Leo Penn; *Writers:* Howard Berk, Pat Robison; *Cast:* Peter Falk, Clive Revill, Jeanette Nolan.

"Up the Rebels," ***Hawaii Five-0***, 60 min. Aired: 15 September 1977. *Director:* Don Weis; *Writer:* Robert Janes; *Cast:* Jack Lord, Stephen Boyd, Elayne Heilveil.

"The Troubles," ***Law and Order***, 60 min. Aired: 26 March 1991. *Director:* John Whitesell; *Writers:* Robert Palm; *Cast:* George Dzundza, Chris Noth, Anthony Heald.

Chapter Notes

Preface

1. MacKillop, *Contemporary Irish Cinema: From* The Quiet Man *to* Dancing at Lughnasa, viii.
2. Ibid.

Introduction

1. Peter Fry and Fiona Somerset, *A History of Ireland* (New York: Barnes and Noble, 1988), 29.
2. Ibid., 67.
3. Ibid., 91.
4. Ibid., 91–94.
5. R. F. Foster, *Modern Ireland 1600–1972* (London: Penguin, 1989), 35.
6. Fry, 112–113.
7. Quoted in Fry, 154.
8. Fry, 154.
9. Paul Johnson, *Ireland: A Concise History from the Twelfth Century to the Present Day* (Chicago: Academy of Chicago, 1980), 55.
10. Fry, 159.
11. Robert Kee, *The Green Flag: A History of Irish Nationalism* (London: Penguin, 1972), 19.
12. Quoted in Fry, 167.
13. Kee, 19.
14. Fry, 163.
15. Johnson, 42.
16. Kee, 19.
17. Johnson, 64.
18. Fry, 228.
19. Johnson, 100.
20. Ibid., 109.
21. Christine Kinealy, "The Spoilers of Our Land," *Irish America*, June/July 2010, 35.
22. Katherine Simms, "The Norman Invasion and the Gaelic Recovery," in *The Oxford History of Ireland*, ed. R. F. Foster, 44–87 (Oxford: Oxford University Press, 1989), 67.
23. Kee, 24–25.
24. Ibid., 81–83.
25. Fry, 208–209.
26. Ibid., 244.
27. Ibid., 218.
28. Ibid., 220–221.
29. Ibid., 222–224.
30. D.J. Hickey and J.E. Doherty, *A Dictionary of Irish History Since 1800* (Totowa, NJ: Barnes and Noble, 1981), 422.
31. Fry, 253–254.
32. Kee, 373.
33. Fry, 255–256.
34. Ibid., 259–260.
35. Gordon Lucy, *The Ulster Covenant: A Pictorial History of the Home Rule Crisis* (Belfast: New Ulster, 1989), 5.
36. Ibid., viii.
37. David Fitzpatrick, "Ireland Since 1870," in *The Oxford History of Ireland*, ed. R. F. Foster, 174–229 (Oxford: Oxford University Press, 1989), 191.
38. Ibid., 191–192.
39. Ibid., 193.

Chapter 1

1. Fry, 276–277.
2. Hickey and Doherty, 210–211.
3. Fry, 282.
4. Hickey and Doherty, 57.
5. Ibid.
6. Max Caulfield, *The Easter Rebellion: Dublin 1916* (Boulder, CO: Roberts Rinehart, 1995), 34–35.
7. Fry, 292.
8. Ibid., 293.
9. Garret Fitzgerald, "The Significance of 1916," *BBC History Online*, British Broadcasting Corporation 2001, Web, 12 May 2010.
10. Ibid.
11. Geoffrey Wheatcroft, "The Evil Legacy of the Easter Rising," *The Guardian*, 9 April 2006, Web, 19 February 2011.
12. Ibid.
13. Kevin Myers, "There Is Nothing to Celebrate in the Easter Rising," *The Belfast Telegraph*, 13 April 2007, Web, 12 May 2010.
14. Mary Lou McDonald, "The Legacy and Lessons of Easter 1916," *Socialist Campaign Group News*, n.d., Web, 12 May 2010.
15. Ibid.
16. Quoted in Alan S. Downer, ed., *Twenty-Five Modern Plays*, 3d ed. (New York: Harper and Row, 1953), 723.
17. O'Casey, *The Plough and the Stars*, 739.
18. Scott Eyman, *Print the Legend: The Life and Times of John Ford* (Baltimore and London: Johns Hopkins University Press, 1999), 178–179.
19. Fry, 296–302.
20. Hickey and Doherty, 597.
21. Fry, 311–312.
22. Quoted in Richard Bennet, *The Black and Tans* (New York: Barnes and Noble, 1995), 186.
23. *The Shadow of Béalnabláth: The Story of Michael Collins.*
24. Quoted in Sarah Bradford, *The Reluctant King: The Life and Reign of George VI 1895–1952* (New York: St. Martin's, 1989), 397.
25. A. O. Scott, "The High Cost of Dignity: Recalling the Troubles in Stark Detail," *The New York Times*, 20 March 2009; Web, 23 January 2011.
26. David Ansen, "Ireland Minus the Blarney," *Newsweek*, 15 March 2007; Web, 5 March 2010.
27. Derek Elley, "The Wind That Shakes the Barley," *Variety*, 18 May 2006; Web, 7 November 2010.
28. Tim Luckhurst, "Director in a Class of His Own," *The Times*, 31 May 2006; Web, 5 May 2010.
29. Ibid.
30. Ibid.
31. Simon Heffer, "Bribe Your Own Voters First, Young George," *The Telegraph*, 3 June 2006; Web, 5 October 2010.
32. Ibid.
33. Ibid.
34. Catherine Shoard, "Ireland Good, Britain Bad," *The Telegraph*, 18 June 2006; Web, 5 May 2010.
35. Ibid.
36. Martin McLoone, *Irish Film: The Emergence of a Contemporary Cinema* (London: British Film Institute, 2000), 14.
37. Tom Barry, *Guerilla Days in Ireland: A Personal Account of the Anglo-Irish War* (Boulder, CO: Roberts Rinehart, 1995), 6–7.
38. "Copper John and His Ruined Mansion," *MailOnline*, 17 August 2005; Web, 16 July 2010.
39. Barry, 113–114.
40. Hal Hinson, "Fools of Fortune," *The Washington Post*, 27 October 1990; Web, 14 July 2010.

Chapter 2

1. Peter Hart, *Mick: The Real Michael Collins* (New York: Penguin, 2005), 426.
2. Ibid.
3. Ibid., 27.
4. Ibid., 65.
5. Tim Pat Coogan, *The Man Who Made Ireland: The Life and Death of Michael Collins* (Niwot, CO: Roberts Rinehart, 1992), 17.
6. Hart, 74–75.
7. Coogan, *The Man Who Made Ireland: The Life and Death of Michael Collins*, 17–18.

8. Hart, 69.

9. Ibid., 91–92.

10. Robert Kee, *The Green Flag: A History of Irish Nationalism* (London: Penguin, 1972), 595.

11. *The Shadow of Béalnáblath: The Story of Michael Collins.*

12. Ibid.

13. Ibid.

14. Ibid.

15. Hart, 195.

16. T. Ryle Dwyer, *The Squad and the Intelligence Operations of Michael Collins* (Douglas Village, Cork, Ireland: Mercier, 2005), 14–15.

17. Ibid., 35.

18. *The Shadow of Béalnabláth: The Story of Michael Collins.*

19. Hickey and Doherty, 46.

20. Martin C. Hartline and M. M. Kaulbach, "Michael Collins and Bloody Sunday," *CIA Historical Review Program* (2 July 1996; Web, 18 January 2009).

21. Bennet, 50.

22. Hart, 180.

23. *The Shadow of Béalnabláth: The Story of Michael Collins.*

24. Hart, 245.

25. *The Shadow of Béalnabláth: The Story of Michael Collins.*

26. Dwyer, 58.

27. Robert Briscoe, *For the Life of Me* (Boston: Little, Brown, 1958), 79–80.

28. Bennett, 51.

29. Dwyer, 133.

30. Ibid., 135.

31. Quoted in Bennet, 118.

32. *The Shadow of Béalnabláth: The Story of Michael Collins.*

33. Dwyer, 20.

34. Ibid., 83.

35. *The Shadow of Béalnabláth: The Story of Michael Collins.*

36. Hart, 240; Coogan, *The Man Who Made Ireland: The Life and Death of Michael Collins*, 157.

37. Hart, 240–241.

38. Ibid., 242.

39. Bennet, 121.

40. James Gleeson, *Bloody Sunday: How Michael Collins's Agents Assassinated Britain's Secret Service in Dublin on November 21, 1920* (Guilford, CT: Lyons, 2004), 143.

41. Quoted in Dwyer, 188.

42. Quoted in Gleeson, xvii.

43. Gleeson, 144.

44. Dwyer, 189.

45. Bennet, 127–128.

46. *The Shadow of Béalnabláth: The Story of Michael Collins.*

47. Hart, 242.

48. Bennett, 116.

49. Hartline and Kaulbach.

50. Hart, 243.

51. Quoted in Dwyer, 203.

52. Coogan, *The Man Who Made Ireland: The Life and Death of Michael Collins*, 207.

53. *The Shadow of Béalnabláth: The Story of Michael Collins.*

54. Quoted in Coogan, *The Man Who Made Ireland: The Life and Death of Michael Collins*, 276.

55. Briscoe, 79.

56. Ibid., 127.

57. Ibid.

59. Ibid., 133–134.

60. Hart, 293.

61. *The Shadow of Béalnabláth: The Story of Michael Collins.*

62. Ibid.

63. Hart, 349–350.

64. *The Shadow of Béalnabláth: The Story of Michael Collins.*

65. Ibid.

66. Ibid.

67. Ibid.

68. Ibid.

69. George Bernard Shaw and Dan H. Laurence, eds., *Bernard Shaw Collected Letters 1911–1925* (New York: Viking Penguin, 1985), 783.

70. Michael Collins, *The Path to Freedom* (Boulder, CO: Robert Rinehart, 1996), 115.

71. Ibid., 118.

72. Ibid. 122.

73. Coogan, *The Man Who Made Ireland: The Life and Death of Michael Collins*, 70.

74. *Hang Up Your Brightest Colours: The Life and Death of Michael Collins.*

75. Ibid.

76. Ibid.

77. Quoted in *Hang Up Your Brightest Colours: The Life and Death of Michael Collins.*

78. Quoted in Tom Peterkin, "Michael Collins Was a Peace Icon, Puttnam Says," *Telegraph.co.uk* (22 August 2007; Web, 12 May 2009).

79. Kevin Myers, "To Say Michael Collins Was a Peacemaker Is Humbug: He Was a Cold-Blooded Killer," *Independent.ie* (21 August 2007; Web, 15 December 2010).

80. Quoted in Peter Berresford Ellis, "'One of a Kind' Welshman and Friend of Ireland," *The Irish Democrat*, 8 August 2006; Web, 17 October 2009.

81. Michael Gray, *Stills, Reels and Rushes: Ireland and the Irish in 20th Century Cinema* (Dublin: Blackhall, 1999), 65

82. Kenneth Turan, "Michael Collins," *Los Angeles Times*, 28 October 1996; Web, 12 May 2010.

83. Steve Daly, "The Fighting Irish: Liam Neeson and Director Neil Jordan Waged a 12-Year Battle of Their Own to Bring the Story of Controversial Irish Revolutionary Michael Collins to the Screen — and the Rest Is History," *Entertainment Weekly* 18 October 1996; Web, 3 December 2009.

84. "The Lying Game," *The Daily Telegraph*, 16 November 1996; Web, 10 May 2009.

85. Daly

86. Raita Merivirta-Chakrabarti, "Between Irish National Cinema and Hollywood: Neil Jordan's *Michael Collins*," *Estudios Irlandeses* 2 (2007): 121.

87. Katie Donovan, "Capturing the Big Fellow on Film," *The Irish Times*, 7 February 1995; Web, 11 December 2009.

88. Quoted in "Michael Collins."

89. Merivirta-Chakrabarti, 122.

90. Quoted in Merivirta-Chakrabarti, 123.

91. Ibid.

92. Fintan O'Toole, "The Man Who Shot Michael Collins," *The Independent*, 3 November 1996; Web, 10 October 2009.

93. Bernard Weintraub, "An Irish Legend's Life and Mysterious Death," *The New York Times*, 9 October 1996, C13.

94. Daly.

95. Ibid.

96. Joan Dean, "Michael Collins in America," *Film West* 27 (n.d.), Galway Film Center; Web, 24 March 2009.

97. Ibid.

98. Ibid.

99. Thom Geier, "One Irish Rebel Films Another," *U.S. News & World Report* 14 (October 1996); Web, 19 May 2009.

100. Terry Golway, "Life in the 90s," *America* 175, no. 12 (26 October 1996): 6.

101. Richard A. Blake, "Some Mother's Son," *America* (15 February 1997): 26.

102. Barbara Shulgasser, "Collins' Terrorist as Hero," *sfgate*, 25 October 1996; Web, 5 May 2010.

103. Christopher Null, "Michael Collins Movie Review," *AMCfilmcritic.com*, 17 October 1996; Web, 15 December 2009.

104. Jonathan Coe, "Michael Collins," *New Statesman*, 8 November 1996; Web, 5 May 2010.

105. Ibid.

106. McIlroy, "History Without Borders: Neil Jordan's *Michael Collins*," in *Contemporary Irish Cinema*, ed. James MacKillop, 22–28 (Syracuse: Syracuse University Press, 1999), 26n.

107. Ibid., 28.

108. Eoghan Harris, "Tally Ho: Not So Funny, Mr. Jordan," *The Irish Times*, 26 October 1996, 8.

109. Neil Jordan, "Tally Ho! Mr. Harris," *The Irish Times*, 23 October 1996; Web, 8 June 2010.

110. Ibid.

111. Ibid.

112. Ibid.

113. Harris.

114. Ibid.

115. Ibid.

116. Ibid.

117. Ibid.
118. Pettitt, "The Film *Michael Collins*," 258.
119. Pramaggiore, *Neil Jordan*, 68.
120. Ibid., 69.
121. Coogan, *The Man Who Made Ireland: The Life and Death of Michael Collins*, 159.

Chapter 3

1. Coogan, *The IRA: A History*, 29.
2. O'Callaghan, *The Easter Lily: The Story of the IRA*, 13.
3. English, *Armed Struggle: The History of the IRA,* 51.
4. Coogan, *The IRA: A History*, 39.
5. English, 51.
6. Ibid., 52.
7. Coogan, *The IRA: A History*, 43.
8. Coogan, *Eamon De Valera: The Man Who Was Ireland*, 470–471.
9. Carter, *The Shamrock and the Swastika*, 96.
10. De Bréadún, "Garda Had Network of Paid IRA Informants in 'Practically Every County.'"
11. Russell, quoted in Coogan, *The IRA: A History*, 89.
12. Coogan, *The IRA: A History*, 91.
13. Ibid.
14. Quoted in Coogan, *Eamon De Valera: The Man Who Was Ireland*, 523.
15. Coogan, *The IRA: A History*, 96–97.
16. "S-Plot."
17. Carter, 24.
18. Bell, *The Secret Army: The IRA*, 150.
19. Ibid., 148.
20. Behan, *Borstal Boy*, 38.
21. "S-Plot."
22. "IRA Ire."
23. Carter, 112–113.
24. Quoted in Coogan, *The IRA: A History*, 155.
25. Coogan, *The IRA: A History*, 155.
26. DeValera, quoted in Coogan, *The IRA: A History,* 97–98.
27. Carter, 24.
28. "Ultimate Cause."
29. English, 70.
30. Carter, 196.
31. O'Donoghue, "Hitler's Strange Bunch of Spies."
32. Whiting, *Hitler's Secret War: The Nazi Espionage Campaign Against the Allies*, 66.
33. Quoted in Coogan, *The IRA: A History*, 160.
34. English, 68.
35. Duggan, *A History of the Irish Army*, 179.
36. Ibid., 186.
37. Quoted in de Valera, "Invasion: Preview and Prevention."
38. Coogan, *Eamon De Valera: The Man Who Was Ireland*, 525.
39. Carter, 27.
40. Coogan, *Eamon De Valera: The Man Who Was Ireland*, 535.
41. Carter, 249.
42. Ibid., 38–39.
43. Ibid., 78.
44. Churchill, *The Gathering Storm, Vol. 1*, 381–382.
45. Carter, 65.
46. Briscoe, 262.
47. Keogh, "Eamon de Valera and Hitler: An Analysis of International Reaction to the Visit to the German Minister, May 1945," 71.
48. Quoted in Keogh, 74–75.
49. Rockett, *Film Censorship: A Cultural Journey from Silent Cinema to Internet Pornography*, 363.
50. Connolly, quoted in Rockett, 335.
51. Ibid.
52. Ibid.
53. Ibid., 336.
54. Ibid., 340.

55. Ibid., 338–339.
56. Ibid., 354–355.
57. Hull, *Film in the Third Reich*, 148.
58. Ibid., 149.
59. Giesen, *Nazi Propaganda Films: A History and Filmography*, 247.
60. Gabler, *An Empire of Their Own: How the Jews Invented Hollywood*, 339.
61. Hull, 149.
62. Ibid.
63. Bourke, "Two Foxes of Glenarvon," 163.
64. Hull, 181.
65. Kehoe, "Surreal Portrayals of Life in Ireland."
66. Moloney, *A Secret History of the IRA*, 49.
67. Montagu, *The Man Who Never Was*, 17–31.
68. Ibid., 50–56.
69. Ibid., 63.
70. Ibid., 93.
71. Ibid., 81–88.
72. Ibid., 110–117.
73. Stripp, "Introduction," *The Man Who Never Was*, 12.
74. Carter, 122.
75. "Richard Harris."
76. Sheehan, "Irish Television in the 1980s."
77. Ibid.
78. Ibid.
79. Behan, *Borstal Boy*, 95–96.
80. O'Sullivan, *Brendan Behan: A Life*, 39–40.
81. Ibid., 41–42.
82. Ibid., 43–44.
83. "Hostage."
84. Quoted in Jeffs, *Brendan Behan: Man and Showman*, 38.

Chapter 4

1. Bell, *The Secret Army: The IRA*, 250.
2. Ibid.
3. Ibid., 257.
4. Ibid., 313.
5. Johnson, 217.
6. Briscoe, 337.
7. Adams, *Free Ireland: Towards a Lasting Peace*, 1.
8. Cronin, *Irish Nationalism: A History of its Roots and Ideology*, 189.
9. Bell, *The Irish Troubles: A Generation of Violence, 1967–1992*, 5.
10. Ibid., 4.
11. Ibid., 3.
12. Conroy, *Belfast Diary: War as a Way of Life*, 123.
13. Lynch, Speech 13 August 1969.
14. Goulding, quoted in English, 17.
15. Cronin, 185.
16. Toolis, *Rebel Hearts: Journeys Within the IRA's Soul*, 24.
17. McKittrick and McVea, *Making Sense of the Troubles: The Story of the Conflict in Northern Ireland*, 128.
18. Ibid., 68.
19. Ibid., 252–254.
20. Teague, "Double Blind: The Untold Story of How British Intelligence Infiltrated and Undermined the IRA."
21. McGartland, *Fifty Dead Men Walking*, 4.
22. Wylie, "He's Belfast's Security Blanket."
23. Conroy, 6.
24. McKittrick and Durman, "Government Will Continue to Pay Ulster Bomb Costs."
25. Moloney, 114–118.
26. Ibid., 105.
27. Coogan, *The Man Who Made Ireland: The Life and Death of Michael Collins*, 303.
28. Toolis, *Rebel Hearts: Journeys Within the IRA's Soul*, 25.
29. McKittrick and McVea, *Making Sense of the Troubles: The Story of the Conflict in Northern Ireland*, 59.
30. LaSalle, "Mayhem 'Nothing Personal.'"

31. McKittrick and McVea, *Making Sense of the Troubles: The Story of the Conflict in Northern Ireland*, 143.
32. Bell, *The Irish Troubles: A Generation of Violence, 1967–1992*, 609.
33. Ibid., 611.
34. Margaret Thatcher, quoted in McKittrick and McVea, *Making Sense of the Troubles: The Story of the Conflict in Northern Ireland*, 144.
35. Conroy, 170.
36. English, 200.
37. Burr, "Hunger: A Look at Hell and the Hunger for Freedom."
38. Scott, "The High Cost of Dignity: Recalling the Troubles in Stark Detail."
39. Cox, "Hunger."
40. Ibid.
41. Ibid.
42. Tookey, "Hunger: More Pro-Terrorist Propaganda."
43. Ibid.
44. Ibid.
45. McGartland, 33.
46. Ingram and Harkin, *Stakeknife: Britain's Secret Agents in Ireland*, 174–177.
47. Peter Taylor, *Behind the Mask: The IRA and Sinn Fein*, 378.
48. Quoted in "1974: Four Dead in Guildford Bomb Blasts"
49. Quoted in Bob Woffinden, "The Trial of the Balcombe Street Four."
50. "1974: Four Dead in Guildford Bomb Blasts."
51. Barton, *Jim Sheridan: Framing the Nation*, 87–92.
52. Taylor, "Behind the Mask."
53. Ibid.
54. Gabriel Megahey, quoted in ibid.
55. McIntyre, *Good Friday: The Death of Irish Republicanism*, 5.
56. "Bobby Sands MP (1954–1981)."
57. Myers, "Staring into Northern Ireland's Moral Abyss."
58. Fachtna Murphy, quoted in Jamison, "Huge Arms Find in County Louth," 2.
59. Production Notes, *Omagh* DVD.
60. Neeson, "A Life Taken."

Chapter 5

1. Ford, *Pappy: The Life of John Ford*, 83–88.
2. Ibid., 87–88.
3. DeFelice, 72.
4. Burns-Bisogno, *Censoring Irish Nationalism*, 61.
5. Ibid., 71.
6. Ibid., 108–109.
7. O'Flaherty, *The Informer*, 182.
8. Ibid.
9. Eyman, *Print the Legend: The Life and Times of John Ford*, 154.
10. Ford, 82.
11. John Ford, quoted in ibid., 23.
12. Ibid., 23–24.
13. Eyman, 154.
14. Ford, 84.
15. Ibid.
16. Green, 45–46.
17. Ibid., 126.
18. DeFelice, 17–18.
19. "BBC Seeks Stars of Belfast Film Noir."
20. DeFelice, 14–15.
21. Quoted in Evans, *Carol Reed*, 78.
22. Carol Reed, quoted in DeFelice, 70.
23. Davidescu, "Identity Politics in Carol Reed's *Odd Man Out* and Neil Jordan's *The Crying Game*."
24. DeFelice, 70.
25. O'Doherty, "Caught in the Crossfire."

Chapter 6

1. Fanning, *The Irish Voice in America: Irish-American Fiction from the 1760s to the 1980s*, 81.
2. O'Brien, *The Wind at My Back: The Life and Times of Pat O'Brien*, 32.

3. Hickey and Doherty, 166.
4. Greeley, *The Irish Americans: The Rise to Money & Power*, 91.
5. Hickey and Doherty, 166.
6. John O'Mahony, quoted in Kee, *The Green Flag: A History of Irish Nationalism*, 317.
7. McCaffrey, *Textures of Irish America*, 145–146.
8. Kee, 339.
9. "Fenian Raids."
10. McCaffrey, 146.
11. "Roberts, William Randall (1830–1897)."
12. Barnes, *Irish-American Landmarks: A Traveler's Guide*, 83.
13. Ibid., 84.
14. Hickey and Doherty, 74.
15. Cronin, 90.
16. Coogan, *Eamon De Valera: The Man Who Was Ireland*, 419.
17. Hickey and Doherty, 128.
18. Ibid., 78.
19. Coogan, *The Man Who Made Ireland: The Life and Death of Michael Collins*, 59–60.
20. Coogan, *Eamon De Valera: The Man Who Was Ireland*, 176.
21. Kobler, *Capone: The Life and World of Al Capone*, 91.
22. Coogan, *The Man Who Made Ireland: The Life and Death of Michael Collins*, 168.
23. Hickey and Doherty, 128.
24. Ibid., 337.
25. Carter, *The Shamrock and the Swastika*, 112–113.
26, Coogan, *The IRA: A History,* 142
27. Bell, *The Irish Troubles: A Generation of Violence, 1967–1992*, 164,
28. Moloney, *A Secret History of the IRA*, 421.
29. Bell, *The Irish Troubles: A Generation of Violence, 1967–1992*, 164.
30. Moloney, *A Secret History of the IRA*, 114.
31. Ibid.
32. George Harrison, quoted in English, 116.
33. McKittrick and McVea, *Making Sense of the Troubles: The Story of the Conflict in Northern Ireland*, 128.
34. English, 117.
35. Glazier, *The Encyclopedia of the Irish in America*, 651.
36. Coogan, *The IRA: A History,* 401.
37. Moloney, *A Secret History of the IRA*, 16.
38. Coogan, *The IRA: A History,* 451.
39. Frank Durkan, quoted in ibid.
40. Bell, *The Irish Troubles: A Generation of Violence, 1967–1992*, 278.
41. Ted Kennedy, quoted in ibid., 254.
42. Roberts, "The Obscenity of Giving Ted Kennedy a Knighthood."
43. Graham Walker, quoted in Coll, "Northern Ireland Remembers Ted Kennedy, the Peacemaker."
44. Heffer, "Honouring Ted Kennedy Is an Insult to IRA's Victims."
45. Roberts.
46. Ted Kennedy, quoted in ibid.
47. Quoted in Molony, "Rep. King and the IRA: The End of an Extraordinary Affair?"
48. Molony, "Rep. King and the IRA: The End of an Extraordinary Affair?"
49. West, "IRA Sympathiser Ted Kennedy Was no Friend of Britain."
50. Ibid.
51. Heffer, "Honouring Ted Kennedy Is an Insult to IRA's Victims."
52. Molony, "Rep. King and the IRA: The End of an Extraordinary Affair?"
53. Liddle, "Cowards Colluding with Terrorists."
54. Fisher, "*The Big Fellah.*"
55. "Patriot Games."
56. Barton, *Irish National Cinema*, 162.
57. "Fiona Glenname."

Chapter 7

1. Moloney, *The Secret Army: The IRA,* 329–331.
2. Ibid., 344.
3. English, 331.
4. Moloney, *The Secret Army: The IRA,* 10.
5. *Ibid.*, 329.

Chapter 8

1. Bell, *The Secret Army: The IRA*, 465.
2. Coogan, *The IRA: A History*, 328.
3. Ibid., 399.
4. McKittrick and McVea, *Making Sense of the Troubles: The Story of the Conflict in Northern Ireland*, 123.
5. Lister, "The IRA PLC Turns from Terror into Biggest Crime Gang in Europe."
6. Pogatchnik, "IRA Crime: The Next Elusive Target of Northern Ireland Peacemaking."
7. Gerry Adams, quoted in ibid.
8. McGartland, 51.
9. Conroy, 88.
10. Ibid., 86.
11. Ibid., 85–86.
12. McGartland, 20.
13. Ibid., 20–21.

Chapter 9

1. *Handbook for Volunteers of the Irish Republican Army*, 1.
2. Ibid., 7.
3. Ibid.
4. Hickey and Doherty, 55.
5. Toolis, *Rebel Hearts: Journeys Within the IRA's Soul*, 194.
6. Ingram and Harkin, *Stakeknife: Britain's Secret Agents in Ireland,* 39.
7. Ibid., 36.
8. Teague, "Double Blind: The Untold Story of How British Intelligence Infiltrated and Undermined the IRA."
9. Ibid.
10. Ibid.
11. Sarma, "Informers and the Battle Against Republican Terrorism: A Review of 30 Years of Conflict."
12. Ibid.
13. Hickey and Doherty, 106.
14. Quoted in ibid., 355.
15. Coogan, *The IRA: A History*, 357.

Chapter 10

1. Quoted in Production Notes, *King of Nothing* DVD.
2. Toolis, "Sinn Fein's Day Has Come, and It Is a Dark One," 18.

Conclusion

1. English, 338.

Bibliography

Adams, Gerry. *Free Ireland: Towards a Lasting Peace.* Niwot, CO: Roberts Rinehart, 1994.

Ansen, David. "Ireland Minus the Blarney." *Newsweek*, 15 March 2007. Web 5 March 2010.

Applebaum, Anne. "The Discreet Charm of the Terrorist Cause." *The Washington Post*, 3 August 2005. Web 9 October 2010.

Barnes, John A. *Irish-American Landmarks: A Traveler's Guide.* Detroit: Visible Ink, 1995.

Barry, Tom. *Guerilla Days in Ireland: A Personal Account of the Anglo-Irish War.* Boulder, CO: Roberts Rinehart, 1995.

Barton, Ruth. *Irish National Cinema.* London: Routledge, 2004.

_____. *Jim Sheridan: Framing the Nation.* Dublin: Liffey Press, 2002.

"BBC Seeks Stars of Belfast Film Noir." *BBC News-Northern Ireland.* BBC, 23 February 2007. Web 5 March 2010.

Behan, Brendan. *Borstal Boy.* New York: Alfred A. Knopf, 1959.

Bell, J. Bowyer. *The Irish Troubles: A Generation of Violence, 1967–1992.* New York: St. Martin's, 1993.

_____. *The Secret Army: The IRA*, Revised 3rd Edition. New Brunswick, NJ: Transaction, 2008.

Bennett, Richard. *The Black and Tans.* New York: Barnes and Noble, 1995.

Blake, Richard A. "Some Mother's Son." *America*, 15 February 1997, 26.

"Bobby Sands MP (1954–1981)." *BBC h2g2.* BBC, 3 September 2009. Web 14 February 2011.

Bourke, Eoin. "Two Foxes of Glenarvon." *Amsterdamer Beiträge zur neueren Germanistik* 63 (1 October 2007): 157–168.

Bradford, Sarah. *The Reluctant King: The Life and Reign of George VI 1895–1952.* New York: St. Martin's, 1989.

Briscoe, Robert. *For the Life of Me.* Boston: Little, Brown, 1958.

Burns-Bisogno, Louisa. *Censoring Irish Nationalism.* Jefferson, NC: McFarland, 1997.

Burr, Ty. "Hunger: A Look at Hell and the Hunger for Freedom." *The Boston Globe* 27, March 2009. Web 23 January 2011.

Cahill, Thomas. "Why Famine Came to Ireland." *Irish America*, June/July 2010, 94–96.

Carter, Carolle J. *The Shamrock and the Swastika.* Palo Alto, CA: Pacific, 1977.

Caulfield, Max. *The Easter Rebellion: Dublin 1916.* Boulder, CO: Roberts Rinehart, 1995.

Churchill, Winston. *The Gathering Storm*, Vol. 1. New York: Bantam, 1961.

Coe, Jonathan. "Michael Collins." *New Statesman.* 8 November 1996. Web 5 May 2010.

Coll, Bryan. "Northern Ireland Remembers Ted Kennedy, The Peacemaker." *Time* 28 (August 2009). Web 9 October 2010.

Collins, Michael. *The Path to Freedom.* Boulder, CO: Robert Rinehart, 1996.

Coogan, Tim Pat. *Eamon DeValera: The Man Who Was Ireland.* New York: HarperCollins, 1993.

_____. *The IRA: A History.* Niwot, CO: Roberts Rinehart, 1994.

_____. *The Man Who Made Ireland: The Life and Death of Michael Collins.* Niwot, CO: Roberts Rinehart, 1992.

"Copper John and His Ruined Mansion." *MailOnline*, 17 August 2005. Web 16 July 2010.

Conroy, John. *Belfast Diary: War as a Way of Life.* Boston: Beacon, 1995.

Cox, David. "Hunger." *The Guardian*, 3 November 2008. Web 23 January 2011.

Cronin, Sean. *Irish Nationalism: A History of Its Roots and Ideology.* New York: Continuum, 1981.

Crowdus, Gary. "Neil Jordan's 'Michael Collins.'" *Cineaste* 22 (Fall 1996). Web 10 October 2009.

Daly, Steve. "The Fighting Irish: Liam Neeson and Director Neil Jordan Waged a 12-Year Battle of Their Own to Bring the Story of Controversial Irish Revolutionary Michael Collins to the Screen — and the Rest Is History." *Entertainment Weekly*, 18 October 1996. Web 3 December 2009.

Davidescu, Radu. "Identity Politics in Carol Reed's *Odd Man Out* and Neil Jordan's *The Crying Game*." *Collected Essays*. Web 10 December 2010.

Dean, Joan. "Michael Collins in America." *Film West* 27 (n.d.), Galway Film Center. Web 24 March 2009.

De Bréadún, Deaglán. "Garda Had Network of Paid IRA Informants in 'Practically Every County.'" *The Irish Times*, 9 February 2009. Web 10 May 2010.

DeFelice, James. *Filmguide to* Odd Man Out. Bloomington: Indiana University Press, 1975.

Donovan, Katie. "Capturing the Big Fellow on Film." *The Irish Times*, 7 February 1995. Web 11 December 2009.

Downer, Alan S., ed. *Twenty-Five Modern Plays*, 3rd Edition. New York: Harper and Row, 1953.

Duggan, John P. *A History of the Irish Army*. Dublin: Gill and Macmillan, 1991.

Dwyer, T. Ryle. *The Squad and the Intelligence Operations of Michael Collins*. Douglas Village, Cork, Ireland: Mercier, 2005.

Elley, Derek. "*The Wind That Shakes the Barley*" *Variety*, 18 May 2006. Web 7 November 2010.

Ellis, Peter Berresford. "'One of a Kind' Welshman and Friend of Ireland." *The Irish Democrat*, 8 August 2006. Web 17 October 2009.

English, Richard. *Armed Struggle: The History of the IRA*. Oxford: Oxford University Press, 2003.

Evans, Peter Williams. *Carol Reed*. Manchester: Manchester University Press, 2005.

Eyman, Scott. *Print the Legend: The Life and Times of John Ford*. Baltimore: Johns Hopkins University Press, 1999.

Fanning, Charles. *The Irish Voice in America: Irish-American Fiction from the 1760s to the 1980s*. Lexington, KY: University Press of Kentucky, 1990.

"Fenian Raids." *Canadian Military*, n.d. Web 9 October 2010.

"Fiona Glenname." *Burn Notice* Character Profiles. *USA Network*. USANetwork.com Web 2 February 2011.

Fisher, Philip. "*The Big Fellah*." *Reviews. The British Theatre Guild*. 2010. Web 10 September 2010.

Fitzgerald, Garret. "The Significance of 1916." *BBC History Online*. British Broadcasting Corporation, 2001. Web 12 May 2010.

Fitzpatrick, David. "Ireland Since 1870." *The Oxford History of Ireland*, ed. R. F. Foster. Oxford: Oxford University Press, 1989, 174–229.

Flynn, Arthur. *The Story of Irish Film*. Dublin: Currach, 2005.

Ford, Dan. *Pappy: The Life of John Ford*. New York: Da Capo, 1998.

Foster, R. F. *Modern Ireland 1600–1972*. London: Penguin, 1989.

Fry, Peter, and Fiona Somerset. *A History of Ireland*. New York: Barnes and Noble, 1988.

Gabler, Neil. *An Empire of Their Own: How the Jews Invented Hollywood*. New York: Crown, 1988.

Geier, Thom. "One Irish Rebel Films Another." *U.S. News & World Report*, 14 October 1996. Web 19 May 2009.

Giesen, Rolf. *Nazi Propaganda Films: A History and Filmography*. Jefferson, NC: McFarland, 2003.

Glazier, Michael, ed. *The Encyclopedia of the Irish in America*. Notre Dame, IN: Notre Dame University Press, 1999.

Gleeson, James. *Bloody Sunday: How Michael Collins's Agents Assassinated Britain's Secret Service in Dublin on November 21, 1920*. Guilford, CT: Lyons, 2004.

Golway, Terry. "Life in the '90s." *America* 175, no. 12 (26 October 1996): 6.

Gray, Michael. *Stills, Reels and Rushes: Ireland and the Irish in 20th Century Cinema*. Dublin: Blackhall, 1999.

Greeley, Andrew M. *The Irish Americans: The Rise to Money and Power*. New York: Harper and Row, 1981.

Green, F. L. *Odd Man Out*. London: Cardinal, 1991.

"Griffith, Kenneth (1921–2006)." Screenonline, n.d. Web 31 October 2009.

Handbook for Volunteers of the Irish Republican Army. General Headquarters, 1956 rept. Boulder, CO: Paladin, 1985.

Harris, Eoghan. "Tally Ho: Not So Funny, Mr. Jordan." *The Irish Times*, 26 October 1996, 8.

Hart, Peter. *Mick: The Real Michael Collins*. New York: Penguin, 2005.

Hartline, Martin C., and M. M. Kaulbach. "Michael Collins and Bloody Sunday." *CIA Historical Review Program*, 2 July 1996. Web 18 January 2009.

Heffer, Simon. "Bribe Your Own Voters First, Young George." *The Telegraph*, 3 June 2006. Web 5 October 2010.

_____. "Honouring Ted Kennedy Is an Insult to IRA's Victims." *The Daily Telegraph*, 7 March 2009. Web 10 September 2010.

Hickey, D.J., & J. E. Doherty. *A Dictionary of Irish History Since 1800*. Totowa, NJ: Barnes and Noble, 1981.

Hinson, Hal. "Fools of Fortune." *The Washington Post*, 27 October 1990. Web 14 July 2010.

"The Hostage." *Internet Broadway Database*, n.d. Web 13 May 2009.

Hull, David Stewart. *Film in the Third Reich*. New York: Touchstone, 1973.

Ignatiev, Noel. *How the Irish Became White*. New York: Routledge, 1995.

Ingram, Martin, and Greg Harkin. *Stakeknife: Britain's Secret Agents in Ireland*. Madison: University of Wisconsin Press, 2004.

"Invasion: Preview and Prevention." *Time*, 3 June 1940. Web 8 July 2010.

"I.R.A. Ire." *Time*, 10 April 1939. Web 8 July 2010.

Jamison, Scott. "Huge Arms Find in County Louth." *Irish Echo*, 13–19 October 2010, 2.

Jeffs, Rae. *Brendan Behan: Man and Showman*. Cleveland: The World, 1968.

Johnson, Paul. *Ireland: A Concise History from the Twelfth Century to the Present Day*. Chicago: Academy of Chicago, 1980.

Jordan, Neil. "Tally Ho! Mr. Harris." *The Irish Times*, 23 October 1996. Web 8 June 2010.

Kee, Robert. *The Green Flag: A History of Irish Nationalism*. London: Penguin, 1972.

Kehoe, Emmanuel. "Surreal Portrayals of Life in Ireland." *The Post.IE*, 4 February 2007. Web 6 June 2008.

Keogh, Dermot. "Eamon de Valera and Hitler: An Analysis of International Reaction to the Visit to the German Minister, May 1945." *Irish Studies in International Affairs* 3, no. 1 (1989): 69–92.

Kinealy, Christine. "The Spoilers of Our Land." *Irish America*, June/July 2010, 32–36.

Kobler, John. *Capone: The Life and World of Al Capone*. Greenwich, CT: Fawcett Crest, 1971.

LaSalle, Mick. "Mayhem 'Nothing Personal.'" *San Francisco Chronicle*, 9 May 1997. Web 10 Aug.

Liddle, Rod. "Cowards Colluding with Terrorists." *The Spectator*, 29 August 2009. Web 10 September 2010.

Lister, David, and Sean O'Neill. "The IRA PLC Turns from Terror Into Biggest Crime Gang in Europe." *The Times*, 25 February 2005. Web 10 December 2010.

Luckhurst, Tim. "Director in a Class of His Own." *The Times*, 31 May 2006. Web 5 May 2010.

Lucy, Gordon. *The Ulster Covenant: A Pictorial History of the Home Rule Crisis*. Belfast: New Ulster, 1989.

"The Lying Game." *The Daily Telegraph*, 16 November 1996. Web 10 May 2009.

Lynch, Jack. Speech, 13 August 1969. *CAIN Web Service* (n.d.). Web 11 February 2011.

Macardle, Dorothy. *The Irish Republic*. New York: Farrar, Straus and Giroux, 1965.

MacKillop, James, ed. *Contemporary Irish Cinema: From* The Quiet Man *to* Dancing at Lughnasa. Syracuse: Syracuse University Press, 1999.

McCaffrey, Lawrence J. *Textures of Irish America*. Syracuse: Syracuse University Press, 1992.

McDonald, Mary Lou. "The Legacy and Lessons of Easter 1916." *Socialist Campaign Group News* (n.d.). Web 12 May 2010.

McGartland, Martin. *Fifty Dead Men Walking*. London: John Blake, 2009.

McIlroy, Brian. "History Without Borders: Neil Jordan's *Michael Collins*." *Contemporary Irish Cinema*, ed. James MacKillop. Syracuse: Syracuse University Press, 1999, 22–28.

McKittrick, David, and Paul Durman. "Government Will Continue to Pay Ulster Bomb Costs." *The Independent*, 9 December 1992. Web 24 December 2010.

McKittrick, David, and David McVea. *Making Sense of the Troubles: The Story of the Conflict in Northern Ireland*. Chicago: New Amsterdam, 2002.

McLoone, Martin. *Irish Film: The Emergence of a Contemporary Cinema*. London: British Film Institute, 2000.

Merivirta-Chakrabarti, Raita. "Between Irish National Cinema and Hollywood: Neil Jordan's *Michael Collins*." *Estudios Irlandeses* 2 (2007): 121–127.

"Michael Collins." *Warner Brothers* (n.d.). Web 11 September 2009.

"Michael Collins: A Man Against an Empire." *Military History*. HistoryNet, 12 June 2006. Web 10 May 2010.

Moloney, Ed. "Rep. King and the IRA: The End of an Extraordinary Affair?" *The New York Sun*, 22 June 2005. Web 10 September 2010.

_____. *A Secret History of the IRA*. New York: Norton, 2002.

Montagu, Ewen. *The Man Who Never Was*. Annapolis: Naval Institute, 2001.

Myers, Kevin. "Staring Into Northern Ireland's Moral Abyss." *Telegraph.co.uk*, 30 March 2008. Web 14 February 2011.

_____. "There Is Nothing to Celebrate in the Easter Rising." *The Belfast Telegraph*, 13 April 2007. Web 12 May 2010.

_____. "To Say Michael Collins Was a Peacemaker Is Humbug: He Was a Cold-Blooded Killer." *Independent.ie*, 21 August 2007. Web 15 December 2010.

Neeson, Anthony. "A Life Taken: Outrage After Omagh Officer Dies in Car Bomb Blast." *The Irish Echo* 84, no. 13 (6–12 April 2011): 1+.

"1974: Four Dead in Guildford Bomb Blasts." *BBC on This Day*. BBC (n.d.). Web 23 April 2011.

Null, Christopher. "Michael Collins." *AMCfilmcritic.com*, 17 October 1996. Web 15 December 2009.

O'Brien, Pat. *The Wind at My Back: The Life and Times of Pat O'Brien*. Garden City, NY: Doubleday, 1964.

O'Callaghan, Sean. *The Easter Lily: The Story of the IRA*. London: Four Square, 1967.

O'Casey, Sean. *The Plough and the Stars*. In *Twenty-Five Modern Plays*, 3rd Edition, edited by Alan S. Downer, 725–763. New York: Harper and Row, 1953.

O'Clery, Conor. "Letter from America." *Newsweek*, February 3, 2003. Web 30 November 2009.

O'Doherty, Malachi. "Caught in the Crossfire." *The Guardian*, 25 August 2006. Web 27 February 2009.

O'Donoghue, David. "Hitler's Strange Bunch of Spies." *The Post.IE*, 1 December 2002. Web 10 May 2010.

O'Flaherty, Liam. *The Informer*. New York: Harcourt Brace Jovanovich, 1980.

O'Sullivan, Michael. *Brendan Behan: A Life*. Boulder, CO: Roberts Rinehart, 1999.

O'Toole, Fintan. "The Man Who Shot Michael Collins." *The Independent*, 3 November 1996. Web 10 October 2009.

"Patriot Games." *Variety*, 1 January 1992. Web 5 August 2010.

Peterkin, Tom. "Michael Collins Was a Peace Icon, Says Puttnam." *Telegraph.co.uk*, 22 August 2007. Web 12 May 2009.

Pettitt, Lance. *Screening Ireland: Film and Television Representation*. Manchester: Manchester University Press, 2000.

Pogatchnik, Shawn. "IRA Crime: The Next Elusive Target of Northern Ireland Peacemaking." *USA Today*, 29 September 2005. Web 7 February 2011.

Pramaggiore, Maria. *Neil Jordan*. Urbana: University of Illinois Press, 2008.

"Richard Harris (Actor)." *Nationmaster Encyclopedia*, Nationmaster.com (n.d.). Web 31 January 2009.

Roberts, Andrew. "The Obscenity of Giving Ted Kennedy a Knighthood." *Mail Online. The Daily Mail*, 5 March 2009. Web 9 October 2010.

"Roberts, William Randall (1830–1897)." *Biographical Directory of the United States Congress 1774–Present*, n.d. Web 10 September 2010.

Rockett, Kevin. *Film Censorship: A Cultural Journey from Silent Cinema to Internet Pornography*. Dublin: Four Courts, 2004.

"Russborough House Has History of Art Thefts." *RTÉ News*, 26 June 2001. Web 27 July 2010.

"S-Plot." *Time*, February 20, 1939. Web 7 June 2010.

Sarma, Kiran. "Informers and the Battle Against Republican Terrorism: A Review of 30 Years of Conflict." *Police Practice and Research* 6, no. 2 (May 2005): 165–180.

Scott, A. O. "The High Cost of Dignity: Recalling the Troubles in Stark Detail." *The New York Times*, 20 March 2009. Web 23 January 2011.

_____. "History, Bloody History." *The New York Times*, 16 March 2007. Web.11 July 2010.

The Shadow of Béalnabláth: The Story of Michael Collins, Dir. Colm Connolly RTE, 1989.

Shaw, George Bernard. *Bernard Shaw Collected Letters, 1911–1925*, ed. Dan H. Laurence. New York: Viking Penguin, 1985.

Sheehan, Helena. "Irish Television Drama in the 1980s." *Irish Television Drama: A Society and Its Stories*. 1987. Web 5 May 2010.

Shoard, Catherine. "Ireland Good, Britain Bad." *The Telegraph*, 18 June 2006. Web 5 May 2010.

Shulgasser, Barbara. "Collins' Terrorist as Hero." *Sfgate*, 25 October 1996. Web 5 May 2010.

Simms, Katharine. "The Norman Invasion and the Gaelic Recovery." *The Oxford History of Ireland*, ed. R. F. Foster. Oxford: Oxford University Press, 1989, 44–87.

Stripp, Alan. "Introduction." *The Man Who Never Was*. Annapolis: Naval Institute, 2001.

Taylor, Peter. "Behind the Mask." Carnegie Council for Ethics in International Affairs, 5 January 1998. *C-Span Video Library*. Web 10 October 2010.

_____. *Behind the Mask: The IRA and Sinn Fein*. New York: TV Books, 1999.

Teague, Matthew. "Double Blind: The Untold Story of How British Intelligence Infiltrated and Undermined the IRA." *The Atlantic*, April 2006. Web 8 March 2010.

Tookey, Chris. "Hunger: More Pro-Terrorist Propaganda." *Mail Online*, 30 October 2008. Web 23 January 2011.

Toolis, Kevin. *Rebel Hearts: Journeys Within the IRA's Soul*. New York: St. Martin's, 1996.

_____. "Sinn Fein's Day Has Come, and It Is a Dark One." *The Times*, 13 December 2010, 18.

Tucker, S. Marion. "Sean O'Casey and His Plays." *Twenty-Five Modern Plays*. 723–724. New York: Harper and Row, 1953.

Turan, Kenneth. "Michael Collins." *Los Angeles Times*, 28 October 1996. Web 12 May 2010.

"Ultimate Cause." *Time*, 19 February 1940. Web 5 May 2009.

Weintraub, Bernard. "An Irish Legend's Life and Mysterious Death." *The New York Times*, 9 October 1996, C 13.

West, Ed. "IRA Sympathiser Ted Kennedy Was no Friend of Britain." *Telegraph Blogs, The Daily Telegraph*, 26 August 2009. Web 10 October 2010.

Wheatcroft, Geoffrey. "The Evil Legacy of the Easter Rising." *The Guardian*, 9 April 2006. Web 19 February 2011.

Whiting, Charles. *Hitler's Secret War: The Nazi Espionage Campaign Against the Allies.* Barnsley: Leo Cooper, 2000.

Woofinton, Bob. "The Trial of the Balcombe Street Four." *Miscarriages of Justice* (n.d.). Web 5 May 2010.

Wylie, Ian. "He's Belfast's Security Blanket." *FastCompany.com*, 19 December 2007. Web 24 December 2010.

Index

Abbey Theatre 16, 18, 19, 97
Abwehr 66–67, 94
Act for the Settling of Ireland 8
Act of Supremacy 8
Act of Union 9, 11
Adams, Gerry 100, 107, 123, 135, 146, 165, 166, 167, 196, 205, 242; film depiction 145
Aherne, Brian 51, 228
Amongst Women 37, 237
Angel 208–209
Anglo-Irish Treaty 22, 44–45; film depictions 25–26, 28, 52–53
Anglo-Irish War (War of Independence) 15, 20, 22, 38, 39, 43, 47, 164, 222, 230; film depictions 23, 24, 26, 29, 30, 34, 49, 55, 60, 242
Ardmore Studios 61

"Battle of the Century," *Boardwalk Empire* 194–196
Behan, Brendan 95–96, 190, 191; film depiction 97–98
Belfast Assassin/Harry's Game 112–113, 216, 243
Bell, J. Bowler 64, 100
Beloved Enemy 50–54, 227, 228, 242
Bergin, Patrick 174, 214, 220, 239
"Big House Dramas" 29–35
Birmingham Six 128; film depiction 128–129
Black and Tans 21; film depictions 23, 24, 25, 26, 27, 31–32, 33, 35, 36, 37, 42, 43, 45, 49, 51, 55, 80, 149, 150, 152, 172, 242
Bloody Sunday 1, 142–144
Bloody Sunday (1920) 42–44; film depictions 49, 50, 55
Bloody Sunday (1972) 142; film depiction 141, 142–144
Blown Away 2, 5, 176–177, 180, 183, 215, 216, 220, 243
Blue Shirts (National Guard) 63
Bogarde, Dirk 5, 82, 83

Boland, Harry 47; film depictions 53–54, 55–56, 61
bombing campaign (S Plan) 64–66
border campaign 100
Borstal Boy 95–99
Boxed 217, 218, 231, 234–235
The Boxer 137–139, 219, 220, 221, 222, 230, 235
Boycott, Charles 12
Boyd, Stephen 88, 90, 189
The Break/A Further Gesture 185–186, 230
Breakfast on Pluto 140–141, 223–224
Breen, Joseph 148
Briscoe, Robert 6, 41–42, 45, 70
British Board of Film Censors 148
Broken Harvest 36–37, 233, 237
Broy, Ned 40–41; film depiction 54–55, 60
Brugha, Cathal 44, 45, 49; film depictions 52, 53, 56
Butt, Isaac 12

Cagney, James 1, 2, 5, 23, 24, 216
Cairo Gang 42
Cal 113–114, 205, 243, 247
Carson, Edward 17
Casement, Roger 16–17, 80, 81
A Casualty of War 169, 199–200, 216, 244
Catholic Church 232
Caught in a Free State 95
censorship 5, 49, 59, 68, 70–71, 148, 149
Chapa, Damian 2, 239–240
Churchill, Winston 6, 38, 44, 48, 50, 53, 55, 57, 69–70, 87, 88, 93–94, 116, 164
Civil War 15, 23; film depictions 36–37
Clan na Gael 62, 64, 66, 163–164
Collins, Michael 2, 6, 38–48; film depictions 50–61
Comer, Marion 234, 237
Connolly, Colm 49, 50

Connolly, James 15, 16, 28, 80; film depiction 18–19
"The Conspirators," *Columbo* 191, 193
Coogan, Tim Pat 38, 47, 49, 61, 62, 242
Cracker: A New Terror 196–197
Cromwell, Oliver 8, 10, 78, 80, 81, 82
The Crying Game 58, 123–124, 219, 231
Cusack, Cyril 23, 25, 88, 91, 156

Dalton, Emmet 16, 44, 46, 49, 53, 61
The Dawning 32–33, 32, 35, 242
The Day They Robbed the Bank of England 169, 205, 220
Day-Lewis, Daniel 131, 137, 138
Dearden, Basil 82, 101, 205
De Valera, Eamon 22–23, 43, 44, 45, 46–47, 63–64, 65, 67–70, 89, 95, 99, 164; film depictions 50, 52, 53–54, 55–56, 57, 95, 194–195, 217
The Devil's Own 177–180, 216, 232
Disappearing in America 186–188, 216
Divorcing Jack 108, 140, 211
Doyle, Tony 37, 53

The Eagle Has Landed 93–95
Easter Rising 2, 16–17, 22–23, 39–40, 47, 54, 64, 102, 163, 230; film depictions 18–20, 228
The Emergency (World War II) 6, 67–70, 95, 99
Emmet, Robert 11
English, Richard 244
An Everlasting Piece 140

The Famine 9–10, 12
Fassbender, Michael 119–120
The Fenian Ram 163
Fenians 11, 161–162, 168
Fianna Fail 23, 63, 241

Fifty Dead Men Walking 109, 214, 225–227, 231, 232
Fine Gael 63, 241
A Fistful of Dynamite 5, 202–203
Fitzgerald, Garret 17, 59
Five Minutes of Heaven 2, 236–237
Flight of the Earls 8
Flight of the Wild Geese 9
Fools of Fortune 30–32, 35, 242
Force Research Unit (FRU) 223
Ford, John 1, 2, 5, 18, 19, 57, 149
48 Angels 237–238
Four Days in July 108, 243
Frankenheimer, John 1, 5
Der Fuchs von Glenarvon 73–75, 78, 217

Gaelic League 15, 41
Gambon, Michael 33, 35, 111
The General 209–210
The Gentle Gunman 82–86, 90, 91, 135, 216, 219, 220, 228, 243
Gere, Richard 5, 182, 218
Gleeson, Brendan 52–53, 185, 209
The Glory Boys 198–199
Good Friday Agreement (Belfast Agreement) 2, 136
Green, F.L. 153–154
Greengrass, Paul 1, 142–144
Griffith, Arthur 15, 20, 22, 44, 45, 53, 149
Griffith, Hugh 205
Griffith, Kenneth 48–49
Guilford Four and Maguire Seven 127; film depiction 129–132

Hang Up Your Brightest Colours: The Life and Death of Michael Collins 48–49
Harris, Eoghan 57, 60–61
Harris, Richard 23, 25, 91–92, 95, 175
Hennessy 133–134, 215, 216, 220
Hidden Agenda 101n, 106n, 125–126, 128n, 189, 217, 218
Hinds, Ciaran 109, 118
Hirschbiegel, Oliver 2, 236
Holland, John 163
Home Rule 12–15, 17, 28, 44, 205, 206
Hopkins, Anthony 1, 5, 32–33
Hoskins, Bob 206–207, 233
Hunger 119–123

I See a Dark Stranger 78–82, 86, 216, 217, 219, 243
In the Name of the Father 2, 129–132, 213–214, 243
The Informant 108, 214, 218, 224–225, 229

The Informer 2, 93, 147, 149–153, 160, 215, 219
The Informer (novel) 148–149
I.R.A. King of Nothing 2, 239–241
Ireland: Act for the Settling of Ireland 8; Act of Supremacy 8; Act of Union 9, 11; Anglo-Irish Treaty 22, 25–26, 28, 44–45, 52–53; Civil War 15, 23, 25–26, 28; early history and invasions 7–9, 10–11; Easter Rising 15–20; The Famine 9–10, 12; Home Rule 12–15, 17, 28, 44, 205, 206; land ownership 9, 12; Nine Years War 9, 10; Norman invasion 7; partition 5, 17, 18, 22, 23, 26, 28, 38, 45, 47, 51, 59, 61, 63, 65, 80, 82, 100, 102, 107, 108, 155, 216; penal laws 8–9; plantation 8; population 9n, 10, 101; Protestant Ascendency 9; rebellions 10–11; reform 11–12; Ulster Covenant 13; War of Independence (Anglo-Irish War) 5, 15, 20, 22, 23, 24, 26, 29, 30, 34, 38, 39, 43, 47, 49, 55, 60, 164, 222, 230, 242; World War I 14, 15; World War II (The Emergency) 6, 67–70, 95, 99
Irish-Americans 16, 62, 65, 77, 89, 163–164, 165–170, 183–184, 190–193, 198, 205, 230; antipathy to Britain 7, 161, 163, 164; Fenians 11, 161–162, 168; film depictions 169–173, 183–185, 189–197
Irish Citizen Army 15, 16
Irish Republican Army (IRA): bombing campaign (S Plan) 64–66; border campaign 100; Civil War 15, 16, 25–26, 28; criminal operations 204–213; formation 6–7; goals 1, 5; international operations 198–203; interwar years 62; "Long War" strategy 107–108; "New IRA" 26, 100; "Old IRA" 6, 26, 29; Operation Dove 66–67, 96; peace process 135–137; Provos 104–105; screen presence 1, 5–6; tactics 217–218; War of Independence (Anglo-Irish War) 5, 15, 20, 22, 23, 24, 26, 29, 30, 34, 38, 39, 43, 47, 49, 55, 60, 164, 222, 230, 242; World War II (The Emergency), 2, 66–67, 78–99
Irish Republican Brotherhood 11, 13, 15, 20, 39, 40, 53, 76, 161, 163
Irish Republicanism 11
Irish Volunteers 14, 15, 40, 163

The Jackal 181–183, 184, 218, 220, 243
Johnny Was 219, 220, 222, 238–239
Jones, Tommy Lee 176, 177
Jordan, Neil 1, 5, 53, 57, 59, 60–61, 123

Kennedy, Ted 166–167, 168
Kiernan, Kitty 47–48; film depiction 54, 55, 56, 57
Kimmich, Max 72–73, 75, 77
King, Peter 146, 166–167, 168

The Land League 12–13
Larkin, John 15
The Last September 33–35
League of Gentlemen 101, 205
Lean, David 1, 5
Lemass, Sean 6, 43, 61
Leone, Sergio 5
Lloyd George 17, 22, 38, 43, 44, 46; film depiction 52–53
Loach, Ken 26–29, 125–126, 128, 189, 217–218
The Long Good Friday 206–208
Long Kesh 115
Lowe, Rob 134, 201, 219
Lynch, Jack 103

MacKillop, James 1
The Man Who Never Was 87–89, 90, 93, 94, 198
Mason, James 1, 5, 148, 155, 244
Maxwell, John 16–17
McBride, Sean 6
McLaglen, Victor 1
McLoone, Martin 29
McSorley, Gerard 137, 144, 145
Mein Leben für Irland 75–78, 229
Merhi, Joseph 1, 180, 205
Merrin, Helen 113, 117
Michael Collins 53–61, 242
Midnight Man 101, 134–135, 219
Mills, John 5, 82, 83
Mitchum, Robert 5, 20, 90, 229
Murray, Don 23–24, 169
My Brother's War 183–185, 205, 215, 218, 220, 222
Myers, Kevin 18, 48, 62, 137

National Guard (Blue Shirts) 63
Nazis 2, 67–70
Neeson, Liam 54, 56, 57, 58, 59, 141, 236, 237
Neligan, Dave 40, 43, 49
Nesbitt, James 142, 144, 236
"New IRA" 26, 100
Nighthawks 201–202
Nine Years War 9, 10
NORAID 59, 165, 166, 167
Northern Ireland 5, 101–104, 105–106; film depictions 108–114, 132

Nothing Personal 111–112, 113, 243

O'Casey, Sean 18–19
O'Connell, Daniel 11–12, 15, 24, 31
Odd Man Out 2, 66, 93, 147, 148, 153–160, 205, 215, 230, 233
Odd Man Out (novel) 153–154
O'Duffy, Eoin 63
O'Flaherty, Liam 26, 148–149
"Old IRA" 6, 26, 29
Omagh 144–146
O'Mahony, John 161, 162
On Dangerous Ground 134, 200–201, 220
O'Neill, Brian 10
Operation Dove 66–67, 96
"Ourselves Alone," *Boardwalk Empire* 194–196
The Outsider 169–171, 173, 187, 216, 224

Paisley, Ian 106, 107, 165
Parnell, Charles Stewart 12–13, 14, 163
partition 5, 17, 18, 22, 23, 26, 28, 38, 45, 47, 51, 59, 61, 63, 65, 80, 82, 100, 102, 107, 108, 155, 216
Patriot Games 2, 132, 174–176, 177, 179, 180, 183, 215, 216, 231, 243
Patriots 171–173, 224
peace process 135–137
Pearse, Padraig 15, 16, 54, 80, 163
penal laws 8–9
Phoenix Park murders 13
Pitt, Brad 1, 5, 178, 180
The Plough and the Stars 18–19, 217, 228, 242
Porter, Eric 5, 123
A Prayer for the Dying 101, 185, 186, 209, 218, 219, 231, 233
priests 232–235
Protestant Ascendency 9
Puttnam, David 48, 57

The Quiet Man 2, 5, 168

The Railway Station Man 188, 220

Rea, Stephen 123–124, 185, 208, 231
Redgrave, Michael 5, 23, 24, 217
Redmond, John 13, 16, 17
Reed, Carol 1, 5, 148, 153–154, 160
Richardson, Miranda 123, 231
Riot 1, 180–181, 205, 216, 243
The Rising of the Moon 230
Roberts, Julia 58, 59
Ronin 210–211, 215
Rourke, Mickey 185, 200, 212, 218, 233
Royal Irish Constabulary (RIC) 21
Run of the Country 132
Russell, Sean 64–67, 96, 164
Ryan, Frank 63, 66–67, 94, 96
Ryan's Daughter 5, 20, 223

Sands, Bobby 114–117, 136, 166, 226, 240, 241, 242; film depictions 117, 118, 119–123
Shadow Dancer 232
The Shadow of Béalnabláth: The Story of Michael Collins 49–50
Shake Hands with the Devil 23–26, 28, 139, 169, 196, 216, 217, 220, 222, 228, 242
Shaw, George Bernard 6, 15, 16, 39, 45, 46, 48
Shergar 211–213, 215
Sheridan, Jim 1, 5, 97, 130
Sheriff, R.C. 154
Sinn Fein 15–16, 20, 22, 23, 40, 42, 104, 107, 115, 117, 136, 137, 166–167, 205, 213, 241; film depictions 118–119, 125, 175, 184, 192, 193, 200, 214
"skirmish funds" 161, 163, 180
Some Mother's Son 2, 117–119, 205, 228, 233
Special Category Status 115
Statutes of Kilkenny 7
Steiger, Rod 133, 198, 202
Stuart, Francis 94
Sturges, John 5, 93

Taylor, Rod 19
terminology 2–3, 6
A Terrible Beauty/The Night Fighters 90–93, 219

Thatcher, Margaret 107, 114, 116, 117, 119, 121, 126, 128, 129, 165
Titanic Town 109–111, 217, 228
Tone, Wolfe 11
The Treaty 52–53, 54, 217, 242
"The Troubles," *Law and Order* 192–193
"Troubles" of Northern Ireland 5, 101–104, 105–106; film depictions 108–114, 132; terminology 2–3, 6

Ulster Covenant 13
Ulster Volunteer Force (UVF) 13
Unionists 1, 2, 6, 13–14, 17, 22, 24, 27, 47, 62, 69, 101–102, 104–106, 110, 136, 161, 165–167, 204; film depictions 60, 176, 235
United Irishmen 11
United States: Clan na Gael 163–164; Fenians 11, 161–162, 168; haven for IRA 185–188; Irish immigration 10; 9/11 Effect 167–168; NORAID 59, 165, 166, 167; source of funds and weapons 163–164, 165–166, 179, 180, 190–191, 194–196
"Up the Rebels" *Hawaii Five-0* 189–191, 192, 215

War of Independence (Anglo-Irish War) 5, 15, 20, 22, 38, 39, 43, 47, 164, 222, 230; film depictions 23, 24, 26, 29, 30, 34, 49, 55, 60, 242
When the Sky Falls 214, 243
Whiteboys 11, 12, 34
Who Bombed Birmingham?/The Investigation: Inside a Terrorist Bombing 128–129, 130, 218
The Wind That Shakes the Barley 26–29, 217, 223, 230, 232, 233, 242
Winter, Ormonde 42
Women in the IRA 227–232
World War I 14, 15
World War II (The Emergency) 2, 67–70, 95, 99

Yeats, William Butler 16, 18
Young Cassidy 19–20, 219, 227